Annual Editions:
Drugs, Society, and Behavior
29/e

**Edited by Mary Maguire, CA State University
Clifford Garoupa, Fresno City College**

http://create.mcgraw-hill.com

ISBN-10: 1259223191   ISBN-13: 9781259223198

Contents

Preface

In publishing ANNUAL EDITIONS we recognize the enormous role played by the magazines, newspapers, and journals of the public press in providing current, first-rate educational information in a broad spectrum of interest areas. Many of these articles are appropriate for students, researchers, and professionals seeking accurate, current material to help bridge the gap between principles and theories and the real world. These articles, however, become more useful for study when those of lasting value are carefully collected, organized, indexed, and reproduced in a low-cost format, which provides easy and permanent access when the material is needed. That is the role played by ANNUAL EDITIONS.

Humanity has developed an ambiguous relationship with substances we have come to define as drugs, particularly those drugs that alter human consciousness and behavior, psychoactive drugs. The use of such substances has resulted in a social circumstance whereby societies struggle to control human behaviors motivated and altered by their use. Although we consider modern society to function based upon logic, science, and reason, closer scrutiny of policy, regulation, and control belies this belief. In effect, such attempts at regulation face an enormous biological and psychological challenge: we humans are designed to alter our consciousness, or to use another term familiar to drug use, to "get high." As a result, to a significant degree, our societies face a seemingly insurmountable challenge: to control and/or manipulate human behavior with regard to drug using or consciousness-altering behaviors. To this end, societies have, presumably in an attempt to protect their members, developed what they perceive to be rational control mechanisms to protect people from themselves.

Unfortunately, the historical foundations upon which drug regulation and control are based, especially in the United States, have their roots in racism and discrimination. This further complicates society's attempts to address, in a logical and coherent sense, what type of role or relationship humans should have with these substances. The reality of our modern world concerning drugs is unequivocal. Despite repeated resolutions by the United State's government in an attempt to achieve a "Drug Free America," and the staggering amount of money spent in the attempt to achieve that end, drugs are ubiquitous in American society; they are here to stay. What has come to be defined as deviant and antisocial behaviors in our attempts to "denormalize" drug use has, in fact, resulted in these activities becoming testimony to people's inherent creativity in their never-ending pursuit of states of altered consciousness. When this penchant to "get high" is combined with the precociousness inherent in our species, one ends up with the current circumstance: new substances are discovered regularly, either by scientific research or common curiosity, and the ritual of consciousness alteration begins anew. We currently find ourselves in a conundrum concerning drugs. For whatever reasons, none of which are based upon science or rationality, some drugs are considered to be acceptable and appropriate, while others are seen to be highly dangerous and a threat. One does not need to be a psychopharmacologist or toxicologist to realize that there is very little difference, for instance, between ethyl alcohol and heroin. As a result, we readily accept and condone the use of one (alcohol) while declaring "war" against the other (heroin). The same situation exists with regard to tobacco, a compound that is among the most toxic and highly addictive known. For these reasons, oftentimes it is in fact impossible to make sense of how modern societies have come to view and address drug using behavior. We hope that the materials presented in this book offer the reader some insight and perspective with regard to understanding the role that drugs play in today's world and how we have come to our current situation concerning drugs and drug use.

The articles contained in Annual Editions: Drugs, Society, and Behavior 29/e are a collection of issues and perspectives designed to provide the reader with a framework for examining current drug-related issues and facts. The book is designed to offer students something to think about and *something with which to think*. It is a unique collection of materials of interest to the casual as well as the serious student of drug-related social phenomena. The first section addresses the significance that drugs have in affecting diverse aspects of American life. It emphasizes the often-overlooked reality that drugs—legal and illegal—have remained a pervasive dimension of past as well as present American history. The unit begins with examples of the multiple ways in which Americans have been and continue to be affected by both legal and illegal drugs. We go on to examine the ways drugs affect the mind and body that result in dependence and addiction and the major drugs of use and abuse, along with issues relative to understanding the individual impacts of these drugs on society. Selections address the impacts produced by the use of legal and illegal drugs and emphasize the alarming nature of widespread prescription drug abuse. We review the dynamic nature of drugs as it relates to changing patterns and trends of use. We give special attention this year to drug trends among youth, particularly those related to prescription drug abuse. Additionally, a section of the book focuses on the social costs of drug abuse and why the costs overwhelm many American institutions. Specific articles have been selected to illustrate the complexity in creating and implementing drug policy, such as that associated with medical marijuana and that associated with foreign drug control policy. The final section concludes the book with discussions of current strategies for preventing and treating drug abuse. Can we deter people from harming themselves with drugs, and can we cure people addicted to drugs? What works and what does not work? Special attention is given to programs that address at-risk youth and programs that reduce criminal offender rehabilitation and recidivism.

Annual Editions: Drugs, Society, and Behavior 29/e contains a number of features that are designed to make the volume user-friendly. These include a table of contents with abstracts that summarize each article, a topic guide to help locate articles on specific individuals or subjects, Learning Outcomes, Critical Thinking questions, and Internet References for each article that can be used to further explore the topics, and help students better understand what they have read.

Editors

Mary H. Maguire
California State University—Sacramento

Dr. Mary Maguire is an Associate Professor of Criminal Justice at California State University–Sacramento, one of the largest Criminal Justice programs in the United States. She teaches Criminology, Research Methods, and Contemporary Issues in Criminal Justice. She has an MA in Psychology, an MSW, and a PhD in Social Work and Social Research. Dr. Maguire has fifteen years of professional experience in behavioral health. She has twelve years of research experience measuring clinical models and behaviors of high-risk populations, including best practices for those with mental illness and co-occurring substance abuse. Dr. Maguire is the recent past President of the Western Society of Criminology and the recipient of the J.D. Lohman Award for Outstanding Service to the Society. She is published in the area of policing, corrections, and criminal justice policy.

Clifford Garoupa
Fresno City College

Mr. Garoupa received his Bachelor of Arts degree from California State University–Fresno in Sociology, his Master's degree in Sociology from The Ohio State University, and his Juris Doctor degree from The San Joaquin College of Law. He worked for many years in the criminal justice system, both in law enforcement and criminal defense, primarily as an investigator but also as a consultant, particularly in homicide and serious drug cases. During his academic career, he has not only served in

an advisory capacity to members of Congress, but also was appointed to the Fresno County Drug and Alcohol Advisory Board, acting for five years as that Board's Chairman. He has been interviewed on National Public Radio concerning European Harm Reduction Policy and Practice, particularly the implementation and effect of drug decriminalization in Portugal. He is the former Program Coordinator for the Drug and Alcohol Counseling program at Fresno City College, which is one of the largest such educational programs in California. He currently teaches both Sociology and Drug Studies.

Academic Advisory Board

Members of the Academic Advisory Board are instrumental in the final selection of articles for *Annual Editions* books and ExpressBooks. Their review of the articles for content, level, and appropriateness provides critical direction to the editor(s) and staff. We think that you will find their careful consideration reflected here.

Correlation Guide

The *Annual Editions* series provides students with convenient, inexpensive access to current, carefully selected articles from the public press. **Annual Editions: Drugs, Society, and Behavior, 29/e** is an easy-to-use reader that presents articles on important topics such as *living with drugs, how drugs work, addiction, use and abuse, trends, social costs of drugs, drug control,* and many more. For more information on *Annual Editions* and other McGraw-Hill Create™ titles, visit www.mcgrawhillcreate.com.

This convenient guide matches the articles in **Annual Editions: Drugs, Society, and Behavior, 29/e** with **Drugs in American Society, 9/e** by Goode.

Drugs in American Society, 9/e by Goode	Annual Editions: Drugs, Society, and Behavior 29/e
Chapter 1: A History of Drug Use	History of Alcohol and Drinking around the World Legalize Drugs—All of Them!
Chapter 2: A History of Drug Control	Drugs 'R' Us
Chapter 3: The Pharmacological Perspective	Tackling Top Teen Problem—Prescription Drugs
Chapter 4: The Sociologist Looks at Drug Use	Did Cocaine Use by Bankers Cause the Global Financial Crisis? Drugs 'R' Us Getting a Fix Old Habits Die Hard for Ageing Addicts Turning the Tide on Drug Reform
Chapter 5: Drugs in the Media	Drugs 'R' Us
Chapter 6: Studying Drug Use	Monitoring the Future: National Results on Adolescent Drug Use, Overview of Key Findings 2011
Chapter 7: Explaining Drug Use	Addiction Diagnoses May Rise Under Guideline Changes
Chapter 8: Legal Drugs Use: Alcohol and Tobacco	Alcoholism Isn't What It Used To Be Engaging Communities to Prevent Underage Drinking History of Alcohol and Drinking around the World Maternal Risk Factors for Fetal Alcohol Spectrum Disorders: Not As Simple As It Might Seem The Genetics of Alcohol and Other Drug Dependence When Booze Comes Off the Battlefield
Chapter 9: Prescription Drugs	A Glut of Antidepressants OxyContin Abuse Spreads from Appalachia across United States OxyContin Maker Closely Guards Its List of Suspect Doctors Prescription Drug Diversion Tackling Top Teen Problem—Prescription Drugs
Chapter 10: Marijuana, LSD, and Club Drugs	Cannabis: Colorado's Budding Industry Why I Changed My Mind on Weed
Chapter 11: Stimulants: Amphetamine, Methamphetamine, Cocaine, and Crack	Diagnosis: Human Did Cocaine Use by Bankers Cause the Global Financial Crisis?
Chapter 12: Heroin and the Narcotics	Getting a Fix How Latin America Is Reinventing the War on Drugs OxyContin Abuse Spreads from Appalachia across United States OxyContin Maker Closely Guards Its List of Suspect Doctors
Chapter 13: Drugs and Crime	California Prisons Spend Big on Anti-Psychotic Drugs
Chapter 14: Trafficking in Illicit Drugs	Do the United States and Mexico Really Want the Drug War to Succeed? 'Legal Highs' Prevalence Makes Ban Policy 'Ridiculous' Secret U.S. Drug Agency Unit Passing Surveillance Information to Authorities
Chapter 15: Law Enforcement, Drug Courts, and Drug Treatment	High-Risk Offenders Participating in Court-Supervised Abuse Treatment: Characteristics, Treatment Received, and Factors Associated with Recidivism Understanding Recovery Barriers: Youth Perceptions about Substance Use Relapse
Chapter 16: Legalization, Decriminalization, and Harm Reduction	Do No Harm: Sensible Goals for International Drug Policy Getting a Fix How Latin America Is Reinventing the War on Drugs 'Legal Highs' Prevalence Makes Ban Policy 'Ridiculous' Legalize Drugs—All of Them! The Needle and the Damage Done: The Case for the Self-Destructing Syringe Turning the Tide on Drug Reform

Topic Guide

All the articles that relate to each topic are listed below the bold-faced term.

Addiction

Addiction Diagnoses May Rise Under Guideline Changes
The Genetics of Alcohol and Other Drug Dependence
Inhalant Abuse
Monitoring the Future: National Results on Adolescent Drug Use,
    Overview of Key Findings 2011
Old Habits Die Hard for Ageing Addicts

Alcohol

Alcoholism Isn't What It Used to Be
Engaging Communities to Prevent Underage Drinking
The Genetics of Alcohol and Other Drug Dependence
History of Alcohol and Drinking around the World
Maternal Risk Factors for Fetal Alcohol Spectrum Disorders: Not As
    Simple As It Might Seem
When Booze Comes Off the Battlefield

Amphetamines

Diagnosis: Human

College

Diagnosis: Human
Drugs 'R' Us
Energy Drink Abuse Worries Health Pros
Prescription Drug Diversion
Why Using Meds for 'Neuroenhancement' Is a Scary Thought

Drinking among college students

Addiction Diagnoses May Rise Under Guideline Changes
Alcoholism Isn't What It Used to Be
The Genetics of Alcohol and Other Drug Dependence

Drug economy

Cannabis: Colorado's Budding Industry
Did Cocaine Use by Bankers Cause the Global Financial Crisis?
Do the United States and Mexico Really Want the Drug War to
    Succeed?
How Latin America Is Reinventing the War on Drugs
Legalize Drugs—All of Them!
The Science of Doping

Epidemiology

Diagnosis: Human
A Glut of Antidepressants
History of Alcohol and Drinking around the World
The Needle and the Damage Done: The Case for the Self-Destructing
    Syringe

Hallucinogens

'Bath Salt' Poisonings Rise as Legislative Ban Tied Up
Transcending the Medical Frontiers: Exploring the Future of
    Psychedelic Drug Research

Heroin use

Engaging Communities to Prevent Underage Drinking
The Genetics of Alcohol and Other Drug Dependence

Monitoring the Future: National Results on Adolescent Drug Use,
    Overview of Key Findings 2011
Old Habits Die Hard for Ageing Addicts
Tackling Top Teen Problem—Prescription Drugs
Understanding Recovery Barriers: Youth Perceptions about Substance
    Use Relapse

Law enforcement

California Prisons Spend Big on Anti-Psychotic Drugs
How Latin America Is Reinventing the War on Drugs
Secret U.S. Drug Agency Unit Passing Surveillance Information to
    Authorities

Legalization

Drugs 'R' Us
How Latin America Is Reinventing the War on Drugs
'Legal Highs' Prevalence Makes Ban Policy 'Ridiculous'
Legalize Drugs—All of Them!
Turning the Tide on Drug Reform

Marijuana

Cannabis: Colorado's Budding Industry
Examination of Over-the-Counter Drug Misuse Among Youth
Tackling Top Teen Problem—Prescription Drugs
Why I Changed My Mind on Weed

Policy

'Bath Salt' Poisonings Rise as Legislative Ban Tied Up
Do No Harm: Sensible Goals for International Drug Policy
Do the United States and Mexico Really Want the Drug War to
    Succeed?
Drugs 'R' Us
Getting a Fix
How Latin America Is Reinventing the War on Drugs
'Legal Highs' Prevalence Makes Ban Policy 'Ridiculous'
Moving the Needle

Prescription drug abuse

Diagnosis: Human
Examination of Over-the-Counter Drug Misuse Among Youth
OxyContin Maker Closely Guards Its List of Suspect Doctors
Prescription Drug Diversion
Tackling Top Teen Problem—Prescription Drugs

Treatment

Addiction Diagnoses May Rise Under Guideline Changes
High-Risk Offenders Participating in Court-Supervised Substance
    Abuse Treatment: Characteristics, Treatment Received, and Factors
    Associated with Recidivism
OxyContin Abuse Spreads from Appalachia across United States
Scientists Are High on Idea That Marijuana Reduces Memory
    Impairment
Understanding Recovery Barriers: Youth Perceptions about Substance
    Use Relapse
When Booze Comes Off the Battlefield

Unit 1

UNIT

Prepared by: Mary Maguire, *California State University—Sacramento*
Clifford Garoupa, *Fresno City College*

Living with Drugs

When attempting to define the U.S. drug experience, one must examine the past as well as the present. Very often, drug use and its associated phenomena are viewed through a contemporary looking glass relative to our personal views, biases, and perspectives. Although today's drug scene is definitely a product of recent historical trends such as the crack trade of the 1980s, the methamphetamine problem, and the turn toward the expanded non-medical use of prescription drugs, it is also a product of the distant past. This past and the lessons it has generated, although largely unknown, forgotten, or ignored, provide one important perspective from which to assess our current status and to guide our future in terms of optimizing our efforts to manage the benefits and control the harm from legal and illegal drugs.

The U.S. drug experience is often defined in terms of a million individual realities, all meaningful and all different. In fact, these realities often originated as pieces of our historical, cultural, political, and personal past that combine to influence present-day drug-related phenomena significantly. The contemporary U.S. drug experience is the product of centuries of human attempts to alter or sustain consciousness through the use of mind-altering drugs. Early American history is replete with accounts of the exorbitant use of alcohol, opium, morphine, and cocaine. Further review of this history clearly suggests the precedents for Americans' continuing pursuit of a vast variety of stimulant, depressant, and hallucinogenic drugs. Drug wars, drug epidemics, drug prohibitions, and escalating trends of alarming drug use patterns were present throughout the early history of the United States. During this period, the addictive properties of most drugs were largely unknown. Today, the addictive properties of almost all drugs are known. So why is it that so many drug-related lessons of the past repeat themselves in the face of such powerful new knowledge? Why does Fetal Alcohol Syndrome remain as the leading cause of mental retardation in infants? How is it that the abuse of drugs continues to defy the lessons of history? How big is the U.S. drug problem and how is it measured?

One important way of answering questions about drug abuse is by conducting research and analyzing data recovered through numerous reporting instruments. These data are in turn used to assess historical trends and make policy decisions in response to what has been learned. For example, one leading source of information about drug use in America is the annual federal Substance Abuse and Mental Health Services Administration's National Survey on Drug Use and Health. It currently reports that there continues to be more than 19 million Americans over 12 years of age who are current users of illicit drugs. The most widely used illicit drug is marijuana with approximately 14 million users—a figure that has remained constant for the past five years. Approximately 51 percent of Americans over 12 are drinkers of alcohol; over 43 percent of full-time enrolled college students are binge drinkers (defined as consuming five or more drinks during a single drinking occasion). Approximately 29 percent of Americans over

12 use tobacco. Almost 23 million people are believed to be drug-dependent on alcohol or illicit drugs. There are approximately five million people using prescription painkillers for nonmedical reasons—an alarming trend. The size of the economy associated with drug use is staggering; Americans continue to spend more than $70 billion a year on illegal drugs alone.

Drugs impact our most powerful public institutions on many fronts. Drugs are the business of our criminal justice system, and drugs compete with terrorism, war, and other major national security concerns as demanding military issues. Over $3 billion per year is committed to the Department of Homeland Security to strengthen drug-related land and maritime border interdictions. The cost of illegal street drugs is up, and the post-9/11 national security infrastructure is impacting historical patterns of trafficking. And the relationship between drug trafficking and terrorism has focused added military emphasis on drug fighting. As the war in Iraq, Afghanistan, and Pakistan continues, U.S. drug agents in those countries are increasing efforts to contain the expanding heroin trade, a major source of funding for the Taliban. As you read through the pages of this book, the pervasive nature of drug-related influences on everyday life will become more apparent.

The lessons of our drug legacy are harsh, whether they are the subjects of public health or public policy. Methamphetamine is now recognized as having produced consequences equal to or surpassing those of crack. The entire dynamic of illicit drug use is changing. Once quiet rural towns, counties, and states have reported epidemics of methamphetamine abuse over the past 10 years, and these suggest comparisons to the inner-urban crack epidemics of the 1980s. The current level of drug-related violence in Mexico is out of control and is firmly in control of the U.S. drug market. This issue is the most dangerous emerging drug problem.

Families, schools, and workplaces continue to be impacted by the many facets of drug abuse. One in three Americans has a close relationship to someone who abuses drugs. It is only because of war, terrorism, and a struggling economy that more public attention toward drug problems has been diverted. The articles and graphics contained in this unit illustrate the evolving nature of issues influenced by the historical evolution of legal and illegal drug use in America. The changing historical evolution of drug-related phenomena is reflected within the character of all issues and controversies addressed by this book. This unit presents examples of the contemporary and diverse nature of current problems, issues, and concerns about drugs and how they continue to impact all aspects of public and private life. The drug-related events of today continue to forecast the drug-related events of tomorrow. The areas of public health, public policy, controlling crime, and education exist as good examples for discussion. As you read this and other literature on drug-related events, the dynamics of past and present drug-related linkages will become apparent.

Article

Prepared by: Mary Maguire, *California State University—Sacramento*
Clifford Garoupa, *Fresno City College*

History of Alcohol and Drinking around the World

DAVID J. HANSON

Learning Outcomes

After reading this article, you will be able to:

- Understand the use of alcohol through history.

- Describe various types of alcohol that people use.

- Identify when different types of alcohol became popular and why.

Alcohol is a product that has provided a variety of functions for people throughout all history. From the earliest times to the present, alcohol has played an important role in religion and worship. Historically, alcoholic beverages have served as sources of needed nutrients and have been widely used for their medicinal, antiseptic, and analgesic properties. The role of such beverages as thirst quenchers is obvious and they play an important role in enhancing the enjoyment and quality of life. They can be a social lubricant, can facilitate relaxation, can provide pharmacological pleasure, and can increase the pleasure of eating. Thus, while alcohol has always been misused by a minority of drinkers, it has proved to be beneficial to most.

Ancient Period

While no one knows when beverage alcohol was first used, it was presumably the result of a fortuitous accident that occurred at least tens of thousands of years ago. However, the discovery of late Stone Age beer jugs has established the fact that intentionally fermented beverages existed at least as early as the Neolithic period (cir. 10,000 B.C.) (Patrick, 1952, pp. 12–13), and it has been suggested that beer may have preceded bread as a staple (Braidwood et al, 1953; Katz and Voigt, 1987); wine clearly appeared as a finished product in Egyptian pictographs around 4,000 B.C. (Lucia, 1963a, p. 216).

The earliest alcoholic beverages may have been made from berries or honey (Blum *et al,* 1969, p. 25; Rouech, 1960, p. 8; French, 1890, p. 3) and winemaking may have originated in the wild grape regions of the Middle East. Oral tradition recorded in the Old Testament (Genesis 9:20) asserts that Noah planted a vineyard on Mt. Ararat in what is now eastern Turkey. In Sumer, beer and wine were used for medicinal purposes as early as 2,000 B.C. (Babor, 1986, p. 1).

Brewing dates from the beginning of civilization in ancient Egypt (Cherrington, 1925, v. 1, p. 404) and alcoholic beverages were very important in that country. Symbolic of this is the fact that while many gods were local or familial, Osiris, the god of wine, was worshiped throughout the entire country (Lucia, 1963b, p. 152). The Egyptians believed that this important god also invented beer (King, 1947, p. 11), a beverage that was considered a necessity of life; it was brewed in the home "on an everyday basis" (Marciniak, 1992, p. 2).

Both beer and wine were deified and offered to gods. Cellars and winepresses even had a god whose hieroglyph was a winepress (Ghaliounqui, 1979, p. 5). The ancient Egyptians made at least seventeen varieties of beer and at least 24 varieties of wine (Ghaliounqui, 1979, pp. 8 and 11). Alcoholic beverages were used for pleasure, nutrition, medicine, ritual, remuneration (Cherrington, 1925, v. 1, p. 405) and funerary purposes. The latter involved storing the beverages in tombs of the deceased for their use in the after-life (King, 1947, p. 11; Darby, 1977, p. 576).

Numerous accounts of the period stressed the importance of moderation, and these norms were both secular and religious (Darby, 1977, p. 58). While Egyptians did not generally appear to define inebriety as a problem, they warned against taverns (which were often houses of prostitution) and excessive drinking (Lutz, 1922, pp. 97, 105–108). After reviewing extensive evidence regarding the widespread but generally moderate use of alcoholic beverage, the historian Darby makes a most important observation: all these accounts are warped by the fact that moderate users "were overshadowed by their more boisterous counterparts who added 'color' to history" (Darby, 1977, p. 590). Thus, the intemperate use of alcohol throughout history receives a disproportionate amount of attention. Those who abuse alcohol cause problems, draw attention to themselves, are highly visible and cause legislation to be enacted. The vast majority of drinkers, who neither experience nor cause difficulties, are not noteworthy. Consequently, observers and writers largely ignore moderation.

Beer was the major beverage among the Babylonians, and as early as 2,700 B.C. they worshiped a wine goddess and other wine deities (Hyams, 1965, pp. 38–39). Babylonians regularly used both beer and wine as offerings to their gods (Lutz, 1922, pp. 125–126). Around 1,750 B.C., the famous Code of Hammurabi devoted attention to alcohol. However, there were no penalties for drunkenness; in fact, it was not even mentioned. The concern was fair commerce in alcohol (Popham, 1978, pp. 232–233). Nevertheless, although it was not a crime, it would appear that the Babylonians were critical of drunkenness (Lutz, 1922, pp. 115–116).

A variety of alcoholic beverages have been used in China since prehistoric times (Granet, 1957, p. 144). Alcohol was considered a spiritual (mental) food rather than a material (physical) food, and extensive documentary evidence attests to the important role it played in the religious life (Hucker, 1975, p. 28; Fei-Peng, 1982, p. 13). "In ancient times people always drank when holding a memorial ceremony, offering sacrifices to gods or their ancestors, pledging resolution before going into battle, celebrating victory, before feuding and official executions, for taking an oath of allegiance, while attending the ceremonies of birth, marriage, reunions, departures, death, and festival banquets" (Fei-Peng, 1982, p. 13).

A Chinese imperial edict of about 1,116 B.C. makes it clear that the use of alcohol in moderation was believed to be prescribed by heaven. Whether or not it was prescribed by heaven, it was clearly beneficial to the treasury. At the time of Marco Polo (1254–1324) it was drunk daily (Gernet, 1962, p. 139) and was one of the treasury's biggest sources of income (Balazs, 1964, p. 97).

Alcoholic beverages were widely used in all segments of Chinese society, were used as a source of inspiration, were important for hospitality, were an antidote for fatigue, and were sometimes misused (Samuelson, 1878, pp. 19–20, 22, 26–27; Fei-Peng, 1982, p. 137; Simons, 1991, pp. 448–459). Laws against making wine were enacted and repealed forty-one times between 1,100 B.C. and A.D. 1,400. (Alcoholism and Drug Addiction Research Foundation of Ontario, 1961, p. 5). However, a commentator writing around 650 B.C. asserted that people "will not do without beer. To prohibit it and secure total abstinence from it is beyond the power even of sages. Hence, therefore, we have warnings on the abuse of it" (quoted in Rouecbe, 1963, p. 179; similar translation quoted in Samuelson, 1878, p. 20).

While the art of wine making reached the Hellenic peninsula by about 2,000 B.C. (Younger, 1966, p. 79), the first alcoholic beverage to obtain widespread popularity in what is now Greece was mead, a fermented beverage made from honey and water. However, by 1,700 B.C., wine making was commonplace, and during the next thousand years wine drinking assumed the same function so commonly found around the world: It was incorporated into religious rituals, it became important in hospitality, it was used for medicinal purposes and it became an integral part of daily meals (Babor, 1986, pp. 2–3). As a beverage, it was drunk in many ways: warm and chilled, pure and mixed with water, plain and spiced (Raymond, 1927, p. 53).

Contemporary writers observed that the Greeks were among the most temperate of ancient peoples. This appears to result from their rules stressing moderate drinking, their praise of temperance, their practice of diluting wine with water, and their avoidance of excess in general (Austin, 1985, p. 11). An exception to this ideal of moderation was the cult of Dionysus, in which intoxication was believed to bring people closer to their deity (Sournia, 1990, pp. 5–6; Raymond, 1927, p. 55).

While habitual drunkenness was rare, intoxication at banquets and festivals was not unusual (Austin, 1985, p. 11). In fact, the symposium, a gathering of men for an evening of conversation, entertainment and drinking typically ended in intoxication (Babor, 1986, p. 4). However, while there are no references in ancient Greek literature to mass drunkenness among the Greeks, there are references to it among foreign peoples (Patrick, 1952, p. 18). By 425 B.C., warnings against intemperance, especially at symposia, appear to become more frequent (Austin, 1985, pp. 21–22).

Xenophon (431–351 B.C.) and Plato (429–347 B.C.) both praised the moderate use of wine as beneficial to health and happiness, but both were critical of drunkenness, which appears to have become a problem. Hippocrates (cir. 460–370 B.C.) identified numerous medicinal properties of wine, which had long been used for its therapeutic value (Lucia, 1963a, pp. 36–40). Later, both Aristode (384–322 B.C.) and Zeno (cir. 336–264 B.C.) were very critical of drunkenness (Austin, 1985, pp. 23, 25, and 27).

Among Greeks, the Macedonians viewed intemperance as a sign of masculinity and were well known for their drunkenness. Their king, Alexander the Great (336–323 B.C.), whose mother adhered to the Dionysian cult, developed a reputation for inebriety (Souria, 1990, pp. 8–9; Babor, 1986, p. 5).

The Hebrews were reportedly introduced to wine during their captivity in Egypt. When Moses led them to Canaan (Palestine) around 1,200 B.C., they are reported to have regretted leaving behind the wines of Egypt (Numbers 20:5); however, they found vineyards to be plentiful in their new land (Lutz, 1922, p. 25). Around 850 B.C., the use of wine was criticized by the Rechabites and Nazarites, two conservative nomadic groups who practiced abstinence from alcohol (Lutz, 1922, p. 133; Samuelson, 1878, pp. 62–63).

In 586 B.C., the Hebrews were conquered by the Babylonians and deported to Babylon. However, in 539 B.C., the Persians captured the city and released the Hebrews from their Exile (Daniel 5:1–4). Following the Exile, the Hebrews developed Judaism as it is now known, and they can be said to have become Jews. During the next 200 years, sobriety increased and pockets of antagonism to wine disappeared. It became a common beverage for all classes and ages, including the very young; an important source of nourishment; a prominent part in the festivities of the people; a widely appreciated medicine; an essential provision for any fortress; and an important commodity. In short, it came to be seen as a necessary element in the life of the Hebrews (Raymond, 1927, p. 23).

While there was still opposition to excessive drinking, it was no longer assumed that drinking inevitably led to drunkenness. Wine came to be seen as a blessing from God and a symbol of joy (Psalms 104; Zachariah 10:7). These changes in beliefs and behaviors appear to be related to a rejection of belief in pagan gods, a new emphasis on individual morality, and the integration of secular drinking behaviors into religious ceremonies and their subsequent modification (Austin, 1985, pp. 18–19; Patai, 1980, pp. 61–73; Keller, 1970, pp. 290–294). Around 525 B.C., it was ruled that the Kiddush (pronouncement of the Sabbath) should be recited over a blessed cup of wine. This established the regular drinking of wine in Jewish ceremonies outside the Temple (Austin, 1985, p. 19).

King Cyrus of Persia frequently praised the virtue of the moderate consumption of alcohol (cir. 525 B.C.). However, ritual intoxication appears to have been used as an adjunct to decision making and, at least after his death, drunkenness was not uncommon (Austin, 1985, p. 19).

Between the founding of Rome in 753 B.C. until the third century B.C., there is consensus among historians that the Romans practiced great moderation in drinking (Austin, 1985, p. 17). After the Roman conquest of the Italian peninsula and the rest of the Mediterranean basin (509 to 133 B.C.), the traditional Roman values of temperance, frugality and simplicity were gradually replaced by heavy drinking, ambition, degeneracy and corruption (Babor, 1986, p. 7; Wallbank & Taylor, 1954, p. 163). The Dionysian rites (Bacchanalia, in Latin) spread to Italy during this period and were subsequently outlawed by the Senate (Lausanne, 1969, p. 4; Cherrington, 1925, v. 1, pp. 251–252).

Practices that encouraged excessive drinking included drinking before meals on an empty stomach, inducing vomiting to permit the consumption of more food and wine, and drinking games. The latter included, for example, rapidly consuming as many cups as indicated by a throw of the dice (Babor, 1986, p. 10).

By the second and first centuries B.C., intoxication was no longer a rarity, and most prominent men of affairs (for example, Cato the Elder and Julius Caesar) were praised for their moderation in drinking. This would appear to be in response to growing misuse of alcohol in society, because before that time temperance was not singled out for praise as exemplary behavior. As the republic continued to decay, excessive drinking spread and some, such as Marc Antony (d. 30 B.C.), even took pride in their destructive drinking behavior (Austin, 1985, pp. 28 and 32–33).

Early Christian Period

With the dawn of Christianity and its gradual displacement of the previously dominant religions, the drinking attitudes and behaviors of Europe began to be influenced by the New Testament (Babor, 1986, p. 11). The earliest biblical writings after the death of Jesus (cir. A.D. 30) contain few references to alcohol. This may have reflected the fact that drunkenness was largely an upper-status vice with which Jesus had little contact (Raymond, 1927, pp. 81–82). Austin (1985, p. 35) has pointed out that Jesus used wine (Matthew 15:11; Luke 7:33–35) and approved of its moderate consumption (Matthew 15:11). On the other hand, he severely attacked drunkenness (Luke 21:34, 12:42; Matthew 24:45–51). The later writings of St. Paul (d. 64?) deal with alcohol in detail and are important to Christian doctrine on the subject. He considered wine to be a creation of God and therefore inherently good (1 Timothy 4:4), recommended its use for medicinal purposes (1 Timothy 5:23), but consistently condemned drunkenness (1 Corinthians 3:16–17, 5:11, 6:10; Galatians 5:19–21; Romans 13:3) and recommended abstinence for those who could not control their drinking.

However, late in the second century, several heretical sects rejected alcohol and called for abstinence. By the late fourth and early fifth centuries, the Church responded by asserting that wine was an inherently good gift of God to be used and enjoyed. While individuals may choose not to drink, to despise wine was heresy. The Church advocated its moderate use but rejected excessive or abusive use as a sin. Those individuals who could not drink in moderation were urged to abstain (Austin, 1985, pp. 44 and 47–48).

It is clear that both the Old and New Testaments are clear and consistent in their condemnation of drunkenness. However, some Christians today argue that whenever "wine" was used by Jesus or praised as a gift of God, it was really grape juice; only when it caused drunkenness was it wine. Thus, they interpret the Bible as asserting that grape juice is good and that drinking it is acceptable to God but that wine is bad and that drinking it is unacceptable. This reasoning appears to be incorrect for at least two reasons. First, neither the Hebrew nor Biblical Greek word for wine can be translated or interpreted as referring to grape juice. Secondly, grape juice would quickly ferment into wine in the warm climate of the Mediterranean region without refrigeration or modern methods of preservation (Royce, 1986, pp. 55–56; Raymond, 1927, pp. 18–22; Hewitt, 1980, pp. 11–12).

The spread of Christianity and of viticulture in Western Europe occurred simultaneously (Lausanne, 1969, p. 367; Sournia, 1990, p. 12). Interestingly, St. Martin of Tours (316–397) was actively engaged in both spreading the Gospel and planting vineyards (Patrick, 1952, pp. 26–27).

In an effort to maintain traditional Jewish culture against the rise of Christianity, which was converting numerous Jews (Wallbank & Taylor, 1954, p. 227), detailed rules concerning the use of wine were incorporated into the Talmud. Importantly, wine was integrated into many religious ceremonies in limited quantity (Spiegel, 1979, pp. 20–29; Raymond, 1927, 45–47). In the social and political upheavals that rose as the fall of Rome approached in the fifth century, concern grew among rabbis that Judaism and its culture were in increasing danger. Consequently, more Talmudic rules were laid down concerning the use of wine. These included the amount of wine that could be drunk on the Sabbath, the way in which wine was to be drunk, the legal status of wine in any way connected with idolatry, and the extent of personal responsibility for behavior while intoxicated (Austin, 1985, pp. 36 and 50).

Roman abuse of alcohol appears to have peaked around mid-first century (Jellinek, 1976, pp. 1,736–1,739). Wine had become the most popular beverage, and as Rome attracted a large influx of displaced persons, it was distributed free or at cost (Babor, 1986, pp. 7–8). This led to occasional excesses at festivals, victory triumphs and other celebrations, as described by contemporaries. The four emperors who ruled from A.D. 37 to A.D. 69 were all known for their abusive drinking. However, the emperors who followed were known for their temperance, and literary sources suggest that problem drinking decreased substantially in the Empire. Although there continued to be some criticisms of abusive drinking over the next several hundred years, most evidence indicates a decline of such behavior (Austin, 1985, pp. 37–44, p. 46, pp. 48–50). The fall of Rome and the Western Roman Empire occurred in 476 (Wallbank & Taylor, 1954, pp. 220–221).

Around A.D. 230, the Greek scholar Athenaeus wrote extensively on drinking and advocated moderation. The extensive attention to drinking, famous drinks, and drinking cups (of which he described 100) reflected the importance of wine to the Greeks (Austin, 1985, pp. 45–46).

The Middle Ages

The Middle Ages, that period of approximately one thousand years between the fall of Rome and the beginning of the High Renaissance (cir. 1500), saw numerous developments in life in general and in drinking in particular. In the early Middle Ages, mead, rustic beers, and wild fruit wines became increasingly popular, especially among Celts, Anglo-Saxons, Germans, and Scandinavians. However, wines remained the beverage of preference in the Romance countries (what is now Italy, Spain and France) (Babor, 1986, p. 11).

With the collapse of the Roman Empire and decline of urban life, religious institutions, particularly monasteries, became the repositories of the brewing and winemaking techniques that had been earlier developed (Babor, 1986, p. 11). While rustic beers continued to be produced in homes, the art of brewing essentially became the province of monks, who carefully guarded their knowledge (Cherrington, 1925, v. 1, p. 405). Monks brewed virtually all beer of good quality until the twelfth century. Around the thirteenth century, hops (which both flavors and preserves) became a common ingredient in some beers, especially in northern Europe (Wilson, 1991, p. 375). Ale, often a thick and nutritious soupy beverage, soured quickly and was made for local consumption (Austin, 1985, pp. 54, 87–88).

Not surprisingly, the monasteries also maintained viticulture. Importantly, they had the resources, security, and stability in that often-turbulent time to improve the quality of their vines slowly over 1986 (p. 11). While most wine was made and consumed locally, some wine trade did continue in spite of the deteriorating roads (Hyams, 1965, p. 151; Wilson, 1991, p. 371).

By the millennium, the most popular form of festivities in England were known as "ales," and both ale and beer were at the top of lists of products to be given to lords for rent. As towns were established in twelfth-century Germany, they were granted the privilege of brewing and selling beer in their immediate localities. A flourishing artisan brewing industry developed in many towns, about which there was strong civic pride (Cherrington, 1925, v. 1, p. 405; Austin 1985, pp. 68, 74, 82–83).

The most important development regarding alcohol throughout the Middle Ages was probably that of distillation. Interestingly, considerable disagreement exists concerning who discovered distillation and when the discovery was made. However, it was Albertus Magnus (1193–1280) who first clearly described the process which made possible the manufacture of distilled spirits (Patrick, 1952, p. 29). Knowledge of the process began to spread slowly among monks, physicians and alchemists, who were interested in distilled alcohol as a cure for ailments. At that time it was called aqua vitae, "water of life," but was later known as brandy. The latter term was derived from the Dutch brandewijn, meaning burnt (or distilled) wine (Seward, 1979, p. 151; Roueche, 1963, pp. 172–173).

The Black Death and subsequent plagues, which began in the mid-fourteenth century, dramatically changed people's perception of their lives and place in the cosmos. With no understanding or control of the plagues that reduced the population by as much as 82% in some villages, "processions of flagellants mobbed city and village streets, hoping, by the pains they inflicted on themselves and each other, to take the edge off the plagues they attributed to God's wrath over human folly" (Slavin, 1973, pp. 12–16).

Some dramatically increased their consumption of alcohol in the belief that this might protect them from the mysterious disease, while others thought that through moderation in all things, including alcohol, they could be saved. It would appear that, on balance, consumption of alcohol was high. For example, in Bavaria, beer consumption was probably about 300 liters per capita a year (compared to 150 liters today) and in Florence wine consumption was about ten barrels per capita a year. Understandably, the consumption of distilled spirits, which was exclusively for medicinal purposes, increased in popularity (Austin, 1985, pp. 104–105, 107–108).

As the end of the Middle Ages approached, the popularity of beer spread to England, France and Scotland (Austin, pp. 118–119). Beer brewers were recognized officially as a guild in England (Monckton, 1966, pp. 69–70), and the adulteration of beer or wine became punishable by death in Scotland (Cherrington, 1929, vol. 5, p. 2,383). Importantly, the consumption of spirits as a beverage began to occur (Braudel, 1974, p. 171).

Early Modern Period

The early modern period was generally characterized by increasing prosperity and wealth. Towns and cities grew in size and number, foreign lands were discovered and colonized, and trade expanded. Perhaps more importantly, there developed a new view of the world. The medieval emphasis on other-worldliness—the belief that life in this world is only a preparation for heaven—slowly gave way, especially among the wealthy and well educated, to an interest in life in the here and now (Wallbank & Taylor, 1954, p. 513).

The Protestant Reformation and rise of aggressive national states destroyed the ideal of a universal Church overseeing a Holy Roman Empire. Rationality, individualism, and science heavily impacted the prevalent emotional idealism, communalism, and traditional religion (Wallbank & Taylor, 1954, pp. 513–518; Slavin, 1973, ch. 5–7).

However, the Protestant leaders such as Luther, Calvin, the leaders of the Anglican Church and even the Puritans did not differ substantially from the teachings of the Catholic Church:

alcohol was a gift of God and created to be used in moderation for pleasure, enjoyment and health; drunkenness was viewed as a sin (Austin, 1985, p. 194).

From this period through at least the beginning of the eighteenth century, attitudes toward drinking were characterized by a continued recognition of the positive nature of moderate consumption and an increased concern over the negative effects of drunkenness. The latter, which was generally viewed as arising out of the increased self-indulgence of the time, was seen as a threat to spiritual salvation and societal well being. Intoxication was also inconsistent with the emerging emphasis on rational mastery of self and world and on work and efficiency (Austin, 1985, pp. 129–130).

However, consumption of alcohol was often high. In the sixteenth century, alcohol beverage consumption reached 100 liters per person per year in Valladolid, Spain, and Polish peasants consumed up to three liters of beer per day (Braudel, 1974, pp. 236–238). In Coventry, the average amount of beer and ale consumed was about 17 pints per person per week, compared to about three pints today (Monckton, 1966, p. 95); nationwide, consumption was about one pint per day per capita. Swedish beer consumption may have been 40 times higher than in modern Sweden. English sailors received a ration of a gallon of beer per day, while soldiers received two-thirds of a gallon. In Denmark, the usual consumption of beer appears to have been a gallon per day for adult laborers and sailors (Austin, 1985, pp. 170, 186, 192).

However, the production and distribution of spirits spread slowly. Spirit drinking was still largely for medicinal purposes throughout most of the sixteenth century. It has been said of distilled alcohol that "the sixteenth century created it; the seventeenth century consolidated it; the eighteenth popularized it" (Braudel, 1967, p. 170).

A beverage that clearly made its debut during the seventeenth century was sparkling champagne. The credit for that development goes primarily to Dom Perignon, the wine-master in a French abbey. Around 1668, he used strong bottles, invented a more efficient cork (and one that could contain the effervescence in those strong bottles), and began developing the technique of blending the contents. However, another century would pass before problems, especially bursting bottles, would be solved and sparkling champagne would become popular (Younger, 1966, pp. 345–346; Doxat, 1971, p. 54; Seward, 1979, pp. 139–143).

The original grain spirit, whiskey, appears to have first been distilled in Ireland. While its specific origins are unknown (Magee, 1980, p. 7; Wilson, 1973, p. 7) there is evidence that by the sixteenth century it was widely consumed in some parts of Scotland (Roueche, 1963, pp. 175–176). It was also during the seventeenth century that Franciscus Sylvius (or Franz de la Boe), a professor of medicine at the University of Leyden, distilled spirits from grain.

Distilled spirit was generally flavored with juniper berries. The resulting beverage was known as junever, the Dutch word for "juniper." The French changed the name to genievre, which the English changed to "geneva" and then modified to "gin" (Roueche, 1963, pp. 173–174). Originally used for medicinal

purposes, the use of gin as a social drink did not grow rapidly at first (Doxat, 1972, p. 98; Watney, 1976, p. 10). However, in 1690, England passed "An Act for the Encouraging of the Distillation of Brandy and Spirits from Corn" and within four years the annual production of distilled spirits, most of which was gin, reached nearly one million gallons (Roueche, 1963, p. 174).

The seventeenth century also saw the Virginia colonists continue the traditional belief that alcoholic beverages are a natural food and are good when used in moderation. In fact, beer arrived with the first colonists, who considered it essential to their well being (Baron, 1962, pp. 3–8). The Puritan minister Increase Mather preached in favor of alcohol but against its abuse: "Drink is in itself a good creature of God, and to be received with thankfulness, but the abuse of drink is from Satan; the wine is from God, but the Drunkard is from the Devil" (quoted in Rorabaugh, 1979, p. 30). During that century the first distillery was established in the colonies on what is now Staten Island (Roueche, 1963, p. 178), cultivation of hops began in Massachusetts, and both brewing and distilling were legislatively encouraged in Maryland (Austin, 1985, pp. 230 and 249).

Rum is produced by distilling fermented molasses, which is the residue left after sugar has been made from sugar cane. Although it was introduced to the world, and presumably invented, by the first European settlers in the West Indies, no one knows when it was first produced or by what individual. But by 1657, a rum distillery was operating in Boston. It was highly successful and within a generation the manufacture of rum would become colonial New England's largest and most prosperous industry (Roueche, 1963, p. 178).

The dawn of the eighteenth century saw Parliament pass legislation designed to encourage the use of grain for distilling spirits. In 1685, consumption of gin had been slightly over one-half million gallons (Souria, 1990, p. 20). By 1714, gin production stood at two million gallons (Roueche, 1963, p. 174). In 1727, official (declared and taxed) production reached five million gallons; six years later the London area alone produced eleven million gallons of gin (French, 1890, p. 271; Samuelson, 1878, pp. 160–161; Watney, 1976, p. 16).

The English government actively promoted gin production to utilize surplus grain and to raise revenue. Encouraged by public policy, very cheap spirits flooded the market at a time when there was little stigma attached to drunkenness and when the growing urban poor in London sought relief from the newfound insecurities and harsh realities of urban life (Watney, 1976, p. 17; Austin, 1985, pp. xxi–xxii). Thus developed the so-called Gin Epidemic.

While the negative effects of that phenomenon may have been exaggerated (Sournia, 1990, p. 21; Mathias, 1959, p. xxv), Parliament passed legislation in 1736 to discourage consumption by prohibiting the sale of gin in quantities of less than two gallons and raising the tax on it dramatically. However, the peak in consumption was reached seven years later, when the nation of six and one-half million people drank over 18 million gallons of gin. And most was consumed by the small minority of the population then living in London and other cities; people in the countryside largely remained loyal to beer, ale and cider (Doxat, 1972, pp. 98–100; Watney, 1976, p.17).

After its dramatic peak, gin consumption rapidly declined. From 18 million gallons in 1743, it dropped to just over seven million gallons in 1751 and to less than two million by 1758, and generally declined to the end of the century (Ashton, 1955, p. 243). A number of factors appear to have converged to discourage consumption of gin. These include the production of higher quality beer of lower price, rising corn prices and taxes which eroded the price advantage of gin, a temporary ban on distilling, a stigmatization of drinking gin, an increasing criticism of drunkenness, a newer standard of behavior that criticized coarseness and excess, increased tea and coffee consumption, an increase in piety and increasing industrialization with a consequent emphasis on sobriety and labor efficiency (Sournia, 1990, p. 22; King, 1947, p. 117; Austin, 1985, pp. xxiii–xxiv, 324–325, 351; Younger, 1966, p. 341).

While drunkenness was still an accepted part of life in the eighteenth century (Austin, 1985, p. xxv), the nineteenth century would bring a change in attitudes as a result of increasing industrialization and the need for a reliable and punctual work force (Porter, 1990, p. xii). Self-discipline was needed in place of self-expression, and task orientation had to replace relaxed conviviality. Drunkenness would come to be defined as a threat to industrial efficiency and growth.

Problems commonly associated with industrialization and rapid urbanization were also attributed to alcohol. Thus, problems such as urban crime, poverty and high infant mortality rates were blamed on alcohol, although "it is likely that gross overcrowding and unemployment had much to do with these problems" (Soumia, 1990, p. 21). Over time, more and more personal, social and religious/moral problems would be blamed on alcohol. And not only would it be enough to prevent drunkenness; any consumption of alcohol would come to be seen as unacceptable. Groups that began by promoting temperance—the moderate use of alcohol—would ultimately become abolitionist and press for the complete and total prohibition of the production and distribution of beverage alcohol. Unfortunately, this would not eliminate social problems but would compound the situation by creating additional problems.

Summary and Conclusion

It is clear that alcohol has been highly valued and in continuous use by peoples throughout history. Reflecting its vital role, consumption of alcohol in moderation has rarely been questioned throughout most of recorded time. To the contrary, "Fermented dietary beverage . . . was so common an element in the various cultures that it was taken for granted as one of the basic elements of survival and self-preservation" (Lucia, 1963b, p. 165). Indicative of its value is the fact that it has frequently been acceptable as a medium of exchange. For example, in Medieval England, ale was often used to pay toll, rent or debts (Watney, 1974, p. 16).

From the earliest times alcohol has played an important role in religion," typically seen as a gift of deities and closely associated with their worship. Religious rejection of alcohol appears to be a rare phenomenon. When it does occur, such rejection may be unrelated to alcohol per se but reflect other considerations. For example, the nomadic Rechabites rejected wine because they associated it with an unacceptable agricultural life style. Nazarites abstained only during the period of their probation, after which they returned to drinking (Sournia, 1990, p. 5; Samuelson, 1878, pp. 62–63). Among other reasons, Mohammed may have forbidden alcohol in order to further distinguish his followers from those of other religions (Royce, 1986, p. 57).

Alcoholic beverages have also been an important source of nutrients and calories (Braudel, 1974, p. 175). In ancient Egypt, the phrase "bread and beer" stood for all food and was also a common greeting. Many alcoholic beverages, such as Egyptian bouza and Sudanese merissa, contain high levels of protein, fat and carbohydrates, a fact that helps explain the frequent lack of nutritional deficiencies in some populations whose diets are generally poor. Importantly, the levels of amino acids and vitamins increase during fermentation (Ghaliounqui, 1979, pp. 8–9). While modern food technology uses enrichment or fortification to improve the nutrition of foods, it is possible to achieve nutritional enrichment naturally through fermentation (Steinkraus, 1979, p. 36).

Alcoholic beverages have long served as thirst quenchers. Water pollution is far from new; to the contrary, supplies have generally been either unhealthful or questionable at best. Ancient writers rarely wrote about water, except as a warning (Ghaliounqui, 1979, p. 3). Travelers crossing what is now Zaire in 1648 reported having to drink water that resembled horse's urine. In the late eighteenth century most Parisians drank water from a very muddy and often chemically polluted Seine (Braudel, 1967, pp. 159–161). Coffee and tea were not introduced into Europe until the mid-seventeenth century, and it was another hundred or more years before they were commonly consumed on a daily basis (Austin, 1985, pp. 251, 254, 351, 359, 366).

Another important function of alcohol has been therapeutic or medicinal. Current research suggests that the moderate consumption of alcohol is preferable to abstinence. It appears to reduce the incidence of coronary heart disease (e.g., Razay, 1992; Jackson et al., 1991; Klatsky et al., 1990, p. 745; Rimm et al., 1991; Miller et al., 1990), cancer (e.g., Bofetta & Garfinkel, 1990) and osteoporosis (e.g., Gavaler & Van Thiel, 1992), among many other diseases and conditions, and to increase longevity (e.g., DeLabry et al., 1992). It has clearly been a major analgesic, and one widely available to people in pain. Relatedly, it has provided relief from the fatigue of hard labor.

Not to be underestimated is the important role alcohol has served in enhancing the enjoyment and quality of life. It can serve as a social lubricant, can provide entertainment, can facilitate relaxation, can provide pharmacological pleasure and can enhance the flavors of food (Gastineau et al., 1979).

While alcohol has always been misused by a minority of drinkers, it has clearly proved to be beneficial to most. In the words of the founding Director of the National Institute on Alcohol Abuse and Alcoholism, ". . . alcohol has existed longer than all human memory. It has outlived generations, nations, epochs and ages. It is a part of us, and that is fortunate indeed. For although alcohol will always be the master of some, for most of us it will continue to be the servant of man" (Chafetz, 1965, p. 223).

References

Hanson, David J. *Preventing Alcohol Abuse: Alcohol, Culture and Control*. Wesport, CT: Praeger, 1995. www2.potsdam.edu/hansondj/controversies/1114796842.html. Retrieved May 2, 2008.

Marley, David. *Chemical Addiction, Drug Use, and Treatment*. MedScape Today 2001 www.medscape.com/viewarticle/418525. Retrieved May 2, 2008.

Critical Thinking

1. Why have patterns related to alcohol use remained consistent around the world for centuries?

2. Consider the theme(s) of alcohol use throughout history as presented in this article and describe how alcohol use today relates to those themes.

Create Central

www.mhhe.com/createcentral

Internet References

National Clearinghouse for Alcohol and Drug Information
www.ncadisamhsa.org

National Institute on Alcoholism and Alcohol Abuse
www.niaaa.nih.gov

Adapted from **DAVID J. HANSON, PHD** *Preventing Alcohol Abuse: Alcohol, Culture, and Control*. Westport, CT: Praeger, 1995.

Article   Prepared by: Mary Maguire, *California State University—Sacramento*
Clifford Garoupa, *Fresno City College*

How Latin America Is Reinventing the War on Drugs

Frustrated with US dictates, countries across the region are floating new ideas to curb drug trafficking, from 'soft' enforcement to legalization.

SARAH MILLER LLANA AND SARA SHAHRIARI

Learning Outcomes

After reading this article, you will be able to:

- Determine how Latin American countries are changing their drug laws.

- Understand why these countries are changing their drug laws.

- Describe how the United States feels about the changes these countries are making.

L ike thousands of other Bolivians, Marcela Lopez Vasquez's parents migrated to the Chapare region, in the Andean tropics, desperate to make a living after waves of economic and environmental upheaval hit farming and mining communities in the 1970s and '80s.

The new migrants, who spread across the undulating green hills here, planted bananas. They planted yucca and orange trees. But it was in the coca leaf that thrives in this climate that they found the salvation of a steady cash crop—and themselves at the nexus of the American "war on drugs."

The coca leaf has been sacred in Andean society for 4,000 years and is a mainstay of Bolivian culture. It is chewed by farmers and miners, enlisted in religious ceremonies, and used for medicinal purposes. "The only resource for maintaining our families is the coca leaf," says Ms. Lopez Vasquez. "With coca we maintain our families: We dress ourselves, take care of our health, and educate our kids."

Coca is also used to make cocaine. To American society, from White House officials to worried parents, the nation's drug problems start in places like the back fields of the Chapare, where neat rows of coca's spindly bushes, bursting with bright green leaves, stand head high. Bolivia is the world's third largest grower of coca, behind Colombia and Peru.

For decades the coca growers here, Lopez Vasquez among them, resisted US-backed forced eradication in a long simmering protest that defined US–Bolivian relations and often turned violent. Growers in the Chapare scored a victory in 2004 when they were granted the right to grow a small plot of coca per family. But a turning point came with the 2006 election of Bolivian President Evo Morales, a former coca grower from the Chapare and still the head of its unions, who promised an end to the old US–Bolivian paradigm. Within three years of his presidency, Mr. Morales kicked out the United States Drug Enforcement Administration (DEA), as well as the US ambassador, accusing both of fomenting opposition. Last year Bolivia became the first country ever to withdraw from the United Nations 1961 Single Convention on Narcotic Drugs for the charter's failure to recognize the traditional use of the coca leaf.

Now the Chapare is once again a nexus—but this time for a new government experiment markedly different from former US drug policy. Today, farmers unions partner with government agencies to control coca production, reducing the amount of the leaf cultivated across Bolivia, as well as the quantities destined for illegal uses. This cooperation is new, and the very acceptance of coca crops in the Chapare defies US wishes.

The US, in fact, has voiced deep skepticism about Bolivia's commitment to the international fight against narcotics, condemning La Paz in a 2012 report for "failing demonstrably" in its antinarcotic obligations.

For the residents of the Chapare, however, the "nationalization" of Bolivia's drug fight means the preservation of a lifestyle and a basic income without the threat of constant conflict.

"I am a coca producer, and they made us take out our crops so cocaine would disappear and narcotraffic would disappear," says Felipe Martinez, who heads a state entity in charge of monitoring and eradicating coca that exceeds legal limits in the Chapare. "But that didn't bring results. It brought blood, sorrow, orphans. We lost the right to be people."

Bolivia's more go-it-alone approach symbolizes a fundamental shift in the drug war in Latin America—one that is creating a tense new relationship between the US and its southern neighbors and could help determine how many drugs ultimately end up on urban streets.

Countries across the region are adopting a more autonomous, sometimes nationalistic, response to narcotics control that increasingly questions Washington's priorities and prescriptions. From Bolivia, where drugs are produced, to Mexico and Guatemala, where they transit through, to Brazil, where they are increasingly consumed, officials are forging new policies or floating ideas to deal with a problem they believe 40 years of US-dictated solutions hasn't curbed.

The relationship between Latin America and the US has always been at its most fraught over the war on drugs, ever since Richard Nixon launched the initiative in the 1970s. Nowhere has Washington's scolding finger been more in the face of its Latin American counterparts. Nowhere has Latin America felt it has fewer options than to just acquiesce, dependent as it is on US aid and military might to overcome the cartels that control narcotics trafficking.

But in the past five years, frustration has mounted. Gruesome drug crimes have brought record levels of violence to swaths of Mexico and Central America, despite the billions that the US has poured into the antinarcotics fight.

Leaders in the region are pleading for new alternatives—some are even discussing legalized drug markets—no matter how much those ideas might alienate the US.

The restiveness reflects a growing political assertiveness in the region. While Latin America has always been weary of the heavy hand of the US, Bolivia and Venezuela have taken their indignation to a new level, refusing to cooperate with the DEA and other US officials. Many countries also seem less inclined to genuflect toward Washington on other issues, from trade to foreign policy.

Yet it is the drug issue that will most define US relations with the hemisphere—and have the most impact around the world. Latin America remains the world's No. 1 supplier of cocaine, and how various countries deal with their coca tracts will not only affect the flow of narcotics, but might lead to new strategies in the drug fight.

For now, the range of ideas and possible routes of action vary widely. Leaders in the most vociferous countries even concede that their ideas might not work. But what seems certain is that the days of policy dictated so heavily from Washington are vanishing.

"There is a desperate call from Latin America for peace, which includes a new model for drug policies," says Milton Romani, Uruguay's ambassador to the Organization of American States (OAS).

Otto Perez Molina is hardly a squeamish liberal. The president of Guatemala, who took office in January, is a retired military general who once served in the country's brutish special forces (Kaibiles). The day after his inauguration, the silver-thatched leader fulfilled a campaign promise to bring an "iron fist" to lawlessness by militarizing the drug fight in Guatemala.

So it stunned the region when the Guatemalan president, in March, floated a provocative initiative to deal with the violence spiraling out of control in another way: He called for an entire rethink of the war on drugs, including the option of the state running a legally regulated drug market.

The idea of pursuing more liberalized drug policies rather than harsher punishments is hardly novel in Latin America. But such notions are usually championed by intellectuals and academics on the left. They have rarely been promoted by sitting presidents.

Yet 2009 marked a hinge moment: A Latin American commission on drug policy headed by three former presidents, from Mexico, Brazil, and Colombia, published a report declaring the war on drugs a failure—one that desperately needed to shift from repression to prevention. Two years later, the group pulled former officials and business leaders from around the world into the Global Commission on Drug Policy, which went further, rallying nations to consider ways to regulate drugs rather than just crack down on their use.

Amid this growing consensus, Mr. Perez Molina, and perhaps even more significant, President Juan Manuel Santos of Colombia, began floating similar ideas. At a talk in London in late 2011, Mr. Santos, a former defense minister, said the war on drugs was stuck on a "stationary bike."

Other leaders rallied to their side, including Laura Chinchilla, the president of Costa Rica. Mexico's conservative president, Felipe Calderón, while not siding with legalization, has said in moments of exasperation that if US consumption cannot be controlled, the hemisphere should consider "market solutions," meaning some kind of regulated legal exchange.

Drug policy became a centerpiece of the OAS Summit held in Cartagena in April, too. The organization set a mandate to study drug policy alternatives and deliver a review in a year's time—what many consider a significant step.

Since then, in the boldest proposal to date, President José Mujica of Uruguay announced the possibility of establishing a legal marijuana market, in which the drug would be produced and distributed under state control. It would be the first market of its kind in the world.

Yet many drug policy experts in the region question whether a state-run exchange could work. Santos in Colombia criticized Mr. Mujica's plan, saying "unilateral" action is not the way forward. Others say corruption—in Guatemala, for instance—would only empower drug traffickers if there were a legal market. Still others note that talk of legalization, which focuses on marijuana, misses the point since cocaine is the big concern and no one is suggesting legalizing it.

But the debate, which has evolved from one led by activists to former presidents to current heads of state in Latin America, suggests that some kind of fundamental change is inevitable.

"For former presidents, it is easy to say 'let's have a debate' on a topic that they cannot do anything about," says Daniel Mejia, who runs a drug policy research center at the University of los Andes in Bogotá. "But having sitting presidents [say that] is a completely new thing that we've seen during the past five years."

While legalization is the buzz word that always draws media attention—and virulent US protests—Latin America is leading the way today in considering a whole range of alternative policy options. It is beginning to focus on drug use as a public health issue, and not a crime, through judicial rulings and legislation, following in the footsteps of Western Europe in the past two decades. Several countries have already introduced decriminalization of possession of small amounts of drugs, mainly marijuana, and are proposing lighter sentences for minor trafficking offenses.

In Argentina, for instance, the Supreme Court ruled in 2009 that it is unconstitutional to punish someone for possessing drugs for personal consumption. Mexico decriminalized personal use that same year, although only for minute quantities. Colombia's Constitutional Court in June upheld an earlier law that decriminalized personal consumption of marijuana and cocaine, while lawmakers in Brazil are debating whether to make possessing small quantities a noncriminal offense as well.

The moves mark a swing back from harsher sentences and an escalation of the war on drugs that have been a hallmark of US influence in the region since the 1980s, according to Martin Jelsma, a drug policy expert at the Transnational Institute in the Netherlands.

Bolivia's changes have been dramatic in their own way. On a recent morning, the Chapare, a New Hampshire-size province in the middle of the country, lies under a heavy mist. Wooden houses propped up on stilts sit among plots of banana trees.

Women in bright velvet skirts and brimmed hats, characteristic of the area's Quechua Indians, shop at local markets. Chickens scour dirt yards and dogs wander the roads. It's a peaceful tableau.

Yet the quietude has only come here recently, residents say. Rosa Montaño, who migrated to the Chapare as a young woman, still farms her legally allotted coca field, called a cato, which helps her maintain her home, a small unpainted wooden room. She lives there with her daughter, Irma Cornejo, who grew up in the height of the coca grower conflict, and her grandchildren. Both say dramatic changes have occurred since Bolivian rural police units, backed by the US, stopped coming in and forcing the eradication of coca.

"They brought my brother here and beat him," Ms. Cornejo says. "Now that doesn't happen. . . . It's calmer now. The kids don't see those beatings that I've seen; and the abuse, it isn't here anymore."

Under the current system, the responsibility for inspecting the size of the coca crops lies with the coca-growing unions and a government-monitoring body. It includes satellite surveillance. The Bolivians are backed in the program, called "social control," with funding from the European Union.

Farmers who consistently grow more than the allotted amount of coca, or who produce it outside designated areas, are subject to forced eradication. Bolivia's antinarcotics forces also still search out cocaine labs and confiscate illegal drug shipments.

"[Bolivia] challenged the United States, and it turned out the United States was not the omnipotent force in drug war policy that it seemed to be," says Kathryn Ledebur, director of the Andean Information Network, a Bolivia-based advocacy group. "And it was important to establish that for everyone in Latin America."

The US isn't completely divorced from the process. It continues to fund the antinarcotics effort in Bolivia through the US embassy, but the aid has dropped from about $40 million in 2006 to $10 million in 2012, according to US State Department figures.

Instead, Bolivia has increasingly been partnering with both the EU and Brazil, with whom it shares a long, porous border. Brazil, which is now the second-largest consumer of cocaine in the world, plans to use drones and other technology to help patrol the Amazonian area that the two countries share.

Brazil's ambassador to Bolivia, Marcel Biato, says the countries have been cooperating more closely since 2010, at the request of La Paz. "I think this link has to do with various internal elements, but also a clear distancing from the US and perhaps greater confidence that Brazil can develop an alternative to all of the historic problems," he says.

As part of the social control program, the coca unions educate local growers about the importance of keeping cultivation at legally accepted limits, which markedly increased during the early years of the Morales administration. When the US government was heavily involved in the eradication effort, before 2004, Bolivia was allowed to plant 46 square miles of coca a year for traditional uses. Since then, the Bolivian government has boosted that amount to 77 square miles.

To further aid growers, Morales is trying to find more legal international markets for the leaf, something the UN charter on narcotics prohibits. In Bolivia, coca is widely used in teas and chewed (bags of leaves are sold on street corners) as well as incorporated into consumer items such as candy, cookies, granola bars, and toothpaste.

The leaf acts as a mild stimulant—it produces no major high like purified cocaine—but can help overcome fatigue, hunger, and thirst. For these reasons, it has long been used as a medicine—something Bolivians have turned to for everything from nosebleeds to indigestion to dealing with childbirth.

The question is how much of it gets made into cocaine. Growers like Lopez Vasquez say there are always people who want to produce more coca than the state allows, or who turn it into cocaine and ship it off to Brazil and as far away as Africa and Europe. But as she stands in a coca field in her hometown, Lopez Vasquez is confident that coca cultivation will decline in the Chapare because the powerful unions are committed to working with, instead of fighting, the government to manage cultivation.

Mr. Martinez, the state official and coca grower, agrees. "More than ever we have applied ourselves to agree on mechanisms between the state and the coca producers so we have positive results," he says in his Chapare office, where he pulls out some coca leaves from his drawer and slips them in his cheek. "We haven't had any deaths. We haven't had any injuries. There has been no blood spilled and no conflicts."

Yet not everyone is convinced the situation is under control. Even though coca leaf cultivation has stabilized in recent years, the US believes that Bolivia is producing far more than even the limits La Paz has set—and thus the potential for cocaine production remains dangerously high.

According to the US's annual International Narcotics Control Strategy Report, the country cultivated 133 square miles of coca in 2010, down slightly from 2009's 135 square mile estimate. From this, the US estimates that the pure cocaine potential remains at 195 metric tons, or 70 percent higher than in 2006.

Further, the US believes Bolivia's ability to arrest major traffickers has eroded since the DEA was kicked out in 2008. "Expelling DEA has seriously harmed Bolivia's counternarcotics capability, especially in regard to interdiction," the report says.

Bolivia has certainly seen setbacks. In 2011, an ex-commander of the nation's antidrug police and current head of a drug intelligence agency was arrested by the DEA in Panama and subsequently pleaded guilty to trafficking. While no reliable evidence has surfaced linking other top Bolivians to the drug trade, accusations swirl that the links go beyond the one official.

"The highest levels of governance in those countries [Bolivia and Venezuela] are complicit in the global drug trade now," says Michael Braun, the former chief of operations for the DEA.

Bolivia represents one of the most extreme examples of countries diverging with the US over drug policy. But others are starting to question elements of America's priorities as well—some of them surprising.

When Mexican President Calderón was elected in 2006 and made fighting the scourge of drug cartels the cornerstone of his presidency, he was feted in American circles. A new era of "co-responsibility" was ushered in as the US signed off on a $1.6 billion aid package to help Mexico fight trafficking.

But as the years wore on and the toll mounted—including more than 50,000 dead in six years, even as top traffickers were caught and extradited to the US—so did public criticism of the strategy. It ultimately cost Calderón's conservative National Action Party the presidency in July elections. The incoming president, Enrique Peña Nieto, who takes office in December, has promised to "reduce violence" instead of focusing single-mindedly on netting traffickers and stanching the flow of drugs.

What that means exactly isn't clear. But ideas are being floated that would make American officials grimace, according to Alejandro Hope, a security analyst and former official in Mexico's intelligence agency.

He argues that Mexico should go after the most violent criminals, not the ones that move the most drugs. He says the country should quietly end eradication efforts, calling it a "pointless exercise." "What Mexico can't do and should not attempt to do is stop the flow of drugs into the US," says Mr. Hope.

US priorities are also under assault in Central America, where violence and trafficking have migrated after crackdowns in Mexico. In Honduras, DEA squadrons have been involved in three fatal shootouts in less than three months. The teams, called Foreign-deployed Advisory and Support Teams (FAST), have been accompanying local forces throughout Honduras and other countries in Central America.

But the program, which was begun quietly in Afghanistan and expanded into Central America, exploded onto the front pages in May after a group of Hondurans, who claim to be innocent victims, were shot at by Honduran forces, accompanied by the DEA, as they plied the waters of the Mosquito Coast in canoes. Four were killed. Since then, the DEA has been involved in two more fatal incidents.

The US and Honduras have defended the raids, and so does Mr. Braun, an architect of the program. "The government of Honduras is asking for more DEA resources, rather than backing away from the incidents. That is pretty telling," says Braun.

A US official echoes those sentiments. He says the success so far of Operation Anvil, under which the FAST teams were dispatched in April, is clear: Honduran forces, with DEA support, have interdicted 2,300 kilograms of cocaine from smuggling flights, mostly coming from Venezuela. "It showed us there is unchallenged illicit air traffic going through Honduras, and Honduras has not been able to control it until now," he says.

More broadly, he notes that the US has put more resources into the "soft" side of the drug fight, not just eradication and hardware but in institution-building and anti-corruption measures. "The old paradigm, the idea of a war on drugs, is long past," he says. "We realize there are a lot of other pieces of it that go well beyond eradicating a coca field."

Still, the incidents in Honduras and the perception of a continued militarization of the fight has provoked an outcry from human rights workers and others in Honduras and beyond. "The use of the military has just caused violence to spiral to levels we have never seen," says Sandino Asturias, head of the Center for Guatemalan Studies.

How far all this change in Latin America, whether in Lopez Vasquez's backyard or in the presidential palace in Bogotá, will go remains uncertain. But the days of Washington dictation seem to be diminishing. As John Walsh at the Washington Office on Latin America puts it: "No one is taking marching orders from the US anymore."

Critical Thinking

1. How long has coca leaf been used in Andean societies?
2. What do the indigenous Andean peoples use coca leaf for traditionally?
3. What exactly do Central and South American countries mean when they say that they want to establish legally regulated drug?

Create Central

www.mhhe.com/createcentral

Internet References

Drug Policy Foundation
   www.drugpolicy.org
Washington Office on Latin America
   www.wola.org

Prepared by: Mary Maguire, *California State University—Sacramento*
Clifford Garoupa, *Fresno City College*

Article

OxyContin Maker Closely Guards Its List of Suspect Doctors

Purdue Pharma has privately identified about 1,800 doctors who may have recklessly prescribed the painkiller to addicts and dealers, yet it has done little to alert authorities.

SCOTT GLOVER AND LISA GIRION

Learning Outcomes

After reading this article, you will be able to:

- Describe what OxyContin is.
- Understand how OxyContin is abused.
- Discuss the extent of OxyContin abuse in the United States.

Over the last decade, the maker of the potent painkiller OxyContin has compiled a database of hundreds of doctors suspected of recklessly prescribing its pills to addicts and drug dealers, but has done little to alert law enforcement or medical authorities.

Despite its suspicions, Purdue Pharma continued to profit from prescriptions written by these physicians, many of whom were prolific prescribers of OxyContin. The company has sold more than $27 billion worth of the drug since its introduction in 1996.

Purdue has promoted the idea that the country's epidemic of prescription drug deaths was fueled largely by pharmacy robberies, doctor-shopping patients, and teens raiding home medicine cabinets. The database suggests that Purdue has long known that physicians also play a significant role in the crisis.

Purdue's database, which contains the names of more than 1,800 doctors, could provide leads for investigators at a time when they are increasingly looking at how reckless prescribing of painkillers contributes to addiction and death.

Purdue has said little about the list since it began identifying doctors in 2002. A company scientist offered a glimpse into the database at a June drug dependency conference in San Diego, noting it was the first time the program had been discussed in public.

In a series of interviews with *The Times*, Purdue attorney Robin Abrams said the company created the database to steer its sales representatives away from risky doctors. Policing physicians, she said, was not Purdue's responsibility.

"We don't have the ability to take the prescription pad out of their hand," she said.

Abrams said the company had alerted law enforcement or medical regulators to 154 of the prescribers—about 8% of those in its database. The company's tally could not be independently verified.

Asked to provide cases reported to law enforcement, she identified three Southern California physicians implicated in major schemes to funnel OxyContin to addicts and dealers.

One of them, Masoud Bamdad of San Fernando, took in $1.5 million a year prescribing OxyContin and other painkillers to young addicts. He is serving a 25-year prison sentence on a drug dealing conviction. Bamdad was linked by prosecutors to six patient deaths.

Another doctor, Eleanor Santiago, is awaiting sentencing on federal charges that she helped flood Los Angeles' black market with more than 1 million illicit doses of OxyContin. Physician Kevin Gohar was linked to a suspected prescription mill in Reseda that authorities say sold OxyContin prescriptions to addicts across Southern California. Gohar died of a drug overdose in 2011 while a criminal investigation was pending.

Mitchell Katz, director of the Los Angeles County Department of Health Services, said Purdue has a duty to report all the doctors on the list, not just a select few.

"There is an ethical obligation," said Katz, a critic of what he says is the overuse of painkillers. "Any drug company that has information about physicians potentially engaged in illegal prescribing or prescribing that is endangering people's lives has a responsibility to report it."

Abrams said that some of the doctors in the database may no longer be active prescribers, but she could not provide a specific number.

OxyContin and other prescription painkillers have fueled a surge in drug overdoses, which in 2009 claimed 39,147 lives, surpassing for the first time traffic accidents as a leading cause of preventable deaths. Two years later, the U.S. Centers for Disease Control and Prevention declared prescription drug overdoses an epidemic.

Last year, a *Times* analysis showed that drugs prescribed by doctors played a role in nearly half the prescription overdose deaths in Southern California from 2006 through 2011. Seventy-one doctors prescribed drugs to three or more patients who fatally overdosed. Oxycodone, the active ingredient in OxyContin, was one of the most often cited drugs in the deaths.

Concerned by the mounting death toll, a congressional oversight committee in June called three top federal officials to testify about the government's response to the prescription drug crisis. Louisiana Republican Rep. Bill Cassidy asked why the government wasn't mining prescribing data to target rogue doctors.

"I'm expecting it's going to be a small percent writing a lot of the inappropriate prescriptions," said Cassidy, himself a physician. "What's the challenge in figuring out which doctors are the bad actors?"

President Obama's drug czar, R. Gil Kerlikowske, testified that the federal government didn't have access to such information.

Unbeknownst to Cassidy and Kerlikowske, Purdue Pharma had a database similar to what the congressman was looking for.

For decades, physicians avoided prescribing narcotic painkillers for anything but cancer and end-of-life pain because they feared the risk of addiction and overdose. But as Purdue and other drug companies pushed for their broad use, doctors began prescribing them for bad backs and other common ailments.

OxyContin—twice as potent as morphine—became one of the nation's most widely prescribed painkillers by marketing its patented time-release formula as safer than other drugs.

But it didn't take long for addicts to discover that "Oxy," as it is known on the streets, produced a heroin-like rush when crushed and snorted, releasing the pill's full potency at once.

By 2001, OxyContin sales hit $1 billion a year. The privately held Stamford, Conn., company was also under fierce attack. Local authorities up and down the East Coast, where problems with OxyContin first emerged, complained that the drug inflicted addiction and crime on their communities. Lawmakers pressed Purdue to do something.

At a hearing on OxyContin abuse that year, Pennsylvania Republican Rep. James C. Greenwood, then the chairman of a House oversight committee, told Purdue's top executives to use sales data to "weed out" bad doctors prescribing their drug.

The next year, Abrams said, Purdue's legal department began training sales representatives to report "red flags" at doctors' offices, including young patients, long lines, people nodding off in waiting rooms and frequent cash transactions.

Abrams said that if she and two other attorneys determine doctors to be too risky, Purdue bars sales representatives from marketing to them and stops paying commissions on the doctors' OxyContin prescriptions. Suspicious doctors are removed from the company's numbered sales territories and assigned to the database known as "Region Zero," she said.

By Purdue's account, the company has fielded 3,200 reports on suspicious doctors and other prescribers. About 75 doctors in the database did not prescribe OxyContin, according to Purdue.

Abrams said putting a doctor into the database is "essentially a judgment call."

"A lot of these are circumstances that if you were to walk into a doctor's office would give you pause and would make you turn around and walk out," said Abrams, a former federal prosecutor who specialized in criminal healthcare fraud cases.

Abrams declined to say precisely how the company decides which cases to refer to authorities. "I don't really want to open up an opportunity for folks to come in here and start looking and second-guessing," she said.

Among the situations that would lead to referrals, she said, are cases in which sales representatives witness apparent drug deals in physicians' parking lots or observe doctors who appear to be under the influence of drugs or alcohol.

Law enforcement, she said, "wouldn't be interested" in more vague reports.

Steve Opferman, who heads a healthcare crime task force for the Los Angeles County Sheriff's Department, said Purdue could be sitting on valuable leads.

"That's definitely data that law enforcement and prosecutors could use," he said.

Purdue used its database this year to bolster an extraordinary argument to the U.S. Food and Drug Administration: The OxyContin it had sold for 14 years was so prone to abuse that generic drug companies should not be allowed to copy it. Purdue said in a letter to the FDA that the argument was based in part on an analysis of prescriptions written by 364 active prescribers of OxyContin in Region Zero.

According to Purdue, when the company introduced a tamper-resistant formulation in August 2010, the doctors' prescriptions for maximum-strength OxyContin—the one favored by addicts—plummeted by 80%. Prescriptions for Opana, a narcotic painkiller made by a rival that could still be crushed and snorted, shot up about 400%, the internal study found. When crush-resistant Opana came out two years later, the same doctors' prescriptions for that drug also plunged.

Purdue concluded that a small number of doctors might account for a "substantial portion" of the nation's black-market supply of prescription painkillers, according to a summary of the unpublished study. The findings held "important implications," Purdue said, for policies aimed at curbing prescription abuse.

The company provided the study to the FDA in a confidential filing; it did not include doctors' names.

On April 16, the day Purdue's patent was set to expire, the FDA agreed that the original OxyContin—the type easily crushed and often abused—was too dangerous to allow generic drugmakers to copy.

At the San Diego conference in June, Purdue epidemiologist Howard Chilcoat made a brief presentation about the study. He said there were doctors in the database who were prescribing painkillers "for what appears to be the wrong reasons."

When he opened the floor to questions, Jane Liebschutz, a medical professor from Boston, made her way to a microphone. "Shouldn't those 364 prescribers be investigated?" she asked.

Chilcoat responded that the company reported doctors to authorities when it deemed it appropriate.

In April 2011, eight months after the introduction of the tamper-resistant OxyContin, Purdue said it gave the names of 82 doctors to officials at the U.S. Drug Enforcement Administration, which is responsible for granting authority to physicians to prescribe narcotic painkillers. The company declined to identify the DEA officials.

Joseph Rannazzisi, the DEA official in charge of the office of prescription drug control, declined to be interviewed.

Abrams said the company waited to share its suspicions until after its analysis "showed some scientific validity" to its theories about the doctors.

"We are doing what we think is the right thing for the right reasons," she said.

Keith Humphreys, a Stanford University professor and former drug policy advisor to Obama, had a different view of Purdue's timing and motives. He noted that Purdue became more vigorous about alerting government authorities to potential problem doctors after it shifted to its tamper-resistant formula and when generic-drug makers were poised to produce the crushable version.

"Those doctors are a gold mine for Purdue Pharma. And the whole time they're taking the money, knowing that something is wrong, and not telling anyone until it gives them a market advantage to do so," he said. "That is really disgusting."

Critical Thinking

1. Why should the maker of OxyContin be concerned about the prescribing?

2. What type of drug is OxyContin?

3. What therapeutic use does OxyContin have?

Create Central

www.mhhe.com/createcentral

Internet References

OxyContin prescription drug abuse
www.ctclearinghouse.org

U.S. Food & Drug Administration
www.fda.gov

Article

Prepared by: Mary Maguire, *California State University—Sacramento*
Clifford Garoupa, *Fresno City College*

Tackling Top Teen Problem— Prescription Drugs

Taking prescription drugs makes you feel "chill," a teenager recently told the *Bulletin*, "and nothing worries you."

GEORGE LAUBY AND KAMIE WHEELOCK

Learning Outcomes

After reading this article, you will be able to:

- Understand why teenagers are taking prescription drugs.
- Discuss the extent of teenage prescription drug use.
- Identify the effects of prescription drug use on teens.

Many people ages 11 to 18 routinely take pills such as Vicodin, Percocet, Xanax, Klonopin, Adderal, Concerta, Ritalin or generic knockoffs of the same.

The illegal use of prescription drugs looms larger than problem drinking or marijuana use, North Platte High School Principal Jim Whitney said.

The drugs are stolen from medicine cabinets, parents' or grandparents' medicine cabinets, or from a friend's house, or even bought off the Internet.

Drugs are passed to friends, either for free or for money. Some pills are reportedly taken by the handful at so-called "pharma parties" where pills are reportedly dumped in a bowl for anyone and everyone, and chased down with beers.

"You are just messed up," a student said of the effects. "You don't even want to move. You just want to lay there and stare off into space."

"Prescription drug abuse has been around in different forms for a long time," Whitney said, "but in the last year and a half it has probably become more popular than alcohol."

In a 2007 Lincoln County survey, 12–14 percent of high school students said they had abused prescription drugs. The same survey found more than 3 percent of sixth graders abused the drugs, and more than 5 percent of eighth graders.

The number who get caught is much lower. Only 12 students have been caught with illegal prescription drugs this year at the high school, Whitney said. Nearly all of them were suspended.

Kids steal drugs not just to chill, but to sell. Many pills bring from $2–5 each. OxyContin can bring $40 each, according to a high school user who asked to remain anonymous.

"Have you ever attended a pharma or pill party?" we asked the student.

"I wouldn't call them pill parties," she said, "but at pretty much any party there's someone who has pills, or is on pills. Recently a couple of people had some Adderal and we were snorting it. Adderal is popular because it makes it so you can drink more and you can stay up all night long."

Adderal is an amphetamine usually prescribed to treat attention deficit hyperactivity.

Taking the Call

The growing problem prompted a group of North Platte residents to fight back. Listeners are hearing hundreds of radio announcements on virtually every North Platte radio station, alerting the public to the problem.

The group has distributed thousands of pamphlets, bundles of posters and dozens of banners.

They have set a day—April 25—aside to collect prescription drugs, including syringes and over-the-counter drugs. They will set up a drive-up drop point at the high school.

The drugs will ultimately be incinerated.

They have lined up a team of powerful speakers who will talk about the danger, the self-destruction that comes with drug abuse.

The group of residents joined together during the Leadership Lincoln County program, wherein 20 people spend a year learning about major businesses and public services so they can get good things done.

In one part of the leadership program, the 20 split into groups of 5–6 people. Each group was challenged to develop a public project that will continue into the future.

The group—Wendy Thompson, Wanda Cooper, Sandy Ross, Bob Lantis, Patrick O'Neil and Connie Cook—kicked around ideas. After a visit with law enforcement officials they agreed to tackle the prescription drug problem at the urging of Capt. Jim Parish of the Nebraska State Patrol.

"The more we learned, the more we got involved," said Cook, a driving force in the project. "The information was riveting—and motivating. We learned about some kids at high school who got in trouble. Their parents were completely shocked. We were shocked. We had no idea."

"Now, we're passionate to do something constructive," Cook said. "It's amazing; every day we learn more and more."

"Have you taken other drugs?" the *Bulletin* asked another student.

"Yeah. I smoke weed like every day and used ecstasy once and I dabbled in coke for a couple of months last year and still do it every once in awhile," he said.

"I tried meth twice, but it made me crazy. I don't want to ever do very much of it; it's bad stuff. I've done mushrooms a couple times too, and of course alcohol is a drug too."

"I'm out of my alcoholic phase but I still drink on the weekends," he said. "I won't buy any drug except weed or alcohol but if someone's offering, I'll do pretty much anything. I'll never do heroin though, but I want to try acid in a few years just to see what it's like."

"Do a lot of your friends take pills?"

"Yeah, pretty much all of them. I have five friends that always have them. They take them pretty much every day."

"What do they think of it?"

"It's not considered a bad thing to do. Pills are the equivalent of smoking weed for people who can't smoke because they are on probation or just don't like pot. Like, the preppy kids do it because their parents would know if they smoked pot because they'd smell it. But most parents have no idea that their kids are getting messed up on pills."

Leadership Is Learning

The leadership group recently dropped posters and flyers at all of Lincoln County's schools, plus Stapleton.

At North Platte's middle schools, they asked the principals if they have caught kids using prescription drugs.

"They told us, 'As far as catching them, no, we've not caught them yet, but we know there are kids here who are stealing drugs so they can sell them to other kids,'" Cook said.

"We want this information out to the public," she said. "We know there is a need to educate those who are all the way from 101 years old to 10 years old. They need to know it's happening and how bad it is for kids, and the environment."

Cook said kids don't understand the dangers.

"What do you take the most?" we asked a North Platte high school student.

"I started out taking Xanax because I got as many as I wanted, for free. Then I had some Percocet. I loved those but they're too addictive to take for a long time. Most people take pain pills (Vicodin/Percocet), anxiety pills (Xanax/Klonopin), or attention deficit disorder pills (Adderal/Concerta/Ritalin)."

"How much would a kid spend on drugs in an average week?"

"People always gave them to me for free, but the average pill popper could probably spend $50–100 a week. The preppies can spend a lot from their lunch-gas-pocket money."

Harm to Creatures Large and Small

Even when the drugs are thrown away, they are usually flushed down the toilet.

Even when drugs are taken properly, traces enter the waste stream that eventually empties into nature, according to the Environmental Protection Agency.

The EPA is becoming more concerned. A study in Boulder, Colo. found female sucker fish outnumber males 5 to 1, and 50 percent of the males have female sex indicators, apparently from estrogen traces from pills for women.

Near Dallas, tiny amounts of Prozac have been found in the livers and brain cells of channel catfish and crappie.

Lots of Help

As part of the leadership project, Cook addressed the Lincoln County noon Rotary in mid-March. She cited national reports that the use of OxyContin increased by 30 percent in one year—2007—among high school seniors. And she said one out of 10 high school seniors that year used Vicodin illegally.

Eighty-one percent of teens who abuse prescription or over-the-counter drugs combine them with alcohol, the national study said.

Hospital emergency room visits involving such drugs increased 21 percent in 2008. Nearly half of those visits were from patients 12 to 20 years old.

The number of teens going into drug treatment has increased 300 percent in the last 10 years.

As Cook painted the alarming picture of abuse and incapacitation, community members offered to help. So far, 24 individuals and businesses have stepped up to sponsor the local education and collection effort.

"The support is overwhelming," Cook said.

"We heard you got into serious medical trouble once from taking too many drugs. Why didn't that stop you from taking more?" we asked a student.

"Well, I know I won't ever take that many again, and it did stop me for the most part. I was getting messed up every day. After that I didn't touch a pill for months. I switched to coke for a couple months, then pot when the person that always gave me coke got sent to rehab."

Featured Speaker—Former Abuser

Former Husker football All-American Jason Peter will speak to the public at the end of the drug collection day, April 25.

Peter, one of the nation's best defensive linemen in 1997, graduated from Nebraska and went to the NFL, where he earned $6.5 million from the Carolina Panthers. But he blew

The Language of Pharming

Big boys, cotton, kicker–Various slang for prescription pain relievers.

Chill pills, french fries, tranqs–Various slang for prescription sedatives and tranquilizers.

Pharming (pronounced "farming")–From the word pharmaceutical. It means kids getting high by raiding their parents' medicine cabinets for prescription drugs.

Pharm parties–Parties where teens bring prescription drugs from home, mix them together into a big bowl (see 'trail mix'), and grab a handful. Not surprisingly, pharm parties are usually arranged while parents are out.

Pilz (pronounced pills)–A popular term used to describe prescription medications. Can also include over-the-counter medications.

Recipe–Prescription drugs mixed with alcoholic or other beverages.

Trail mix–A mixture of various prescription drugs, usually served in a big bag or bowl at pharm parties.

most of the money on illegal drugs, taking up to 80 pain killers a day.

Jason Peter's life finally crashed. A series of injuries took him off the NFL roster.

He managed to clean up and wrote a book, "Heros of the Underground" and now hosts an ESPN talk show from his hometown of Lincoln. He spends his spare time traveling, talking about the dangers of drug abuse.

"Prescription drugs are a lot more addictive than people realize," another North Platte student told the *Bulletin*.

"You can get into big-time trouble," he said. "Possession of a controlled substance is a felony. They can even charge you for each pill in your possession. If they think you're selling them you get possession of a controlled substance with intent to distribute, which is prison time."

National Obsession

"Our national pastime—self-destruction," writer Jerry Stahl said in a review of Jason Peter's book.

"We are a nation obsessed with pharmaceuticals," Cook said as she addressed the Rotary. "We spend vast sums to manage our health, and we pop pills to address every conceivable symptom. In this nation, we abuse prescription drugs . . . daily."

Persons 65 and older take one-third of all prescribed medications even though they comprise 13 percent of the population, Cook said. Older patients are more likely to have multiple prescriptions, which can lead to unintentional misuse, more drugs stored in medicine cabinets for kids to steal.

The leadership group advises to keep medicine containers closed, even locked. Keep a record of prescriptions and the amount on hand. Reinforce a message of caution and restraint to your children. Start early, long before adolescence. Build a solid foundation for resisting temptations and outside influences.

North Platte Therapist: Most Clients Abuse Prescriptions

Young people steal grandma's pills and distribute them at school. Senior citizens falsify prescriptions for more pain medication. Babysitters take pills from cabinets.

An Ohio real estate agent lost her license for pilfering pills from bathrooms at open houses.

The appeal is obvious—the drugs can be legally obtained, the stigma of going to a street pusher can be avoided, and the price isn't steep.

There are an estimated 800,000 websites which sell prescription drugs on the Internet and will ship them to households no questions asked.

Today, about one-third of all U.S. drug abuse is prescription drug abuse.

Approximately 1.9 million persons age 12 or older have used OxyContin (pain reliever, like morphine) non-medically at least once in their lifetime, according to Columbia University's National Center on Addiction and Substance Abuse.

Vicki Dugger, a therapist with New Beginnings Therapy Associates in North Platte, said about 75 percent of the patients she treats admitted abusing prescription drugs.

Dugger said many more people are aware of it today than in the 1980s and 1990s. Still, much more awareness is needed.

"There's a misconception that abusing prescription medication is not harmful," Dugger said. "The fact is, it can have deadly results."

Dugger said, kids have died after attending pharming parties. She has some tips for parents to help keep their teenagers safe:

- Consider your own drug behavior and the message you are sending.
- Do a drug inventory. Forgotten or expired prescriptions or leftover over-the-counter meds could be appealing to kids, so get rid of them. Put new drugs away.
- Reach out and have a discussion. Dugger said research showed that kids who learn a lot about drug risks from their parents are up to half as likely to use drugs as kids who haven't had that conversation from mom and dad.
- Look on the computer. Try conducting your own web search to see how easily one can buy prescription meds without a prescription.
- Watch for warning signs. These may include unexplained disappearance of meds from medicine cabinets, declining grades, loss of interest in activities, changes in friends and behaviors, disrupted sleeping or eating patterns and more.

Dugger said she recently had a mother of a teen ask her about all the Musinex boxes around her house.

Musinex is a medication that is used for temporary relief of coughs caused by certain respiratory tract infections but teens have been known to abuse it by taking more than the recommended amounts to get high.

Dugger said she advised the mother to have a conversation with her teen immediately.

Critical Thinking

1. Do you see an abuse of prescription drugs among your friends or fellow classmates? How will you know when abuse exists?

2. What, in your opinion, needs to take place in the wider society to lessen dependency and prevent the abuse of prescription drugs?

Create Central

www.mhhe.com/createcentral

Internet References

Free Vibe Drug Facts
www.freevibe.com/drug_facts

Parents the Anti Drug
www.theantidrug.org

The entire *Bulletin* staff contributed to this report. It was first published April 1 in the *Bulletin* print edition.

Prepared by: Mary Maguire, *California State University—Sacramento*
Clifford Garoupa, *Fresno City College*

Article

A Glut of Antidepressants

RONI CARYN RABIN

Learning Outcomes

After reading this article, you will be able to:

- Understand the nature and extent of antidepressant use in the United States.

- Determine what the D.S.M criteria for diagnosis of depression is.

- Identify who is most often misdiagnosed as suffering from depression.

Over the past two decades, the use of antidepressants has skyrocketed. One in 10 Americans now takes an antidepressant medication; among women in their 40s and 50s, the figure is one in four.

Experts have offered numerous reasons. Depression is common, and economic struggles have added to our stress and anxiety. Television ads promote antidepressants, and insurance plans usually cover them, even while limiting talk therapy. But a recent study suggests another explanation: that the condition is being overdiagnosed on a remarkable scale.

The study, published in April in the journal *Psychotherapy and Psychosomatics,* found that nearly two-thirds of a sample of more than 5,000 patients who had been given a diagnosis of depression within the previous 12 months did not meet the criteria for major depressive episode as described by the psychiatrists' bible, the *Diagnostic and Statistical Manual of Mental Disorders* (or D.S.M.).

The study is not the first to find that patients frequently get "false positive" diagnoses for depression. Several earlier review studies have reported that diagnostic accuracy is low in general practice offices, in large part because serious depression is so rare in that setting.

Elderly patients were most likely to be misdiagnosed, the latest study found. Six out of seven patients age 65 and older who had been given a diagnosis of depression did not fit the criteria. More educated patients and those in poor health were less likely to receive an inaccurate diagnosis.

The vast majority of individuals diagnosed with depression, rightly or wrongly, were given medication, said the paper's lead author, Dr. Ramin Mojtabai, an associate professor at the Johns Hopkins Bloomberg School of Public Health.

Most people stay on the drugs, which can have a variety of side effects, for at least two years. Some take them for a decade or more.

"It's not only that physicians are prescribing more, the population is demanding more," Dr. Mojtabai said. "Feelings of sadness, the stresses of daily life and relationship problems can all cause feelings of upset or sadness that may be passing and not last long. But Americans have become more and more willing to use medication to address them."

By contrast, the Dutch College of General Practitioners last year urged its members to prescribe antidepressants only in severe cases, and instead to offer psychological treatment and other support with daily life. Officials noted that depressive symptoms may be a normal, transient reaction to disappointment or loss.

Ironically, while many patients in the United States are inappropriately diagnosed with depression, many who actually have it suffer without treatment. Dr. Mark Olfson, a professor of clinical psychiatry at Columbia University Medical Center, noted that from the time they develop major depression, it takes Americans eight years on average to seek care.

Diagnosing depression is an inherently subjective task, said Dr. Jeffrey Lieberman, the president of the American Psychiatric Association.

"It would be great if we could do a blood test or a lab test or do an EKG," Dr. Lieberman said, noting that similar claims of overtreatment have been made about syndromes like attention deficit hyperactivity disorder. "A diagnosis is made by symptoms and history and observation."

The new study drew 5,639 individuals who had been diagnosed with depression from among a nationally representative sample of over 75,000 adults who took part in the National Survey of Drug Use and Health in 2009 and 2010. The subjects were then interviewed in person with questions based on the D.S.M.-4 criteria.

Only 38.4 percent of the participants met these criteria for depression during the previous year, Dr. Mojtabai said.

It's possible some of the participants did not appear to be depressed because they had already been successfully treated, said Dr. Jeffrey Cain, the president of the Academy of Family Physicians. Their improved mood may also have colored the way they responded to questions about the past.

"If I'm checking people who are being treated for high blood pressure and taking medication, I would expect it to be better when I'm checking them," Dr. Cain said.

According to the D.S.M., a diagnosis of major depressive episode is appropriate if the patient has been in a depressed mood and felt no interest in activities for at least two weeks, and also has *at least five symptoms that impair functioning almost every day*. These include unintentional weight gain or loss, problems sleeping, agitation or slowed reactions noticed by others, fatigue and low energy, feelings of excessive guilt or worthlessness, difficulty concentrating and recurrent thoughts of death.

"We're not just talking about somebody who's having a bad day or got into an argument with their spouse," Dr. Lieberman said. "We're talking about something that is severe, meaning it's disabling and distressing and is not transient."

Many doctors have long prescribed antidepressants soon after the death of a family member, even though the D.S.M. urges clinicians to differentiate between normal grief and pathological bereavement.

One 50-year-old New York City woman said her doctor prescribed an antidepressant a few weeks after her husband died, even though she thought her feelings of shock and sadness were appropriate.

"He told me, 'You have to function, you have to keep your job, you have a daughter to raise,' " said the woman, who asked that her name be withheld because few friends or family members knew she was taking antidepressants.

Most of the study participants were not receiving specialty mental health care, but Dr. Cain pointed out that it was not clear who was making the misdiagnoses: a psychiatrist, non-psychiatrist physician or other provider, like a nurse practitioner.

But while a psychiatrist may spend up to 90 minutes with a patient before making a diagnosis, patients often are more comfortable with their primary care doctors, who rarely have that kind of time.

Dr. Lieberman suggested watchful waiting may be appropriate in some cases, and more integrated forms of health care may soon make it easier to send patients to a mental health provider "down the hall."

Doctors need to improve their diagnostic skills, Dr. Mojtabai said, and must resist the temptation "to take out the prescription pad and write down an antidepressant and hand it to the patient."

Critical Thinking

1. What is the D.S.M?
2. What is the principal way depression is treated?
3. Is everyone diagnosed as suffering from depression treated?

Create Central

www.mhhe.com/createcentral

Internet References

American Psychological Association
  www.apa.org
National Alliance on Mental Illness
  www.nami.org

Article

Prepared by: Mary Maguire, *California State University—Sacramento*
Clifford Garoupa, *Fresno City College*

Scientists Are High on Idea That Marijuana Reduces Memory Impairment

EMILY CALDWELL

Learning Outcomes

After reading this article, you will be able to:

- Understand the effects of marijuana on memory.
- Define what delta-9 tetrahydrocannabiol is.
- Understand what the endocannabinoid sytem is and what it does.

Columbus, Ohio—The more research they do, the more evidence Ohio State University scientists find that specific elements of marijuana can be good for the aging brain by reducing inflammation there and possibly even stimulating the formation of new brain cells.

The research suggests that the development of a legal drug that contains certain properties similar to those in marijuana might help prevent or delay the onset of Alzheimer's disease. Though the exact cause of Alzheimer's remains unknown, chronic inflammation in the brain is believed to contribute to memory impairment.

Any new drug's properties would resemble those of tetrahydrocannabinol, or THC, the main psychoactive substance in the cannabis plant, but would not share its high-producing effects. THC joins nicotine, alcohol and caffeine as agents that, in moderation, have shown some protection against inflammation in the brain that might translate to better memory late in life.

"It's not that everything immoral is good for the brain. It's just that there are some substances that millions of people for thousands of years have used in billions of doses, and we're noticing there's a little signal above all the noise," said Gary Wenk, professor of psychology at Ohio State and principal investigator on the research.

Wenk's work has already shown that a THC-like synthetic drug can improve memory in animals. Now his team is trying to find out exactly how it works in the brain.

The most recent research on rats indicates that at least three receptors in the brain are activated by the synthetic drug, which is similar to marijuana. These receptors are proteins within the brain's endocannabinoid system, which is involved in memory as well as physiological processes associated with appetite, mood and pain response.

This research is also showing that receptors in this system can influence brain inflammation and the production of new neurons, or brain cells.

"When we're young, we reproduce neurons and our memory works fine. When we age, the process slows down, so we have a decrease in new cell formation in normal aging. You need those cells to come back and help form new memories, and we found that this THC-like agent can influence creation of those cells," said Yannick Marchalant, a study coauthor and research assistant professor of psychology at Ohio State.

Could people smoke marijuana to prevent Alzheimer's disease if the disease is in their family? We're not saying that, but it might actually work. What we are saying is it appears that a safe, legal substance that mimics those important properties of marijuana can work on receptors in the brain to prevent memory impairments in aging. So that's really hopeful, Wenk said.

Marchalant described the research in a poster presentation Wednesday (11/19/08) at the Society for Neuroscience meeting in Washington, D.C.

Knowing exactly how any of these compounds work in the brain can make it easier for drug designers to target specific systems with agents that will offer the most effective anti-aging benefits, said Wenk, who is also a professor of neuroscience and molecular virology, immunology and medical genetics.

"Could people smoke marijuana to prevent Alzheimer's disease if the disease is in their family? We're not saying that, but it might actually work. What we are saying is it appears that a safe, legal substance that mimics those important properties of marijuana can work on receptors in the brain to prevent memory impairments in aging. So that's really hopeful," Wenk said.

One thing is clear from the studies: Once memory impairment is evident, the treatment is not effective. Reducing inflammation and preserving or generating neurons must occur before the memory loss is obvious, Wenk said.

Marchalant led a study on old rats using the synthetic drug, called WIN-55212-2 (WIN), which is not used in humans because of its high potency to induce psychoactive effects.

The researchers used a pump under the skin to give the rats a constant dose of WIN for three weeks–a dose low enough to induce no psychoactive effects on the animals. A control group of rats received no intervention. In follow-up memory tests, in which rats were placed in a small swimming pool to determine how well they use visual cues to find a platform hidden under the surface of the water, the treated rats did better than the control rats in learning and remembering how to find the hidden platform.

"Old rats are not very good at that task. They can learn, but it takes them more time to find the platform. When we gave them the drug, it made them a little better at that task," Marchalant said.

In some rats, Marchalant combined the WIN with compounds that are known to block specific receptors, which then offers hints at which receptors WIN is activating. The results indicated the WIN lowered the rats' brain inflammation in the hippocampus by acting on what is called the TRPV1 receptor. The hippocampus is responsible for short-term memory.

With the same intervention technique, the researchers also determined that WIN acts on receptors known as CB1 and CB2, leading to the generation of new brain cells—a process known as neurogenesis. Those results led the scientists to speculate that the combination of lowered inflammation and neurogenesis is the reason the rats' memory improved after treatment with WIN.

The researchers are continuing to study the endocannabinoid system's role in regulating inflammation and neuron development. They are trying to zero in on the receptors that must be activated to produce the most benefits from any newly developed drug.

What they already know is THC alone isn't the answer.

"The end goal is not to recommend the use of THC in humans to reduce Alzheimer's," Marchalant said. "We need to find exactly which receptors are most crucial, and ideally lead to the development of drugs that specifically activate those receptors. We hope a compound can be found that can target both inflammation and neurogenesis, which would be the most efficient way to produce the best effects."

References

The National Institutes of Health supported this work.
Coauthors on the presentation are Holly Brothers and Lauren Burgess, both of Ohio State's Department of Psychology.

Critical Thinking

1. What role does chronic inflammation in the brain play in Alzheimer's disease?
2. What is THC and how does it affect the brain?
3. What is the endocannabinoid system? What is it responsible for in the brain?

Create Central

www.mhhe.com/createcentral

Internet References

Drug Policy Foundation
www.drugpolicy.org
NORML
www.norml.com

Unit 2

UNIT

Prepared by: Mary Maguire, *California State University—Sacramento*
Clifford Garoupa, *Fresno City College*

Understanding How Drugs Work—Use, Dependency, and Addiction

Understanding how drugs act upon the human mind and body is a critical component to the resolution of issues concerning drug use and abuse. An understanding of basic pharmacology is requisite for informed discussion on practically every drug-related issue and controversy. One does not have to look far to find misinformed debate, much of which surrounds the basic lack of knowledge about how drugs work.

Different drugs produce different bodily effects and consequences. All psychoactive drugs influence the central nervous system, which, in turn, sits at the center of how we physiologically and psychologically interpret and react to the world around us. Some drugs, such as methamphetamine and LSD, have great, immediate influence on the nervous system, while others, such as tobacco and marijuana, elicit less-pronounced reactions. Almost all psychoactive drug effects on the body are mitigated by the dosage level of the drug taken, the manner in which it is ingested, and the physiological and emotional state of the user. For example, cocaine smoked in the form of crack versus snorted as powder produces profoundly different physical and emotional effects on the user.

Even though illegal drugs often provide the most sensational perspective from which to view drug effects, the abuse of prescription drugs is being reported as an exploding new component of the addiction problem. Currently, the non-medical use of pain relievers such as oxycodone and hydrocodone is continuing at alarming rates. This trend has been increasing steadily since 1994, and it currently competes with methamphetamine abuse as the most alarming national trend of drug abuse. Currently, more than 5 million Americans use prescription pain medications for non-medical reasons. Molecular properties of certain drugs allow them to imitate and artificially reproduce certain naturally occurring brain chemicals that provide the basis for the drugs' influence.

The continued use of certain drugs and their repeated alteration of the body's biochemical structure provide one explanation for the physiological consequences of drug use. The human brain is the quintessential master pharmacist and repeatedly altering its chemical functions by drug use is risky. Doing such things may produce profound implications for becoming addicted. For example, heroin use replicates the natural brain chemical endorphin, which supports the body's biochemical defense to pain and stress. The continued use of heroin is believed to deplete natural endorphins, causing the nervous system to produce a painful physical and emotional reaction when heroin is withdrawn. Subsequently, one significant motivation for continued use is realized.

A word of caution is in order, however, when proceeding through the various explanations for what drugs do and why they do it. Many people, because of an emotional and/or political relationship to the world of drugs, assert a subjective predisposition when interpreting certain drugs' effects and consequences. One person is an alcoholic while another is a social drinker. People often argue, rationalize, and explain the perceived nature of drugs' effects based upon an extremely superficial understanding of diverse pharmacological properties of different drugs. A detached and scientifically sophisticated awareness of drug pharmacology may help strengthen the platform from which to interpret the various consequences of drug use. Drug addiction results as a continuum comprised of experimentation, recreational use, regular use, and abuse. The process is influenced by a plethora of physiological, psychological, and environmental factors. Although some still argue that drug dependence is largely a matter of individual behavior—something to be chosen or rejected—most experts agree that new scientific discoveries clearly define the roots of addiction to live within molecular levels of the brain. Powerful drugs, upon repeated administration, easily compromise the brain's ability to make decisions about its best interests.

One theory used to describe specific drugs as more addictive or less addictive explains a process referred to as "reinforcement." Simply explained, reinforcement is a form of psychological conditioning that results from a drug's influence on a person's brain. Reinforcement is the term used to describe a person's behavior that expresses the uncontrollable need to repeatedly introduce the drug to the body. Powerful drugs such as the stimulant cocaine and the depressant oxycodone influence the brain's reward pathway and promote behavior in which drug seeking is recognized by the brain as actions necessary for survival. Persons addicted to drugs known to be strongly reinforcing typically report that they care more about getting the drug than about anything else—even in the face of self-destruction. Drug addiction and the rate at which it occurs must compete with certain physiological and psychological, as well as environmental, variables that are unique to individuals. A drug user with a greater number of biological markers known to be associated with drug addiction, such as mental illness, alcoholism, and poor physical health, may encourage drug dependency sooner than a person with fewer biological markers. Similarly, a person's positive environmental associations, or "natural reinforcers," such as a strong family structure and healthy personal and professional relationships may not only make experimentation unappealing, it may delay a user's developing drug addiction. Subsequently, one's liability for drug addiction is closely associated with genetics, environment, and the use of psychoactive drugs. Understanding the concept of addiction requires an awareness of these factors. For many people, drug addiction and the reasons that contribute to it are murky concepts.

The articles in this unit illustrate some of the current research and viewpoints on the ways that drugs act upon the human body. New science is suggesting that a new era has begun relative to understanding drugs and their pharmacological influence on the human body. This new science is critical to understanding the assorted consequences of drug use and abuse. Science has taken us closer to understanding that acute drug use changes brain function profoundly and that these changes may remain with the user long after the drug has left the system. New research investigating the liabilities produced by adolescents smoking tobacco suggests that even small amounts produce a remarkable susceptibility for addiction. Subsequently, many new issues have emerged for drug and health-related public policy. Increasingly, drug abuse competes with other social maladies as public enemy number one. Further, the need for a combined biological, behavioral, and social response to this problem becomes more evident. Many healthcare professionals and healthcare educators, in addition to those from other diverse backgrounds, argue that research dollars spent on drug abuse and addiction should approach that spent on heart disease, cancer, and AIDS. The articles in this unit provide examples of how some new discoveries have influenced our thinking about addiction. They also provide examples of how, even in light of new knowledge, breaking addictions is so very hard to do.

Article   Prepared by: Mary Maguire, *California State University—Sacramento*
Clifford Garoupa, *Fresno City College*

Prescription Drug Diversion

AMELIA M. ARRIA

Learning Outcomes

After reading this article, you will be able to:

• Identify individuals who are at risk for prescription drug abuse.

• Describe the resultant risks of prescription drug abuse.

• Discuss mechanisms to reduce prescription drug abuse in the youth population.

Statement of Amelia M. Arria, PhD Director, Center on Young Adult Health and Development University of Maryland School of Public Health

Committee on House Energy and Commerce Subcommittee on Commerce, Manufacturing and Trade

April 14, 2011

Chairman Bono-Mack, Ranking Member Butterfield, Members of the Subcommittee, other distinguished guests and members of the audience: thank you for highlighting the seemingly intractable problem of prescription drug abuse in the United States—and for the opportunity for me to lend my voice to the others invited here today.

Today I testify on the problem as it manifests among our nation's youth, college age and even younger. And I come at this issue from my perspective as a researcher at the University of Maryland and the Treatment Research Institute in Philadelphia. Since 2003, with my dedicated staff, I have led the College Life Study, a NIDA-funded investigation of the health risk behaviors, including drinking and drug use, of more than 1200 young adults who were originally enrolled as college students. For eight years, on an annual basis, we have gathered a large amount of data from this cohort of young adults, whether or not they continue attending college. These data tell a compelling story that is consistent with the work of several others in our field.

The first major finding is that nonmedical prescription drug use among our nation's youth is a symptom of a much larger problem. It does not occur in isolation—individuals who use prescription drugs nonmedically are very likely to be heavy drinkers and/or users of illicit drugs. Although the prescription drug problem receives a lot of visibility because of some

unique features, it is tightly linked to the larger drug abuse problem in the United States. We can, and must, deal with this "symptom"—because it is real, potentially dangerous, and threatens the futures of the youth of this nation. But even if policy makers, or practitioners, researchers, parents, or others are successful in alleviating this manifestation of the problem, we must also address the root issue or in five years you will be calling another hearing to discuss a new manifestation of the same problem.

Consider the following findings from the College Life Study:

By the fourth year of college, 13% of college students used a prescription tranquilizer nonmedically, that is, without having a legitimate prescription. By the same point, 23% had used prescription analgesics—again, non-medically and, finally 30% nonmedically used prescription stimulants.

Importantly, the overlap with other drug use was significant. In the past year prior to being assessed, 88% of nonmedical stimulant users had used marijuana, 30% had used hallucinogens, and 15% had used cocaine. Other findings from the College Life Study show that nonmedical use is fueled by sharing or selling of prescription medications, usually between friends or acquaintances. More than one third of students in our study who had been prescribed any type of psychoactive medication diverted it to someone else at least once in their lifetime. The most commonly diverted class of prescription medications on college campuses are prescription stimulants, medications prescribed for ADHD, such as Adderall, Ritalin and Concerta, with an estimated 61% of students with ADHD in our study diverting their medications to another person.

Let me sharpen the focus on this particular aspect of this problem of nonmedical use of prescription stimulants. We know that these drugs are widely available on college campuses for nonmedical use, owing in part to their ability to increase wakefulness. This particular class of drugs is attractive to college students with high task demands, and especially to those experiencing academic difficulties. There is a popular assumption—widely believed by the young adults themselves, and sometimes reinforced by the media that taking stimulants nonmedically confers an "academic edge," and is therefore beneficial for passing exams and writing papers. With headlines referencing "smart drugs" and "smart doping," the popular media have perpetuated the general notion that nonmedical use of prescription stimulants increases academic performance and that stimulants are used nonmedically by the best students.

Scientific evidence tells us quite the opposite, however. Nonmedical prescription stimulant use is associated with lower academic performance; it is not primarily the academically successful students who use prescription stimulants nonmedically, but the academically unsuccessful students.

Compared to non-users, our data show that nonmedical users of prescription drugs are more likely to meet criteria for dependence on alcohol and marijuana, skip class more frequently, and spend less time studying. And digging even deeper to the root of this issue, we see that these academic performance problems are linked to heavy drinking and marijuana use. In summary, what the research shows is that nonmedical prescription stimulant use is an unsuccessful shortcut, an attempt to compensate for declining academic performance, and is really a "red flag" for an underlying alcohol and/or drug problem in a college student.

Although stimulant medications when used safely under proper medical supervision for the treatment of ADHD can be instrumental in achieving therapeutic goals related to academic performance, there is no basis for making the assumption that similar benefits are attained through nonmedical use. It is necessary to dispel the powerful myths that parents, students and the media use to rationalize the nonmedical use of prescription stimulants. Prescribing physicians and college health centers need to emphasize why this behavior should be of concern, rather than a benign or normative behavior. In fact, the nonmedical use of prescription stimulants should trigger an assessment for possible underlying drug use, academic problems, and possible mental health issues.

[Data from] my supplementary materials shows the relationship between nonmedical prescription stimulant use and alcohol/illicit drug use data taken from 15 separate studies. On the point of prescription drug diversion, research findings consistently show that individuals who divert prescription drugs share characteristics with individuals who use prescription drugs for nonmedical purposes, and often times are nonmedical users themselves. Again, we are not dealing with separate issues—they are tightly linked to one another and represent similar problems.

What can policy makers do to address this "symptom" of the issue? The single best thing is to help tighten the "chain of custody" that ultimately governs supply of prescription drugs. Putting better prescription monitoring programs in place is one critical thing policy makers can do.

But physicians also have roles to play to reform their dosing practices, and be vigilant about underlying alcohol and drug issues when they prescribe psychoactive drugs to their adolescent and young adult patients.

Moreover, patients and parents need to do their part in tightening the supply chain by curtailing sharing of prescription medications among adults and becoming more aware of the whereabouts of leftover medication.

However, because the prescription drug problem has complicated the landscape of existing drug threats to our nation's youth and young adults, we need to redouble our efforts to develop innovative solutions to the public health problem of drug abuse and addiction. What specific strategies should be proposed? Today, I recommend two things related to prevention and early intervention:

1. Modernize the nation's infrastructure for early detection to address drug problems in youth and young adults. Decades of research tell us that we can identify those who are at highest risk for drug problems, just like knowing who is at risk for other chronic health conditions. Youth who develop drug problems share certain identifiable characteristics. With an approach that involves standardized assessments, early intervention, and promotes teamwork between parents, physicians and educators, we can put these young people back on track to fulfill their potential. To this end, NIH research has yielded valuable information about the risk and resiliency factors involved in the various stages of youth drug involvement, the interplay between genetics and environment on the escalation of drug problems, and the natural history and course of addiction. Finding effective solutions to this enormous threat to public health will require continued funding for NIH research.

2. Connect the dots between drug use and academic problems. The link between drug use and educational outcomes cannot be ignored any longer. Making this connection loud and clear will get the attention of parents who want more than anything else to see their child succeed. Tacit approval by parents and students of underage drinking as normative and college as a "five year party," especially when there are stimulant drugs as a last-resort pathway to "success," is a completely misguided but, regrettably, an all too common notion. Parents must be empowered to recognize a myth when they see one and respond with appropriate communication, emphasizing that attending class, completing assignments and using the time in college constructively is the best strategy to achieve superior academic performance.

Similarly, we must engage the leaders of our nation's education system who are concerned about the high school dropout crisis and less than optimal college graduation rates. With full recognition that academic problems can sometimes place a child at risk for drug use, we must also recognize the very real and contributory role of drug problems to poor academic achievement. Sustaining our economy and navigating future challenges will require a clear mind and sharp focus, which is inconsistent with underage and excessive drinking, and illicit and nonmedical use of prescription drugs, among our nation's secondary school and college students.

Again, I thank the Chair, ranking member, and all other members of this Subcommittee for shedding light on this continuing public health problem and allowing me to contribute to the discussion on solutions.

Critical Thinking

1. Analyze the risks of illicit prescription drug use in the youth population.

2. Describe the links between illicit prescription drug use and abuse of other substances.

3. Discuss policies that might help to alleviate the abuse of prescription drug use.

Create Central

www.mhhe.com/createcentral

Internet References

National Institute on Drug Abuse
www.drugabuse.gov/publications/drugfacts/high-school-youth-trends

NIDA for Teens
http://teens.drugabuse.gov/drug-facts/prescription-drugs

From *FDCH Congressional Testimony*, April 14, 2011. Public Domain.

Article

Prepared by: Mary Maguire, *California State University—Sacramento*
Clifford Garoupa, *Fresno City College*

The Genetics of Alcohol and Other Drug Dependence

Danielle M. Dick and Arpana Agrawal

Learning Outcomes

After reading this article, you will be able to:

- Describe the genetic factors related to alcohol use.
- Describe the genetic factors related to drug use.
- Identify the limitations of genetics in our understanding of alcohol and drug abuse.

This article explores the hypothesis that certain genetic factors increase a person's risk of both alcohol abuse and dependence and other drug abuse and dependence. It first reviews the evidence suggesting that certain genetic factors contribute to the development of alcohol and other drug (AOD) use disorders, as well as to the development of a variety of forms of externalizing psychopathology—that is, psychiatric disorders characterized by disinhibited behavior, such as antisocial personality disorder, attention deficit/hyperactivity disorder, and conduct disorder. After summarizing the difficulties associated with, and recent progress made in, the identification of specific genes associated with AOD dependence, the article then discusses evidence that implicates several genes in a person's risk for dependence on both alcohol and illicit drugs.

Genetic Epidemiology of AOD Dependence

Alcohol dependence frequently co-occurs with dependence on illicit drugs (Hasin et al. 2007). Both alcohol use disorders (i.e., alcohol abuse and alcohol dependence) and drug use disorders (drug abuse and drug dependence) are influenced by several factors. For example, family, twin, and adoption studies have convincingly demonstrated that genes contribute to the development of alcohol dependence, with heritability estimates ranging from 50 to 60 percent for both men and women (McGue 1999). Dependence on illicit drugs only more recently has been investigated in twin samples, but several studies now suggest that illicit drug abuse and dependence also are under significant genetic influence. In these studies of adult samples, heritability estimates ranged from 45 to 79 percent (for reviews, see Agrawal and Lynskey 2006; etc. Kendler et al. 2003a; Tsuang et al. 2001).

Twin studies also can be used to assess the extent to which the *co-occurrence* of disorders is influenced by genetic and/or environmental factors. Thus, a finding that the correlation between alcohol dependence in twin 1 and drug dependence in twin 2 is higher for identical (i.e., monozygotic) twins, who share 100 percent of their genes, than for fraternal (i.e., dizygotic) twins, who share on average only 50 percent of their genes, indicates that shared genes influence the risk of both alcohol and drug dependence. The twin studies conducted to date support the role of such shared genetic factors. For example, in the largest twin study of the factors underlying psychiatric disorders, Kendler and colleagues (2003b) analyzed data from the Virginia Twin Registry and found that a common genetic factor contributed to the total variance in alcohol dependence, illicit drug abuse and dependence, conduct disorder, and adult antisocial behavior. This pattern also has been identified in several other independent twin studies (Krueger et al. 2002; Young et al. 2000). Taken together, these findings suggest that a significant portion of the genetic influence on alcohol dependence and drug dependence is through a general predisposition toward externalizing disorders, which may manifest in different ways (e.g., different forms of AOD dependence and/or antisocial behavior) (see Figure). However, some evidence also suggests that disorder-specific genetic influences contribute to AOD dependence (Kendler et al. 2003b). These specific influences likely reflect the actions of genes that are involved in the metabolism of individual drugs.

The idea that alcohol and drug dependence share a genetic liability with each other, as well as with other forms of externalizing psychopathology, is further supported by electrophysiological studies recording the brain's electrical activity. These studies, which are conducted using electrodes placed on the person's scalp, provide a noninvasive, sensitive method of measuring brain function in humans. They generate a predictable pattern in the height (i.e., amplitude) and rate (i.e., frequency) of brain waves that can show characteristic abnormalities in people with certain types of brain dysfunction. For example, electrophysiological abnormalities have been observed in people with a variety of externalizing disorders as well as in unaffected children of these people. These findings suggest that electrophysiological measurements can be used as markers of a genetic vulnerability to externalizing disorders.

One commonly measured electrophysiological characteristic is the so-called P3 component of an event-related potential—that is, a spike in brain activity that occurs about 300 milliseconds after a person is exposed to a sudden stimulus (e.g., a sound or light). Researchers have observed that the amplitude of the P3 component is reduced in alcohol-dependent people and their children, suggesting that this abnormality is a marker for a genetic predisposition to alcohol dependence (Porjesz et al. 1995). However, the abnormal P3 response is not specific to alcohol dependence but appears to be associated with a variety of disinhibitory disorders, including other forms of drug dependence, childhood externalizing disorders, and adult antisocial personality disorder, again suggesting a shared underlying predisposition to multiple forms of AOD dependence and other externalizing problems (Hicks et al. 2007).[1]

Interestingly, electrophysiological abnormalities are most pronounced in alcohol-dependent people who also have a diagnosis of illicit drug abuse or dependence (Malone et al. 2001). This observation is consistent with data from twin and family studies suggesting that co-morbid dependence on alcohol and another drug represents a more severe disorder with higher heritability than dependence on one drug alone (Johnson et al. 1996; Pickens et al. 1995). This conclusion also appears to be supported by new studies exploring the roles of specific genes, which are discussed later in this article.

Identifying Specific Genes Related to AOD Dependence

With robust evidence indicating that genes influence both alcohol dependence and dependence on illicit drugs, efforts now are underway to identify specific genes involved in the development of these disorders. This identification, however, is complicated by many factors. For example, numerous genes are thought to contribute to a person's susceptibility to alcohol and/or drug dependence, and affected people may carry different combinations of those genes. Additionally, environmental influences have an impact on substance use, as does gene–environment interaction (Heath et al. 2002). Finally, the manifestation of AOD dependence varies greatly among affected people, for example, with respect to age of onset of problems, types of symptoms exhibited (i.e., symptomatic profile), substance use history, and presence of co-morbid disorders.

Despite the complications mentioned above, the rapid growth in research technologies for gene identification in recent years has led to a concomitant increase in exciting results. After suffering many disappointments in early attempts to identify genes involved in complex behavioral outcomes (i.e., phenotypes), researchers now are frequently succeeding in identifying genes that help determine a variety of clinical phenotypes. These advances have been made possible by several factors. First, advances in technologies to identify a person's genetic makeup (i.e., genotyping technology) have dramatically lowered the cost of genotyping, allowing for high-throughput analyses of

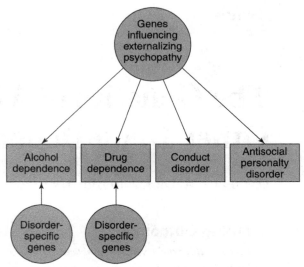

Figure Schematic representation of a model to illustrate the influence of genetic factors on the development of alcohol dependence, dependence on other drugs, and other externalizing disorders (e.g., conduct disorder or antisocial personality disorder). Some of the proposed genetic factors are thought to have a general influence on all types of externalizing conditions, whereas others are thought to have a disorder-specific influence.

the entire genome. Second, the completion of several large-scale research endeavors, such as the Human Genome Project, the International HapMap Project,[2] and other government and privately funded efforts, have made a wealth of information on variations in the human genome publicly available. Third, these developments have been complemented by advances in the statistical analysis of genetic data.

Several large collaborative projects that strive to identify genes involved in AOD dependence currently are underway. The first large-scale project aimed at identifying genes contributing to alcohol dependence was the National Institute on Alcohol Abuse and Alcoholism (NIAAA)-sponsored Collaborative Study on the Genetics of Alcoholism (COGA), which was initiated in 1989. This study, which involves collaboration of investigators at several sites in the United States, examines families with several alcohol-dependent members who were recruited from treatment centers across the United States. This study has been joined by several other gene identification studies focusing on families affected with alcohol dependence, including the following:

- A sample of Southwestern American Indians (Long et al. 1998);
- The Irish Affected Sib Pair Study of Alcohol Dependence (Prescott et al. 2005*a*);
- A population of Mission Indians (Ehlers et al. 2004);
- A sample of densely affected families collected in the Pittsburgh area (Hill et al. 2004); and
- An ongoing data collection from alcohol-dependent individuals in Australia.

Importantly, most of these projects include comprehensive psychiatric interviews that focus not only on alcohol use and alcohol use disorders but which also allow researchers to collect information about other drug use and dependence. This comprehensive approach permits researchers to address questions about the nature of genetic influences on AOD dependence, as discussed below.

More recently, additional studies have been initiated that specifically seek to identify genes contributing to various forms of illicit drug dependence as well as general drug use problems (for more information, see www.nida.nih.gov/about/organization/Genetics/consortium/index.html). Through these combined approaches, researchers should be able to identify both genes with drug-specific effects and genes with more general effects on drug use. The following sections focus on several groups of genes that have been identified by these research efforts and which have been implicated in affecting risk for dependence on both alcohol and illicit drugs.

Genes Encoding Proteins Involved in Alcohol Metabolism

The genes that have been associated with alcohol dependence most consistently are those encoding the enzymes that metabolize alcohol (chemically known as ethanol). The main pathway of alcohol metabolism involves two steps. In the first step, ethanol is converted into the toxic intermediate acetaldehyde; this step is mediated by the alcohol dehydrogenase (ADH) enzymes. In a second step, the acetaldehyde is further broken down into acetate and water by the actions of aldehyde dehydrogenase (ALDH) enzymes. The genes that encode the ADH and ALDH enzymes exist in several variants (i.e., alleles) that are characterized by variations (i.e., polymorphisms) in the sequence of the DNA building blocks. One important group of ADH enzymes are the ADH class I isozymes ADH1A, ADH1B, and ADH1C. For both the genes encoding ADH1B and those encoding ADH1C, several alleles resulting in altered proteins have been identified, and the proteins encoded by some of these alleles exhibit particularly high enzymatic activity in laboratory experiments (i.e., in vitro) (Edenberg 2007). This suggests that in people carrying these alleles, ethanol is more rapidly converted to acetaldehyde.[3] Several studies have reported lower frequencies of both the ADH1B*2 and ADH1C*1 alleles, which encode some of the more active proteins, among alcoholics than among non-alcoholics in a variety of East Asian populations (e.g., Shen et al. 1997) and, more recently, in European populations (Neumark et al. 1998; Whitfield et al. 1998).

In addition, genome-wide screens to identify genes linked to alcoholism and alcohol-related traits have been conducted in three independent samples consisting largely of people of European descent—the COGA study (Saccone et al. 2000), the Irish Affected Sib Pair Study of Alcohol Dependence (Prescott et al. 2005a), and an Australian sample (Birley et al. 2005). These studies have found evidence that a region on chromosome 4 containing the ADH gene cluster shows linkage to the phenotypes studied. This cluster contains, in addition to the genes encoding ADH class I isozymes, the genes ADH4, ADH5, ADH6, and ADH7, which encode other ADH enzymes.

Polymorphisms exist for each of these genes, some of which also have been associated with alcohol dependence (Edenberg et al. 2006; Luo et al. 2006a,b; Prescott et al. 2005b).

Interestingly, the effects of these genes do not appear to be limited to alcohol dependence. One study compared the frequency of alleles that differed in only one DNA building block (i.e., single nucleotide polymorphisms [SNPs]) throughout the genome between people with histories of illicit drug use and/or dependence and unrelated control participants. This study detected a significant difference for a SNP located near the ADH gene cluster (Uhl et al. 2001). More recent evidence suggests that genetic variants in the ADH1A, ADH1B, ADH1C, ADH5, ADH6, and ADH7 genes are associated with illicit drug dependence and that this association is not purely attributable to co-morbid alcohol dependence (Luo et al. 2007). The mechanism by which these genes may affect risk for illicit drug dependence is not entirely clear. However, other observations[4] also indicate that enzymes involved in alcohol metabolism may contribute to illicit drug dependence via pathways that currently are unknown but independent of alcohol metabolism (Luo et al. 2007).

Genes Encoding Proteins Involved in Neurotransmission

AODs exert their behavioral effects in part by altering the transmission of signals among nerve cells (i.e., neurons) in the brain. This transmission is mediated by chemical messengers (i.e., neurotransmitters) that are released by the signal-emitting neuron and bind to specific proteins (i.e., receptors) on the signal-receiving neuron. AODs influence the activities of several neurotransmitter systems, including those involving the neurotransmitters γ-aminobutyric acid (GABA), dopamine, and acetylcholine, as well as naturally produced compounds that structurally resemble opioids and cannabinoids. Accordingly, certain genes encoding components of these neurotransmitter systems may contribute to the risk of both alcohol dependence and illicit drug dependence.

Genes Encoding the GABA$_A$ Receptor

GABA is the major inhibitory neurotransmitter in the human central nervous system—that is, it affects neurons in a way that reduces their activity. Several lines of evidence suggest that GABA is involved in many of the behavioral effects of alcohol, including motor incoordination, anxiety reduction (i.e., anxiolysis), sedation, withdrawal signs, and preference for alcohol (Grobin et al. 1998). GABA interacts with several receptors, and much of the research on alcohol's interactions with the GABA system has focused on the GABA$_A$ receptor. This receptor also is the site of action for several medications that frequently are misused and have high addictive potential, such as benzodiazepines, barbiturates, opiates, α-hydroxybutyrates, and other sedative–hypnotic compounds. Accordingly, this receptor likely is involved in dependence on these drugs as well (Orser 2006).

The GABA$_A$ receptor is composed of five subunits that are encoded by numerous genes, most of which are located in clusters. Thus, chromosome 4 contains a cluster comprising the genes *GABRA2, GABRA4, GABRB1,* and *GABRG1;* chromosome 5 contains *GABRA1, GABRA6, GABRB2,* and *GABRG2;* and chromosome 15 contains *GABRA5, GABRB3,* and *GABRG3* (see www.ncbi.nlm.nih.gov/sites/entrez?db=gene).

Interest in the GABA$_A$ receptor genes on chromosome 4 grew when this region consistently was identified in genome-wide scans looking for linkage with alcohol dependence (Long et al. 1998; Williams et al. 1999). Subsequently, COGA investigators systematically evaluated short DNA segments of known location (i.e., genetic markers) that were situated in the GABA$_A$ receptor gene cluster on chromosome 4. These studies found that a significant association existed between multiple SNPs in the *GABRA2* gene and alcohol dependence (Edenberg et al. 2004). This association has been replicated in multiple independent samples (Covault et al. 2004; Fehr et al. 2006; Lappalainen et al. 2005; Soyka 2007). In addition, the same SNPs in the *GABRA2* gene have been shown to be associated with drug dependence in both adults and adolescents (Dick et al. 2006*a*), as well as with the use of multiple drugs in another independent sample (Drgon et al. 2006).

Variations in the *GABRA2* gene are associated not only with AOD dependence but also with certain electrophysiological characteristics (i.e., endophenotypes) in the COGA sample (Edenberg et al. 2004). As reviewed above, these electrophysiological characteristics are not unique to alcohol dependence but also are found in individuals with other forms of externalizing psychopathology. This association supports the hypothesis that the *GABRA2* gene generally is involved in AOD use and/or externalizing problems. Interestingly, subsequent analyses investigating the role of *GABRA2* in drug dependence (Agrawal et al. 2006) found that the association with *GABRA2* was strongest in people with co-morbid AOD dependence, with no evidence of association in people who were only alcohol dependent. This observation supports the assertion that co-morbid AOD dependence may represent a more severe, genetically influenced form of the disorder.

Several other GABA$_A$ receptor genes have yielded more modest evidence of association with different aspects of AOD dependence. Thus, *GABRB3* (Noble et al. 1998) and *GABRG3* (Dick et al. 2004) are modestly associated with alcohol dependence, *GABRA1* (Dick et al. 2006*b*) is associated with alcohol-related phenotypes (e.g., history of alcohol-induced blackouts and age at first drunkenness), and *GABRG2* (Loh et al. 2007) is associated with aspects of drug dependence. These findings await confirmation in independent samples.

Genes Involved in the Cholinergic System

The cholinergic system includes neurons that either release the neurotransmitter acetylcholine or respond to it. Acetylcholine generally has excitatory effects in the human central nervous system—that is, it affects neurons in a way that enhances their activity. It is thought to be involved in such processes as arousal, reward, learning, and short-term memory. One of the receptors through which acetylcholine acts is encoded by a gene called *CHRM2*. In the COGA sample, linkage was observed between a region on chromosome 7 that contains the *CHRM2* gene and alcohol dependence, and subsequent experiments confirmed

that an association existed between alcohol dependence and the *CHRM2* gene (Wang et al. 2004). This association has been replicated in a large independent study (Luo et al. 2005) that also found evidence that the gene was associated with drug dependence.

As with the *GABRA2* gene described above, the association between *CHRM2* and alcohol dependence in the COGA sample was strongest in people who had co-morbid AOD dependence (Dick et al. 2007). Additional analyses in the COGA sample have suggested that *CHRM2* is associated with a generally increased risk of externalizing disorders, including symptoms of alcohol dependence and drug dependence (Dick et al. 2008). This potential role of *CHRM2* in contributing to the general liability of AOD use and externalizing disorders is further supported by findings that *CHRM2*, like *GABRA2*, also is associated with certain electrophysiological endophenotypes (Jones et al. 2004).

Genes Involved in the Endogenous Opioid System

Endogenous opioids are small molecules naturally produced in the body that have similar effects as the opiates (e.g., morphine and heroin) and which, among other functions, modulate the actions of other neurotransmitters. The endogenous opioid system has been implicated in contributing to the reinforcing effects of several drugs of abuse, including alcohol, opiates, and cocaine. This is supported by the finding that the medication naltrexone, which prevents the normal actions of endogenous opioids (i.e., is an opioid antagonist), is useful in the treatment of alcohol dependence and can reduce the number of drinking days, amount of alcohol consumed, and risk of relapse.

Research on the role of the endogenous opioids in AOD dependence has centered mainly on a gene called *OPRM1*, which encodes one type of opioid receptor (i.e., the μ-opioid receptor), although the results so far have been equivocal. This gene contains a polymorphism resulting in a different protein product (i.e., a non-synonymous polymorphism) that in one study was found to bind one of the endogenous opioids (i.e., β-endorphin) three times as strongly as the main variant of the gene (Bond et al. 1998); other studies, however, could not confirm this finding (Befort et al. 2001; Beyer et al. 2004).

Laboratory studies have suggested that *OPRM1* is associated with sensitivity to the effects of alcohol (Ray and Hutchison 2004). In addition, several studies have reported evidence of an association between *OPRM1* and drug dependence (e.g., Bart et al. 2005). Other studies, however, have failed to find such an association (e.g., Bergen et al. 1997), and a combined analysis of several studies (i.e., a meta-analysis) concluded that no association exists between the most commonly studied *OPRM1* polymorphism and drug dependence (Arias et al. 2006). However, this finding does not preclude the possibility that other genetic variants in *OPRM1* and/or other genes related to the endogenous opioid system are involved in risk for drug dependence. For example, a recent study determining the genotypes of multiple genetic variants across the gene uncovered evidence of association with *OPRM1* and AOD dependence (Zhang et al. 2006).

Researchers also have investigated genetic variations in other opioid receptors and other components of the endogenous opioid system; however, the results have been mixed. One study (Zhang et al. 2007) found modest support that the genes *OPRK1* and *OPRD1*—which encode the κ- and δ-opioid receptors, respectively—are associated with some aspects of drug dependence. Other researchers (Xuei et al. 2007) reported evidence that the genes *PDYN, PENK,* and *POMC*—which encode small molecules (i.e., peptides) that also bind to opioid receptors—may be associated with various aspects of drug dependence.

Genes Involved in the Endogenous Cannabinoid System

Endogenous cannabinoids are compounds naturally produced in the body that have a similar structure to the psychoactive compounds found in the cannabis plant and which bind cannabinoid receptors. The endogenous cannabinoid system is thought to regulate brain circuits using the neurotransmitter dopamine, which likely helps mediate the rewarding experiences associated with addictive substances. The main cannabinoid receptor in the brain is called CB1 and is encoded by the *CNR1* gene, which is located on chromosome 6. This gene is an excellent candidate gene for being associated with AOD dependence because the receptor encoded by this gene is crucial for generating the rewarding effects of the compound responsible for the psychoactive effects associated with cannabis use (i.e., Δ9-tetrahydrocannabinol). However, the findings regarding the association between *CNR1* and AOD dependence to date have been equivocal, with some studies producing positive results (e.g., Zhang et al. 2004) and others producing negative results (e.g., Herman et al. 2006). Most recently, Hopfer and colleagues (2006) found that a SNP in the *CNR1* gene was associated with cannabis dependence symptoms. Moreover, this SNP was part of several sets of multiple alleles that are transmitted jointly (i.e., haplotypes), some of which are associated with developing fewer dependence symptoms, whereas others are associated with an increased risk for cannabis dependence. Finally, a recent case-control study found that multiple genetic variants in *CNR1* were significantly associated with alcohol dependence and/or drug dependence (Zuo et al. 2007).

Conclusions

For both alcohol dependence and drug dependence, considerable evidence suggests that genetic factors influence the risk of these disorders, with heritability estimates of 50 percent and higher. Moreover, twin studies and studies of electrophysiological characteristics indicate that the risk of developing AOD dependence, as well as other disinhibitory disorders (e.g., antisocial behavior), is determined at least in part by shared genetic factors. These observations suggest that some of a person's liability for AOD dependence will result from a general externalizing factor and some will result from genetic factors that are more disorder specific.

Several genes have been identified that confer risk to AOD dependence. Some of these genes—such as *GABRA2* and *CHRM2*—apparently act through a general externalizing phenotype. For other genes that appear to confer risk of AOD dependence—such as genes involved in alcohol metabolism and in the endogenous opioid and cannabinoid systems—however, the pathways through which they affect risk remain to be elucidated. Most of the genes reviewed in this article originally were found to be associated with alcohol dependence and only subsequently was their association with risk for dependence on other illicit drugs discovered as well. Furthermore, studies that primarily aim to identify genes involved in dependence on certain types of drugs may identify different variants affecting risk, underscoring the challenge of understanding genetic susceptibility to different classes of drugs.

This review does not exhaustively cover all genes that to date have been implicated in alcohol and illicit drug dependence. For example, several genes encoding receptors for the neurotransmitter dopamine have been suggested to determine at least in part a person's susceptibility to various forms of drug dependence. In particular, the *DRD2* gene has been associated with alcohol dependence (Blum et al. 1990) and, more broadly, with various forms of addiction (Blum et al. 1996). This association remains controversial, however, and more recent studies suggest that the observed association actually may not involve variants in the *DRD2* gene but variants in a neighboring gene called *ANKK1* (Dick et al. 2007*b*). Studies to identify candidate genes that influence dependence on illicit drugs, but not on alcohol, are particularly challenging because of the high co-morbidity between alcohol dependence and dependence on illicit drugs. Therefore, meaningful studies require large sample sizes to include enough drug-dependent people with no prior history of alcohol dependence.

The increasingly rapid pace of genetic discovery also has resulted in the identification of several genes encoding other types of proteins that appear to be associated with alcohol use and/or dependence. These include, for example, two genes encoding taste receptors (i.e., the *TAS2R16* gene [Hinrichs et al. 2006] and the *TAS2R38* gene [Wang et al. 2007]) and a human gene labeled *ZNF699* (Riley et al. 2006) that is related to a gene previously identified in the fruit fly *Drosophila* as contributing to the development of tolerance to alcohol in the flies. Future research will be necessary to elucidate the pathways by which these genes influence alcohol dependence and/or whether they are more broadly involved in other forms of drug dependence.

Notes

1. Abnormalities in the P3 response also have been associated with risk for other psychiatric disorders, such as schizophrenia (van der Stelt et al. 2004).

2. The International HapMap Project is a multicountry effort to identify and catalog genetic similarities and differences in human beings by comparing the genetic sequences of different individuals in order to identify chromosomal regions where genetic variants are shared. Using the information obtained in

the HapMap Project, researchers will be able to find genes that affect health, disease, and individual responses to medications and environmental factors.

3. Rapid acetaldehyde production can lead to acetaldehyde accumulation in the body, which results in highly unpleasant effects, such as nausea, flushing, and rapid heartbeat, that may deter people from drinking more alcohol.

4. For example, the medication disulfiram, which inhibits another enzyme involved in alcohol metabolism called aldehyde dehydrogenase 2 (ALDH2) and is used for treatment of alcoholism, has demonstrated a treatment effect in cocaine dependence (Luo et al. 2007).

5. The SNP was not located in one of those gene regions that encode the actual receptor (i.e., in an exon) but in a region that is part of the gene but is eliminated during the process of converting the genetic information into a protein product (i.e., in an intron).

Critical Thinking

1. Why are electrophysiological abnormalities most pronounced in alcohol-dependent people who also have a diagnosis of illicit drug abuse or dependence?

2. What are risk factors for cannabis dependence? Explain.

Create Central

www.mhhe.com/createcentral

Internet References

Addiction and Recovery
www.addictionsandrecovery.org/is-addiction-a-disease.htm

Genetic Science Learning Center
http://learn.genetics.utah.edu/content/addiction

DANIELLE M. DICK, PhD, is an assistant professor of psychiatry, psychology, and human genetics at the Virginia Institute for Psychiatric and Behavioral Genetics, Virginia Commonwealth University, Richmond, Virginia. **ARPANA AGRAWAL, PhD,** is a research assistant professor in the Department of Psychiatry, Washington University, St. Louis, Missouri.

Acknowledgments—Danielle M. Dick is supported by NIAAA grant AA–15416 and Arpana Agrawal is supported by National Institute on Drug Abuse (NIDA) grant DA–023668. The COGA project is supported by grant U10–AA–08401 from NIAAA and NIDA.

From *Alcohol Research and Health,* vol. 31, No. 2, 2008. Published by National Institute on Alcohol Abuse and Alcoholism (NIAAA).

Maternal Risk Factors for Fetal Alcohol Spectrum Disorders: Not As Simple As It Might Seem by Philip A. May and J. Phillip Gossage

41

Article

Prepared by: Mary Maguire, *California State University—Sacramento*
Clifford Garoupa, *Fresno City College*

Maternal Risk Factors for Fetal Alcohol Spectrum Disorders

Not As Simple As It Might Seem

Gathering information about drinking during pregnancy is one of the most difficult aspects of studying fetal alcohol spectrum disorders (FASD). This information is critical to linking specific risk factors to any particular diagnosis within the FASD continuum. This article reviews highlights from the literature on maternal risk factors for FASD and illustrates that maternal risk is multidimensional, including factors related to quantity, frequency, and timing of alcohol exposure; maternal age; number of pregnancies; number of times the mother has given birth; the mother's body size; nutrition; socioeconomic status; metabolism; religion; spirituality; depression; other drug use; and social relationships. More research is needed to more clearly define what type of individual behavioral, physical, and genetic factors are most likely to lead to having children with FASD.

PHILIP A. MAY AND J. PHILLIP GOSSAGE

Learning Outcomes

After reading this article, you will be able to:

- Discuss a robust and comprehensive definition of Fetal Alcohol Spectrum.

- Analyze the contributors to Fetal Alcohol Syndrome.

- Describe the effects of alcohol use during pregnancy on infants.

Over the almost 40 years since fetal alcohol syndrome (FAS) was first described as a clinical diagnosis by Jones and Smith (Jones et al. 1973), several general maternal risk factors have been described in a number of studies using various approaches, including questionnaire-based surveys in prenatal clinics, surveillance using a variety of records, and population-based epidemiologic studies (May et al. 2009). One of the most difficult aspects of any research on fetal alcohol spectrum disorders (FASD) has been gathering accurate, honest, and detailed information on specific drinking patterns and actual or estimated blood alcohol concentration (BAC) levels and linking them to exact times of exposure in individual fetuses and children. Information on specific prenatal drinking behaviors that are the necessary causal factors for FASD has been elusive, and this has, in fact, limited the ability to determine the true prevalence of FASD more than any other factor (Eriksson 2007).

There are three major factors that must be addressed in the diagnosis of FASD in an individual: (1) physical growth, development, and structural defects (i.e., dysmorphology); (2) cognitive function and neurobehavior; and (3) maternal exposure and risk (Stratton et al. 1996). Of these three domains, detailed information on maternal drinking and cofactors of risk is most often missing for many cases. Without accurate and detailed maternal risk information, it is difficult to link specific, individual risk factors, or combinations thereof, to any particular diagnosis within the continuum of damage called FASD (Eriksson 2007). This article reviews highlights from the literature on maternal risk factors for FASD and illustrates that maternal risk is multidimensional, as there are a wide variety of variables that influence the development of a child with FASD. More research is needed to most clearly define what type of individual behavioral, physical, and genetic factors are most likely to lead to having a child with FASD.

When the diagnosis of fetal alcohol syndrome (FAS) was new in the medical literature in the mid-1970s, the link between alcohol use during pregnancy and FAS seemed simple. The literature was at first characterized by defining the unique traits of children with FAS, the most severe form of alcohol damage to the fetus (Clarren and Smith 1978; Jones and Smith 1973). Later, in 1981, the first Surgeon General's warning on FAS simply stated: "The Surgeon General advises women who are pregnant (or considering pregnancy) not to drink alcoholic beverages and to be aware of the alcoholic content of foods and drugs" (U.S. Surgeon General 1981, p. 9). The simple truth reflected in the Surgeon General's warning was that any woman who drank substantial amounts of alcohol during pregnancy could produce a child with FAS. But, to a great degree, no one was fully aware then of how much prenatal exposure to alcohol in any particular individual woman was necessary to cause the recognizable features of FAS that met the diagnostic criteria at the time. Some researchers believed that there might be a critical level of alcohol, a minimum "threshold" BAC that, once exceeded, would uniformly guarantee or produce FAS in children of the typical woman. However, as both early human and animal studies have shown, there is indeed a great deal of variation in the traits or features of FASD produced by individual mothers, different species of laboratory animals, and different animal strains within a species (Maier and West 2001; Thomas et al. 1996; West and Goodlett 1990). Because alcohol damage in humans ranges from mild to severe, examination of a variety of maternal behaviors and traits that might explain some or all of this variation is needed. Although some part of the differential vulnerability for the development of FASD likely is the result of genetic and epigenetic factors in the mother and/or fetus (Warren and Li 2005), evidence gathered to date suggests that the most substantial contributor to the variability in dysmorphology and other developmental deficits arises from differences in the extent of alcohol exposure, drinking pattern, and other maternal risk factors.

Describing a Spectrum of Damage

At least two concepts emerged in research in response to the variable nature of the effects of prenatal alcohol exposure described in the literature from clinical and laboratory studies. The first was the concept that FAS is manifested in various levels of severity. The term fetal alcohol effects (FAE) (Aase et al. 1995) was first used to describe a number of traits similar to those found in FAS and, although less severe in their manifestation than in children with FAS, were linked to prenatal alcohol exposure and were evident in certain children born to mothers who were known to misuse alcohol. Traits of FAE were first recognized and the term coined in studies of laboratory animals. Some researchers questioned whether it was a viable term for use with humans in clinical settings and whether it was productive to label or provide a diagnostic term for these less severe manifestations of prenatal alcohol exposure in humans (Aase et al. 1995). Later, this continuum of effects was expanded to four different diagnoses by a committee of the Institute of Medicine (Stratton et al. 1996). The four diagnoses, from most dysmorphic to least dysmorphic, were designated as FAS, partial FAS (pFAS), alcohol-related birth defects (ARBDs), and alcohol-related neurodevelopmental disorder (ARND). The overarching term later coined to describe these four diagnoses was FASD (Warren et al. 2004).

Clinicians currently are more likely to diagnose children with FAS or pFAS than they are the less dysmorphic and growth-retarded cases such as ARND (Hoyme et al. 2005; Stratton et al. 1996). There are a number of reasons for this, but the following are two major factors: Severe dysmorphology

and growth retardation represent the most recognizable traits of FASD, and the exact, unique neurobehavioral phenotype of FASD (especially ARND) has not yet been fully defined or developed. Furthermore, all population–based studies of FASD, to date, have used first-stage screening techniques based on dysmorphic features and physical growth retardation because dysmorphology currently is the most likely identifier of FASD.

The second concept that arose in an attempt to explain the variability of traits in alcohol-exposed children was the breakdown of maternal alcohol consumption by the quantity, frequency, and timing (QFT) of exposure. Defining alcohol consumption by specific traits of quantity, frequency, and variability (QFV) was first developed in epidemiologic studies of adult drinking (Mulford and Miller 1959, 1960). Using the concepts of QFV, these studies empirically described, in a manner that was particularly useful for researchers, the various drinking styles and patterns from survey data. This concept subsequently was adapted to the study of maternal drinking practices as they influence FASD. Briefly stated, the severity of damage to an individual child was, to a great degree, believed to be a function of the quantity (amount) of alcohol consumed by a mother during a pregnancy, the frequency (how often) that she consumed alcohol during that pregnancy, and the timing of the drinking during the gestation of the child (e.g., heavy drinking during the specific days when a particular anatomical feature of the fetus was developing) (May 1995).

Therefore, maternal risk for FASD initially was viewed within the two major frameworks outlined above. These held that if a woman drinks alcohol during a particular pregnancy, the child would be born affected to some degree, from mild to severe, depending on how much she drinks, how often, and the particular timing of the consumption during the pregnancy. Over the years, researchers (both basic scientists and epidemiologists) and clinicians have learned that it is not that simple. Other maternal traits and behaviors have been shown to play important roles in the variable nature of the features exhibited in alcohol-exposed offspring with and without FASD. The following sections will highlight first the QFT variables that are influential in maternal risk for FASD and then move on to describe other important maternal traits that have been linked to variation in severity of FASD traits in children across a number of studies.

Binge Drinking and Severity of FASD: Quantity and Frequency Considered

The National Institute on Alcohol Abuse and Alcoholism (NIAAA) defines binge drinking among women as a pattern of drinking that brings BAC to 0.08 gram percent or above. For the typical adult woman, this pattern corresponds to consuming four or more drinks in about 2 hours (NIAAA 2004). Some studies of FASD have revised this definition to three or more drinks per occasion, as this level of drinking correlates highly with child dysmorphology and behavior (May et al. 2007, 2008). Binge drinking has been found to be the most damaging

Maternal Risk Factors for Fetal Alcohol Spectrum Disorders: Not As Simple As It Might Seem by Philip A. May and J. Phillip Gossage

43

form of alcohol consumption on fetal development because it produces the highest BAC, and it is the peak BAC that affects the developing fetus most negatively (Abel 1998; Livy et al 2003; Maier and West 2001; Pierce and West 1986; West and Goodlett 1990).

Populations that have the highest rates of frequent binge drinking generally have been found to have the greatest number of babies born with FASD, particularly the most severe forms—FAS and pFAS (May et al. 1983, 2000, 2002, 2007; Urban 2008; Viljoen et al. 2005). Populations in which alcohol is consumed in a more moderate pattern, with lower amounts consumed over an extended period of time, generally will have fewer cases of FASD overall, more cases of pFAS than FAS, and more cases of ARND than FAS (May et al. 2006), but the ability of most clinicians to diagnose the majority of the less severe cases that are thought to exist still is limited.

By examining the ratio of only the two most severe forms of FASD to one another, one can gain an idea of the importance of binge drinking as a determinant of FASD severity. Table 1 shows the ratio of FAS to pFAS for several population-based studies. The populations listed in the top of the table have the highest proportion of heavy binge drinkers, and overall, the ratio of FAS cases to pFAS cases is higher in the communities where binge drinking is more prevalent. South Africa has a higher ratio of FAS cases to pFAS cases, primarily because it has the highest prevalence and most consistent pattern of weekly binge drinking, whereas Italy has the lowest occurrence of binge drinking. The normative pattern of drinking in Italy is moderate consumption of alcohol with meals, whereas heavy (binge) drinking on Friday and Saturday nights is the norm in the South African communities studied.

Quantity of Alcohol Consumed

Longitudinal studies have documented lower overall cognitive and behavioral abilities among children born to women who report moderate or light drinking with infrequent binges (Jacobson and Jacobson 1994; Streissguth and LaDue 1985). In these studies, the mean IQ and other cognitive measures indicate that cohorts of children born to drinking mothers are deficient when compared with children of nondrinking mothers. The mothers' alcohol use in these cohorts generally is not characterized as particularly heavy drinking or binge drinking; rather, the criteria are that the child was exposed to alcohol prenatally and the mean daily consumption exceeded 0.3 to 0.5 or more standard drinks per day as averaged across 7 days.

Therefore, quantity of alcohol consumed, particularly over a short period of time as in binge drinking, is the major factor in producing FASD. Alcohol is, as the name of the disorder indicates, the necessary condition. Moderate use of alcohol may not be a sufficient condition to produce FASD, although it can affect development, as noted above.

Frequency of Alcohol Use

Frequency of use over 9 months of pregnancy also is a necessary condition to produce a child with FASD. Abel (1998) suggested that for FAS to occur, there must be frequent, heavy drinking over the course of the pregnancy and not just a few isolated episodes. Without regular occurrences of heavy drinking (e.g., weekly), then a diagnosable condition within the FASD spectrum is not likely to occur. In South Africa, study populations practice extremely regular binge drinking. Mothers of children with FAS and pFAS binge drink an average of 2 days every weekend, almost without fail, consuming an average of 6.6 standard drinks per evening (see table 2) on Friday and Saturday (May et al. 2000, 2007; Viljoen et al. 2005). In doing so, these particular women are producing BACs that are high enough and regular enough that their offspring have severe FASD (Khaole et al. 2004). In other words, given the composition of the population of this area, and the circumstances under which they live,

Table 1   Cases of Fetal Alcohol Syndrome (FAS) and Partial FAS (pFAS) in Various Population Studies by Frequency, Percent, and Ratio

Community Studies Organized from Top to Bottom by Proportion of Binge Drinking	FAS n (%)	pFAS n (%)	Ratio of FAS per pFAS
South Africa I	40 (91)	4 (9)	10 to 1
South Africa II	37 (56)	29 (44)	1.3 to 1
South Africa III	55 (75)	18 (25)	3.1 to 1
Total South Africa*	**132 (72)**	**51 (28)**	**2.6 to 1**
Plains USA**	56 (45)	69 (55)	0.81 to 1
Western City, USA (1 & 2)*	6 (33)	12 (67)	0.5 to 1
Italy (1 & 2)*	8 (18)	36 (82)	0.22 to 1

NOTES: *All of these studies were school-based studies in which all consenting first-grade children were screened if their growth in height, weight, and head circumference was found to be below the 10th centile or they were picked randomly from the entire first-grade population as control subjects.
**Plains USA was an active-case ascertainment study in which children (birth to age 18 years) were recruited from seven communities to referral clinics for FASD and related developmental disabilities if they had physical features, behavior, or learning problems similar to those characteristics of FASD.

Table 2 Maternal Risk and Protective Factors from Studies of FASD: Selected Findings

Variable	South Africa 1997, 1999, 2002 (n = 433) Mothers of:		Italy 2004, 2005 (n = 115) Mothers of:		Western City, USA 2007, 2008 (n = 72) Mothers of:		Northern Plains, USA 1997–2009 (n = 136) Mothers of:	
	FASD subjects	Control subjects	FASD subjects	Control subjects	FASD subjects	Control subjects	FASD subjects	Control subjects
Age of delivery for index pregnancy [mean (SD)]	27.7 (6.5)	25.9 (6.1)**	31.1 (5.0)	29.3 (5.4)	26.8 (6.5)	28.2 (5.5)	26.6 (6.0)	24.1 (5.2)*
Rural residence during pregnancy (%)	51.4	26.6***	12.5	18.7*	0.0	0.0	75.8	93.1***
Educational attainment (years) [mean (SD)]	5.1 (3.2)	8.0 (3.0)***	Senior high school or higher (%)		High school or GED or higher (%)		High school or GED or higher (%)	
			37.5	71.1*	63.6	100.0***	54.8	92.0***
Involved in religion (%)	92.1	98.0**	85.7	93.4	90.9	91.5	86.7	93.3
Marital status (married) (%)	25.5	38.9***	100.0	92.4	54.5	83.3*	23.7	36.8*
Childbearing								
Gravidity [mean (SD)]	3.6 (1.6)	2.9 (1.3)***	3.4 (3.4)	2.4 (1.1)*	4.4 (2.1)	3.2 (1.6)*	5.2 (1.8)	3.7 (1.5)***
Miscarriages [mean (SD)]	0.3 (0.7)	0.2 (0.4)**	—	—	0.9 (1.4)	0.2 (0.7)*	0.6 (0.8)	0.3 (0.6)
Stillbirths [mean (SD)]	0.05 (0.2)	0.01 (0.1)*	—	—	0.0 (0.0)	0.0 (0.2)	0.1 (0.3)	0.1 (0.3)
Parity [mean (SD)]	3.3 (1.4)	2.7 (1.2)***	2.4 (2.7)	1.9 (0.6)	3.5 (1.9)	2.8 (1.2)	4.5 (1.9)	3.1 (1.4)***
Women's body profile								
Height (cm) [mean (SD)]	154.0 (5.9)	157.3 (7.0)***	156.3 (5.2)	162.8 (6.2)**	161.5 (7.6)	167.4 (7.6)*	163.6 (7.4)	163.3 (6.1)
Weight (kg) [mean (SD)]	58.0 (15.0)	68.2 (16.2)***	57.9 (8.3)	61.9 (8.8)	68.4 (12.9)	74.5 (18.6)	72.0 (17.6)	85.9 (18.8)***
Head circumference (cm) [mean (SD)]	54.4 (1.6)	54.8 (1.6)	—	—	—	—	55.2 (2.0)	56.0 (1.5)
BMI (kg/m^2) [mean (SD)]	24.4 (5.9)	27.5 (6.5)***	23.0 (2.0)	23.3 (3.3)	26.4 (6.2)	26.7 (5.7)	26.9 (5.8)	32.4 (6.8)***
Alcohol/drug use								
Among drinkers, number of drinks consumed over 30 days by father of child during index pregnancy [mean (SD)]	110.9 (147.8)	83.6 (193.5)	—	—	78.2 (115.2)	33.4 (55.3)	276.1 (231.6)	142.2 (214.5)*
Age woman began drinking regularly [mean (SD)]	20.8 (4.3)	21.0 (4.4)	22.6 (7.8)	22.2 (6.8)	18.7 (3.1)	20.0 (5.6)	18.8 (4.5)	17.8 (3.2)

(Cont'd)

Maternal Risk Factors for Fetal Alcohol Spectrum Disorders: Not As Simple As It Might Seem by Philip A. May and J. Phillip Gossage

45

Variable	South Africa 1997, 1999, 2002 (n = 433) Mothers of:		Italy 2004, 2005 (n = 115) Mothers of:		Western City, USA 2007, 2008 (n = 72) Mothers of:		Northern Plains, USA 1997–2009 (n = 136) Mothers of:	
	FASD subjects	Control subjects	FASD subjects	Control subjects	FASD subjects	Control subjects	FASD subjects	Control subjects
Among drinkers, number of drinks consumed by woman in week preceding interview [mean (SD)]	13.2 (12.1)	7.0 (6.6)***	16.6 (22.3)	2.1 (3.1)***	6.0 (0.0)	3.3 (2.9)	12.3 (11.9)	9.6 (6.0)
Among drinkers, number of drinking days by woman in week preceding interview [mean (SD)]	2.0 (1.0)	2.0 (1.3)	—	—	1.0 (0.0)	1.8 (1.0)	1.4 (0.9)	1.3 (0.5)
Woman used tobacco during index pregnancy (%)	77.7	34.8***	50.0	32.4	40.0	16.4	66.2	26.7***
Woman used other drugs during index pregnancy (%)	0.0	0.7	0.0	0.9	10.0	1.6	25.0	1.3***

NOTES: *P < .05;
**P ≤ .01;
***P ≤ .001; — Indicates that comparable data across populations do not exist in these individual studies, or maternal risk factor data have not yet been analyzed for these entire samples; SD = Standard deviation.
SOURCE: See May et al. 2006 for Italy; and Viljoen et al. 2002 and May et al. 2005 and 2008 for South Africa Waves I, II, and III. Specific details of the other two studies are not yet published independently.

the quantity and frequency of alcohol consumed are sufficient to produce very high rates of FAS and pFAS. The rate of FAS and pFAS combined in the most recent studies of the northern and western Cape provinces of South Africa have been 88 to 89 per 1,000 children (or 8.8 to 8.9 percent) in population-based studies (May et al. 2007; Urban et al. 2008).

The first population-based study of FAS (May 1991) provides another example of the necessity of both quantity and frequency occurring together for severe FASD to result. In the southwestern United States, seven communities of American Indians of three different cultural traditions were studied for FAS and what were at that time called FAE. The rates of FAS were highly variable between the different cultural groups, and the variation was based on the normative pattern of drinking, which affected frequency of drinking. Two of the communities were of tribal cultures that were more tolerant of heavy binge drinking on a sporadic basis than were the tribes of the other five communities. These two communities of Southwestern Plains tribal groups had the highest rates of FAS and FAE combined, because the sporadic binge drinking that was practiced among their women of childbearing age produced very high BACs. If the binge drinking did occur too frequently (e.g., daily or more than two times per week), it was not considered a serious breach of expectations within certain families and peer groups. In other words, the drinking was heavy but sporadic. Three of the other communities in this study were intolerant of heavy drinking among women in their tribal communities, especially of those women who had reached childbearing age. In these three communities, women who drank heavily were punished, jailed, or made to feel very uncomfortable. They often were ostracized (self-imposed in most cases) to off-reservation communities where the supply of alcohol was greater and the constraints on heavy consumption fewer, and therefore heavy drinking was more frequent. In these latter groups, the ratio of FAS to FAE was much higher (4.4 FAS cases to each case of FAE) because both quantity and frequency of drinking were high. In contrast, in the groups that were more tolerant of sporadic bingeing, quantities of alcohol consumed were high, but the frequency was not as great. This produced a rather equal number of FAS and FAE cases (1.4 FAS cases to each case of FAE) (May 1991).

Survey and Questionnaire Information on Drinking During Pregnancy

Data on the extent of drinking during pregnancy in the United States and most other countries are believed to be inaccurate in that they may grossly underreport drinking in the prenatal period. The Centers for Disease Control and Prevention (CDC) has indicated that about 10.2 to 16.2 percent of pregnant women report drinking during the previous month, and 2 percent report binge drinking during that same time frame (CDC 2009). Yet studies of drinking prior to pregnancy recognition and retrospective studies have reported significantly higher levels, because recent studies have concluded that women who have reported their alcohol use after the fact, often long after the birth of a child and outside of prenatal clinics, are more truthful and accurate (Alvik 2006; Czarnicki 1990; Floyd et al. 1999; Hannigan et al. 2010; May et al. 2008). Fear of revealing prenatal drinking information prior to a child's birth causes inaccurate reporting motivated by avoidance of shame and stigmatization. There have been a number of attempts to devise brief and somewhat indirect screening methods to determine whether there is alcohol exposure in a particular pregnancy (Chang 2001). These screening tools, although generally useful for clinical purposes, are inadequate for research purposes, which require data on differential levels and timing of exposure. Therefore, data on QFT obtained in prenatal clinics likely are very inaccurate (Hannigan et al. 2010), and prenatal clinics may provide the least accurate research information on drinking during the prenatal period. In fact, Hannigan and colleagues (2010) found that retrospective reports 14 years postpartum identified 10.8 times more women as at risk than in antenatal reports for the same women. Another excellent illustration of underreporting is a study from Sweden. Wurst and colleagues (2008) found that 8.7 percent of women in antenatal clinics interviewed with the AUDIT[1] questionnaire reported drinking. The women also submitted urine and hair samples at the same time. When the samples were analyzed for fatty acid ethyl esters (FAEEs) and ethyl glucuronide (EtG), metabolites of alcohol that indicate recent consumption, the percentage of women who had actually consumed alcohol rose to 25.2 percent. Therefore, the methods and techniques for gathering accurate and specific research data on maternal risk have been inadequate in the past, especially in prenatal clinics. These must improve in the future with new, more effective questionnaire designs administered in appropriate settings and at times when the respondents will be most truthful and accurate (Alvik et al. 2006; Goransson et al. 2006; King 1994; Whaley and O'Connor 2003). Furthermore, better techniques of determining exposure by QFT, including biomarkers, are needed (Litten et al. 2010). Such improvements will not only improve research accuracy and understanding, but they also will aid clinicians in detecting alcohol use and abuse in prenatal clinics for intervention and prevention.

Timing of Maternal Drinking and Effect on Children's Physiology and Behavior

The timing of maternal drinking is critical as to which anatomical features are affected (Hoyme et al. 2005; Stratton et al. 1996; Sulik 2005; Sulik et al. 1981). Because of the sequential development of the fetus over an 8- to 9-month period, drinking during critical periods of gestation will produce various anatomical defects or brain-based cognitive or behavioral deficits, depending on the stage of development when a significant drinking episode occurs. For example, the key facial features that are commonly used to diagnose FAS and pFAS include short eye openings, thin border between the upper lip and facial skin, flat middle groove in the upper lip (i.e., philtrum), underdeveloped midface, wide distance between the right and left inner corners of the eyes (i.e., inner canthal distance), and droopy eyelid (i.e., ptosis). Each of these conditions

develops during the sixth through the ninth week of gestation. If a woman's drinking produces high BACs during this window of fetal gestation, then one or more of these features likely may be negatively affected and abnormal.

Timing also may be critical as to the particular cognitive and behavioral traits that are produced in a particular child. Even though the central nervous system, including the brain, is developing the entire 9 months of a normal pregnancy, particular critical regions (e.g., the hippocampus, regions of the frontal lobe, or corpus collosum) may have key windows in time when damage can result from a heavy binge or chronic drinking (Guerri et al. 2009; Mattson et al. 2001; Riley and McGee 2005). As studies continue to determine and define the specific nature of the behavioral characteristics of children with FASD, researchers may learn which regions of the brain are linked to particular deficits and behaviors and also when they are most at risk from the teratogenic effects of alcohol.

Therefore, the major necessary determinants of maternal risk factors for producing a child with diagnosable FASD are the quantity of alcohol consumed per occasion, the frequency with which drinking occurs, and the timing of these drinking episodes as they occur in relation to the specific gestational stages of the individual, developing fetus. Even though these conditions are necessary, and theoretically sufficient in the face of very high and frequent drinking episodes, they are not always sufficient as drinking is practiced by individual women and subgroups in society. That is, particular QFT levels of alcohol consumption that would produce FAS or pFAS in the offspring of a particular pregnancy of a particular mother may not do so in another pregnancy of another woman with different individual traits or cofactors of risk. Therefore, certain levels of alcohol exposure may not be sufficient to produce a child with FASD in the absence of certain other known cofactors of risk such as those detailed below.

Maternal Characteristics That Modify Risk and Outcome: Age, Gravidity, and Parity

Given relatively similar reported QFT of drinking across pregnancies, it is possible for some children to be significantly more affected than others, even if they share the same mother. The sections below will examine the factors responsible for differential degrees of damage in the offspring of individual women (or individual pregnancies) who have reported drinking similar amounts of alcohol over similar time periods during pregnancy.

The first three maternal cofactors of risk that were identified by researchers are maternal age (chronological years), gravidity (number of previous pregnancies), and parity (number of previous births). Women who are higher on any of these three variables, on average, have been found to have children who are more severely affected than those borne to other women (Jacobson et al. 1996, 1998; May et al. 1983, 2005, 2006, 2007, 2008). In other words, the older the drinking pregnant woman is and the more pregnancies and children she has had, the greater the average likelihood that she will have a more severely affected child compared with other women drinking in a similar manner and at similar levels. Table 2 highlights these variables for

Maternal Risk Factors for Fetal Alcohol Spectrum Disorders: Not As Simple As It Might Seem by Philip A. May and J. Phillip Gossage

47

studies from South Africa, Italy, and the Northern Plains of the United States. In each of these studies and populations, the mean gravidity and parity are higher in the maternal group bearing FASD children, and maternal age is higher in FASD mothers in all studies except one. Table 2 also shows that women who have children with FASD also have more miscarriages and stillbirths.

Further Modifiers of Risk: Body Size, Nutrition, and Socioeconomic Status

In epidemiologic studies of FASD children in South Africa, Italy, and the United States, experience has shown that smaller women tend to be overrepresented in the FASD maternal group. As shown in table 2, the average height, weight, and BMI of the FASD mothers is lower than the control subjects in each country and sample. These differences are consistently and statistically significant in the larger samples such as the South African studies. In at least one cohort of the South Africa studies, head circumference of the mothers of FAS children was significantly smaller than the comparison group (May et al. 2005). This may indicate that some of the mothers of FASD children may have FAS or pFAS themselves.

As indicated in table 3, the average drinks per drinking day (DDD) measure is highest for the mothers of FAS children and lower for the other two groups: the mothers of pFAS children and the 24 percent of mothers of the randomly selected control children (children without FASD) who reported drinking during pregnancy. Interestingly, the average DDD measures of the mothers of some of the control children are equal to or

higher than the average levels of the mothers of the pFAS children. Turning to the estimated average BAC levels for the three groups, however, the expected spectrum emerges as the BAC of the mothers of FAS children is highest, the pFAS mothers next highest, and the mothers of the control children the lowest. A major reason for this pattern likely is found in the maternal BMI. The mothers of the control children have the highest mean BMI, which reduces the BAC per drink and therefore, reduces alcohol exposure to the fetus. Body mass obviously and significantly moderates risk for FASD.

Nutrition and FASD Risk

Nutrition studies of the average daily intake of foods among mothers in a small town and surrounding rural areas of South Africa have revealed that both mothers of children with severe FASD and mothers of control children have major nutritional deficiencies, placing them well below the recommended daily intake of both the United States and South Africa. This is undoubtedly one explanation for the very high rate of severe FASD in this region. Nevertheless, a comparison of the FASD mothers' diet and that of control subjects indicates that the mothers of the FASD children have significantly lower intake of riboflavin, calcium, and DPA (one of the omega-3 fatty acids) than the mothers of non-FAS control subjects (May et al. 2004). Other nutrients, such as zinc and B vitamins, also may play a key role (Tamura et al. 2004). In fact, a recent study (Keen et al. 2010) indicates that a zinc deficiency was found in drinking mothers in both Russia and the Ukraine when compared with nondrinking mothers in the same antenatal clinics. Furthermore, a copper deficiency also was found in the Ukraine sample. The authors state that "select micronutrient deficiencies increase the risk for the occurrence of FASD in high risk populations. In theory these

Table 3 Average Drinks per Drinking Day, Estimated Peak BAC Levels,**** and Body Mass Index (BMI) Data from Interviews with South African Women (*n* = 175)

	Drinking Mothers of Children with FAS	Drinking Mothers of Children with pFAS	Drinking Mothers of Children without FAS or pFAS[†]
1st trimester			
D.D.D.*** (SD)	5.7 (3.8)	3.9 (1.4)	3.8 (3.4)*
BAC [mean (SD)]	0.197 (.17)	0.155 (.07)	0.122 (.11)
2nd trimester			
D.D.D. (SD)	5.7 (3.7)	3.2 (1.9)	3.7 (3.4)*
BAC (SD)	0.200 (.17)	0.124 (.09)	0.084* (.09)
3rd trimester			
D.D.D. (SD)	5.5 (3.9)	2.7 (2.0)	3.7 (3.5)*
BAC (SD)	0.191 (.17)	0.102 (.12)	0.076 (.09)
Body Mass Index (SD)	22.5 (5.6)	23.5 (5.6)	27.4 (6.9)**

NOTES: *p < .05.
**p < .001.
***D.D.D. = avg. drinks per drinking day.
****-BAC estimated by the BACCuS technique (accounts for mother's weight, quantity consumed, and duration of drinking).
[†] This group was selected from mothers of randomly selected non-FASD children in a community study of first-graders. Specifically, this sample represents the 24 percent of mothers in this group who reported drinking during pregnancy.
SD = Standard deviation.
Source: May et al. 2008.

nutritional deficiencies can arise as a consequence of poor diets as well as a consequence of tissue injury-induced alterations in the metabolism of select nutrients" (Keen at al. 2010, p. 131). Therefore, undernutrition of a variety of nutrients is a risk factor for FASD for a variety of reasons over and above its effect on BMI. Although this is not a new concept to some basic scientists, it now is an increasing focus for researchers of FASD. Some researchers specifically are looking at using supplementation of particular nutrients (e.g., choline) both as a cofactor related to FASD damage and as a partial solution for reducing the damage caused by prenatal alcohol use (Thomas et al. 2004).

Socioeconomic Status and FASD Risk

Although women of any socioeconomic status (SES) can bear children with FASD, the more severe forms of FAS and pFAS most frequently have been found in the lower SES categories in various countries. One classic study (Bingol et al. 1987) of the influence of SES in the United States found that the risk of bearing a child with FAS was 15.8 times higher for women of lower SES even with comparable drinking levels. Abel (1995) also identified lower SES as an important risk factor for FAS.

The SES of mothers of children with FASD is consistently lower than control subjects in epidemiologic studies as well. For example, all population-based studies of FASD in South Africa have indicated that the highest rates are found among women who live on the poorest rural farms where the living conditions are the worst, nutrition of the women is poorest, and weekend binge drinking is a regular practice. In most population-based studies, women with FASD children have lower levels of education and more frequently are unemployed or underemployed. Table 2 indicates clearly that this pattern holds in the South African, Italian, and U.S. studies represented, as maternal educational attainment is lower in all groups.

An overarching trait that may modify or enhance all of the above cofactors of risk is "weathering" (Holzman et al. 2009). Weathering is a concept put forth to explain the cumulative effect of poor living conditions, inadequate nutrition, and high levels of stress on childbearing. Research (Abel and Hannigan 1995; Bingol et al. 1987) has described the fact that women with lower SES on average have children characterized by lower birth weight and length, smaller heads, more malformations, and more attention deficit disorder, whether alcohol-exposed or not, and that diet and lower levels of nutrition, particularly antioxidants, are all enhanced risk factors in low-SES populations. Some studies in the United States have found that an early age of initiating regular drinking (May et al. 2005) may accelerate the weathering process by increasing the amount of time that alcohol can affect vital biophysiological processes such as the production of liver isoenzymes for alcohol metabolism, a change in the electrolyte balance in the digestive system, and longer-term exposure of the ovum to the teratogenic effects of alcohol.

Metabolism and Known Genetic Influences

In the general clinical literature and in animal studies (Badger et al. 2005; Frezza et al. 1990; Shankar et al. 2006, 2007), it is known that alcohol metabolism varies from one individual woman to the next and that pregnancy affects alcohol and general metabolism in a variety of ways. This variance has both genetic and environmental influences. In a study in South Africa, researchers examined the effects of both metabolism and a known genetic polymorphism linked to alcohol metabolism among 10 women who had given birth to children with FAS, compared with 20 control women who had also consumed alcohol during pregnancy but borne unaffected children in the same birth cohort in the same town (Khaole et al. 2004). None of the women were pregnant at the time. They were allowed to drink beer or another beverage of choice at their own pace in a controlled situation in their own residence with the researchers present to monitor BAC via breathalyzer. The researchers found that the mothers of FAS children drank faster and produced high (peak) BACs of 0.20 more quickly. Furthermore, blood samples drawn from these women indicated that the mothers of FAS children were significantly less likely than the control women to have the protective genetic variants of the enzyme alcohol dehydrogenase[2] (ADH) (i.e., $ADH1B*2$ and $ADH1B*3$). In other words, the mothers of the FAS children had the normal ADH variant of $ADH1B*1$ commonly found among the majority of human populations, those who can drink with fewer negative metabolism—related consequences (Khaole et al. 2004). Similar findings have been reported by others with the $ADH1B$ pattern in other populations and studies (Jacobson et al. 2006; Viljoen et al. 2001; Warren and Li 2005).

Abel and Hannigan (1995) differentiate influential variables by classifying some as "permissive" and others as "provocative." The permissive condition variables are those that "are predisposing behavioral, social, or environmental factors . . . that create the differential reaction to alcohol responsible for the occurrence/ non-occurrence of FASD" (Abel 1988, p. 159). The provocative condition variables are those that are "related to physiological changes in the internal milieu . . . that increase vulnerability to alcohol's toxic effects" (Abel 1988, p. 159). In this model, alcohol metabolism is considered in relationship to conditions and mechanisms that may permit and provoke the expression of traits of FASD. Key to this model is that undernutrition is associated with antioxidant deficiency, which permits the accumulation of free radicals. Free radicals increase the likelihood of cell damage and therefore make FASD traits more likely. Therefore, low SES, undernutrition, advanced maternal age, high parity, and overall weathering increase the risk for FASD trait expression in this scenario (Abel and Hannigan 1995).

Religion, Spirituality, Depression, Other Drug Use, and Social Relations as Cofactors of Risk

In several studies in South Africa, two in Italy, and two in the United States (see table 2), women who reported less adherence to a major religion and less practice of prayer and regular church attendance were overrepresented in the maternal FAS group when compared with control subjects (May et al. 2005a, b, 2008; Viljoen et al. 2002). One of the Italian studies did prove to be a partial exception, as Italian women in the

Maternal Risk Factors for Fetal Alcohol Spectrum Disorders: Not As Simple As It Might Seem by Philip A. May and J. Phillip Gossage

49

first study who gave birth to children with FASD were more likely to report a higher level of church attendance than control subjects (May et al. 2006) but were not necessarily higher on other measures of religiosity. Generally, women who are more likely to adhere to and practice a religious/spiritual tradition on a frequent basis (e.g., daily prayer) are less likely to drink and to drink to excesses that would cause FASD.

Depression has been reported to be more common among mothers of children with FASD (Flynn and Chermack 2008; Rubio et al. 2008; Trujillo Lewis 2008). Women who drink heavily and who have borne children with FASD are likely to have heavy drinking in their families of origin and procreation and also in their peer groups (Abel 1998b; May et al. 2005, 2008; Viljoen et al. 2002). The partners of women who bear FASD children are virtually always heavy drinkers or even very heavy drinkers of either a binge or chronic consumption style (see table 2).

Many studies indicate that mothers of FASD children in some countries use other drugs in addition to alcohol, as is evident in the two U.S. samples in table 2. South African and Italian women, however, are almost exclusively users of alcohol. Smoking also is much more common among mothers of FASD children (and drinkers in general) in all samples in table 2.

Domestic violence such as spousal abuse and poor domestic relations between parents of FASD children also are significantly higher in some studies (May et al. 2005, 2008). Households and families where FASD children are conceived, born, and raised tend to be less stable and more chaotic, which also may enhance the negative behavior traits that are often associated with children who have FASD.

A Comprehensive Scheme for Organizing the Overall Risk for FASD

As described above, many maternal factors affect FASD risk; figure 1 provides a useful scheme for organizing these variables.

Using a standard public health classification (MacMahon and Pugh 1970) of associated and causal factors to organize the multiple, interdisciplinary variables that influence maternal risk for FASD in humans, a list emerges that may assist in clarifying our understanding of the multiple maternal influences on FASD. This schematic listing also may serve to guide further research, prevention, and intervention programming (May 1995). The three topical categories of variables are the host (the individual woman), the agent (alcohol as a teratogenic agent exposed to the fetus via the mother), and the environment (the social and natural setting of the pregnant woman's life).

Conclusions

Although research over the past four decades has identified many factors that contribute to the development of children with FASD, much work remains. Most importantly, detailed and accurate studies are needed to define the specific or average QFT of maternal alcohol consumption in women from specific populations that are found to produce children with each of the diagnoses within the continuum of FASD. For example, how many drinks per episode, how many episodes per week, and at which times during pregnancy does it take to produce a child with FAS, pFAS, or ARND among women in the general population of the United States (Hannigan et al. 2010; Robles et al. 1990)? Animal models provide many clues, but more accurate and specific studies of alcohol consumption in humans are greatly needed for advancements in research on maternal risk factors. Second, once this level of specificity is attained from improved maternal interviewing and other forms of data gathering from mothers, then other cofactors of risk can be controlled in statistical analyses, and the differential effects of variables such as gravidity, maternal age, body mass, nutrition, and other influences can be factored into the equation of risk and/or causation.

The major conclusion from this selective review, then, is that new and highly focused attention needs to be paid to gathering accurate and detailed data on maternal risk from mothers of

Figure 1 Commonly Recognized Maternal Risk Factors for FASD from the Literature: A Public Health Variable Summary

Host	Agent Exposure	Environment
• Mother's age ≥ 25	• High BAC from large quantities of EtOH	• Low SES
• Gravidity ≥ 3	• Binge drinking (3+ per occasion)	• Not married, but living with partner
• Parity ≥ 3	• Length of drinking career	• Culture accepting of heavy drinking
• Higher rates of stillbirth and miscarriage	• Frequent smoker (lower birth weight)	• Family of origin of heavy drinkers
• Infrequent practice of religion/spirituality	• Beer is beverage of choice of a majority of FASD mothers in most populations	• Partner is a heavy & frequent drinker
• Low maternal education		• Alcohol-centered recreation popular
• Smokes cigarettes	• Drinking outside of meals	• Social isolation from mainstream economy & society
• Depression/psychological distress	• Polysubstance abuse in urban studies	
• Short stature	• Change in gastric ADH activity	• Little or no knowledge or awareness of FASD
• Low weight	• Change in nutritional status during pregnancy	
• Low BMI		
• Nutritional deficiency		
• Particular alcohol dehydrogenase polymorphisms		

FASD children with all levels of severity; from mothers who drank, but did not bear children with FASD; and also from those who do not drink. With specific and detailed data covering the variety of maternal risk factors over the entire course of pregnancies in representative, general populations, we can begin to definitively answer the complex questions of maternal risk for FASD. Improved methods of collecting maternal risk data are needed in order to make progress in this area of human study, especially since most people are reluctant to share such revealing and potentially stigmatizing information about themselves.

In 2005, the Surgeon General's office updated the advisory on alcohol use and pregnancy. The new advisory reads: "We do not know what, if any, amount of alcohol is safe. But we do know that the risk of a baby being born with any of the fetal alcohol spectrum disorders increases with the amount of alcohol a pregnant woman drinks, as does the likely severity of the condition. And when a pregnant woman drinks alcohol, so does her baby. Therefore, it is in the child's best interest for a pregnant woman to simply not drink alcohol" (U.S. Surgeon General 2005, p. 1).

Therefore, although much has been learned about individual maternal factors that both increase and decrease risk of FASD in individual offspring, the general warning appropriate for public health advice to the general population of women remains much the same: don't drink alcohol when pregnant.

References

Aase, J.M.; Jones, K.L.; Clarren, S.K. Do we need the term "FAE"? *Pediatrics* 95:428–430, 1995. PMID: 7862486

Abel, E.L. An update on incidence of FAS: FAS is not an equal opportunity birth defect. *Neurotoxicology and Teratology* 17:437–443, 1995. PMID: 7565490

Abel, E.L. *Fetal Alcohol Abuse Syndrome.* New York: Plenum Press, 1998a.

Abel, E.L. Fetal Alcohol Syndrome in Families. *Neurotoxicology and Teratology* 10:1–2, 1998b. PMID: 3352564

Abel, E.L.; Hannigan, J.H. Maternal risk factors in fetal alcohol syndrome: Provocative and permissive influences. *Neurotoxicology and Teratology* 17:445–462, 1995. PMID: 7565491

Alvik, A.; Haldorsen, T.; Groholt, B.; and Lindemann, R. Alcohol consumption before and during pregnancy comparing concurrent and retrospective reports. *Alcoholism: Clinical and Experimental Research* 30:510–515, 2006. PMID: 16499492

Babor, T.F.; Biddle-Higgins, J.C.; Saunders, J.B.; and Monteiro, M.G. *AUDIT: The Alcohol Use Disorders Identification Test: Guidelines for Use in Primary Health Care.* Geneva, Switzerland: World Health Organization, 2001.

Badger, T.M.; Hidestrand, M.; Shankar, K.; et al. The effects of pregnancy on ethanol clearance. *Life Sciences* 77:2111–2126, 2005. PMID: 15925387

Bingol, N.; Schuster, C.; Fuchs, M.; et al. The influence of socioeconomic factors on the occurrence of fetal alcohol syndrome. *Advances in Alcohol & Substance Abuse* 6:105–118, 1987. PMID: 3425475

Centers for Disease Control and Prevention (CDC). Alcohol use among women of childbearing age: United States, 1991–2005. *MMWR: Morbidity and Mortality Weekly Report* 58:529–532, 2009. PMID: 19478721

Chang, G. Alcohol screening instruments for pregnant women. *Alcohol Research & Health* 25:204–209, 2001. PMID: 11810959

Clarren, S.K., and Smith, D.W. The fetal alcohol syndrome. *New England Journal of Medicine* 298:1063–1067, 1978. PMID: 347295

Czarnecki, D.M.; Russell, M.; Cooper, M.L.; and Salter, D. Five-year reliability of self-reported alcohol consumption. *Journal of Studies on Alcohol* 51:68–76, 1990. PMID: 2299853

Eriksson, U.J. Fetal ethanol exposure during pregnancy: How big is the problem and how do we fix it? *Acta Paediatrica* 96:1557–1559, 2007. PMID: 17937681

Floyd, R.L.; Decouflé, P.; Hungerford, D.W. Alcohol use prior to pregnancy recognition. *American Journal of Preventive Medicine* 17(2):101–107, 1999. PMID: 10490051

Flynn, H.A., and Chermack, S.T. Prenatal alcohol use: The role of lifetime problems with alcohol, drugs, depression, and violence. *Journal of Studies on Alcohol and Drugs* 69:500–509, 2008. PMID: 18612565

Frezza, M.; di Padova, C.; Pozatto, G.; et al. High blood alcohol levels in women: The role of decreased gastric alcohol dehydrogenase activity and first-pass metabolism. *New England Journal of Medicine* 322:95–99, 1990. PMID: 2248624

Goransson, M.; Magnusson, A.; and Heilig, M. Identifying hazardous alcohol consumption during pregnancy: Implementing a research-based model in real life. *Acta Obstetricia et Gynecologica Scandinavica* 85:657–662, 2006. PMID: 16752255

Guerri, C., Bazinet, A., and Riley, E.P. Foetal Alcohol Spectrum Disorders and alterations in brain and behaviour. *Alcohol and Alcoholism* 44:108–114, 2009. PMID: 19147799

Hannigan, J.H.; Chiodo, L.M.; Sokol, R.J.; et al. A 14-year retrospective maternal report of alcohol consumption in pregnancy predicts pregnancy and teen outcomes. *Alcohol* 44(7–8); 583–594, 2010. PMID: 20036487

Holzman, C.; Eyster, J.; Kleyn, M.; et al. Maternal weathering and risk of preterm delivery. *American Journal of Public Health* 99:1864–1871, 2009. PMID: 19696383

Hoyme, H.E.; May, P.A.; Kalberg, W.O.; et al. A practical clinical approach to diagnosis of fetal alcohol spectrum disorders: Clarification of the 1996 Institute of Medicine criteria. *Pediatrics* 115:39–47, 2005. PMID: 15629980

Jacobson, J.L., and Jacobson, S.W. Prenatal alcohol exposure and neurobehavioral development. *Alcohol Health and Research World* 18:30–36, 1994.

Jacobson, J.L.; Jacobson, S.W.; and Sokol, R.J. Increased vulnerability to alcohol-related birth defects in the offspring of mothers over 30. *Alcoholism: Clinical and Experimental Research* 20:359–363, 1996. PMID: 8730230

Jacobson, J.L.; Jacobson, S.W.; Sokol, R.J.; and Ager, J.W., Jr. Relation of maternal age and pattern of pregnancy drinking to functionally significant cognitive deficit in infancy. *Alcoholism: Clinical and Experimental Research* 22:345–351, 1998. PMID: 9581639

Jacobson, S.W.; Jacobson, J.L.; Sokol, R.J. et al. Maternal recall of alcohol, cocaine, and marijuana use during pregnancy. *Neurotoxicology and Teratology* 13:535–540, 1991. PMID: 1758408

Jacobson, S.W.; Carr, L.G.; Croxford, J.; et al. Protective effects of the alcohol dehydrogenase-ADH1B allele in children exposed to alcohol during pregnancy. *Journal of Pediatrics* 148:30–37, 2006. PMID: 16423594

Maternal Risk Factors for Fetal Alcohol Spectrum Disorders: Not As Simple As It Might Seem by Philip A. May and J. Phillip Gossage

51

Jones, K.L., and Smith, D.W. Recognition of the fetal alcohol syndrome in early infancy. *Lancet* 302:999–1001, 1973. PMID: 4127281

Jones, K.L.; Smith, D.W.; Ulleland, C.N.; and Streissguth, A.P. Pattern of malformation in offspring of chronic alcoholic mothers. *Lancet* 1:1267–1271, 1973. PMID: 4126070

Keen, C.L.; Uriu-Adams, J.Y.; Skalny, A.; et al. The plausibility of maternal nutritional status being a contributing factor to the risk for fetal alcohol spectrum disorders: The potential influence of zinc status as an example. *Biofactors* 36:125–135, 2010. PMID: 20333752

Khaole, N.C.; Ramchandani, V.A.; Viljoen, D.L.; and Li, T.K. A pilot study of alcohol exposure and pharmacokinetics in women with or without children with fetal alcohol syndrome. *Alcohol and Alcoholism* 39:503–508, 2004. PMID: 15351745

King, A.C. Enhancing the self-report of alcohol consumption in the community: Two questionnaire formats. *American Journal of Public Health* 84:294–296, 1994. PMID: 8296958

Litten, R.Z.; Bradley, A.M.; and Moss, H.B. Alcohol biomarkers in applied settings: Recent advances and future opportunities. *Alcoholism: Clinical and Experimental Research* 34:955–967, 2010. PMID: 20374219

Livy, D.J.; Miller, E.K.; Maier, S.E.; and West, J.R. Fetal alcohol exposure and temporal vulnerability: Effects of binge-like alcohol exposure on the developing rat hippocampus. *Neurotoxicology and Teratology* 25:447–458, 2003. PMID: 12798962

Maier, S.E., and West, J.R. Drinking patterns and alcohol-related birth defects. *Alcohol Research & Health* 25:168–174, 2001. PMID: 11810954

MacMahon, B., and Pugh, T.F. *Epidemiology.* Boston: Little Brown, 1970.

Mattson, S.N.; Schoenfeld, A.M.; and Riley, E.P. Teratogenic effects of alcohol on brain and behavior. *Alcohol Research & Health* 25:185–191, 2001. PMID: 11810956

May, P.A. Fetal alcohol effects among North American Indians: Evidence and implications for society. *Alcohol Health and Research World* 15(3):239–248, 1991.

May, P.A. A multiple-level, comprehensive approach to the prevention of fetal alcohol syndrome (FAS) and other alcohol-related birth defects (ARBD). *International Journal of the Addictions* 30:1549–1602, 1995. PMID: 8557409

May, P.A.; Brooke, L.; Gossage, J.P.; et al. The epidemiology of fetal alcohol syndrome in a South African community in the Western Cape Province. *American Journal of Public Health* 90:1905–1912, 2000. PMID: 11111264

May, P.A.; Fiorentino, D.; Gossage, J.P.; et al. Epidemiology of FASD in a province in Italy: Prevalence and characteristics of children in a random sample of schools. *Alcoholism: Clinical & Experimental Research* 30:1562–1575, 2006. PMID: 16930219

May, P.A.; Gossage, J.P.; Brooke, L.E.; et al. Maternal risk factors for fetal alcohol syndrome in the Western Cape Province of South Africa: A population-based study. *American Journal of Public Health* 95:1190–1199, 2005. PMID: 15933241

May, P.A.; Gossage, J.P.; Marais, A.S.; et al. The epidemiology of fetal alcohol syndrome and partial FAS in a South African community. *Drug and Alcohol Dependence* 88:259–271, 2007. PMID: 17127017

May, P.A.; Gossage, J.P.; Marais, A.S.; et al. Maternal risk factors for fetal alcohol syndrome and partial fetal alcohol syndrome in South Africa: A third study. *Alcoholism: Clinical and Experimental Research* 32:738–753, 2008. PMID: 18336634

May, P.A.; Gossage, J.P.; Kalberg, W.O.; et al. The prevalence and epidemiologic characteristics of FASD from various research methods with an emphasis on recent in-school studies. *Developmental Disabilities Research Reviews* 15:176–192, 2009. PMID: 19731384

May, P.A.; Hamrick, K.J.; Brooke, L.E.; et al. Nutrition: Its possible contribution to fetal alcohol syndrome among Coloured women in the Western Cape Province of South Africa. *Alcoholism: Clinical & Experimental Research* 28(5):125A, 2004.

May, P.A.; Hymbaugh, K.J.; Aase, J.M.; and Samet, J.M. Epidemiology of fetal alcohol syndrome among American Indians of the Southwest. *Social Biology* 30:374–387, 1983. PMID: 6336013

May, P.A.; McCloskey, J.; and Gossage, J.P. Fetal alcohol syndrome among American Indians: Epidemiology, issues, and research review. Mail, P.D.; Heurtin-Roberts, S.; Martin, S.E.; Howard, J.; Eds. *Alcohol Use among American Indians and Alaska Natives: Multiple Perspectives on a Complex Problem.* Bethesda, MD: U.S. Dept. of Health and Human Services, 2002, pp. 321–369 (NIAAA Monograph No. 37).

Mulford, H.A., and Miller, D.E. Drinking behavior related to definitions of alcohol: A report of research in progress. *American Sociological Review* 24:385–389, 1959.

Mulford, H.A., and Miller, D.E. Drinking in Iowa: III. A scale of definitions of alcohol related to drinking behavior. *Quarterly Journal of Studies on Alcohol* 21:267–278, 1960. PMID: 14425112

National Institute on Alcohol Abuse and Alcoholism (NIAAA). National Institute of Alcohol Abuse and Alcoholism Council approves definition of binge drinking. *NIAAA Newsletter.* 2004. Winter. Available at: http://pubs.niaaa.nih.gov/publications/newsletter/winter2004/newsletter_number3.htm0.

Pierce, D.R., and West, J.R. Blood alcohol concentration: A critical factor for producing fetal alcohol effects. *Alcohol* 3:269–272, 1986. PMID: 3638973

Riley, E.P., and McGee, C.L. Fetal alcohol spectrum disorders: An overview with emphasis on changes in brain and behavior. *Experimental Biology and Medicine* 30:357–365, 2005. PMID: 15956765

Robles, N., and Day, N.L. Recall of alcohol consumption during pregnancy. *Journal of Studies on Alcohol* 51:403–407, 1990. PMID: 2232792

Rubio, D.M.; Kraemer, K.L.; Farrell, M.H.; and Day, N.L. Factors associated with alcohol use, depression, and their co-occurrence during pregnancy. *Alcoholism: Clinical and Experimental Research* 32:1543–1551, 2008. PMID: 18540924

Shankar, K.; Hidestrand, M.; Liu, X.; et al. Physiologic and genomic analyses of nutrition-ethanol interactions during gestation: Implications for fetal ethanol toxicity. *Experimental Biology and Medicine* 231:1379–1397, 2006. PMID: 16946407

Shankar, K.; Ronis, M.J.; and Badger, T.M. Effects of pregnancy and nutritional status on alcohol metabolism. *Alcohol Research & Health* 30:55–59, 2007. PMID: 17718402

Stratton, K.R.; Howe, C.J.; and Battaglia, F.C. *Fetal Alcohol Syndrome Diagnosis, Epidemiology, Prevention, and Treatment.* Washington, DC: Institute of Medicine (Division of Biobehavioral Sciences and Mental Disorders, Committee to Study Fetal Alcohol Syndrome and National Institute on Alcohol Abuse and Alcoholism), National Academy Press, 1996.

Streissguth, A.P., and LaDue, R.A. Psychological and behavioral effects in children prenatally exposed to alcohol. *Alcohol Health and Research World* 10:6–12, 1985.

Sulik, K.K. Genesis of alcohol-induced craniofacial dysmorphism. *Experimental Biology and Medicine* 230:366–375, 2005. PMID: 15956766

Sulik, K.K., Johnston, M.C., and Webb, M.A. Fetal alcohol syndrome: Embryogenesis in a mouse model. *Science* 214:936–938, 1981. PMID: 6795717

Tamura, T.; Goldenberg, R.L.; Johnston, K.E.; and Chapman, V.R. Relationship between pre-pregnancy BMI and plasma zinc concentrations in early pregnancy. *British Journal of Nutrition* 91:773–777, 2004. PMID: 15137929

Thomas, J.D.; Garrison, M.; and O'Neill, T.M. Perinatal choline supplementation attenuates behavioral alterations associated with neonatal alcohol exposure in rats. *Neurotoxicology and Teratology* 26:35–45, 2004. PMID: 15001212

Thomas, J.D.; Wasserman, E.A.; West, J.R.; and Goodlett, C.R. Behavioral deficits induced by bingelike exposure to alcohol in neonatal rats: Importance of developmental timing and number of episodes. *Developmental Psychobiology* 29:433–452, 1996. PMID: 8809494

Trujillo Lewis, P. "The Relationship of Selected Demographic, Behavioral, and Psychological Characteristics of American Indian Mothers to the Prevalence of a FASD." Albuquerque, NM: University of New Mexico. Master's Thesis, July 2008.

Urban, M.; Chersich, M.F.; Fourie, L.A.; et al. Fetal alcohol syndrome among grade 1 schoolchildren in Northern Cape Province: Prevalence and risk factors. *South African Medical Journal* 98:877–882, 2008. PMID: 19177895

U.S. Surgeon General. Surgeon General's advisory on alcohol and pregnancy. *FDA Drug Bulletin* 11:9–10, 1981. PMID: 7250574

U.S. Surgeon General. *U.S. Surgeon General's Advisory on Alcohol Use in Pregnancy*. Washington, DC: U.S. Department of Health and Human Services Press Office, 2005. Available at: http://www.surgeongeneral.gov/pressreleases/sg02222005.html. Accessed October 5, 2010.

Viljoen, D.L.; Carr, L.G.; Foroud, T.M.; et al. Alcohol dehydrogenase-2*2 allele is associated with decreased prevalence of fetal alcohol syndrome in the mixed-ancestry population of the Western Cape Province, South Africa. *Alcoholism: Clinical and Experimental Research* 25:1719–1722, 2001. PMID: 11781503

Viljoen, D.L.; Croxford, J.; Gossage, J.P.; et al. Characteristics of mothers of children with fetal alcohol syndrome in the Western Cape Province of South Africa: A case control study. *Journal of Studies on Alcohol* 63:6–17, 2002. PMID: 11925060

Viljoen, D.L.; Gossage, J.P.; Brooke, L.; et al. Fetal alcohol syndrome epidemiology in a South African community: A second study of a very high prevalence area. *Journal of Studies on Alcohol* 66:593–604, 2005. PMID: 16331845

Warren, K.; Floyd, L.; Calhoun, F.; et al. *Consensus Statement on FASD*. Washington, DC: National Organization on Fetal Alcohol Syndrome, 2004.

Warren, K.R., and Li, T.K. Genetic polymorphisms: Impact on the risk of fetal alcohol spectrum disorders. *Birth Defects Research Part A: Clinical and Molecular Teratology* 73:195–203, 2005. PMID: 15786496

West, J.R., and Goodlett, C.R. Teratogenic effects of alcohol on brain development. *Annals of Medicine* 22:319–325, 1990. PMID: 2291839

Whaley, S.E., and O'Connor, M.J. Increasing the report of alcohol use among low-income pregnant women. *American Journal of Health Promotion* 17:369–372, 2003. PMID: 12858616

Wurst, F.M.; Kelso, E.; Weinmann, W.; et al. Measurement of direct ethanol metabolites suggests higher rate of alcohol use among pregnant women than found with the AUDIT: A pilot study in a population-based sample of Swedish women. *American Journal of Obstetrics and Gynecology* 198(4):407.e1–e5, 2008. PMID: 18221928

Notes

1. The AUDIT (Babor et al. 2001) is a 10-item screening questionnaire with three questions on the amount and frequency of drinking, three on alcohol dependence, and four on problems caused by alcohol.

2. Alcohol dehydrogenase (ADH) is one of the major enzymes involved in alcohol metabolism and converts alcohol to acetaldehyde, a toxic compound that can be damaging to the liver and other body organ systems. People with the ADH1B*2 and ADH1B*3 variants of the enzyme tend to have a more intense response to alcohol and a reduced risk for alcohol abuse and alcoholism.

Critical Thinking

1. Discuss why the effects of fetal alcohol syndrome are worse in low SES populations, even when prenatal alcohol use is the same.

2. Discuss the benefits and challenges of FAS screening tools.

3. Discuss the co-factors of risk for FAS.

Create Central

www.mhhe.com/createcentral

Internet References

National Organization for Fetal Alcohol Syndrome
www.nofas.org

US National Library of Medicine PubMed Health
www.ncbi.nlm.nih.gov/pubmedhealth/PMH0001909

PHILIP A. MAY, PHD, is professor of sociology and of family and community medicine; J. PHILLIP GOSSAGE, PHD, is a senior research scientist, both at the University of New Mexico Center on Alcoholism, Substance Abuse, and Addictions, Albuquerque, New Mexico.

Acknowledgments: Much of the research that supported this manuscript was funded by NIAAA grants R01 AA–9440, R01/U01 AA–11685, and R01 AA–15134.

Special thanks are given to all of our many exceptional and dedicated colleagues in large epidemiological studies of the prevalence, characteristics, and maternal risk factors of FASD.

Prepared by: Mary Maguire, *California State University—Sacramento*
Clifford Garoupa, *Fresno City College*

Article

Examination of Over-the-Counter Drug Misuse Among Youth[1]

ERIN J. FARLEY AND DANIEL J. O'CONNELL

Learning Outcomes

After reading this article, you will be able to:

- Discuss the factors that contribute to the prevalence of over-the-counter drug misuse by teens.

- Analyse the contribution of gender to over-the-counter drug misuse by teens.

- Discuss possible policy or practice efforts to decrease over-the-counter drug misuse by teens.

Introduction

Potential harm from the intentional misuse of over-the-counter (OTC) medicines among youth has become an area of increased concern among medical practitioners and researchers (Bryner et al. 2006; Lessenger et al. 2008; Substance Abuse and Mental Health Services Administration (SAMHSA) 2006). Although the likelihood of death from overdose is rare, research has revealed an increase in dextromethorphan (a key ingredient in numerous cough and cold medicines) abuse cases reported to poison control centers (Bryner et al. 2006). Equally important is the suspicion that OTC use may be a stepping stone to other forms of drug misuse and abuse.

While OTC misuse has garnered increased media coverage, it has not yet attracted an equivalent interest among researchers. Further, it is possible that research to date has inappropriately specified the relationship between OTC and other drug misuse. Extant research has examined the relationship between OTC misuse and illicit drug use by utilizing a single construct, limiting the ability to completely flesh out the dimensions of this relationship between drug use. One area that needs further attention is if and how OTC misuse among youth is associated with other types of drug use. By combining all categories of drugs under a single construct, the nuances of how particular drugs relate to OTC use is diminished. This paper examines the current state of knowledge on OTC misuse by examining the prevalence of OTC misuse and its relationship with other types of drug use among a specific cohort to expand the current understanding of the problem.

Prevalence of OTC Misuse

OTC cough and cold medicines (e.g., Coricidin and Nyquil) can be easily purchased from pharmacies and drug stores. Adolescents typically ingest OTC medicines for the ingredient dextromethorphan (DXM). DXM is a synthetic drug related to opiates, which has the ability to produce effects similar to psychotropic drugs (Bobo et al. 2004; SAMHSA 2006). These effects include sensory enhancement, perceptual distortion, and hallucinations. DXM can be found in as many as 140 different cold and cough medications (Bobo et al. 2004; SAMHSA 2008). Misuse of these types of OTC drugs often involve youth seeking inexpensive and easily accessible substitute for other drugs that are more difficult to obtain.

Misuse of OTC drugs, especially in combination with other types of drugs, can lead to a variety of serious health problems, including confusion, blurred vision, slurred speech, loss of coordination, paranoia, high blood pressure, loss of consciousness, irregular heartbeat, seizure, panic attacks, brain damage, coma, and possibly death (Bobo et al. 2004; Food and Drug Administration 2005). Yet, there is a growing concern that youth who intentionally misuse OTC drugs misperceive that they are safe because these types of drugs are legal and prevalent (Johnston et al. 2006). If this misperception is contributing to the misuse of OTC drugs, the consequences can be serious. On the other hand, this same misperception also points towards potentially efficacious prevention programs focused on educating youth to the harm posed by these drugs.

Prevalence by Age

The abuse or misuse of OTC drugs appears to be mostly a problem among younger persons. A Drug Abuse Warning Network (DAWN) report revealed that 12,584 emergency department visits were associated with DXM use in 2004 (SAMHSA 2006). Among these, 44% (5,581) were associated with the nonmedical use of DXM products among patients aged 12 to 20. Findings from this report highlight that negative consequences associated with OTC misuse are more likely to occur among youth and young adults. For example, the rate of visits to the emergency department resulting from nonmedical use of

DXM was 7.1 per 100,000 youths ages 12 to 20. For older age groups the rate was 2.6 visits or fewer per 100,000 (Bobo and Fulton 2004). In addition, a recent National Survey on Drug Use and Health (NSDUH) report highlighted OTC misuse as a significant problem among youth and young adults (SAMHSA 2008). According to this report, respondents age 12 to 17 years were more likely than those age 18 to 25 years to report past year misuse of OTCs (SAMHSA 2008).

One signal that OTC misuse is becoming of greater concern among researchers is the addition of an OTC measure ("to get high") by both the Monitoring the Future and the National Drug Use and Health in 2006 into their annual surveys. The 2007 Monitoring the Future (MTF) survey revealed that 4% of eighth graders, 5% of tenth graders and 6% of twelfth graders report past year use of OTCs to get high (Johnston et al., 2008). For eighth graders in particular, self-report misuse of OTCs was lower than past year marijuana (10%), inhalant (8%), and alcohol (32%) use. However, OTC misuse was higher than past year hallucinogen (2%), ecstasy (2%), Oxycontin (2%), Vicodin (3%), Ritalin (2%), and tranquilizer (2%) use.

Prevalence by Gender, Race, and Ethnicity

Extant research reveals significant gender differences in OTC misuse. A 2008 NSDUH report found an interaction of age and gender on self-report OTC misuse. While females age 12 to 17 years were more likely than males in the same age group to report past year OTC misuse, males age 18 to 25 years were more likely to report past year OTC misuse in comparison to females in the same age group (SAMHSA 2008). Other research has found significant gender differences in OTC misuse. For instance, both Steinman's (2006) analysis of 39,345 high school students from Ohio and Ford's (2009) examination of the 2006 National Survey on Drug Use and Health data (ages 12 to 17) revealed significant gender differences with females more likely to report OTC misuse than males (Ford 2009; Steinman 2006).

Research on racial and ethnic differences in OTC misuse is less clear. While Steinman's (2006) findings revealed Native Americans were more likely to report misuse, followed by white, "other/mixed," Hispanic, Asian, and African-American, the national survey conducted by SAMHSA (2008) revealed whites were more likely to report OTC misuse, followed by Hispanic and African-American. Misuse by Native Americans may be an additional area of concern, but the extant data indicate that whites and females are particularly at risk.

OTC Misuse Association with Prescription and Illicit Drugs

While the existing literature of OTC misuse is scant, there are key observations to be noted from research on the nonmedical use of prescription drugs (NMUPDs). Prior research on the NMUPDs has repeatedly highlighted the strong relationship between illicit prescription drug use and cigarette, alcohol, marijuana, and other drug use (Boyd et al. 2006; McCabe et al. 2004; McCabe et al. 2005; Simoni-Wastila et al. 2004). These findings suggest that nonmedical users of prescription drugs may not be a qualitatively different category of drug users, but are in fact part of well-established group of poly-drug users. It is unclear from available research whether the relationship between OTC and street drugs is the same as prescribed drugs.

Current research suggests there is reason to be concerned about the phenomena of youth mixing cough and cold medicines with other types of drugs. A 2006 DAWN report revealed that among those emergency department visits that involved DXM, 13% of 12 to 17 year old visits and 36% of 18 to 20 year old visits involved combinations of DXM and alcohol. In addition, Steinman's (2006) research on OTC misuse in Ohio high schools revealed OTC misuse was associated with alcohol, cigarette, marijuana, and other illicit drug use (e.g., cocaine, LSD, and ecstasy). Research by Ford (2009) also found a significant relationship between OTC misuse and binge drinking, marijuana use, prescription drug use, and other illicit drug use. Steinman (2006) emphasized the strong association between OTC misuse with alcohol and other illicit drugs suggesting that OTC misuse is not a "gateway" drug, but only one of a number of substance utilized by adolescents.

OTC as the Gateway?

The gateway drug concept suggests that there are lower tiered drugs that open the way towards other drugs, and that drug use itself is responsible for opening the gate (Kandel 1975; Kandel et al. 1975; Kandel et al. 2002). Other studies have attempted to refute this concept, suggesting that more serious drug users may in fact use harder drugs prior to drugs like marijuana (Mackesy-Amiti et al. 1997). Early teen drug use may largely be dictated by what drugs are available to adolescents, as well as a desire to alter one's consciousness. Access to most drugs, however, is not evenly distributed. Marijuana use by older youth may provide access to a small group of marijuana users, while another group might have access to prescription drugs, and another, access to drugs like cocaine. Unlike these other substances, almost all youth have access to OTC drugs.

While it has been shown empirically that "drug users use drugs," that is, using any substance increases the probability of using any other substance, this pattern may not be exclusively based on availability. In our modern consumer culture, adolescents are faced with multiple choices, and increasingly, the type of drug is one of them. Recognizing that the choice of drug is related to both availability and preference, it is important to understand the pattern of correlation between different drugs. Just as there are more choices in terms of which drugs, there are also more choices regarding where to obtain drugs. Those involved in traditional street drugs like marijuana and ecstasy are getting drugs from those who sell them, necessitating some link to a criminal element. Those using OTC drugs and prescription drugs can sidestep this path, which has important considerations for prevention policy.

The Current Study

This study intends to tease out the relationship between OTC misuse and the use of different types of drugs. Previous analyses have tended to lump "other illegal drugs" together in one category. If early teen usage is related to drug choice and availability, combining drugs may mask relationships that exist among individual drugs. The current study utilized a large enough sample to examine drugs both individually and in groups, and attempted to investigate which drugs are associated with OTC use.

The objective of the current study is twofold: First, the prevalence of OTC misuse among a sample of eighth grade public school students is examined, including gender and race differences in OTC misuse; Second, the relationship between OTC misuse and other substance use is examined to identify patterns of use, with a specific focus on whether estimating the effects of other illegal drugs individually provides more insight than using a single construct.

Methods

Data for the current study are from the 2005 Delaware School Survey. Data was collected by The Center for Drug and Alcohol Studies (CDAS) at the University of Delaware. CDAS has conducted an annual survey of eighth grade public school students since 1995 (the annual survey also measures fifth and eleventh graders). In order to ensure confidentiality and foster honesty, survey administrators are University personnel and not teachers. Passive parental and active student consent is solicited before administrating the survey. The purpose of the survey is to track prevalence rates of drug use among Delaware public school students.

A single question, "how often do you use OTC drugs (cough & cold meds, Nyquil) to get high?" measured eighth grade self-reports of OTC misuse. Response options included "never," "before, but not in past year," "a few times in past year," "once or twice a month," "once or twice a week," and "almost everyday." This measure was recoded into a dichotomous variable (0 = not in past year, 1 = in past year).

Other substance questions included past year cigarette, alcohol, and marijuana use. Binge drinking was also measured and defined as three drinks at a time in the last two weeks. Other drug use (with the intent of getting high) questions included: uppers (speed, meth, crank, diet pills), sedatives (tranquilizers, barbiturates, Xanax), heroin, inhalants, ecstasy, hallucinogens, pain relievers, stimulants (Ritalin, Adderall, Cylert etc.), albuterol, and crack/cocaine. All drug measures were recoded into dichotomous variables (0 = not in past year, 1 = in past year).

First, univariate and bivariate analyses were utilized to examine the prevalence of OTC use and the relationship with other substances; second a series of logistic regressions were used to demonstrate the difference between using a single construct "other illicit drug use" differs from utilizing each drug measure individually.

Results

A total of 7,815 eighth graders completed the 2005 survey (50% female and 50% male). The racial and ethnic distribution of students sampled consisted of 53% (3,975) white, 28% (2,065) black, 8% (632) Puerto Rican or Mexican, 2.6% (198) Asian,

1.9% (142) American Indian/Native Alaskan, and 6.8% (509) "Other." With Steinman's (2006) findings that Native Americans reported the highest levels of OTC misuse, we conducted a crosstabulation as an initial examination into racial variation. While American Indians/Native Alaskans represented only 2.5% of the students reporting OTC misuse in the past year, this represented 13% of American Indians/Native Alaskans students, this being the highest rate of use in comparison to the other racial categories. This finding lends support to Steinman's (2006) findings. Due to small cell counts the race categories for Puerto Rican, Mexican, Asian, American Indian/Native Alaskan and "other" were collapsed into one encompassing "other" category. Subsequent crosstabulation analysis revealed no significant variation between White, Black and "other" students. As a result, the race variable was collapsed into white and nonwhite (0 = white, 1 = non-white) for use in the multivariate models.

The past year OTC misuse prevalence in eighth grade Delaware sample was 10% (n = 704). Table 1 displays the breakdown of student self-reports: 86% of eighth graders reported never misusing OTCs, 9% report past year use, and 4% report misusing OTC in the past month.

Table 2 demonstrates a significant difference between male and female past year misuse of OTC drugs but no significant difference between white and nonwhite students.

Crosstabulations of OTC and other drugs are presented in Table 3. The percent of people using OTC drugs is given for those who used and did not use each substance in the past year. For example, the first substance column alcohol is interpreted

Table 1 Eighth Grade Self-Reports of OTC Abuse to Get High

	Percentage
Never	86%
Before, but not in past year	5%
Few times in past year	5%
Once or twice a month	3%
Once or twice a week	1%
Almost everyday	0%*

*Note: Less than one-half of one percent.

Table 2 Crosstabulation of OTC Abuse by Gender and Race

	Past Year OTC Abuse
Gender*	
Male	8%
Female	12%
Race	
White	10%
NonWhite	10%

*Note: Significant at the .001 level.

as 5.6% of those who did not use alcohol in the past year used OTC drugs, while 15.1% of those who did use alcohol used OTC drugs. The distribution is not uniform across drug types. There is a clear distribution of the type of adolescents most likely to be misusing OTC drugs. There appear to be four steps in the distribution in Table 3. First, youth who do not report using a given substance remain below 10% across all substances. Second, those youth who used alcohol and marijuana used OTC drugs at the lowest rate among users, hovering between 15% and 22% (Binge drinkers). Third, those using the more traditional street drugs such as ecstasy, hallucinogens, inhalants, heroin and cocaine formed a middle tier, reporting OTC use on the 25% to

30% range. Fourth and final, there is a group of persons using prescription drugs who are more likely to use OTC drugs as well. Those youths who used sedatives, amphetamines, pain relievers and stimulants were substantially more likely to use OTC drugs, with all categories reporting over 40% OTC users and 56% of those who use pain relievers using OTC drugs as well. In order to further investigate how these relationships function, we next employed regression techniques to control for the effect of other drugs.

The multivariate analyses begin in Table 4, with findings from the initial logistic regression (Model 1). This model tested the traditional means of measuring the effects of other illicit drugs by utilizing a single construct. Of the 7 variables, three did not reach significance (nonwhite, past year binge drinking and past year marijuana use). The odds of females misusing OTC drugs are 1.6 times greater (OR = 1.603, p = .000) than their male counterparts, holding all other variables constant. The odds of past year cigarette users misusing OTC drugs is 1.4 times greater (OR = 1.385, p = .011) than nonusers. The odds of past year alcohol users misusing OTC drugs is 1.8 times greater (OR = 1.779, p = .000) than nonusers. Using the single construct other illicit drugs category produced the largest effect, returning an odds ratio of 7.7 (OR = 7.685, p = .000), indicating that youth who reported using any of the other drugs reported in Table 3 increased the odds of using OTC drugs in the past year by 7.7 times.

The suggestion is that combining all other drugs into one construct misses variation among individual drugs. In order to tease out this concept, a logistic regression analysis examining the effect of other illicit drugs measured individually is presented as Model 2 in Tables 4A (Model 1) and 4B (Model 2). When compared to Model 1, there are no major differences in

Table 3   Percent of OTC Use or Nonuse of Other Substances

	Did Not Use Drug	Used Drug
Alcohol	5.6%	15.1%
Binge Drink	8.1%	22%
Marijuana	7.8%	17.3%
Ecstasy	9.3%	31.0%
Hallucinogen	9.2%	31.0%
Sedatives	9.0%	48.3%
Albuterol	7.8%	28.2%
Amphetamines	8.9%	44.0%
Inhalants	8.3%	35.2%
Pain Relievers	7.1%	56.2%
Ritalin	8.8%	45.8%
Heroin	9.4%	25.4%
Crack/Cocaine	9.1%	32.5%

Table 4A   Reduced Logistic Regression Predicting Past Year OTC Misuse (Model 1)

	B	S.E.	Wald	Sig.	OR	95% CI
Constant	−.316	.108	1122.595	.000	.027	
Female	.472	.092	26.451	.000	1.603	1.339, 1.918
NonWhite	.085	.091	.806	.354	1.088	.910, 1.301
Past Year Cigarette Use	.325	.128	6.446	.011	1.385	1.077, 1.780
Past Year Alcohol Use	.576	.108	28.653	.000	1.779	1.441, 2.197
Binge Drinking	.180	.132	1.859	.173	.197	.924, 1.549
Past Year Marijuana Use	−.144	.129	1.259	.262	.866	.673, 1.114
Other Illegal Drug Use	2.039	.094	469.024	.000	7.685	6.390, 9.243
Past Year Ecstasy	-	-	-	-	-	-
Past Year Hallucinogens	-	-	-	-	-	-
Past Year Albuterol	-	-	-	-	-	-
Past Year Sedatives	-	-	-	-	-	-
Past Year Amphetamines	-	-	-	-	-	-
Past Year Inhalants	-	-	-	-	-	-
Past Year Pain Relievers	-	-	-	-	-	-
Past Year Ritalin	-	-	-	-	-	-
Past Year Heroin	-	-	-	-	-	-
Past Year Crack/Cocaine	-	-	-	-	-	-

the effects of the lower tiered drugs on OTC misuse, when other variables were accounted for. The exceptions to this are the smokeable substances, cigarettes and marijuana, both of which lose significance in Model 2.

The odds of females misusing OTC drugs remained approximately 1.5 times greater (OR = 1.497, p = .000) than their male counterparts, holding all other variables constant. Modest effects were again found for cigarettes smokers (OR = 1.333, p < .05) and alcohol users (OR = 1.766, p = .000). The largest effects, however, were among users of pain relievers. The odds of students who reported past year use of illicit pain relievers reporting OTC drug misuse were over 9 times more likely than those who did not report pain reliever use (OR = 9.920, p = .000). Similarly, albuterol (or other asthma medicine) misusers were 4 times more likely to report OTC misuse in comparison to nonusers (OR = 4.071, p = .000). In addition, inhalant misusers were approximately twice as likely to report OTC misuse (OR = 2.302, p = .000). Similar effects were found for cocaine use (OR = 2.560, p < .01), and Ritalin use to get high (OR = 1.964, p < .01). Finally, heroin use significantly declined among those students who reported past year OTC drug misuse (OR = .321, p < .05).

Discussion and Conclusion

This study questioned whether combining all drugs into one construct is an appropriate measure in the current drug environment in which youth have more choices in terms of type of drug and routes of acquiring the drugs. While the current study

replicates the findings of prior research indicating that OTC use is correlated with other drug use, the study demonstrated that this relationship is by no means uniform, and that combining drugs other than marijuana and alcohol into a single "other drug" construct misses the nuanced variation between drugs.

The objective of this study was to examine the relationship between past year OTC misuse and other drug types including other illicit drugs and the NMUPDs. Bivariate analyses revealed that nonmedical users of prescription drugs were more likely to use OTC drugs, and users of drugs like alcohol and marijuana were least likely to misuse OTC drugs. Our full model (Tables 4A and 4B) revealed that modeling drugs individually and allowing them to essentially "fight it out" in a regression analysis showed that past year nonmedical use of pain relievers and albuterol were by far the strongest predictors of OTC misuse.

Unlike Steinman's (2006) findings which led him to explore answers to the question of why is OTC misuse associated with more serious drug use, our findings lead us to ask the question, why is OTC misuse significantly associated with the NMUPDs? The significant association between OTC misuse and the NMUPDs (i.e., pain relievers, albuterol, and Ritalin) may be due to the similar accessibility or mode of acquisition for the two types of drugs. For example, both OTC drugs and prescription drugs may be easily accessible from friends at school, at home in the medicine cabinet, or, in the case of OTC drugs, from their local drug store. Acquiring OTC or prescription drugs does not require contact with a traditional drug dealer which some students do not have access to and others might find discomforting.

Table 4B   Full Logistic Regression Predicting Past Year OTC Misuse (Model 2)

	B	S.E.	Wald	Sig.	OR	95% CI
Constant	−3.502	.110	1008.918	.000	.030	
Female	.403	.098	16.794	.000	1.497	1.234, 1.816
NonWhite	.141	.098	2.058	.151	1.151	.959, 1.395
Past Year Cigarette Use	.297	.141	4.139	.042	1.333	1.011, 1.757
Past Year Alcohol Use	.569	.113	25.248	.000	1.766	1.415, 2.205
Binge Drinking	.154	.150	1.059	.303	1.167	.870, 1.565
Past Year Marijuana Use	−.107	.141	.573	.449	.899	.682, 1.185
Other Illegal Drug Use	-	-	-	-	-	-
Past Year Ecstasy	−.307	.396	.600	.439	.736	.338, 1.600
Past Year Hallucinogens	−.533	.365	1.916	.166	.587	.276, 1.248
Past Year Albuterol	1.404	.122	132.464	.000	4.071	3.205, 5.170
Past Year Sedatives	.290	.320	.821	.365	1.336	.714, 2.499
Past Year Amphetamines	.138	.311	.197	.657	1.148	.624, 2.113
Past Year Inhalants	.834	.172	23.449	.000	2.302	1.643, 3.227
Past Year Pain Relievers	2.295	.148	239.336	.000	9.920	7.418, 13.267
Past Year Ritalin	.675	.244	7.662	.006	1.964	1.218, 3.169
Past Year Heroin	−1.137	.536	4.505	.034	.321	.112, .917
Past Year Crack/Cocaine	.940	.344	7.487	.006	2.560	1.306, 5.019

The widespread and growing prevalence of OTC misuse is partially facilitated by its easy accessibility and the perception that OTC drugs are not as harmful as more traditional drugs. The relationship between these OTC and NMUPD may be due to the misperception that OTC and prescription drugs are safer than other types of drugs.

One relationship which appears counterintuitive to the finding that OTC use is more prominently associated with the NMUPD is the significant relationship between OTC misuse and crack/cocaine use. Not only did crack/cocaine use have a larger effect on OTC misuse than cigarette use, alcohol use, inhalant use, and illicit Ritalin use, crack/cocaine use is also a notable step into more serious types of drug use. One possible explanation is that crack/cocaine users often use some type of depressant to "take the edge off." It may thus be that some youth who are using crack/cocaine are also using OTC drugs to ease the "crash" from crack/cocaine. Further research is needed to explore the dimensions of this relationship.

What appears to emerge from this study is that misusers of OTC drugs are more likely to be using pills (sedatives, stimulants, pain relievers) and asthma drugs to get high than they are the traditional marijuana, cocaine, and hallucinogens of earlier eras (See Table 2). MTF data have already shown the new drug users are more likely to initiate use through prescription drugs rather than marijuana (Mackesy-Amiti et al. 1997). That finding, coupled with those above lead us to question whether there may be a shift in adolescent drug use on the horizon or even occurring currently.

A general awareness about the misuse potential of OTC drugs among adolescents already exists. This awareness can be seen in the recent movement to place OTC drugs behind cashier counters and also limiting the number of OTC drugs an individual can buy at one time. The findings from this analysis help to further our understanding of OTC misuse among youth.

Research limitations need to be acknowledged. The data utilized for the current analysis was cross-sectional data and limits our ability to examine directionality of drug misuse. The sample was drawn from a single state, thus limiting its generalizability. In addition, no survey data is available for students who were absent the day the survey was administered. Further, the OTC measure utilized represented one general question about OTC drug misuse instead of a list of OTC drugs by type. This general OTC measure limits our ability to interpret differences in misuse by type of OTC drug.

Based on the findings from this study, the authors emphasize continued education for adolescents on the dangers of misusing OTC drugs. Combating misuse should involve educating parents about the dangers of the drugs in their house and the potential for misuse, especially among youth who may not already be known for misusing or abusing drugs. OTC drug use occurs among inexperienced drug users and traditional signs of drug use among youth may not be successful in identifying youth who are abusing OTC drugs.

References

Bobo, William V. and Robert B. Fulton. 2004. "Commentary on: Severe Manifestations of Coricidin Intoxication." *American Journal of Emergency Medicine* 22: 624–625.

Boyd, Carol J., Sean E. McCabe, and Christian J. Teter. 2006. "Medical and Nonmedical Use of Prescription Pain Medication by Youth in a Detroit-Area Public School District." *Drug and Alcohol Dependence* 81: 37–45.

Bryner, Jodi K., Uerica K. Wang, Jenny W. Hui, Merlin Bedodo, Conan MacDougall, and Ilene B. Anderson. 2006. "Dextromethorphan Abuse in Adolescence: An Increasing Trend: 1999–2004." *Archives of Pediatrics & Adolescent Medicine* 160:1217–1222.

Food and Drug Administration. 2005. "FDA Warns Against Abuse of Dextromethorphan (DXM). (Talk Paper T05–23). Rockville, MD: National Press Office. (Also available at http://www.fda/gov/bbs/topics/answers/2005/ans01360.html.)

Ford, Jason A. 2009. "Misuse of Over-the-Counter Cough or Cold Medications Among Adolescents: Prevalence and Correlates in a National Sample." *Journal of Adolescent Health* 44: 505–507.

Johnston, Lloyd D., Patrick M. O'Malley, Jerald G. Bachman, and John E. Schulenberg. 2006. National press release, Teen drug use continues down in 2006, particularly among older teens; but use of prescription-type drugs remains high. University of Michigan News Service, Ann Arbor.

Johnston, Lloyd D., Patrick M. O'Malley, Jerald G. Bachman, and John E. Schulenberg. 2008. "Monitoring the Future National Results on Adolescent Drug Use, Overview of Key Findings, 2007." (*NIH Publication No. 08-6418*). Bethesda, MD: National Institution on Drug Use.

Kandel, Denise and Richard Faust. 1975. "Sequence and Stages in Patterns of Adolescent Drug Use." *Archives of General Psychiatry* 32: 923–932.

Kandel, Denise. 1975. "Stages in Adolescent Involvement in Drug Use." *Science* 190: 912–914.

Kandel, D. and K. Yamaguchi. 2002. "Stages of Drug Involvement in the US Population." Pp. 65–89 in *Stages and Pathways of Drug Involvement: Examining the Gateway Hypothesis*, edited by Denise B. Kandel. New York, Cambridge University Press.

Lessenger, James E. and Steven D. Feinberg. 2008. "Abuse of Prescription and Over-the-Counter Medications." *Journal of the American Board of Family Medicine* 21: 45–54.

Mackesy-Amiti, Mary Ellen, Michael Fendrich, and Paul J. Goldstein. 1997. "Sequence of Drug Use Among Serious Drug Users: Typical vs Atypical Progression." *Drug and Alcohol Dependence* 45: 185–96.

McCabe, Sean E., Carol J. Boyd, and Christian J. Teter. 2005. "Illicit Use of Opioid Analgesics by High School Seniors." *Journal of Substance Abuse Treatment* 28: 225–230.

McCabe, Sean E., Christian J. Teter, and Carol J. Boyd. 2004. "The Use, Misuse, and Diversion of Prescription Stimulants Among Middle and High School Students." *Substance Use and Misuse* 39: 1095–1116.

Steinman, Kenneth J. 2006. "High School Students' Misuse of Over-The-Counter Drugs: A Population-Based Survey in an Urban Area." *Journal of Adolescent Health* 38: 445–447.

Substance Abuse and Mental Health Services Administration (SAMHSA). 2006. The New Dawn Report: Emergency Department visits Involving Dextromethorphan. Office of Applied Studies. Rockville, MD.

Substance Abuse and Mental Health Services Administration (SAMHSA). 2008. "The NSDUH Report: Misuse of Over-the-Counter Cough and Cold Medications among Persons Aged 12 to 25." Office of Applied Studies. Rockville, MD.

Simoni-Wastila, Linda, Grant Ritter, and Gail Strickler. 2004. "Gender and Other Factors Associated with Nonmedical use of Abusable Prescription Drugs." *Substance Use and Misuse* 39: 1–23.

Note

1. Original study supported by Delaware Health and Human Services, Division of Substance Abuse and Mental Health, through the Substance Abuse Prevention and Treatment Block Grant from the Substance Abuse and Mental Health Services Administration (SAMHSA), U.S. Department of Health and Human Services. Support for this study also received from The Delaware Legislature through the Delaware Health Fund.

Critical Thinking

1. Discuss the factors that contribute to the prevalence of over-the-counter drug misuse by teens.

2. Are their gender differences in misuse of over-the-counter misuse of drugs? If so, why do you think this is? If not, why not?

Create Central

www.mhhe.com/createcentral

Internet References

Stop Medicine Abuse
http://stopmedicineabuse.org/what-does-abuse-look-like

United States Army Public Health Command
http://phc.amedd.army.mil/topics/healthyliving/asm/Pages/Over-the-CounterMedicationMisuse.aspx

Article

Prepared by: Mary Maguire, *California State University—Sacramento*
Clifford Garoupa, *Fresno City College*

Why Using Meds for 'Neuroenhancement' Is a Scary Thought

CHRISTOPHER LANE

Learning Outcomes

After reading this article, you will be able to:

- Identify what is meant by "brain doping" and discuss its prevalence.
- Discuss two perspectives related to the use of neuroenhancing drugs among college students.
- Identify the risks of the use of neuroenhancing drugs.

A basic fear in today's competitive society is not measuring up. "Brain Gain," Margaret Talbot's insightful and troubling article in *The New Yorker* in April 2009, opened the way to broader public discussion about the pros and cons of "neuroenhancement," the use and misuse of prescription stimulants by those seeking better mental cognition to offset worries about falling behind or otherwise falling short.[1] According to Peter D. Kramer, the prominent psychiatrist and author of *Listening to Prozac,* the term "encompasses a set of medical interventions in which the goal is not to cure illness but rather to alter normal traits and abilities."[2] That would be altering for the better, Kramer hopes, because the drugs carry a long list of side effects. Indeed, despite its upbeat title, Talbot's article also came with a darker subtitle, "The Underground World of 'Neuroenhancing' Drugs," as if questioning whether the term is accurate or misleading.

Talbot's article covered the widespread off-label abuse of Adderall, Ritalin, and Provigil by often panicky college students seeking a cognitive advantage. (Off-label abuse means taking medications, like Adderall, commonly prescribed to those with attention-deficit hyperactivity disorder, for conditions not approved by the Food and Drug Administration.) Abusers typically get their hands on the pills through friends' prescriptions and online pharmacies with lax requirements and poor safety regulations. Talbot referenced surveys calculating that 6.9 percent of students in U.S. universities have used prescription stimulants to try to overcome academic performance anxieties or being bested by their peers, with the greatest frequency at highly competitive schools.[3]

The article also quoted prominent scholars at Stanford, Harvard, and Penn arguing that concerns are overstated because "cognitive enhancement has much to offer individuals and society, and a proper societal response will involve making enhancements available while managing their risks."[4] Talbot's piece further referenced the British Medical Association (BMA) arguing in one upbeat 2007 discussion paper, "Boosting Your Brainpower," "Universal access to enhancing interventions would bring up the base-line of cognitive ability, which is generally seen to be a good thing"[5] and, thus nothing to be worried about.

Increasing cognitive ability is of course a good thing, and there are many ways to achieve it, including through education. But to what extent can chemically-raised expectations about academic performance be said to be a real or lasting improvement? And what might the BMA be missing about unanticipated medical risks? (Adderall is comprised of mixed amphetamine salts whose side effects include loss of appetite, headaches, extreme fatigue, fever, heartburn, and cardiac arrhythmia.)

Talbot led off by interviewing a recent Harvard graduate dubbed "Alex," a history major who daily took Adderall off-label, without a medical or psychiatric diagnosis, in hopes of ramping up his output as he juggled an ever-greater number of extracurricular activities. These included running a student organization, a task sometimes eating up 40 hours per week, as well as bouts of weekend partying. A rebalancing of priorities was doubtless in order. "Since, in essence, this life was impossible," Talbot comments, "Alex began taking Adderall to make it possible."

Like many of the thousands of students across American campuses who routinely take medications off-label, Alex wanted to accomplish more than time and body permitted. As he put it, summing up the rationale of taking the drug off-label, "it's often people—mainly guys—who are looking in some way to compensate for activities that are detrimental to their performance."

But female students do this too. The British *Guardian* newspaper published an April article, "Are 'Smart Drugs' Safe for Students?" that featured, among other bright students, Lucy, a postgraduate at Cambridge, who uses the drugs "less from a lack of diligence than an excess of it. Extremely hard working, she takes modafinil [originally developed to treat narcolepsy] once or twice a week." "With study, work and sport I have a very full timetable," she reports. "I want to do everything, but I don't want to do any of it at a mediocre level. Taking modafinil helps me to do it all."[6]

"So popular have these drugs become," writes Catherine Nixey, author of *The Guardian* article, that Barbara Sahakian, professor of clinical neuropsychology at Cambridge University, "warned that their use has 'enormous implications' and that universities must act on them—even mentioning dope testing as one possibility. But this is not happening. 'What universities are doing about [them] is nothing,' she says," adding, "It's a real worry that students are taking these drugs."

In 2005, notes Talbot, a team led by a professor at the University of Michigan's Substance Abuse Research Center "reported that in the previous year 4.1 percent of American undergraduates had taken prescription stimulants for off-label use." Three years earlier, another study "at a small college found that more than 35 percent of the students had used prescription stimulants nonmedically in the previous year."

Given these figures, Talbot wanted to understand what was driving the phenomenon. According to Alex, the primary student Talbot interviewed, some students taking Adderall off-label find they spend hours doing nothing more productive than reorganizing their music collection. Another group, more stupefied, will research a paper obsessively, but endlessly postpone getting down to writing it. When they do manage to grind out essays, the results are, unsurprisingly, unconvincing and verbose. Multiply that effect across any number of American campuses and the net result begins to look not only dispiriting, intellectually, but also troubling, nationally.

Talbot interviews Johns Hopkins University psychiatrist Paul McHugh about cosmetic neurology, a term he coined to explain the rising numbers of undergraduate and high school students who misuse medication in hopes of boosting their mental performance. "At least once a year," Talbot writes, "in his private practice [McHugh] sees a young person—usually a boy—whose parents worry that his school performance could be better, and want a medication that will assure it." McHugh counters in his 2006 book *The Mind Has Mountains* that "the truth [more often] is that the son does not have the superior I.Q. of his parents, though the boy may have other qualities that surpass those of his parents—he may be handsome, charming, athletic, graceful." Adds Talbot, "McHugh sees his job as trying to get the parents to 'forget about adjusting him to their aims with medication or anything else.' "[7]

That may be easier said than done. "Neuroenhancement" has passionate defenders and powerful advocates such as Stanford University bioethicist Henry Greely and University of Pennsylvania neuropsychologist Martha J. Farah. What's not to like about the word "enhancement"? What's the cause of distress? To be against "enhancement" seems like you're against progress and self-improvement. Indeed, "neuroenhancement" seems as if it's already settled an argument.

Advocates often see the ethics of the matter as squarely on their side: Why hold on to "self-limiting" behaviors when there are chemical opportunities to extend our reach? As one proponent put it in Talbot's article, "Why would you *want* an upward limit on the intellectual capabilities of a human being? And, if you have a very nationalist viewpoint, why wouldn't you want our country to have the advantage over other countries, particularly in what some people call a knowledge-based economy?" "Using neuroenhancers," this proponent insists, "is like customizing yourself—customizing your brain. . . . It's fundamentally a choice you're making about how you want to experience consciousness."

This libertarian view, also a type of scare tactic, is backed by several prominent bioethicists. We can have "responsible use of cognitive-enhancing drugs by the healthy," declared Greely and a team of scholars in the journal *Nature* in December 2008. " 'Enhancement' is not a dirty word," the group insisted, even as they declined to define what "responsible" means in "responsible use," a phrase appearing only in their subtitle.[8] A raft of letters followed, however, with scholars worldwide pointing out the obvious: "The risks and benefits may turn out to be finely balanced." "Stimulants and other drugs proposed as potential cognitive enhancers are known to create a profound state of dependence." Indeed, "the pressure that leads people to enhance their performance might also be a crucial trigger to mental disorder." "Most seasoned physicians," a Penn neurologist summed up, "have had the sobering experience of prescribing medications that, despite good intentions, caused bad outcomes."[9]

I share these concerns. There is indeed much to be worried about. We need to distinguish between "performance" and "understanding" in the bioethicist debates, especially when students churning out essays while on Adderall and Ritalin may well find that the drugs make their thinking and writing *less* effective. Statements of free choice over such experimentation also conveniently ignore that new norms and practices put even greater pressure on students: raising expectations about performance tied *solely* to medication rather than to greater effort and knowledge.

Even an advocate of "selective neuroenhancement," a professional poker player, conceded in Talbot's article, "I don't think we need to be turning up the crank another notch on how hard we work."

The issue concerns not only student and public health, but also academic honesty. A teacher myself, I don't like the thought of students self-medicating—cheating—on an assignment. Another person Talbot interviewed, an evolutionary biologist, put it this way, disabusing the fantasy of an intellectual transformation after popping a pill, or what he called "brain doping": "In the end, you're only as good as the ideas you've come up with."

Yet in Nixey's *Guardian* article, students deny these accusations. "I'm not cheating," insists Lucy. "Taking a pill is no different to having a cup of coffee." Another student agrees: "I don't think this is cheating. I read a nice analogy, which said that people with a bad memory are no different to people who have bad eyesight. You let people with bad eyesight have glasses; why not let people with a bad memory have these pills?"

That analogy is strained to the point of absurdity. This is a mistaken belief that brain doping is an acceptable way of coping with academic and other forms of stress. The solution is to avoid overscheduling, nurture one's health, and prioritize one's studies.

To my mind, the most powerful moment in Talbot's article comes when she sums up these issues and reveals her own feelings about them. "All this may be leading to a kind of society I'm not sure I want to live in: a society where we're even more overworked and driven by technology than we already are, and where we have to take drugs to keep up; a society where we give children academic steroids along with their daily vitamins."

What a scary thought.

Critical Thinking

1. Discuss your position on the use of neuroenhancing drugs among college students.

2. What can or should colleges and universities do to manage the use of neuroenhancers?

3. Either support or refute the argument that students are not engaging in "free choice" when they use neuroenhancers to improve academic performance.

Create Central

www.mhhe.com/createcentral

Internet References

Neuroenhancers
www.neuroenhancers.net
US National Library of Medicine EMBO Reports
www.ncbi.nlm.nih.gov/pmc/articles/PMC3059919

CHRISTOPHER LANE, the Pearce Miller Research Professor of Literature at Northwestern University, is the author of several books including *Shyness: How Normal Behavior Became a Sickness* (Yale, 2007), a history of social anxiety disorder. His next book, forthcoming from Yale in spring 2011, is *The Age of Doubt: Tracing the Roots of Our Religious Uncertainty.* Lane writes a blog for *Psychology Today* magazine called "Side Effects" (www.psychologytoday.com/blog/side-effects). Born and educated in London, Lane earned English degrees from University of East Anglia (B.A.), University of Sussex (M.A.), and University of London (Ph.D.). Email him at clane@northwestern.edu.

Lane, Christopher. Reprinted from 'Phi Kappa Phi Forum,' vol. 90, no. 3 (Fall 2010). Copyright © by Christopher Lane. By permission of the publishers.

Unit 3

Prepared by: Mary Maguire, *California State University—Sacramento*
Clifford Garoupa, *Fresno City College*

UNIT

The Major Drugs of Use and Abuse

The following articles discuss those drugs that have evolved historically to become the most popular drugs of choice. Although pharmacological modifications emerge periodically to enhance or alter the effects produced by certain drugs or the manner in which various drugs are used, basic pharmacological properties of the drugs remain unchanged. Crack is still cocaine, ice is still methamphetamine, and black tar is still heroin. In addition, all tobacco products supply the drug nicotine, coffee and a plethora of energy drinks provide caffeine, and alcoholic beverages provide the drug ethyl alcohol. All these drugs influence the way we act, think, and feel about ourselves and the world around us. They also produce markedly different effects within the body and within the mind.

To understand why certain drugs remain popular over time, and why new drugs become popular, one must be knowledgeable about the effects produced by individual drugs. Why people use drugs is a bigger question than why people use tobacco. However, understanding why certain people use tobacco, or cocaine, or marijuana, or alcohol is one way to construct a framework from which to tackle the larger question of why people use drugs in general. One of the most complex relationships is the one between Americans and their use of alcohol. More than 76 million Americans have experienced alcoholism in their families.

The most recent surveys of alcohol use estimate that 127 million Americans currently use alcohol. The use of alcohol is a powerful influence that serves to shape our national consciousness about drugs. The relationship between the use of alcohol and tobacco and alcohol and illicit drugs provides long-standing statistical relationships. The majority of Americans, however, believe that alcohol is used responsibly by most people who use it, even though approximately 10 percent of users are believed to be suffering from various stages of alcoholism.

Understanding why people initially turn to the nonmedical use of drugs is a huge question that is debated and discussed in a voluminous body of literature. One important reason why the major drugs of use and abuse, such as alcohol, nicotine, cocaine, heroin, marijuana, amphetamines, and a variety of prescription, designer, over-the-counter, and herbal drugs, retain their popularity is because they produce certain physical and psychological effects that humans crave. They temporarily restrain our inhibitions; reduce our fears; alleviate mental and physical suffering; produce energy, confidence, and exhilaration; and allow us to relax. Tired, take a pill; have a headache, take a pill; need to lose weight, take a pill; need to increase athletic performance, the options seem almost limitless. There is a drug for everything. Some drugs even, albeit artificially, suggest a greater capacity to transcend, redefine, and seek out new levels of consciousness. And they do it upon demand. People initially use a specific drug, or class of drugs, to obtain the desirable effects historically associated with the use of that drug.

Heroin and opiate-related drugs such as OxyContin and Vicodin produce, in most people, a euphoric, dreamy state of well-being. The abuse of these prescription painkillers is one of the fastest growing (and alarming) drug trends. Methamphetamine and related stimulant drugs produce euphoria, energy, confidence, and exhilaration. Alcohol produces a loss of inhibitions and a state of well-being. Nicotine and marijuana typically serve as relaxants. Ecstasy and other "club drugs" produce stimulant as well as relaxant effects. Various over-the-counter and herbal drugs attempt to replicate the effects of more potent and often prohibited or prescribed drugs. Although effects and side effects may vary from user to user, a general pattern of effects is predictable from most major drugs of use and their analogs. Varying the dosage and altering the manner of ingestion is one way to alter the drug's effects. Some drugs, such as LSD and certain types of designer drugs, produce effects on the user that are less predictable and more sensitive to variations in dosage level and to the user's physical and psychological makeup.

Although all major drugs of use and abuse have specific reinforcing properties perpetuating their continued use, they also produce undesirable side effects that regular drug users attempt to mitigate. Most often, users attempt to mitigate these effects with the use of other drugs. Cocaine, methamphetamine, heroin, and alcohol have long been used to mitigate each other's side effects. A good example is the classic "speedball" of heroin and cocaine. When they are combined, cocaine accelerates and intensifies the euphoric state of the heroin, while the heroin softens the comedown from cocaine. Add to this the almost limitless combinations of prescription drugs, mixed and traded at "pharming" parties, and an entirely new dimension for altering drugs' physiological effects emerges. Additionally, other powerful influences on drug taking, such as advertising for alcohol, tobacco, and certain prescription drugs, significantly impact the public's drug-related consciousness. The alcohol industry, for example, dissects numerous layers of society to specifically market alcoholic beverages to subpopulations of Americans, including youth. The same influences exist with tobacco advertising. What is the message in Philip Morris's advertisements about its attempts to mitigate smoking by youth? Approximately 500,000 Americans die each year from tobacco-related illness. Add to the mix advertising by prescription-drug companies for innumerable human maladies and one soon realizes the enormity of the association between business and drug taking. Subsequently, any discussion of major drugs could begin and end with alcohol, tobacco, and prescription drugs.

Article

Prepared by: Mary Maguire, *California State University—Sacramento*
Clifford Garoupa, *Fresno City College*

'Bath Salt' Poisonings Rise as Legislative Ban Tied Up

As the number of accidental poisonings explodes and parents recount horror stories of crazed teenagers high on synthetic marijuana and "bath salts," federal attempts to outlaw the chemicals have stalled.

DONNA LEINWAND LEGER

Learning Outcomes

After reading this article, you will be able to:

- Describe the possible and varied chemical compounds of bath salts.
- Discuss the patterns of use of bath salts.
- Discuss law enforcement and legistative response to the manufacture and use of bath salts.

The House has passed legislation that would outlaw "bath salts" and other chemical concoctions, sold at convenience stores and on the Internet as legal highs—and implicated in deaths and accidental poisonings around the country. But the legislation is stuck in the Senate, where Sen. Rand Paul, R-Ky., is keeping it from reaching a floor vote.

As the Senate dukes it out, the clock is running on the Drug Enforcement Administration's year-long emergency bans, and casualties are growing.

The number of calls to poison control centers nationwide involving "bath salts" soared in 2011, to 6,138 from 304 in 2010. The drugs come in powder and crystal form, which resemble conventional bath salts. Users looking for a high will snort or eat the powder.

Poison control centers fielded nearly 7,000 calls about synthetic marijuana in 2011, up from 2,906 in 2010.

"It is poison," said Republican Sen. Chuck Grassley of Iowa, a sponsor of a bill to outlaw synthetic marijuana. "People are spraying chemicals on a pile of plant clippings, putting that in an envelope and selling it to kids."

Dozens of teens and young adults have been hospitalized in recent months—and some have died—after smoking, snorting or swallowing the chemicals, which mimic the highs associated with popular illegal drugs such as marijuana, cocaine and Ecstasy.

Users have arrived in hospital emergency rooms gravely ill, and occasionally violent, with puzzling symptoms that confound doctors, said Debbie Carr, executive director of the American Association of Poison Control Centers. Carr said the unusual spike in cases "caused national alarm."

- In Blaine, Minn., a 22-year-old man pleaded guilty to murder last month and faces 20 years in prison after he shared 2 C-E, a synthetic hallucinogen he purchased on the Internet, with friends at a party. One teenager who tried the drug died.
- In Casper, Wyo., last month, public health officials warned people to avoid the synthetic drugs after three people who smoked or swallowed "blueberry spice" went into kidney failure and at least a dozen others needed medical help. "We are viewing use of this drug as a potentially life-threatening situation," said Tracy Murphy, state epidemiologist with the Wyoming Department of Health.
- In Bowling Green, Ky., Ashley Stillwell, a recent high school graduate, took a hit of a synthetic marijuana known as 7H while hanging out at a hookah bar with friends last year and was hospitalized, her mother, Amy Stillwell, said. "Within three minutes, she was paralyzed," her mother said.

The teen could hear her friends talking about her, including discussing how they could dispose of her body in a river should she die, Amy Stillwell said.

When she finally recovered enough to call her parents, they took her to the hospital, where she complained that her heart felt as if it was beating out of her chest. A drug screen didn't detect anything, so doctors called poison control to figure out how to treat her.

DEA Administrator Michelle Leonhart has used the agency's emergency powers to temporarily outlaw the substances while the FDA conducts the scientific and medical studies needed to include the chemicals under the Controlled Substances Act, making them the equivalent of marijuana, cocaine and other illicit drugs.

A year-long ban on three synthetic stimulants used to make "bath salts" expires Oct. 21. The ban on synthetic marijuana expires in September.

Leonhart believes the chemicals pose "an imminent danger" to the public, said Special Agent Gary Boggs of the DEA's Office of Diversion Control.

Manufacturers of the mixtures evade federal FDA regulations by printing a warning on the labels that says they are not for human consumption, Boggs said.

"What that means is that people are taking things that are manufactured under unregulated and unlicensed conditions," he said. "These aren't really bath salts. These things are made in basements and garages and warehouses."

At least 39 states have taken steps to ban synthetic marijuana, and 34 states have outlawed baths salts. The latest laws ban broad classes of the chemicals to prevent chemists from tweaking formulas to make them fall outside the ban. A permanent federal ban would allow the agents to act against people who import the drugs, sell them on the Internet and ship them across state lines.

Paul, a libertarian who says criminal justice is the purview of the states, placed a hold on the federal legislation that prevents the Senate from debating it. "He's a doctor. He understands these compounds are dangerous," said Paul spokeswoman Moira Bagley. "Our state has already made it illegal. It would be great to do that in all the states."

Sen. Amy Klobuchar, D-Minn., a former prosecutor who proposed legislation to ban the synthetic hallucinogens, said she and several other senators are trying to persuade Paul to lift his block and allow debate on the Senate floor.

"We've had many instances in our state of people who nearly died," Klobuchar said. "These synthetic drugs are often worse than the illegal drugs they claim to be."

Critical Thinking

1. What makes bath salts harder to regulate than other illegal drugs, and how might issues of regulation be addressed?

2. Discuss the effects of bath salts on the human body.

3. What do you predict the future of synthetic drugs will be and why?

Create Central

www.mhhe.com/createcentral

Internet References

Centers for Disease Control
www.cdc.gov/mmwr/preview/mmwrhtml/mm6019a6.htm

Drug Free.org
www.drugfree.org/drug-guide/bath-salts?gclid=COKokKHxyLoCFUlyQg odwxoA0A

Article

Prepared by: Mary Maguire, *California State University—Sacramento*
Clifford Garoupa, *Fresno City College*

Inhalant Abuse

Learning Outcomes

After reading this article, you will be able to:

- Describe the scope of chemical compounds that are used as inhalants.

- Describe the effects of inhalant abuse.

- Describe the patterns of use of inhalants in the United States.

What Are Inhalants?

Inhalants are volatile substances that produce chemical vapors that can be inhaled to induce a psychoactive, or mind-altering, effect. Although other abused substances can be inhaled, the term "inhalants" is used to describe a variety of substances whose main common characteristic is that they are rarely, if ever, taken by any route other than inhalation. This definition encompasses a broad range of chemicals that may have different pharmacological effects and are found in hundreds of different products. As a result, precise categorization of inhalants is difficult. One classification system lists four general categories of inhalants—volatile solvents, aerosols, gases, and nitrites—based on the forms in which they are often found in household, industrial, and medical products.

Volatile solvents are liquids that vaporize at room temperature. They are found in a multitude of inexpensive, easily available products used for common household and industrial purposes. These include paint thinners and removers, dry-cleaning fluids, degreasers, gasoline, glues, correction fluids, and felt-tip markers.

Aerosols are sprays that contain propellants and solvents. They include spray paints, deodorant and hair sprays, vegetable oil sprays for cooking, and fabric protector sprays.

Gases include medical anesthetics as well as gases used in household or commercial products. Medical anesthetics include ether, chloroform, halothane, and nitrous oxide (commonly called "laughing gas"). Nitrous oxide is the most abused of these gases and can be found in whipped cream dispensers and products that boost octane levels in racing cars. Other household or commercial products containing gases include butane lighters, propane tanks, and refrigerants.

Nitrites often are considered a special class of inhalants. Unlike most other inhalants, which act directly on the central nervous system (CNS), nitrites act primarily to dilate blood vessels and relax the muscles. While other inhalants are used

---

From the Director:

Although many parents are appropriately concerned about illicit drugs such as marijuana, cocaine, and LSD, they often ignore the dangers posed to their children from common household products that contain volatile solvents or aerosols. Products such as glues, nail polish remover, lighter fluid, spray paints, deodorant and hair sprays, whipped cream canisters, and cleaning fluids are widely available yet far from innocuous. Many young people inhale the vapors from these sources in search of quick intoxication without being aware that using inhalants, even once, can have serious health consequences.

National surveys indicate that nearly 21.7 million Americans aged 12 and older have used inhalants at least once in their lives. NIDA's Monitoring the Future (MTF) survey reveals that 13.1 percent of 8th-graders have used inhalants. Parents and children need to know that even sporadic or single episodes of inhalant abuse can be extremely dangerous. Inhalants can disrupt heart rhythms and cause death from cardiac arrest, or lower oxygen levels enough to cause suffocation. Regular abuse of these substances can result in serious harm to vital organs, including the brain, heart, kidneys, and liver.

Through scientific research, we have learned much about the nature and extent of inhalant abuse, its pharmacology, and its consequences. This research has brought the picture of inhalant abuse in the Nation into focus and pointed to the dangers and the warning signs for parents, educators, and clinicians. We hope this compilation of the latest scientific information will help alert readers to inhalant abuse and its harmful effects and aid efforts to deal with this problem effectively.

Nora D. Volkow, M.D.
Director
National Institute on Drug Abuse

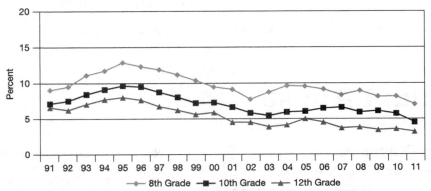

Past-Year Inhalant Use Among 8th-, 10th-, and 12th-Graders, 1991–2011.
Source: University of Michigan, 2011 Monitoring the Future Study

to alter mood, nitrites are used primarily as sexual enhancers. Nitrites include cyclohexyl nitrite, isoamyl (amyl) nitrite, and isobutyl (butyl) nitrite and are commonly known as "poppers" or "snappers." Amyl nitrite is used in certain diagnostic procedures and was prescribed in the past to treat some patients for heart pain. Nitrites now are prohibited by the Consumer Product Safety Commission but can still be found, sold in small bottles labeled as "video head cleaner," "room odorizer," "leather cleaner," or "liquid aroma."

Generally, inhalant abusers will abuse any available substance. However, effects produced by individual inhalants vary, and some users will go out of their way to obtain their favorite inhalant. For example, in certain parts of the country, "Texas shoeshine," a shoe-shining spray containing the chemical toluene, is a local favorite.

What Is the Scope of Inhalant Abuse?

According to the 2010 National Survey on Drug Use and Health (NSDUH), there were 793,000 persons aged 12 or older who had used inhalants for the first time within the past 12 months; 68.4 percent were under the age of 18. In fact, inhalants—particularly volatile solvents, gases, and aerosols—are often the easiest and first options for abuse among young children who use drugs. NIDA's annual MTF survey of 8th-, 10th-, and 12th-graders consistently reports the highest rates of current, past-year, and lifetime inhalant use among 8th-graders.

Inhalant use has decreased significantly among 8th-, 10th-, and 12th-graders compared to its peak years in the mid-1990s (see figure). According to the 2011 MTF survey, past-year use was reported as 7.0, 4.5, and 3.2 percent, for 8th-, 10th-, and 12th-graders, respectively. Data compiled by the National Capital Poison Center also show a decrease in the prevalence of inhalant cases reported to U.S. poison control centers—down 33 percent from 1993 to 2008. The prevalence was highest among children aged 12 to 17, peaking among 14-year-olds.

Demographic differences in inhalant use have been identified at different ages. The MTF survey indicates that in 2011, 8.6 percent of 8th-grade females reported using inhalants in the past year, compared with 5.5 percent of 8th-grade males.

In terms of ethnicity, Hispanics have the highest rates of past-year use among 8th- and 10th-graders, compared to both Blacks and Whites.

People from both urban and rural settings abuse inhalants. Further, research on factors contributing to inhalant abuse suggests that adverse socioeconomic conditions, a history of childhood abuse, poor grades, and school dropout are associated with inhalant abuse.

How Are Inhalants Used?

Inhalants can be breathed in through the nose or the mouth in a variety of ways, such as—

- "sniffing" or "snorting" fumes from containers;
- spraying aerosols directly into the nose or mouth;
- "bagging"—sniffing or inhaling fumes from substances sprayed or deposited inside a plastic or paper bag;
- "huffing" from an inhalant-soaked rag stuffed in the mouth; and
- inhaling from balloons filled with nitrous oxide.

Inhaled chemicals are absorbed rapidly into the bloodstream through the lungs and are quickly distributed to the brain and other organs. Within seconds of inhalation, the user experiences intoxication along with other effects similar to those produced by alcohol. Alcohol-like effects may include slurred speech; the inability to coordinate movements; euphoria; and dizziness. In addition, users may experience lightheadedness, hallucinations, and delusions.

Because intoxication lasts only a few minutes, abusers frequently seek to prolong the high by inhaling repeatedly over the course of several hours, which is a very dangerous practice. With successive inhalations, abusers can suffer loss of consciousness and possibly even death. At the least, they will feel less inhibited and less in control. After heavy use of inhalants, abusers may feel drowsy for several hours and experience a lingering headache.

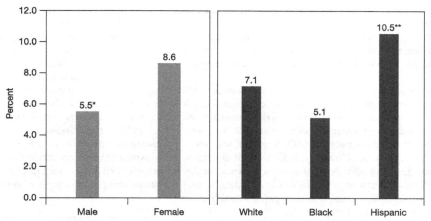

Gender and Race/Ethnicity Differences in Past-Year Inhalant Use Among 8th-Graders, 2011.
*Level of significance of difference between Male and Female = .05
**Level of significance of difference between Whites and Hispanics and Blacks and Hispanics = .001
Source: University of Michigan, 2011 Monitoring the Future Study*

Most inhalants produce a rapid high that resembles alcohol intoxication, with initial excitation then drowsiness, disinhibition, lightheadedness, and agitation.

How Do Inhalants Produce Their Effects?

Many brain systems may be involved in the anesthetic, intoxicating, and reinforcing effects of different inhalants. Nearly all abused inhalants (other than nitrites) produce a pleasurable effect by depressing the CNS. Nitrites, in contrast, dilate and relax blood vessels rather than act as anesthetic agents.

Evidence from animal studies suggests that a number of commonly abused volatile solvents and anesthetic gases have neurobehavioral effects and mechanisms of action similar to those produced by CNS depressants, which include alcohol and medications such as sedatives and anesthetics.

A 2007 animal study indicates that toluene, a solvent found in many commonly abused inhalants—including model airplane glue, paint sprays, and paint and nail polish removers—activates the brain's dopamine system. The dopamine system has been shown to play a role in the rewarding effects of nearly all drugs of abuse.

How Can Inhalant Abuse Be Recognized?

Early identification and intervention are the best ways to stop inhalant abuse before it causes serious health consequences. Parents, educators, family physicians, and other health care practitioners should be alert to the following signs:

- Chemical odors on breath or clothing
- Paint or other stains on face, hands, or clothes
- Hidden empty spray paint or solvent containers, and chemical-soaked rags or clothing
- Drunk or disoriented appearance
- Slurred speech
- Nausea or loss of appetite
- Inattentiveness, lack of coordination, irritability, and depression

What Are the Short- and Long-Term Effects of Inhalant Use?

Although the chemical substances found in inhalants may produce various pharmacological effects, most inhalants produce a rapid high that resembles alcohol intoxication, with initial excitation followed by drowsiness, disinhibition, lightheadedness, and agitation. If sufficient amounts are inhaled, nearly all solvents and gases produce anesthesia—a loss of sensation—and can lead to unconsciousness.

The chemicals found in solvents, aerosol sprays, and gases can produce a variety of additional effects during or shortly after use. These effects are related to inhalant intoxication and may include belligerence, apathy, impaired judgment, and impaired functioning in work or social situations; nausea and vomiting are other common side effects. Exposure to high doses can cause confusion and delirium. In addition, inhalant abusers may experience dizziness, drowsiness, slurred speech, lethargy, depressed reflexes, general muscle weakness, and stupor. For example, research shows that toluene can produce headache, euphoria, giddy feelings, and the inability to coordinate movements.

Inhaled nitrites dilate blood vessels, increase heart rate, and produce a sensation of heat and excitement that can last for several minutes. Other effects can include flush, dizziness, and headache.

A strong need to continue using inhalants has been reported by many individuals, particularly those who have abused inhalants for prolonged periods over many days. Compulsive use and a mild withdrawal syndrome can occur with long-term inhalant abuse. A recent survey of 43,000 American adults suggests that inhalant users, on average, initiate use of cigarettes, alcohol, and almost all other drugs at younger ages and display a higher lifetime prevalence of substance use disorders, including abuse of prescription drugs, when compared with substance abusers without a history of inhalant use.

What Are the Other Medical Consequences of Inhalant Abuse?

Inhalant abusers risk an array of other devastating medical consequences. The highly concentrated chemicals in solvents or aerosol sprays can induce irregular and rapid heart rhythms and lead to fatal heart failure within minutes of a session of prolonged sniffing. This syndrome, known as "sudden sniffing death," can result from a single session of inhalant use by an otherwise healthy young person. Sudden sniffing death is associated particularly with the abuse of butane, propane, and chemicals in aerosols. Inhalant abuse also can cause death by—

- **asphyxiation**—from repeated inhalations that lead to high concentrations of inhaled fumes, which displace available oxygen in the lungs;
- **suffocation**—from blocking air from entering the lungs when inhaling fumes from a plastic bag placed over the head;
- **convulsions or seizures**—from abnormal electrical discharges in the brain;
- **coma**—from the brain shutting down all but the most vital functions;
- **choking**—from inhalation of vomit after inhalant use; or
- **fatal injury**—from accidents, including motor vehicle fatalities, suffered while intoxicated.

Based on independent studies performed over a 10-year period in three different states, the number of inhalant-related fatalities in the United States is approximately 100–200 per year.

Animal and human research shows that most inhalants are extremely toxic. Perhaps the most significant toxic effect of chronic exposure to inhalants is widespread and long-lasting damage to the brain and other parts of the nervous system. For example, chronic abuse of volatile solvents, such as toluene or naphthalene (the volatile ingredient in mothballs), damages the protective sheath around certain nerve fibers in the brain and peripheral nervous system. This extensive destruction of nerve fibers is clinically similar to that seen with neurological diseases such as multiple sclerosis.

The neurotoxic effects of prolonged inhalant abuse include neurological syndromes that reflect damage to parts of the brain involved in controlling cognition, movement, vision, and hearing. Cognitive abnormalities can range from mild impairment to severe dementia.

Inhalants also are highly toxic to other organs. Chronic exposure can produce significant damage to the heart, lungs, liver, and kidneys. Although some inhalant-induced damage to the nervous and other organ systems may be at least partially reversible when inhalant abuse is stopped, many syndromes caused by repeated or prolonged abuse are irreversible.

Abuse of inhalants during pregnancy also may place infants and children at increased risk of developmental harm. Animal studies designed to simulate human patterns of inhalant abuse

---

Hazards of Chemicals Found in Commonly Abused Inhalants

amyl nitrite, butyl nitrite
("poppers," "video head cleaner")
sudden sniffing death syndrome, suppressed immunologic function, injury to red blood cells (interfering with oxygen supply to vital tissues)

benzene
(found in gasoline)
bone marrow injury, impaired immunologic function, increased risk of leukemia, reproductive system toxicity

butane, propane
(found in lighter fluid, hair and paint sprays)
sudden sniffing death syndrome via cardiac effects, serious burn injuries (because of flammability)

freon
(used as a refrigerant and aerosol propellant)
sudden sniffing death syndrome, respiratory obstruction and death (from sudden cooling/cold injury to airways), liver damage

methylene chloride
(found in paint thinners and removers, degreasers)
reduction of oxygen-carrying capacity of blood, changes to the heart muscle and heartbeat

nitrous oxide *("laughing gas")*, **hexane**
death from lack of oxygen to the brain, altered perception and motor coordination, loss of sensation, limb spasms, blackouts caused by blood pressure changes, depression of heart muscle functioning

toluene
(found in gasoline, paint thinners and removers, correction fluid)
brain damage (loss of brain tissue mass, impaired cognition, gait disturbance, loss of coordination, loss of equilibrium, limb spasms, hearing and vision loss), liver and kidney damage

trichloroethylene
(found in spot removers, degreasers)
sudden sniffing death syndrome, cirrhosis of the liver, reproductive complications, hearing and vision damage

Glossary

Anesthetic: An agent that causes insensitivity to pain and is used for surgeries and other medical procedures.

Central nervous system: The brain and spinal cord.

Dementia: A condition of deteriorated mental function.

Dopamine: A brain chemical, classified as a neurotransmitter, found in regions of the brain that regulate movement, emotion, motivation, and pleasure.

Naphthalene: Volatile, active ingredient in mothballs.

Toxic: Causing temporary or permanent effects that are detrimental to the functioning of a body organ or group of organs.

Withdrawal: Symptoms that occur after chronic use of a drug is reduced abruptly or stopped.

suggest that prenatal exposure to toluene can result in reduced birth weights, occasional skeletal abnormalities, delayed neurobehavioral development, and altered regulation of metabolism and body composition in males, as well as food intake and weight gain in both sexes. A number of case reports note abnormalities in newborns of mothers who chronically abuse solvents, and there is evidence of subsequent developmental impairment in some of these children. However, no well-controlled prospective study of the effects of prenatal exposure to inhalants in humans has been conducted, and it is not possible to link prenatal exposure to a particular chemical to a specific birth defect or developmental problem.

Finally, a 2008 survey of over 13,000 high school students has identified an association between disordered eating (defined as a positive response to one or more of three questions about engaging in inappropriate behaviors for weight control during the past 30 days) and inhalant use among both male and female students.

What Are the Unique Risks Associated with Nitrites Abuse?

Nitrites are abused mainly by older adolescents and adults. Typically, individuals who abuse nitrites are seeking to enhance sexual function and pleasure. Research shows that abuse of these drugs in this context is associated with unsafe sexual practices that greatly increase the risk of contracting and spreading infectious diseases such as HIV/AIDS and hepatitis.

Animal research raises the possibility that there may also be a link between abuse of nitrites and the development and progression of infectious diseases and tumors. The research indicates that inhaling nitrites depletes many cells in the immune system and impairs mechanisms that fight infectious diseases. A study found that even a relatively small number of exposures to butell nitrite can produce dramatic increases in tumor incidence and growth rate in animals.

References

Bowen, S.E.; Batis, J.C.; Paez-Martinez, N.; and Cruz, S.L. The last decade of solvent research in animal models of abuse: Mechanistic and behavioral studies. *Neurotoxicol Teratol* 28(6):636–647, 2006.

Bowen, S.E.; Daniel, J.; and Balster, R.L. Deaths associated with inhalant abuse in Virginia from 1987 to 1996. *Drug Alcohol Depend* 53(3):239–245, 1999.

Bowen, S.E.; Wiley, J.L.; Evans, E.B.; Tokarz, M.E.; and Balster, R.L. Functional observational battery comparing effects of ethanol, 1,1,1-trichloroethane, ether, and flurothyl. *Neurotoxicol Teratol* 18(5):577–585, 1996.

Fung, H.L., and Tran, D.C. Effects of inhalant nitrites on VEGF expression: A feasible link to Kaposi's sarcoma? *J Neuroimmune Pharmacol* 1(3):317–322, 2006.

Hall, M.T.; Edwards, J.D.; and Howard, M.O. Accidental deaths due to inhalant misuse in North Carolina: 2000–2008. *Subst Use Misuse* 45(9):1330–1339, 2010.

Institute for Social Research. *Monitoring the Future, 2011* (Study Results). Ann Arbor, MI: University of Michigan, 2012. Data retrieved 7/19/2012 from www.monitoringthefuture.org.

Jarosz, P.A.; Fata, E.; Bowen, S.E.; Jen, K.L.; and Coscina, D.V. Effects of abuse pattern of gestational toluene exposure on metabolism, feeding and body composition. *Physiol Behav* 93(4–5):984–993, 2008.

Jones, H.E., and Balster, R.L. Inhalant abuse in pregnancy. *Obstet Gynecol Clin North Am* 25(1):153–167, 1998.

Lubman, D.I.; Yücel, M.; and Lawrence, A.J. Inhalant abuse among adolescents: Neurobiological considerations. *Br J Pharmacol* 154(2):316–326, 2008.

Marsolek, M.R.; White, N.C.; and Litovitz, T.L. Inhalant abuse: Monitoring trends by using poison control data, 1993–2008. *Pediatrics* 125(5):906–913, 2010.

Maxwell, J.C. Deaths related to the inhalation of volatile substances in Texas: 1988–1998. *Am J Drug Alcohol Abuse* 27(4):689–697, 2001.

Mimiaga, M.J.; Reisner, S.L.; Vanderwarker, R.; Gaucher, M.J.; O'Connor, C.A.; Medeiros, M.S.; and Safren, S.A. Polysubstance use and HIV/STD risk behavior among Massachusetts men who have sex with men accessing Department of Public Health mobile van services: Implications for intervention development. *AIDS Patient Care STDS* 22(9):745–751, 2008.

Pisetsky, E.M.; Chao, Y.M.; Dierker, L.C.; May, A.M.; and Striegel-Moore, R.H. Disordered eating and substance use in high-school students: Results from the Youth Risk Behavior Surveillance System. *Int J Eat Disord* 41(5):464–470, 2008.

Riegel, A.C.; Zapata, A.; Shippenberg, T.S.; and French, E.D. The abused inhalant toluene increases dopamine release in the nucleus accumbens by directly stimulating ventral tegmental area neurons. *Neuropsychopharmacology* 32(7):1558–1569, 2007.

Sakai, J.T.; Hall, S.K.; Mikulich-Gilbertson, S.K.; and Crowley, T.J. Inhalant use, abuse, and dependence among adolescent patients: Commonly comorbid problems. *J Am Acad Child Adolesc Psychiatry* 43(9):1080–1088, 2004.

Schepis, T.S., and Krishnan-Sarin, S. Characterizing adolescent prescription misusers: A population-based study. *J Am Acad Child Adolesc Psychiatry* 47(7):745–754, 2008.

Sharp, C.W., and Rosenberg, N. Inhalant-related disorders. In: Tasman, A., Kay, J., and Lieberman, J.A., eds. *Psychiatry, Vol. 1.* Philadelphia, PA: W.B. Saunders, 1997. pp. 835–852.

Sharp, C.W., and Rosenberg, N.L. Inhalants. In: Lowinson, J.H., Ruiz, P., Millman, R.B., and Langrod, J.G., eds. *Substance Abuse: A Comprehensive Textbook (3d ed.).* Baltimore, MD: Williams & Wilkins, 1996. pp. 246–264.

Soderberg, L.S. Increased tumor growth in mice exposed to inhaled isobutyl nitrite. *Toxicol Lett* 104(1–2):35–41, 1999.

Substance Abuse and Mental Health Services Administration, Office of Applied Studies. Results from the *2010 National Survey on Drug Use and Health: Summary of National Findings.* HHS Pub. No. (SMA) 11–4658, Rockville, MD: SAMHSA, 2011.

Weintraub, E.; Gandhi, D.; and Robinson, C. Medical complications due to mothball abuse. *South Med J* 93(4):427–429, 2000.

Woody, G.E.; Donnell, D.; Seage, G.R.; Metzgera, D.; Michael, M.; Kobling, B.A.; Buchbinderh, S.; Grossd, M.; Stoneh, B.; and Judsoni, F.N. Noninjection substance use correlates with risky sex among men having sex with men: Data from *HIV/NET. Drug Alcohol Depend* 53(3):197–205, 1999.

Wu, L.T.; Howard, M.O.; and Pilowsky, D.J. Substance use disorders among inhalant users: Results from the national epidemiologic survey on alcohol and related conditions. *Addict Behav* 33(7):968–973, 2008.

Critical Thinking

1. Discuss the implications of the rates of inhalant use among United States youth.
2. What are the unique dangers of inhalant abuse?
3. How might schools and families address the risks of inhalant use in young adolescents?

Create Central

www.mhhe.com/createcentral

Internet References

Inhalant Abuse
www.inhalant.org/?gclid=CJ3T4YiDyboCFceDQgod-l0AGQ

Mayo Clinic
www.mayoclinic.com/health/inhalant-abuse/HQ00923

From *National Institute on Drug Abuse Research Report*, July 2012. Published 2012 by National Institute on Drug Abuse/National Institutes of Health.

Article

Prepared by: Mary Maguire, *California State University—Sacramento*
Clifford Garoupa, *Fresno City College*

The Science of Doping

Behind the scenes at the Games is a fierce competition between those top athletes who secretly use illicit substances to gain an edge and the scientists racing to catch them. This summer, the stakes are higher than ever.

CHRISTIE ASCHWANDEN

Learning Outcomes

After reading this article, you will be able to:

- Discuss a brief history of doping for athletic performance.

- Describe the different types of performance enhancing drugs and their effects.

- Describe the connection between athletic doping and organized crime.

DeeDee Trotter was on an airplane in 2006 when she overheard a passenger seated behind her discussing the steroids scandal. Federal investigators in the Balco case, named for a lab that produced supplements, would eventually implicate more than two dozen athletes for the use of performance-enhancing drugs, including Barry Bonds, baseball's home run king, and Marion Jones, the track-and-field star, who would end up in jail, stripped of five Olympic medals.

"This guy was reading the newspaper and he said, 'Oh, they're all on drugs,'" recalls Trotter, a runner who won a gold medal in the 4 × 400 meter relay at the 2004 Olympics. She was furious. "I turned around and said, 'Hey—excuse me, I'm sorry, but that's not true. I'm a professional athlete and Olympic gold medalist, and I'm not on drugs. I've never even considered it.'" Currently vying to join the U.S. team and appear in her third Olympics, Trotter projects a sassy confidence. "It really upset me that it's perceived that way—that if she runs fast, then she's on drugs. I hated that and I gave him a little attitude."

That airplane conversation prompted Trotter to create a foundation called Test Me, I'm Clean! "It gave us clean athletes a chance to defend ourselves," says Trotter. "If you see someone wearing this wristband"—she holds up a rubbery white bracelet emblazoned with the group's name—"it means that I am a clean athlete. I do this with hard work, honesty and honor. I don't take any outside substances."

As Trotter tells me this story, I catch myself wondering if it's all just a bunch of pre-emptive PR. It pains me to react this way, but with doping scandals plaguing the past three Summer Olympics and nearly every disgraced athlete insisting, at least initially, that he or she is innocent, it's hard to take such protestations at face value.

My most profound disillusionment came from a one-time friend, Tyler Hamilton, my teammate on the University of Colorado cycling team. When he won a gold medal in the time trial at the 2004 Olympics, I was thrilled to see someone I'd admired as honest and hardworking reach the top of a sport that had been plagued by doping scandals. But in the days that followed, a new test implicated Hamilton for blood doping. His supporters began hawking "I Believe Tyler" T-shirts, and he took donations from fans to fund his defense. The evidence against him seemed indisputable, but the Tyler I knew in college was not a cheat or liar. So I asked him straight-out if he was guilty. He looked me in the eye and told me he didn't do it. Last year, after being subpoenaed by federal investigators, Hamilton finally confessed and returned his medal.

The downfall of Olympic heroes has cast a cloud of suspicion over sports. And the dopers' victims aren't just the rivals from whom they stole their golden podium moments but every clean athlete whose performance is greeted with skepticism.

Doping, or using a substance to enhance performance, is nothing new. Contrary to romantic notions about the purity of Olympic sports, ancient Greeks ingested special drinks and potions to give them an edge, and at the 1904 Games, athletes downed potent mixtures of cocaine, heroin and strychnine. For most of Olympic history, using drugs wasn't considered cheating. Then, in the 1960 Olympics, Danish cyclist Knut Jensen passed out during a race, cracked his skull and later died. The coroner blamed the death on amphetamines, and the case led to anti-doping rules. Drug testing began with the 1968 Games, with a goal to protect athlete health. In addition to short-term damage, certain drugs also appear to increase the risk of heart disease and possibly cancer.

The original intent of anti-doping rules was to prevent athletes from dropping dead of overdoses, but over the years the rules have come to focus just as intently on protecting the integrity of the Games. The complex task of upholding the standards falls to the World Anti-Doping Agency (WADA) and its American counterpart, the U.S. Anti-Doping Agency (USADA), established in 1999 and 2000, respectively. These agencies oversee drug testing and work with Olympic organizers to manage testing at the Games.

Previously, testing was carried out by the U.S. Olympic Committee and cases were judged by each sport's governing body but governing bodies promote their sports, solicit sponsorship money and help deliver the astounding performances that fans crave. No sport wanted a dirty reputation, and officials were reluctant to tarnish their stars. Though performance-enhancing drugs were prohibited, in some sports the ban was treated the same way many drivers view speed limits—go ahead and speed, just don't get caught.

The creation of independent testing agencies changed all that, says USADA's Travis Tygart. "We said, we're not going to allow the culture to be different than what the rules are—that kind of moral relativism won't be tolerated." Tygart joined the agency in 2002 as director of legal affairs and became CEO in 2007. Although he's officially a rule-enforcer, he says that his number one job is "to ensure the integrity of competition, and uphold the rights of clean athletes."

WADA's prohibited list currently includes more than 200 banned substances and methods:

Anabolic steroids: Made famous by bodybuilders who use them to bulk up, anabolic steroids can also enhance recovery and allow endurance athletes to train harder with less rest. They're easily detectable in urine tests, so athletes use them in microdoses on days they're unlikely to be tested. The Balco (Bay Area Laboratory Co-operative) case involved a steroid called "the clear" designed to evade detection. After a track coach sent anti-doping officials a sample of the drug, scientists developed a specific test for it. The scandal implicated several dozen athletes.

Blood doping: Increasing the blood's oxygen-carrying capacity can improve muscle performance and enhance endurance by as much as 15 percent. The original technique was for an athlete to withdraw blood and freeze it, then re-inject some just prior to competition. The strategy became easier in 1989 with the approval of erythropoietin (EPO) as a medical treatment for anemia based on a naturally occurring hormone that spurs red blood cell production. When experts learned to detect illicit EPO use by athletes, dopers changed their doses to evade the test. In 2004, researchers unveiled a test to detect a blood transfusion from a donor—which is how Tyler Hamilton was caught blood doping at the 2004 Tour of Spain and the 2004 Athens Olympics. Scientists are currently working on a test to identify transfusions of the athlete's own blood from chemicals that leach into blood during storage.

Hormones: Because they're produced naturally in the body, insulin, IGF-1 and human growth hormone are some of the most difficult substances to detect. Elite athletes have used them illicitly to increase muscle mass and speed recovery. Insulin has become popular in recent years, but taken in the wrong dose, it can kill. Sprinter and three-time Olympic medalist Alvin Harrison received a four-year suspension in 2004 after admitting to using six performance-enhancing drugs, including insulin and human growth hormone. (He kept his Olympic medals, which he won before the admitted doping.)

Asthma medications: Also known as beta-2 agonists, salmeterol and clenbuterol act as muscle-building agents if taken in large doses. The drugs are detectable in urine. Last summer, David Clinger received a lifetime ban from cycling for testing positive for clenbuterol during an out-of-competition test conducted near the end of his two-year ban for testosterone and the stimulant modafinil.

Hormone antagonists or modulators: Dopers who take steroids or hormones can trip up their bodies' natural hormone balances, so they may take substances to counteract these reactions. A large dose of testosterone may stimulate a body to produce additional estrogen, with unwanted results in men such as enlarged breasts. USADA slapped Houston-based cyclist Mitch Comardo with a two-year suspension in 2009 after he tested positive for tamoxifen, a drug that blocks estrogen.

Experimental substances: To stay ahead of testers, cheaters regularly turn to drugs still in development, often obtaining them on the black market. WADA is partnering with the pharmaceutical industry to develop tests to detect experimental drugs. In November 2009, the International Olympic Committee (IOC) announced sanctions against five 2008 Olympians for using CERA, a third-generation EPO drug.

Olympic organizers plan to conduct 5,000 drug tests—an unprecedented number—during the London Games. Nearly half of the 14,000 athletes competing, including all medalists, will be taken aside after their event and brought to a private testing room. There, they'll produce a urine or blood sample under an anti-doping official's watch. The athlete will label, sign and seal the samples before they're sent to a state-of-the-art, WADA-certified facility directed by scientists at King's College London.

This year's tests will screen for more than 240 illegal substances, from growth hormones to asthma medications to experimental drugs not yet on the market. It sounds impressive, but competition-day testing is not especially effective. Many performance-enhancing drugs aren't used during competition but during training. Athletes can easily load up on anabolic steroids to increase their muscle mass and allow themselves to work harder during training, then stop before an event to test clean, says Daniel Eichner, executive director of the WADA-accredited Sports Medicine Research and Testing Laboratory in Salt Lake City. Similarly EPO continues to enhance performance long after the drug can be detected in the body.

For this reason, out-of-competition testing has become a cornerstone of WADA's approach. Athletes must keep anti-doping agencies apprised of their whereabouts via a confidential system they can access from the Internet and smartphones. Testers, in turn, target athletes during the times they're most likely to dope, such as pre-season training periods and the weeks leading up to competition. "Our testing is now very strategic," Tygart says. "We have two goals—maximum deterrence and maximum detection."

Through candid discussions with reformed dopers, officials keep tabs on the unexpected ways that illicit drug users enhance performance. For instance, they've learned that power jocks like weight lifters and sprinters wanting to bulk up aren't the only ones using steroids. Endurance athletes such as marathon runners and distance swimmers use them, at low doses, to train harder with less rest. Revelations like these have changed USADA's approach.

"Traditionally, anti-doping was reactionary," Eichner says. "They would wait for a drug to be brought on the market, and then they would think, well, maybe athletes are using it, so we better prohibit it and then work out a test." WADA has spent more than $54 million to date on anti-doping research to predict and prepare for new drugs that might enhance performance.

The agency can also catch past cheaters. WADA rules permit samples to be stored for up to eight years so they can be subjected to new tests that are developed well after an event. The IOC will soon retest samples from the 2004 Games. This kind of retrospective testing cost Rashid Ramzi his 1,500-meter run gold medal from the 2008 Olympics after he came up positive for CERA months after the Games had ended. Had Ramzi known that the test was imminent, he might have abstained. Because CERA was covered under WADA's detailed list of prohibited substances and methods, the agency could unveil its new test without fanfare, a strategy meant to keep dopers on the defensive.

WADA's most ambitious project yet is what the agency calls a biological passport—a type of physiological profile used to spot subtle signs of doping. Traditional tests are like police radar—easily avoided if you know when to be on the lookout, Eichner says. The passport, by contrast, doesn't detect doping products themselves, but the physiological changes they provoke. "Instead of trying to catch you speeding," Eichner says, "we measure how long it takes to get from Point A to Point B, and then calculate how fast you were going." Researchers have three types of passports in the works: for blood boosting, steroids and hormones.

The blood passport, which was developed first, analyzes blood samples over the course of a season to flag discrepancies that indicate doping. For instance, the passport tracks levels of newly formed red blood cells, called reticulocytes. Taking a drug like EPO that promotes red blood cell production creates a rapid increase in reticulocyte numbers, while blood transfusions cause reticulocytes to drop, as the body shuts down its own blood cell production. Hemoglobin, a molecule that carries oxygen in the blood, also rises and falls in response to various blood-doping regimens, so testers can keep tabs on its levels to look for signs of doping.

Passports make doping more difficult, but they won't entirely eliminate it, Eichner says. "The passport catches a lot of people, but it's clear that some athletes have adapted to the program and have found ways to avoid triggering any flags." History has shown that every new test spurs a workaround.

"We're fighting the dark side," WADA director general David Howman told reporters at a meeting of the Partnership for Clean Competition in New York City last December. "Marion Jones competed for seven years without one positive test result. For seven years, she said, 'I'm clean, I've been tested more than any other athlete in the world,'" Howman says, adding: "Just because you're tested, doesn't mean you're clean, we know that."

A growing challenge, Howman says, is organized crime. "The underworld is substantially involved in providing and distributing these substances—the profits are extraordinary. With an investment of $100, you can make $1,000 or maybe $100,000. WADA has to make sure that stops." The testing group recently hired a chief investigations officer to gather intelligence and collaborate with law enforcement agencies. "There have been doping control officers bribed, there have been people working in labs bribed. It's happening and we need to stop it," Howman says.

And then there's the entourage problem. Howman estimates that sports is worth $800 billion annually, and athletes are surrounded and influenced by coaches, trainers, agents and lawyers who stand to profit. Tygart says athletes have been talked out of confessing to illicit drug use by lawyers who would earn more in a lengthy litigation process. "Those within the system who are preying on our athletes need to be held accountable, and we'll do everything in our power to kick those people out of sport," Tygart says.

Track standout Michelle Collins was shocked the first time that someone in her inner circle offered her THG, a steroid designed to evade drug tests. The Olympic sprinter and former world champion was told the drug would make her stronger and speed recovery after training. "I was never actually told what it was," says Collins, who was caught in the Balco scandal for using THG and EPO. She first encountered drugs while making the leap from collegiate to professional competition, an especially vulnerable period in an athlete's career. "That's where a lot of athletes get scooped up and grabbed by coaches promising to take them to the next level," says Collins. "There's a lot of brainwashing that goes on." Athletes are convinced that they must dope to be competitive, she says. "I definitely believed that."

Likewise, Tyler Hamilton, in an interview with CBS News' "60 Minutes," described receiving his package of performance-enhancing drugs for the first time as a sort of rite of passage, an invitation to the big time.

"Good people make mistakes," Tygart says, and mentions Collins, who, after initial denials, admitted to doping. Tygart recalls seeing her after her confession. "It was a transformation. Her whole posture and personality was completely changed. It was amazing." Collins left sports and works as a licensed massage therapist with her own practice near Dallas. Now "very content," she regrets taking dope. "If I could go back in time, I would say no," she told me. "I was already talented. I'd made an Olympic team without drugs. I didn't really need to go there."

When the Olympics begin this summer, all eyes will focus on the medal counts and podium ceremonies. While those who fall short of a medal may comfort themselves in having fought a good fight, the truth is, winning still matters. In the world of sports, nothing commands greater regard than an Olympic gold medal. Yet the question remains, at what cost? Will that shiny gold medal represent integrity and sportsmanship, or a value system that puts winning ahead of everything else? This is a question that the athletes themselves must answer.

I was skeptical when DeeDee Trotter first told me about her Test Me, I'm Clean! pledge, but I've chosen to trust her. I believe Trotter, because I believe that authenticity still exists in sports. For every medal-stealing fraud like Tyler Hamilton or Marion Jones, there are other athletes who choose to do the right thing. The Olympics still provide a stage for human excellence. It's not too late to save sports. But it will take athletes like Trotter standing up to the doping culture. The fight against doping is nothing less than a culture war, one that can be won only from within.

Critical Thinking

1. What are the effects of professional doping on young amateur athletes?
2. Other than the individual athlete's desire to excel, what are the factors influencing the doping business?
3. Develop a comprehensive plan to weaken the doping industry.

Create Central

www.mhhe.com/createcentral

Internet References

World Anti-Doping Agency
www.wada-ama.org/en/anti-doping-community/athletes-

American Society for Biochemistry and Molecular Biology
www.asbmb.org/asbmbtoday/asbmbtoday_article.aspx?id=17038

Article

Prepared by: Mary Maguire, *California State University—Sacramento*
Clifford Garoupa, *Fresno City College*

Monitoring the Future

National Results on Adolescent Drug Use, Overview of Key Findings 2011

LLOYD D. JOHNSTON ET AL.

Learning Outcomes

After reading this article, you will be able to:

- Define the role and goals of Monitoring the Future.
- Describe at least two prevalent drugs of misuse among the youth population.
- Discuss possible responses to youth drug abuse.

Introduction

Monitoring the Future (MTF) is a long-term study of American adolescents, college students, and adults through age 50. It has been conducted annually by the University of Michigan's Institute for Social Research since its inception in 1975 and is supported under a series of investigator-initiated, competing research grants from the National Institute on Drug Abuse.

The need for a study such as MTF is clear. Substance use by American young people has proven to be a rapidly changing phenomenon, requiring frequent assessments and reassessments. Since the mid-1960s, when it burgeoned in the general youth population, illicit drug use has remained a major concern for the nation. Smoking, drinking, and illicit drug use are leading causes of morbidity and mortality, during adolescence as well as later in life. How vigorously the nation responds to teenage substance use, how accurately it identifies the emerging substance abuse problems, and how well it comes to understand the effectiveness of policy and intervention efforts largely depend on the ongoing collection of valid and reliable data. Monitoring the Future is uniquely designed to generate such data in order to provide an accurate picture of what is happening in this domain and why, and the study has served that function well for the past 37 years. Policy discussions in the media, in government, education, public health institutions, and elsewhere have been informed by the ready availability of extensive and consistently accurate information from the study relating to a large number of substances. Similarly, the work of organizations and agencies providing prevention and treatment services is informed by MTF.

The 2011 the MTF survey encompassed about 46,700 8th-, 10th-, and 12th-grade students in 400 secondary schools nationwide. The first published results are presented in this report. Recent trends in the use of licit and illicit drugs are emphasized, as well as trends in the levels of perceived risk and personal disapproval associated with each drug. This study has shown these beliefs and attitudes to be particularly important in explaining trends in use. In addition, trends in the perceived availability of each drug are presented.

A synopsis of the design and methods used in the study and an overview of the key results from the 2011 survey follow this introductory section. These are followed by a separate section for each individual drug class, providing figures that show trends in the overall proportions of students at each grade level (a) using the drug, (b) seeing a "great risk" associated with its use (perceived risk), (c) disapproving of its use (disapproval), and (d) saying they could get it "fairly easily" or "very easily" if they wanted to (perceived availability). For 12th graders, annual data are available since 1975, and for 8th and 10th graders, since 1991, the first year they were included in the study.

For the sake of brevity, we present these prevalence statistics here only for the 1991–2011 interval, but statistics on 12th graders are available for earlier years in other MTF publications. For each prevalence period, the tables indicate which of the most recent one-year changes (between 2010 and 2011) are statistically significant. The graphic depictions of multiyear trends often indicate gradual, continuing change that may not reach significance in a given one-year interval.

A much more extensive analysis of the study's findings on secondary school students may be found in *Volume I,* the second monograph in this series, which will be published later in 2012.[2] *Volume I* contains a more complete description of the study's methodology as well as an appendix explaining how to test the significance of differences between groups and of trends over time. The most recent such volume is always available on the MTF website, www.monitoringthefuture.org, listed under Publications.

MTF's findings on American college students and adults through age 50 are not covered in this early *Overview* report because the data from those populations become available later in the year. These findings will be covered in *Volume II,* the third monograph in this annual series, which will be published later in 2012.[3] A fourth monograph, *HIV/AIDS; Risk and Protective Behaviors Among Young Adults,* dealing with national trends in HIV/AIDS-related risk and protective behaviors among young adults 21 to 30 years old, was added to the series in 2009.[4] For the publication years prior to 2010, the volumes in these annual series are available from the NIDA Drug Publications Research Dissemination Center at 877-NIDA-NIH (877-643-2644); or by e-mail at drugpubs.drugabuse.gov. Beginning with the 2010 publication date, the volumes are available electronically at the MTF website. Further information on the study, including its latest press releases, a listing of all publications, and the text of many of them may be found at www.monitoringthefuture.org.

Study Design and Methods

Monitoring the Future's main data collection involves a series of large, annual surveys of nationally representative samples of public and private secondary school students throughout the coterminous United States. Every year since 1975 a national sample of 12th graders has been surveyed. In 1991 the study was expanded to include comparable, independent national samples of 8th and 10th graders. The year 2011 marked the 37th national survey of 12th graders and the 21st national survey of 8th and 10th graders.

Sample Sizes

The 2011 sample sizes were about 16,500, 15,400, and 14,900 in 8th, 10th, and 12th grades, respectively. In all, about 46,700 students in 400 secondary schools participated. Because multiple questionnaire forms are administered at each grade level to increase coverage of attitudinal and behavioral domains relevant to substance use, and because not all questions are contained in all forms, the number of cases upon which a particular statistic is based may be less than the total sample size. The tables here contain notes on the number of forms used for each statistic if less than the total sample is used.

Field Procedures

University of Michigan staff members administer the questionnaires to students, usually in their classrooms during a regular class period. Participation is voluntary. Parents are notified well in advance of the survey administration and are provided the opportunity to decline their child's participation. Questionnaires are self-completed and are formatted for optical scanning.

In 8th and 10th grades the questionnaires are completely anonymous, and in 12th grade they are confidential (name and address information is gathered to permit the longitudinal follow-up surveys of random subsamples of participants after high school). Extensive, carefully designed procedures are followed to protect the confidentiality of the participants and their data. All procedures are reviewed and approved on an annual basis by the University of Michigan's Institutional Review Board (IRB) for compliance with federal guidelines for the treatment of human subjects.

Measures

A standard set of three questions is used to determine *usage* levels for the various drugs (except for cigarettes and smokeless tobacco). For example, we ask, "On how many occasions (if any) have you used marijuana . . . (a) . . . in your lifetime? (b) . . . during the past 12 months? (c) . . . during the last 30 days?" Each of the three questions is answered on the same answer scale: 0, 1–2, 3–5, 6–9, 10–19, 20–39, and 40 or more occasions.

For the psychotherapeutic drugs (amphetamines, sedatives [barbiturates], tranquilizers, and narcotics other than heroin), respondents are instructed to include only use ". . . on your own—that is, without a doctor telling you to take them." A similar qualification is used in the question on use of anabolic steroids, OxyContin, Vicodin and several other drugs.

For cigarettes, respondents are asked two questions about use. First they are asked, "Have you ever smoked cigarettes?" The answer categories are "never," "once or twice," and so on. The second question asks, "How frequently have you smoked cigarettes during the past 30 days?" The answer categories are "not at all," "less than one cigarette per day," "one to five cigarettes per day," "about one-half pack per day," etc.

Smokeless tobacco questions parallel those for cigarettes.

Alcohol use is measured using the three questions illustrated above for marijuana. A parallel set of three questions asks about the frequency of being drunk. A different question asks, for the prior two-week period, "How many times (if any) have you had five or more drinks in a row?"

Perceived risk is measured by a question asking, "How much do you think people risk harming themselves (physically or in other ways), if they . . ." ". . . try marijuana once or twice," for example. The answer categories are "no risk," "slight risk," "moderate risk," "great risk," and "can't say, drug unfamiliar."

Disapproval is measured by the question "Do YOU disapprove of people doing each of the following?" followed by "trying marijuana once or twice," for example. Answer categories are "don't disapprove," "disapprove," and "strongly disapprove." In the 8th- and 10th-grade questionnaires, a fourth category—"can't say, drug unfamiliar"—is provided and included in the calculations.

Perceived availability is measured by the question "How difficult do you think it would be for you to get each of the following types of drugs, if you wanted some?" Answer categories are "probably impossible," "very difficult," "fairly difficult," "fairly easy," and "very easy." For 8th and 10th graders, an additional answer category—"can't say, drug unfamiliar"—is offered and included in the calculations.

Summary of Key Findings

One important finding of the MTF study is that cohort effects—lasting differences between different cohorts entering secondary school—have emerged, beginning with increases in drug use during the early 1990s. Such cohort effects mean that usage rates (and sometimes attitudes and beliefs about various drugs) reach peaks and valleys in different years for different grades. We have seen such cohort effects for cigarette smoking throughout most of the life of the study, but they were much less evident for illicit drugs until the mid-1990s. Since then, 8th graders have tended to be the first to show turnarounds in illicit drug use, and have generally shown the greatest proportional declines from recent peak levels of use, attained for the most part during the 1990s, while the proportional declines have generally been smallest among 12th graders.

In 2008, we introduced a set of tables providing an overview of drug use trends for the *three grades combined*. While there are important differences by grade, this approach gives a more succinct summary of the general nature of historical trends over the last several years.

A number of interesting findings emerged from the 2011 survey, relating in particular to the three substances most widely used by adolescents—cigarettes, alcohol, and marijuana. We begin by discussing marijuana and two other illegal drugs of concern, then return to cigarettes and alcohol.

Marijuana use, which had been rising among teens for the past three years, continued to rise in 2011 in all prevalence periods for 10th and 12th graders. The recent rise in use stands in stark contrast to the long, gradual decline that had been occurring over the preceding decade. (Among 8th graders there was some decrease in annual prevalence in 2011 although annual prevalence has been rising overall since 2004.) It is relevant that perceived risk for marijuana has been falling for the past five years, and disapproval declined for the past three to four years. (The decline in perceived risk in particular may be related to the increased public discussions concerning medical marijuana.) Of particular importance, ***daily marijuana use*** increased significantly in all three grades in 2010, rising further in all three grades in 2011, though the one-year increase was not statistically significant. Daily use now stands at 1.3%, 3.6%, and 6.6% in grades 8, 10, and 12. That means that roughly one in fifteen high school seniors today is a current daily, or near-daily, marijuana user.

Synthetic marijuana

Which goes by such names as Spice and K-2, is an herbal drug mixture that usually contains designer chemicals that fall into the cannibinoid family. Until March of 2011 these drugs were not scheduled by the Drug Enforcement Administration, so they were readily available on the Internet and in head shops, gas stations, etc. The DEA did schedule them under its emergency authority for one year, beginning March 1, 2011, making their possession and sale no longer legal. MTF first addressed the use of synthetic marijuana in its 2011 survey, asking 12th graders about use in the prior 12 months, which would have covered a considerable period of time prior to the drugs being

scheduled. Some 11.4% indicated use in the prior 12 months. Next year's survey results should reflect any effects of the scheduling by the DEA.

Ecstasy

After a decline of several years in perceived risk and disapproval of ecstasy use—which we had been warning could presage a rebound in use—ecstasy use does now appear to be rebounding, primarily among the older teens.

Alcohol use, including *binge drinking*, continued its longer term decline among teens, reaching historically low levels in 2011 in all three grades under study. Use has been in a long-term pattern of decline since about 1980, with the interruption of a few years in the early 1990s during which alcohol use increased along with the use of cigarettes and almost all illicit drugs. Among 12th graders in 1981, 41% reported having five or more drinks in a row on at least one occasion in the two weeks prior to the survey (sometimes called binge drinking). This statistic fell to 28% by 1992, prior to the rebound in the 1990s, but has now fallen even further, reaching 22% in 2011—a decline of nearly one half since 1981.

Cigarettes

After decelerating considerably in recent years, the long-term decline in *cigarette* use, which began in the mid-1990s, appeared to come to a halt in the lower grades in 2010. Indeed, both 8th and 10th graders showed evidence of a slight increase in smoking in 2010, though the increases did not reach statistical significance. Perceived risk and subsequently disapproval had both leveled off some years ago. In 2011, however, the decline in teen smoking resumed in the lower grades (there was a significant drop in use among the 10th graders) and also continued among 12th graders. Perceived risk and disapproval rose in all three grades, significantly for both among 10th graders. Availability also dropped significantly among 8th and 10th graders but more than half of the 8th graders and nearly three quarters of the 10th graders still say it would be "fairly easy" or "very easy" for them to get cigarettes if they wanted some.

Use of any illicit drug

Because marijuana is by far the most prevalent drug included in the *any illicit drug* use index, an increase in prevalence occurred for that index in 2011, as well as for marijuana for the two upper grades. The proportions using *any illicit drug other than marijuana* had been declining gradually since about 2001, but no further decline occurred in 2010 and only slight (non-significant) declines occurred in 2011 for 8th and 10th graders; the 2011 levels are similar to the 2008 levels.

Other Drugs Declining in Use

Several other drugs showed signs of decreased use in 2011. These include: ***inhalants, cocaine powder, crack cocaine,*** the narcotic drug ***Vicodin,*** the amphetamine ***Adderall, sedatives, tranquilizers,*** and ***over-the-counter cough and cold medicines*** used to get high.

Inhalants

The annual prevalence of inhalant use fell in all grades in 2011 (significantly so in 8th and 10th grades), continuing modest declines occurring since the mid-2000s. This is surprising in light of the fact that perceived risk for inhalant use fell considerably among 8th and 10th graders from 2001 through 2008 before leveling, which we have interpreted as generational forgetting of the risks of inhalant use. Usually, when this occurs, there is a resurgence in use; but for whatever reason, such a resurgence has not yet occurred. (Twelfth graders are not asked about perceived risk for this drug.)

Powdered cocaine use continued gradual declines in 8th and 10th grades in 2011, while use among 12th graders leveled. All three grades are at their lowest levels of use since recent peak years. Use of *crack* continued to decline in 2011 with a significant decline among 12th graders. In 2011 *Vicodin,* the most widely used of the narcotic drugs, continued to decline among 8th graders, declined significantly among 10th graders but showed no further decline among 12th graders. Use of *Adderall,* the most widely used amphetamine and a drug used in the treatment of ADHD, declined in the lower grades and there was no further change among 12th graders. *Sedative* (barbiturates) use, which is reported only for 12th graders, continued its slow, non-significant decline in 2011. *Tranquilizer* use declined significantly for 8th graders but only slightly for 10th graders. There was no further change among 12th graders, but they remain at their lowest point in 12 years. The misuse of *over-the-counter (OTC) cough and cold medicines* to get high dropped some for 8th graders, increased a bit for 10th graders and dropped significantly for 12th graders. These OTC drugs usually contain the cough suppresant dextromethorphan, which can have hallucinogenic effects when taken in large quantities.

Drugs Holding Steady in 2011

Use of drugs in several categories held fairly steady in 2011. These included an index of the use of *any illicit drug other than marijuana, LSD, hallucinogens other than LSD, salvia, heroin* used with and without a needle, *narcotics other than heroin, OxyContin* specifically, *amphetamines* (and *Ritalin* specifically), several so-called "club drugs" (*Rohypnol, GHB,* and *Ketamine*), *methamphetamine, crystal methamphetamine, Provigil* (a stay-awake drug), and *anabolic steroids.* Use of most of these drugs is well below their recent peak levels attained in the past 15 years. Two exceptions are "any prescription drug" and salvia. While the proportion of students using any illicit drug has increased in the upper grades this year, due primarily to the rise in marijuana use, the proportion using any of the other illicit drugs held steady and may have even declined slightly in the lower grades. One group of drugs that is not down much from peak levels is *narcotics other than heroin;* their continued high rate of use is a disturbing finding.

The *psychotherapeutic drugs* now make up a larger part of the overall U.S. drug problem than was true 10–15 years ago, in part because use increased for many prescription drugs over that period, and in part because use of a number of street drugs has declined substantially since the mid-1990s. It seems likely that young people are less concerned about the dangers of using these prescription drugs outside of medical regimen, likely because they are widely used for legitimate purposes. (Indeed, the low levels of perceived risk for sedatives and amphetamines observed among 12th graders illustrate this point.) Also, prescription psychotherapeutic drugs are now being advertised directly to the consumer, which implies both that they are widely used and safe to use. Fortunately, the use of most of these drugs has either leveled or begun to decline in the past few years. The proportion of 12th graders misusing *any* of these prescription drugs (i.e., amphetamines, sedatives, tranquilizers, or narcotics other than heroin) in the prior year has leveled at 15.2%—about where it has been since 2008 and down slightly from 17.1% in 2005.

Implications for Prevention

The wide divergence in historical trajectories of the various drugs over time helps to illustrate that, to a considerable degree, the determinants of use are often specific to each drug. These determinants include both perceived benefits and perceived adverse outcomes that young people come to associate with each drug.

Unfortunately, word of the supposed benefits of using a drug usually spreads much faster than information about the adverse consequences. Supposed benefits take only rumor and a few testimonials, the spread of which have been hastened and expanded greatly by the media and Internet. It usually takes much longer for the evidence of adverse consequences (e.g., death, disease, overdose, addiction) to cumulate and then be disseminated. Thus, when a new drug comes onto the scene, it has a considerable grace period during which its benefits are alleged and its consequences are not yet known. We believe that ecstasy illustrated this dynamic. Synthetic marijuana and so-called "bath salts" are two more recent examples where evidence of adverse outcomes is only beginning to catch up to the push that these drugs have received through the Internet and the media.

To a considerable degree, prevention must occur drug by drug, because people will not necessarily generalize the adverse consequences of one drug to the use of others. Many beliefs and attitudes held by young people are drug specific. The figures in this *Overview* on perceived risk and disapproval for the various drugs—attitudes and beliefs that we have shown to be important in explaining many drug trends over the years—amply illustrate this assertion. These attitudes and beliefs are at quite different levels for the various drugs and, more importantly, often trend quite differently over time.

"Generational Forgetting" Helps Keep the Drug Epidemic Going

Another point worth keeping in mind is that there tends to be a continuous flow of new drugs onto the scene and of older ones being rediscovered by young people. Many drugs have made a comeback years after they first fell from popularity, often because knowledge among youth of their adverse consequences faded as generational replacement took place. We call this process "generational forgetting." Examples include LSD and methamphetamine, two drugs used widely in the 1960s that made a comeback in the 1990s after their initial popularity faded as a result of their adverse consequences becoming widely recognized during periods of high use. Heroin, cocaine, PCP, and crack are some others that have followed a similar pattern. At present, *LSD, inhalants,* and *ecstasy* are all showing some effects of generational forgetting—that is, perceived risk has declined appreciably for those drugs—which puts future cohorts at greater risk of having a resurgence in use. In the case of LSD, perceived risk among 8th graders has declined appreciably and more are saying that they are not familiar with the drug. It would appear that a resurgence in availability (which declined very sharply after about 2001, most likely due to the FDA closing a major lab in 2000) could generate another increase in use.

As for newly emerging drugs, examples include nitrite inhalants and PCP in the 1970s; crack and crystal methamphetamine in the 1980s; Rohypnol, GHB, and ecstasy in the 1990s; dextromethorphan, salvia and synthetic marijuana in the 2000s, and "bath salts" more recently. The frequent introduction of new drugs (or new forms or new modes of administration of older drugs, as illustrated by crack, crystal methamphetamine, and noninjected heroin) helps keep this nation's drug problem alive. Because of the lag times described previously, the forces of containment are always playing catch-up with the forces of encouragement and exploitation. Organized efforts to reduce the grace period experienced by new drugs would seem to be among the most promising responses for minimizing the damage they will cause. Such efforts regarding ecstasy by the National Institute on Drug Abuse and others appeared to pay off.

Cigarettes and Alcohol

The findings concerning use of the licit drugs—cigarettes and alcohol—remain a basis for considerable concern.

Cigarettes

Four in every ten American young people (40%) have tried cigarettes by 12th grade, and nearly one in five (19%) 12th graders is a current smoker. (These proportions would be higher if high school dropouts were included in the study's coverage.) Even as early as 8th grade, nearly one in five (18%) has tried cigarettes, and 1 in 16 (6%) has already become a current smoker. Fortunately, there has been some real improvement in these statistics since the mid- to late 1990s, following a dramatic increase in adolescent smoking earlier in the 1990s. Some of the improvement was simply regaining lost ground; however, in 2011, cigarette use reached the lowest levels recorded in the life of the MTF study, going back over 36 years in the case of 12th graders and 20 years in the case of 8th and 10th graders.

Thirty-day prevalence of cigarette use reached a peak in 1996 at grades 8 and 10, capping a rapid climb from the 1991 levels (when data were first gathered on these grades). Between 1996 and 2011, current smoking fell considerably in these grades (by 71% and 61%, respectively). However, the decline in use had decelerated in recent years, and in 2010 there was evidence of some increase in smoking rates among 8th and 10th graders (though not statistically significant). In 2011 use decreased among 8th graders and decreased significantly for

10th graders. For 12th graders, peak use occurred a year later, in 1997, and has since shown a more modest decline, dropping to 19.2% by 2010 and then to 18.7% in 2011. Because of the strong cohort effect that we have consistently observed for cigarette smoking, we expect use at 12th grade to continue to show declines, as the lighter using cohorts of 8th and 10th graders become 12th graders. Overall increases in perceived risk and disapproval appear to have contributed to the downturn. Perceived risk increased substantially and steadily in all grades from 1995 through 2004, after which it leveled in 8th and 10th grades; however, it continued rising in 12th grade until 2006, after which it leveled and then declined some in 2008. Disapproval of smoking had been rising steadily in all grades since 1996. After 2004, the rise decelerated in the lower grades through 2006—again, reflecting a cohort effect in this attitude. All three grades showed an increase in perceived risk and in disapproval in 2011. (The increases for both measures were significant for 10th graders.)

It seems likely that some of the attitudinal change surrounding cigarettes is attributable to the adverse publicity suffered by the tobacco industry in the 1990s, as well as a reduction in cigarette advertising and an increase in antismoking advertising reaching children.

Various other attitudes toward smoking became more unfavorable during that interval, as well, though some have since leveled off. For example, among 8th graders, the proportions saying that they "prefer to date people who don't smoke" rose from 71% in 1996 to 81% by 2004, about where it remains in 2011. Similar changes occurred in 10th and 12th grades, as well. Thus, at the present time, smoking is likely to make an adolescent less attractive to the great majority of potential romantic partners. However, most of the negative connotations of smoking and smokers have leveled off in the past few years. In addition to changes in attitudes and beliefs about smoking, price likely also played an important role in the decline in use. Cigarette prices rose appreciably in the late 1990s and early 2000s as cigarette companies tried to cover the costs of the tobacco settlement, and as many states increased excise taxes on cigarettes.

Smokeless tobacco use had also been in decline for some years, continuing into the early 2000s, but the decline ended in all grades by about 2007. Indeed, the 30-day prevalence rates for smokeless tobacco were down by about half from peak levels, but all grades showed an increase in use from about 1997 through 2009, before leveling in 2011. Appreciable increases in both perceived risk and disapproval in prior years likely contributed to the decline in use, but then they both showed a small reversal for a couple of years. In 2011 both measures increased at all grades except for perceived risk among 8th graders.

Alcohol remains the most widely used drug by today's teenagers. Despite recent declining rates, seven out of every ten students (70%) have consumed alcohol (more than just a few sips) by the end of high school, and one third (33%) has done so by 8th grade. In fact, half (51%) of 12th graders and more than one sixth (15%) of 8th graders in 2011 report having been drunk at least once in their life.

Alcohol use began a substantial decline in the 1980s. To a considerable degree, alcohol trends have tended to parallel the trends in illicit drug use. These include a modest increase in binge drinking (defined as having five or more drinks in a row at least once in the past two weeks) in the early and mid-1990s, though it was a proportionally smaller increase than was seen for cigarettes and most of the illicit drugs. Fortunately, binge drinking rates leveled off eight to eleven years ago, just about when the illicit drug rates began to turn around, and in 2002 a drop in drinking and drunkenness resumed in all grades. Gradual declines continued into 2011, and we are now seeing the study's lowest rates of teen drinking and drunkeness in all three grades.

The longer term trend data available for 12th graders show that alcohol usage rates, and binge drinking in particular, are now substantially below peak levels measured in the early 1980s.

Any Illicit Drug

Monitoring the Future routinely reports three different indexes of illicit drug use—"any illicit drug," "any illicit drug other than marijuana," and "any illicit drug including inhalants." In this section we discuss only the first two.

In order to make comparisons over time, we have kept the definitions of these indexes constant. Levels are little affected by the inclusion of newer substances, primarily because most individuals using them are also using the more prevalent drugs included in the indexes. The major exception has been inhalants, the use of which is quite prevalent in the lower grades, so in 1991 a special index was added that includes inhalants.

Trends in Use

In the late 20th century, young Americans reached extraordinarily high levels of illicit drug use by U.S. as well as international standards. In 1975, when MTF began, the majority of young people (55%) had used an illicit drug by the time they left high school. This figure rose to two thirds (66%) in 1981 before a long and gradual decline to 41% in 1992—the low point. After 1992 the proportion rose considerably, reaching a recent high point of 55% in 1999; it then declined gradually to 47% in 2007 through 2009, before rising to 50% in 2011 as marijuana use has been rising again.

Trends for annual, as opposed to lifetime, prevalence . . . are quite parallel to those for lifetime prevalence, but at a lower level. Among 8th graders, a gradual and continuing fall off occurred after 1996. Peak rates since 1991 were reached in 1997 in the two upper grades and declined little for several years. Between 2001 and 2007 all three grades showed declines, but annual use rates in all three grades have risen since then except for 8th grade in 2011. Because marijuana is much more prevalent than any other illicit drug, trends in its use tend to drive the index of any illicit drug use. Thus we also report an index that excludes marijuana, and shows the proportions of students who use the other, so-called "harder" illicit drugs. In 1975 over one third (36%) of 12th graders had tried some illicit drug other than marijuana. This figure rose to 43% by 1981, then declined for a long period to a low of 25% in 1992. Some increase followed in the 1990s as the use of a number of drugs rose steadily, and it reached 30% by 1997. (In 2001 it was 31%, but this apparent upward shift in the estimate was an artifact due to a change in the question wording for "other hallucinogens"

and tranquilizers.[5]) Lifetime prevalence among 12th graders then fell slightly, to 25% in 2011. The fourth panel presents the *annual* prevalence data for any illicit drug other than marijuana, which shows a pattern of change over the past few years similar to the index of any illicit drug use, but with much less pronounced change since 1991. It leveled in all three grades in 2010 and then dropped slightly in the two lower grades in 2011.

Overall, these data reveal that, while use of individual drugs (other than marijuana) may fluctuate widely, the proportion using *any* of them is much more stable. In other words, the proportion of students prone to using such drugs and willing to cross the normative barriers to such use changes more gradually. The usage rate for each individual drug, on the other hand, reflects many more rapidly changing determinants specific to that drug: how widely its psychoactive potential is recognized, how favorable the reports of its supposed benefits are, how risky its use is seen to be, how acceptable it is in the peer group, how accessible it is, and so on.

Marijuana

Marijuana has been the most widely used illicit drug throughout MTF's 37 year history. It can be taken orally, mixed with food, and smoked in a concentrated form as hashish—the use of which is much more common in Europe. The great majority of consumption in the U.S. involves smoking it in rolled cigarettes ("joints"), in pipes or water pipes, or in hollowed-out cigars ("blunts").

Trends in Use

Annual marijuana prevalence peaked among 12th graders in 1979 at 51%, following a rise that began during the 1960s. Then use declined fairly steadily for 13 years, bottoming at 22% in 1992—a decline of more than half. The 1990s, however, saw a resurgence of use. After a considerable increase (one that actually began among 8th graders a year earlier than among 10th and 12th graders), annual prevalence rates peaked in 1996 at 8th grade and in 1997 at 10th and 12th grades. After these peak years, use declined among all three grades through 2006, 2007, or 2008; since then there has been an upturn in use in all three grades, indicating another possible resurgence in use although in 2011 there was some decline in use among 8th graders. In 2010 there was a significant increase in *daily use* in all three grades, followed by a nonsignificant increase in 2011 reaching 1.3%, 3.6%, and 6.6% in grades 8, 10, and 12, respectively. The rate for 12th graders is the highest rate since 1981, when it was 7.0%.

Perceived Risk

The proportion of students seeing great risk from using marijuana regularly fell during the rise in use in the 1970s, and again during the subsequent rise in the 1990s. Indeed, at 10th and 12th grades, perceived risk declined a year before use rose in the upturn of the 1990s, making perceived risk a leading indicator of change in use. (The same may have happened at 8th grade as well, but we lack data starting early enough to know.) The decline in perceived risk halted in 1996 in 8th and 10th grades; the increases in use ended a year or two later, again making perceived risk a leading indicator. From 1996 to 2000, perceived risk held fairly steady and the decline in use in the upper grades stalled. After some decline prior to 2002, perceived risk increased in all grades through 2004 as use decreased. Perceived risk fell after 2004 and 2005 in 8th and 12th grades respectively, (and since 2008 in 10th grade) pre-saging the more recent increase in use. In 2011 perceived risk continued to decline in grades 10 and 12 and leveled in grade 8.

Disapproval

Personal disapproval of trying marijuana use fell considerably among 8th graders between 1991 and 1996 and among 10th and 12th graders between 1992 and 1997—by 17, 21, and 19 percentage points, respectively, over those intervals of increasing use. After that there was some modest increase in disapproval among 8th graders, but not much among 10th and 12th graders until 2004, when the lower grades showed increases. From 2003 to 2007 (2008 in the case of 10th graders) disapproval increased in all three grades, but has declined some since then as use rose.

Availability

Ever since the MTF study began in 1975, between 81% and 90% of 12th graders each year have said that they could get marijuana fairly easily or very easily if they wanted some. It has been considerably less accessible to younger adolescents. Still, in 2011 38% of 8th graders, 68% of 10th graders, and 82% of 12th graders reported it as being fairly or very easy to get. It thus seems clear that marijuana has remained a highly accessible drug.

Inhalants

Inhalants are any gases or fumes that can be inhaled for the purpose of getting high. These include many household products—the sale and possession of which is legal—including glue, nail polish remover, gasoline, solvents, butane, and propellants used in certain commercial products such as whipped cream dispensers. Unlike nearly all other classes of drugs, their use is most common among younger adolescents and tends to decline as youth grow older. The use of inhalants at an early age may reflect the fact that many inhalants are cheap, readily available (often in the home), and legal to buy and possess. The decline in use with age likely reflects their coming to be seen as "kids' drugs," in addition to the fact that a number of other drugs become available to older adolescents, who are also more able to afford them.

Trends in Use

According to the long-term data from 12th graders, inhalant use (excluding the use of nitrite inhalants) rose gradually from 1976 to 1987, which was somewhat unusual as most other forms of illicit drug use were in decline during the 1980s. Use rose among 8th and 10th graders from 1991, when data were first gathered on them, through 1995; it rose among 12th graders from 1992 to 1995. All grades then exhibited a fairly steady and substantial decline in use through 2001 or 2002. After 2001 the grades diverged somewhat in their trends: 8th graders showed a

significant increase in use for two years, followed by a decline from 2004 to 2007; 10th graders showed an increase after 2002 but some decline since 2007 including a significant decrease in 2011; 12th graders showed some increase from 2003 to 2005, but a decline since then.

Perceived Risk

Only 8th and 10th graders have been asked questions about the degree of risk they associate with inhalant use. Relatively low proportions think that there is a "great risk" in using an inhalant once or twice. However, significant increases in this belief were observed between 1995 and 1996 in both 8th and 10th grades, probably due to an anti-inhalant advertising initiative launched by The Partnership for a Drug-Free America at that time. That increase in perceived risk marked the beginning of a long and important decline in inhalant use, and no other drugs showed a turnaround in use at that point. However, the degree of risk associated with inhalant use declined steadily between 2001 and 2008 among both 8th and 10th graders, perhaps explaining the turnaround in use in 2003 among 8th graders and in 2004 in the upper grades. The hazards of inhalant use were communicated during the mid-1990s; but a generational forgetting of those hazards has likely been taking place, as replacement cohorts who were too young to get that earlier message have entered adolescence. The decline in perceived risk is worrisome, though the decline did halt as of 2008, and perceived risk has not changed much since then. In this case, the decline in perceived risk (between 2002 and 2008) did not translate into a surge in use.

Disapproval

Over 80% of students say that they would disapprove of even trying an inhalant. There was a very gradual upward drift in this attitude among 8th and 10th graders from 1995 through about 2001, with a gradual fall off since then among 8th graders. Among 10th graders there was some decrease after 2004 but the decline halted after 2007.

Availability

Respondents have not been asked about the availability of inhalants. It seems reasonable to assume that these substances are universally available to young people in these age ranges.

LSD

For some years, LSD was the most widely used drug within the larger class of hallucinogens. This is no longer true, due to sharp decreases in its use combined with an increasing use of psilocybin.

Trends in Use

Annual prevalence of LSD use among 12th graders has been below 10% since MTF began. Use declined some for the first 10 years among 12th graders, likely continuing a decline that had begun before 1975. Use was fairly level in the latter half of the 1980s but, as was true for a number of other drugs, rose in all three grades between 1991 and 1996. Between 1996 and

2006 or so, use declined in all three grades, with particularly sharp declines between 2001 and 2003. Since then use has remained at historically low levels.

Perceived Risk

We think it likely that perceived risk for LSD use increased during the early 1970s, before MTF began, as concerns grew about possible neurological and genetic effects (most of which were never scientifically confirmed) as well as "bad trips" and "flashbacks." However, there was some decline in perceived risk in the late 1970s, after which it remained fairly level among 12th graders through most of the 1980s. A substantial decline occurred in all grades in the early 1990s, as use rose. Since about 2000, perceived risk has declined steadily and substantially among 8th graders, declined considerably among 10th graders before leveling in 2011, but held fairly steady among 12th graders through 2009 before dropping a bit. The decline in the lower grades suggests that younger teens are less knowledgeable about this drug's effects than their predecessors—through what we have called "generational forgetting"—making them vulnerable to a resurgence in use.

The decline of LSD use in recent years, despite a fall in perceived risk, suggests that some factors other than a change in underlying attitudes and beliefs were contributing to the downturn—prior to 2001 some displacement by ecstasy may have been a factor, while more recently a decline in availability (discussed below) likely is a factor.

Disapproval

Disapproval of LSD use was quite high among 12th graders through most of the 1980s, but began to decline after 1991 along with perceived risk. All three grades exhibited a decline in disapproval through 1996, with disapproval of experimentation dropping 11 percentage points between 1991 and 1996 among 12th graders. After 1996 a slight increase in disapproval emerged among 12th graders, accompanied by a leveling among 10th graders and some further decline among 8th graders. Since 2001, disapproval of LSD use has diverged among the three grades, declining considerably among 8th graders, declining less among 10th graders, and increasing significantly among 12th graders. Note, however, that the percentages of 8th and 10th graders who respond with "can't say, drug unfamiliar" increased over the years (a finding consistent with the notion that generational forgetting has been occurring); thus the base for disapproval has shrunk, suggesting that the real decline of disapproval among the younger students is less than it appears here. Regardless of these diverging trends, use fell sharply in all grades before leveling in 2004, with little change since then.

Availability

Reported availability of LSD by 12th graders fell considerably from 1975 to 1979, declined a bit further until 1986, and then began a substantial rise, reaching a peak in 1995. LSD availability also rose somewhat among 8th and 10th graders in the early 1990s, reaching a peak in 1995 or 1996. Since those peak years, there has been considerable fall off in availability in all three grades, including a significant decrease for 10th graders

in 2011—quite possibly in part because fewer students have LSD-using friends from whom they could gain access. There was also very likely a decrease in supply due to the closing of a major LSD-producing lab by the Drug Enforcement Administration in 2000. It is clear that attitudinal changes cannot explain the recent declines in use.

Cocaine

Cocaine was used almost exclusively in powder form for some years, though "freebasing" emerged for a while. Then the early 1980s brought the advent of crack cocaine. Our original questions did not distinguish among different forms of cocaine or modes of administration. Since 1987, though, we have asked separate questions about the use of crack and "cocaine other than crack," which has consisted almost entirely of powder cocaine use. Data on overall cocaine use are presented in the figures in this section, and results for crack alone are presented in the next section.

Trends in Use

There have been some important changes in the levels of overall cocaine use over the life of MTF. Use among 12th graders originally burgeoned in the late 1970s and remained fairly stable through the first half of the 1980s before starting a precipitous decline after 1986. Annual prevalence among 12th graders dropped by about three quarters between 1986 and 1992. Between 1992 and 1999, use reversed course again and doubled before declining by 2000. Use also rose among 8th and 10th graders after 1992 before reaching recent peak levels in 1998 and 1999. Over the last decade, use declined in all three grades; 12th-grade use stands at an historical low at just 2.9% in 2011, with use by 8th and 10th graders still lower.

Perceived Risk

General questions about the dangers of cocaine have been asked only of 12th graders. The results tell a fascinating story. They show that perceived risk for experimental use fell in the latter half of the 1970s (when use was rising), stayed level in the first half of the 1980s (when use was level), and then jumped very sharply in a single year (by 14 percentage points between 1986 and 1987), just when the substantial decline in use began. The year 1986 was marked by a national media frenzy over crack cocaine and also by the widely publicized cocaine-related death of Len Bias, a National Basketball Association first-round draft pick. Bias' death was originally reported as resulting from his first experience with cocaine. Though that was later proven to be incorrect, the message had already "taken." We believe that this event helped to persuade many young people that use of cocaine at any level is dangerous, no matter how healthy the individual. Perceived risk continued to rise through 1991 as the fall in use continued. From 1991 to 2000, perceived risk declined modestly. Perceived risk has leveled in recent years at far higher levels than existed prior to 1987, and there is as yet little evidence of generational forgetting of cocaine's risks—at least among the 12th graders.

Disapproval

Questions about disapproval of cocaine have been asked only of 12th graders. Disapproval of cocaine use by 12th graders followed a cross-time pattern similar to that for perceived risk, although its seven-percentage-point jump in 1987 was not quite as pronounced. There was some decline from 1991 to 1997, followed by a period of stability. In recent years there has been a slight drift upwards in disapproval.

Availability

The proportion of 12th graders saying that it would be "fairly easy" or "very easy" for them to get cocaine if they wanted some was 33% in 1977, rose to 48% by 1980 as use rose, and held fairly level through 1982; then, after a one-year drop, it increased steadily to 59% by 1989 (in a period of rapidly *declining* use). Perceived availability then fell back to about 47% by 1994. After 2007 it dropped significantly and stands at 31% in 2011. Note that the pattern of change does not map well onto the pattern of actual use, suggesting that changes in overall availability have not been a major determinant of use—particularly during the sharp decline in use in the late 1980s. The advent of crack cocaine in the early 1980s, however, provided a lower cost form of cocaine, thus reducing the prior social class differences in use.

Crack

Several indirect indicators suggest that crack use grew rapidly in the period 1983–1986, beginning before we had direct measures of its use. In 1986 a single usage question was included in one of the five 12th-grade questionnaire forms, asking those who indicated any cocaine use in the prior 12 months if they had used crack. After that, we introduced into several questionnaire forms three questions about crack use covering our usual three prevalence periods.

Trends in Use

Clearly crack use rose rapidly in the early 1980s, judging by the 4% prevalence reached in 1986; but, after 1986 there was a precipitous drop in crack use among 12th graders—a drop that continued through 1991. After 1991 for 8th and 10th graders (when data were first available) and after 1993 for 12th graders, all three grades showed a slow, steady increase in use through 1998. Since then, annual prevalence dropped by roughly six tenths in all three grades. As with many drugs, the decline at 12th grade lagged behind those in the lower grades due to a cohort effect.

Perceived Risk

By the time we added questions about the perceived risk of using crack in 1987, crack was already seen by 12th graders as one of the most dangerous illicit drugs: 57% saw a great risk in even trying it. This compared to 54% for heroin, for example. (See the previous section on cocaine for a discussion

of changes in perceived risk in 1986.) Perceived risk for crack rose still higher through 1990, reaching 64% of 12th graders who said they thought there was a great risk in taking crack once or twice. (Use was dropping during that interval.) After 1990 some fall off in perceived risk began, well before crack use began to increase in 1994. Thus, here again, perceived risk was a leading indicator. Between 1991 and 1998 there was a considerable fall off in this belief in grades 8 and 10, as use rose quite steadily. Perceived risk leveled in 2000 in grades 8 and 12 and a year later in grade 10. We think that the declines in perceived risk for crack and cocaine during the 1990s may well reflect an example of generational forgetting, wherein the class cohorts that were in adolescence when the adverse consequences were most obvious (i.e., in the mid-1980s) were replaced by newer cohorts who had heard much less about the dangers of this drug as they were growing up; nevertheless, it is still seen as a relatively dangerous drug.

Disapproval

Disapproval of crack use was not included in the MTF study until 1990, by which time it was also at a very high level, with 92% of 12th graders saying that they disapproved of even trying it. Disapproval of crack use declined slightly but steadily in all three grades from 1991 through about 1997. After a brief period of stability, disapproval increased some, but is now level.

Availability

Crack availability did not change dramatically across most of the interval for which data are available. Eighth and 10th graders reported some modest increase in availability in the early 1990s. This was followed by a slow, steady decrease from 1995 through 2004 in 8th grade (followed by a leveling) and sharper drops among 10th and 12th graders beginning in 1999 and 2000, respectively. Since 2007, availability has declined, particularly in the upper grades.

Amphetamines

Amphetamines, a class of psychotherapeutic stimulants, had a relatively high prevalence of use in the youth population for many years. The behavior reported here excludes any use under medical supervision. Amphetamines are controlled substances—they cannot be bought or sold without a doctor's prescription—but some are diverted from legitimate channels, and some are manufactured and/or imported illegally.

> ## Note
>
> The distinction between crack cocaine and other forms of cocaine (mostly powder) was made several years after the study's inception.

Trends in Use

The use of amphetamines rose in the last half of the 1970s, reaching a peak in 1981—two years after marijuana use peaked. We believe that the usage rate reached among 12th graders in 1981 (annual prevalence of 26%) may have been an exaggeration of true amphetamine use because "look-alikes" were in common use at that time. After 1981 a long and steady decline in 12th graders' use of amphetamines began, and ended in 1992.

As with many other illicit drugs, amphetamines made a comeback in the 1990s. Use peaked in the lower two grades by 1996. Since then, use declined steadily in 8th grade and sporadically in 10th grade. Only after 2002 did it begin to decline in 12th grade. The decline in 8th grade paused in 2008, but has since continued. In 10th grade there was a pause in the decline in 2009 and 2010, but the decline resumed in 2011. In 12th grade there has been a reversal of the decline since 2009. Since the recent peaks in use, annual prevalence is down by about six tenths in 8th grade, by about half in 10th grade, and by about one fourth in 12th grade.

Perceived Risk

Only 12th graders are asked about the amount of risk they associate with amphetamine use. For a few years, changes in perceived risk were not correlated with changes in usage levels (at the aggregate level). Specifically, in the interval 1981–1986, risk was quite stable even though use fell considerably, likely as a result of some displacement by cocaine. There was, however, a decrease in risk during the period 1975–1981 (when use was rising), some increase in perceived risk in 1986–1991 (when use was falling), and some decline in perceived risk from 1991 to 1995 (in advance of use rising again). Perceived risk has generally been rising in recent years, very likely contributing to the decline in use that was occurring among 12th graders after 2002; but it appears to have leveled since 2007. In 2011 the examples of specific amphetamines provided in the text of the questions on perceived risk, disapproval, and availability were updated with the inclusion of Adderall and Ritalin. This led to some discontinuities in the trend lines in 2011.

Disapproval

Disapproval of amphetamine use is asked in 12th grade only. Relatively high proportions of 12th graders have disapproved of even trying amphetamines throughout the life of the study. Disapproval did not change in the late 1970s despite an increase in use. From 1981 to 1992, disapproval rose gradually from 71% to 87% as perceived risk rose and use steadily declined. In the mid-1990s it declined along with perceived risk, but it has increased fairly steadily since 1996, again along with perceived risk.

Availability

When the MTF study started in 1975, amphetamines had a high level of reported availability. The level fell by about 10 percentage points by 1977, drifted up a bit through 1980, jumped sharply in 1981, and then began a long, gradual decline through 1991. There was a modest increase in availability at all three grade levels in the early 1990s, as use rose, followed by a long-term decline after that. Some further decline occurred in all grades in 2009 and 2010, but a comparison for 2011 is not possible due to the necessary question change.

Methamphetamine and Crystal Methamphetamine (Ice)

One subclass of amphetamines is called methamphetamine ("speed"). This subclass has been around for a long time and gave rise to the phrase "speed kills" in the 1960s. Probably because of the reputation it got at that time as a particularly dangerous drug, it was not popular for some years, so we did not include a full set of questions about its use in MTF's early questionnaires. One form of methamphetamine, crystal methamphetamine or "ice," grew in popularity in the 1980s. It comes in crystallized form, as the name implies, and the chunks can be heated and the fumes inhaled, much like crack.

Trends in Use

For most of the life of the study, the only question about methamphetamine use has been contained in a single 12th-grade questionnaire form. Respondents who indicated using any type of amphetamines in the prior 12 months were asked in a sequel question to indicate on a prespecified list the types they had used during that period. Methamphetamine was one type on the list, and data exist on its use since 1976. In 1976, annual prevalence on this measure was 1.9%; it then roughly doubled to 3.7% by 1981 (the peak year), before declining for over a decade all the way down to 0.4% by 1992. Use then rose again in the 1990s, as did use of a number of drugs, reaching 1.3% by 1998. In other words, it has followed a cross-time trajectory fairly similar to that for amphetamines as a whole.

In 1990, in the 12th-grade questionnaires only, we introduced our usual set of three questions for *crystal methamphetamine,* measuring lifetime, annual, and 30-day use. Among 12th graders in 1990, 1.3% indicated any use in the prior year; use then climbed to 3.0% by 1998, and has generally been declining since. This variable is charted on the first facing panel.

Responding to the growing concern about methamphetamine use in general—not just crystal methamphetamine use—we added a full set of three questions about the use of any methamphetamine to the 1999 questionnaires for all three grade levels.

These questions yield a somewhat higher annual prevalence for 12th graders: 4.3% in 2000, compared to the sum of the methamphetamine and crystal methamphetamine answers in the other, branching question format, which totaled 2.8%. It would appear, then, that the long-term method we had been using for tracking methamphetamine use probably yielded an understatement of the absolute prevalence level, perhaps because some proportion of methamphetamine users did not correctly categorize themselves initially as amphetamine users (even though methamphetamine was given as one of the examples of amphetamines). We think it likely that the shape of the trend curve was not distorted, however.

The newer questions for methamphetamine show annual prevalence rates in 2011 of 0.8%, 1.4%, and 1.4% for 8th, 10th, and 12th graders, respectively. All of these levels are down considerably from the first measurement taken in 1999, when they were 3.2%, 4.6%, and 4.7%. So, despite growing public concern about the methamphetamine problem in the United States, use actually has shown a fairly steady decline over the past 12 years, at least among secondary school students. (A similar decline in methamphetamine use did not begin to appear among college students and young adults until after 2004, likely reflecting a cohort effect.)

Other Measures

No questions have yet been added to the study on perceived risk, disapproval, or availability with regard to overall methamphetamine use.

Clearly the perceived risk of crystal methamphetamine use has risen considerably since 2003, very likely explaining much of the decline in use since then. Perceived availability has been falling in all three grades since 2006, perhaps in part because there are many fewer users.

Heroin

For many decades, heroin—a derivative of opium—was administered primarily by injection into a vein. However, in the 1990s the purity of available heroin reached very high levels, making other modes of administration (such as snorting and smoking) practical alternatives. Thus, in 1995 we introduced questions that asked separately about using heroin with and without a needle in order to determine whether noninjection use explained the upsurge in heroin use we were observing.

Trends in Use

The annual prevalence of heroin use among 12th graders fell by half between 1975 and 1979, from 1.0% to 0.5%. The rate then held amazingly steady until 1994. Use rose in the mid- and late-1990s, along with the use of most drugs; it reached peak levels in 1996 among 8th graders (1.6%), in 1997 among 10th graders (1.4%), and in 2000 among 12th graders (1.5%). Since those peak levels, use has declined, with annual prevalence in all three grades fluctuating between 0.7% and 0.9% from 2005 through 2011.

Because the questions about use with and without a needle were not introduced until the 1995 survey, they did not encompass much of the period of increasing heroin use. Responses to the new questions showed that by then about equal proportions of all 8th-grade users were taking heroin by each method of ingestion, and some—nearly a third of users—were using both means. At 10th grade a somewhat higher proportion of all users took heroin without a needle, and at 12th grade the proportion was even higher. Much of the remaining increase in overall heroin use beyond 1995 occurred in the proportions using it without injecting, which we strongly suspect was true in the immediately preceding period of increase as well. Likewise, most of the decrease in use since the recent peak levels has been due to decreasing use of heroin without a needle. Use with a needle has fluctuated less over time, though in 2010 12th

graders showed a significant increase to 0.7%, about where it remained in 2011 (0.6%).

Perceived Risk

Students have long seen heroin to be one of the most dangerous drugs, which no doubt helps to account both for the consistently high level of personal disapproval of use and the quite low prevalence of use. Nevertheless, there have been some changes in perceived risk levels over the years. Between 1975 and 1986, perceived risk gradually declined, even though use dropped and then stabilized in that interval. Then there was a big spike in 1987 (the same year that perceived risk for cocaine jumped dramatically), where it held for four years. In 1992, perceived risk dropped to a lower plateau again, presaging an increase in use a year or two later. Perceived risk then rose again in the latter half of the 1990s, and use leveled off and subsequently declined. Based on the short interval for which we have such data from 8th and 10th graders, the tables at the end of this report illustrate that perceived risk of use without a needle rose in the lower grades between 1995 and 1997, foretelling an end to the increase in use. Note that perceived risk has served as a leading indicator of use for this drug as well as a number of others. During the 2000s, perceived risk has been relatively stable in all three grades along with use.

Disapproval

There has been little fluctuation in the very high disapproval levels for heroin use over the years, and the small changes that have occurred have been generally consistent with changes in perceived risk and use.

Availability

The proportion of 12th-grade students saying they could get heroin fairly easily if they wanted some remained around 20% through the mid-1980s; it then increased considerably from 1986 to 1992 before stabilizing at about 35% from 1992 through 1998. At the lower grade levels, reported availability has been markedly lower. Availability has declined gradually since the late 1990s in all three grades.

Other Narcotic Drugs, Including OxyContin and Vicodin

There are a number of narcotic drugs other than heroin—all controlled substances. Many are analgesics that can be prescribed by physicians and dentists for pain. Like heroin, many are derived from opium, but there are also a number of synthetic analogues in use today, including OxyContin and Vicodin.

Throughout the life of the MTF study, we have asked about the use of any narcotic drug other than heroin without specifying which one. Examples of drugs in the class are provided in the question stem. In one of the six 12th-grade questionnaire forms, however, respondents indicating that they had used any narcotic in the past 12 months were then asked to check which of a fairly long list of such drugs they used. Table E-4 in *Volume I* of this annual monograph series provides trends in their annual prevalence data. In the late 1970s, opium and codeine were among the narcotics most widely used. In recent years Vicodin, codeine, Percocet, and OxyContin have been the most prevalent.

Trends in Use

Use is reported only for 12th graders, because we considered the data from 8th and 10th graders to be of questionable validity. Twelfth graders' use of narcotics other than heroin generally trended down from about 1977 through 1992, dropping considerably. After 1992 use rose rather steeply, with annual prevalence nearly tripling from 3.3% in 1992 to 9.5% in 2004, before leveling. (In 2002 the question was revised to add Vicodin, OxyContin, and Percocet to the examples given, which clearly had the effect of increasing reported prevalence. So the extent of the increase over the full time span likely is exaggerated, but probably not by much, because these drugs came onto the scene later, during the rise. They simply were not being fully reported by the late 1990s.)

OxyContin use increased some in all grades from 2002 (when it was first measured) through 2011, though the trend lines have been irregular. Annual prevalence in 2011 was 1.8%, 3.9%, and 4.9% in grades 8, 10, and 12, respectively. Use of Vicodin, on the other hand, remained fairly steady at somewhat higher levels since 2002, though use among 10th and 12th graders has declined sharply since 2009. In 2011 annual prevalence rates were 2.1%, 5.9%, and 8.1% in grades 8, 10, and 12.

Availability

Questions were asked about the availability of other narcotics, taken as a class. Perceived availability increased gradually among 12th graders from 1978 through 1989, even as reported use was dropping. Among 12th graders, perceived availability rose gradually from 1991 through 2001, as use rose more sharply. In contrast, perceived availability has declined among 8th and 10th graders since the late 1990s. (A change in question wording in 2010 to include OxyContin and Vicodin as examples presumably accounts for the considerable jump in reported availability.) Availability declined further in all three grades in 2011.

Tranquilizers

Tranquilizers are psychotherapeutic drugs that are legally sold only by prescription, like amphetamines. They are central nervous depressants and, for the most part, comprise benzodiazepines (minor tranquilizers), although some nonbenzodiazepines have been introduced. Respondents are instructed to exclude any medically prescribed use from their answers. At present, Valium and Xanax are the two tranquilizers most commonly used by students. In 2001 the examples given in the tranquilizer question were modified to reflect changes in the drugs in common use—Miltown was dropped and Xanax was added.

Trends in Use

During the late 1970s and all of the 1980s, tranquilizers fell steadily from popularity, with 12th graders' use declining by three fourths over the 15-year interval between 1977 and 1992. Their use then increased, as happened with many other drugs

during the 1990s. Annual prevalence more than doubled among 12th graders, rising steadily through 2002, before leveling. Use also rose steadily among 10th graders, but began to decline some in 2002. Use peaked much earlier among 8th graders, in 1996, and then declined slightly for two years. Tranquilizer use has remained relatively stable since then among 8th graders, at considerably lower levels than the upper two grades, though they did show a significant decline in 2011. From 2002 to 2005 there was some decline among 10th graders, followed by a leveling, while among 12th graders there was a very gradual decline from 2002 through 2007, before leveling. This staggered pattern of change suggests that a cohort effect has been at work. At present the prevalence of use of these prescription-type drugs is modestly lower than their recent peak levels, with annual prevalence rates of 2.0%, 4.5%, and 5.6% in grades 8, 10, and 12, respectively.

Perceived Risk and Disapproval

Data have not been collected on perceived risk and disapproval primarily due to questionnaire space limitations.

Availability

As the number of 12th graders reporting non-medically prescribed tranquilizer use fell dramatically during the 1970s and 1980s, so did the proportion saying that tranquilizers would be fairly or very easy to get. Whether declining use caused the decline in availability or vice versa is unclear. However, 12th graders' perceived availability has continued to fall since then, even as use rebounded in the 1990s; it is now down by more than three fourths over the life of the study—from 72% in 1975 to 17% by 2011. Availability has fallen fairly continuously since 1991 in the lower grades as well, though not as sharply.

Sedatives (Barbiturates)

Like tranquilizers, sedatives are prescription-controlled psychotherapeutic drugs that act as central nervous system depressants. They are used to assist sleep and relieve anxiety.

Though for many years respondents have been asked specifically about their use of barbiturate sedatives, they likely have been including other classes of sedatives in their answers. In 2004 the question on use was revised to say "sedatives/barbiturates"—a change that appeared to have no impact on reported levels of use. Respondents are told for what purposes sedatives are prescribed and are instructed to exclude from their answers any use under medical supervision. Usage data are reported only for 12th graders because we believe that 8th- and 10th-grade students tend to overreport use, perhaps including in their answers their use of nonprescription sleep aids or other over-the-counter drugs.

Trends in Use

As with tranquilizers, the use of sedatives (barbiturates) fell steadily among 12th graders from the mid-1970s through the early 1990s. From 1975 to 1992 annual prevalence fell by three fourths, from 10.7% to 2.8%. As with many other drugs, a gradual, long-term resurgence in sedative use occurred after 1992, and use continued to rise steadily through 2005, well beyond the point where the use of many illegal drugs began falling. Use has declined some since 2005, and by 2011 the annual prevalence rate is down by about four tenths from its recent peak. The sedative methaqualone has been included in the MTF study from the very beginning, and has never been as popular as barbiturates; use rates have generally been declining since 1975, reaching an annual prevalence of just 0.5% in 2007, about where it has remained since.

Perceived Risk

Trying sedatives (barbiturates) was never seen by most students as very dangerous. But then perceived risk shifted up some through 1991 while use was still falling. It dropped back some through 1995, as use was increasing, and then remained relatively stable for a few years. Perceived risk has generally been at quite low levels, which may help to explain why the use of this class of psychotherapeutic drugs (and likely others) has stayed at relatively high levels in the first half of the decade of the 2000s. However, it began to rise a bit after 2000, foretelling the decline in use that began after 2005. When the term "sedatives" was changed to "sedatives/barbiturates" in 2004, the trend line shifted down slightly, but perceived risk has continued to climb some. As perceived risk has risen, use has declined some.

Disapproval

Like many illicit drugs other than marijuana, sedative (barbiturate) use has received the disapproval of most high school seniors since 1975, with some variation in disapproval rates that have moved consistently with usage patterns. The necessary change in question wording in 2004 appeared to lessen disapproval slightly. There has been some modest increase in disapproval since 2000.

Availability

The perceived availability of sedatives (barbiturates) has generally been declining during most of the life of the study, except for one upward shift that occurred in 1981—a year in which look-alike drugs became more widespread. (The necessary change in question text in 2004 appears to have had the effect of increasing reported availability among 12th graders but not among those in the lower grades.)

Ecstasy (MDMA) and Other "Club Drugs"

There are a number of "club drugs," so labeled because they have been popular at night clubs and "raves." They include LSD, MDMA ("ecstasy"), methamphetamine, GHB (gammahydroxybutyrate), ketamine ("special K"), and Rohypnol. Because previous sections in this *Overview* have dealt with LSD and methamphetamine, they will not be discussed further here.

Rohypnol and GHB, both of which can induce amnesia while under the influence, have also been labeled "date rape drugs." The annual prevalence of GHB use in 2011 was 0.6%, 0.5%, and 1.4% in grades 8, 10, and 12, respectively, and the annual prevalence of ketamine use was 0.8%, 1.2%, and 1.7%, respectively. Both have shown considerable drops since their recent peak levels of use. There are no questions on risk, disapproval, or availability for GHB, ketamine, or Rohypnol.

Trends in Ecstasy Use

Ecstasy (3,4-methylenedioxymethamphetamine or MDMA) is used more for its mildly hallucinogenic properties than for its stimulant properties. Questions on ecstasy use were added to the high school surveys in 1996 (and have been asked of college students and adults since 1989).

Annual prevalence of ecstasy use in 10th and 12th grades in 1996 was 4.6%—considerably higher than among college students and young adults at that time—but it fell in both grades over the next two years. Use then rose sharply in both grades from 1999 to 2001, bringing annual prevalence up to 6.2% among 10th graders and 9.2% among 12th graders. From 2000 to 2001, use also began to rise among 8th graders, to 3.5%. In 2002, use decreased sharply—by about one fifth—in all three grades, followed by an even sharper decline in 2003. The drops continued in 2004, but decelerated considerably. By 2005 the decline had halted among 8th and 10th graders, but it continued for another year among 12th graders. For two or three years there was some rebound in use among 10th and 12th graders, raising the concern that a new epidemic of ecstasy use may be developing; however, after 2007 the trend lines leveled off in all grades until annual prevalence increased significantly in the lower grades between 2009 and 2010 (from 1.3% to 2.4% in 8th grade and from 3.7% to 4.7% in 10th grade), but then declined in 2011 in both grades. Use among 12th graders did increase in 2011.

Perceived Risk of Ecstasy Use

There was little change in 12th graders' perceived risk of ecstasy use until 2001, when it jumped by eight percentage points, and then by another seven percentage points in 2002. Significant increases occurred again in 2003 for all grades. This very sharp rise likely explains the turnaround in use that we had predicted in advance. However, since 2004, we have seen a troubling drop in perceived risk, first among 8th and 10th graders, then among 12th graders. This shift corresponded to the increase in use in the upper two grades, and then in all three grades, suggesting that there may be a generational forgetting of the dangers of ecstasy use resulting from generational replacement. The decline in perceived risk continued into 2010 in the upper grades, and then into 2011 in 8th and 12th grades.

Disapproval of Ecstasy Use

Disapproval of ecstasy use had been declining slightly after 1998, but increased significantly in all three grades in 2002, perhaps because of the rise in perceived risk. The significant increases in disapproval continued through 2003 for 8th graders, 2004 for 10th graders, and 2006 for 12th graders, suggesting some cohort effect. After those peaks, disapproval dropped sharply among 8th graders before leveling, dropped by less among 10th graders before leveling, and did not drop among 12th graders until 2010—suggesting a cohort effect. We previously stated that the erosion in perceived risk and disapproval—which has been sharpest among 8th graders—left these age groups more vulnerable to a possible rebound in ecstasy use: some rebound appears to have occurred.

Availability of Ecstasy

The figure shows a dramatic rise in 12th graders' perceived availability of ecstasy after 1991, particularly between 1999 and 2001, consistent with informal reports about growing importation of the drug. Perceived availability then declined considerably in all grades after 2001 but has been fairly level since 2009.

Alcohol

Alcoholic beverages have been among the most widely used psychoactive substances by American young people for a very long time. In 2011 the proportions of 8th, 10th, and 12th graders who reported drinking an alcoholic beverage in the 30-day period prior to the survey were 13%, 27%, and 40%, respectively. Here we focus on episodic heavy or "binge" drinking (i.e., having five or more drinks in a row during the prior two-week interval at least once)—the pattern of alcohol consumption that is probably of greatest concern from a public health perspective. But it is important to mention that in 2011 all measures of alcohol use—lifetime, annual, 30-day, and binge drinking in the prior two weeks—reached historic lows over the life of the study, following a long period of gradual declines.

Trends in Use

Among 12th graders, binge drinking peaked at about the same time as overall illicit drug use, in 1979. It held steady for a few years before declining substantially from 41% in 1983 to a low of 28% in 1992 (also the low point of any illicit drug use). This was a drop of almost one third in binge drinking. Although illicit drug use rose by considerable proportions in the 1990s, binge drinking rose by only a small fraction, followed by some decline in binge drinking at all three grades. By 2011, proportional declines since the recent peaks reached in the 1990s are 52%, 39%, and 31% for grades 8, 10, and 12, respectively.

It should be noted that there is no evidence of any displacement effect in the aggregate between alcohol and marijuana—a hypothesis frequently heard. The two drugs have moved much more in parallel over the years than in opposite directions, at least until the past four years, during which time alcohol continued to decline while marijuana reversed course and rose. Moreover, these two behaviors have consistently been positively correlated at the individual level.

Perceived Risk

Throughout most of the life of the MTF study, the majority of 12th graders have not viewed binge drinking on weekends as carrying a great risk.

However, an increase from 36% to 49% occurred between 1982 and 1992. There then followed a decline to 43% by 1997 as use rose, before it stabilized. Since 2003, perceived risk has risen some in all grades including in 2011. These changes are consistent with changes in actual binge drinking. We believe that the public service advertising campaigns in the 1980s against drunk driving, as well as those that urged use of designated drivers when drinking, may have contributed to the increase in perceived risk of binge drinking generally. As we have published elsewhere, drunk driving by 12th graders declined during that period by an even larger proportion than binge drinking.[6] Also, we have demonstrated that increases in the minimum drinking age during the 1980s were followed by reductions in drinking and increases in perceived risk associated with drinking.

Disapproval

Disapproval of weekend binge drinking moved fairly parallel with perceived risk, suggesting that such drinking (and very likely the drunk-driving behavior associated with it) became increasingly unacceptable in the peer group. Note that the rates of disapproval and perceived risk for binge drinking are higher in the lower grades than in 12th grade. As with perceived risk, disapproval has increased appreciably in all grades, though it has leveled some in recent years.

Availability

Perceived availability of alcohol, which until 1999 was asked only of 8th and 10th graders, was very high and mostly steady in the 1990s. Since 1996, however, there have been significant declines in 8th and 10th grades. For 12th grade, availability has declined only modestly with 89% still saying that it would be fairly easy or very easy for them to get alcohol. It appears that states, communities, and parents have been successful at reducing access to alcohol among the younger students, however.

Cigarettes

Cigarette smoking is the leading cause of preventable disease and mortality in the United States, and is usually initiated in adolescence. That makes what happens in adolescence particularly important.

Trends in Use

Differences in smoking rates between various birth cohorts (or, in this case, school class cohorts) tend to stay with those cohorts throughout the life cycle. This means that it is critical to prevent smoking very early. It also means that the trends in a given historical period may differ across various grade levels as changes in use occurring earlier in adolescence work their way up the age spectrum (i.e., "cohort effects").

Among 12th graders, 30-day prevalence of smoking reached a peak in 1976, at 39%. (The peak likely occurred considerably earlier at lower grade levels as these same class cohorts passed through them in previous years.) There was about a one quarter drop in 12th-grade 30-day prevalence between 1976 and 1981, when the rate reached 29%, and remained there until 1992 (28%). In the 1990s, smoking began to rise sharply, after 1991 among 8th and 10th graders and 1992 among 12th graders. Over the next four to five years, smoking rates increased by about one half in the lower two grades and by almost one third in grade 12—very substantial increases to which MTF drew public attention. Smoking peaked in 1996 for 8th and 10th graders and in 1997 for 12th graders before beginning a fairly steady and substantial decline that continued through 2004 for 8th and 10th graders (12th graders increased a bit in 2004). Between the peak levels in the mid-1990s and 2004, 30-day prevalence of smoking declined by 56% in 8th grade, 47% in 10th, and 32% in 12th. It is noteworthy, however, that this important decline in adolescent smoking decelerated sharply after about 2002. There was some further decline after 2004 in all grades, but the declines appeared to end in the lower two grades in 2010. In 2011, however, declines occurred in all three grades, with the decline in 10th grade reaching statistical significance.

Perceived Risk

Among 12th graders, the proportion seeing great risk in pack-a-day smoking rose before and during the first period of decline in use in the late 1970s. It leveled in 1980 (before use leveled), declined a bit in 1982, but then started to rise again gradually for five years. (It is possible that cigarette advertising effectively offset the influence of rising perceptions of risk during that period.) Perceived risk fell some in the early 1990s at all three grade levels as use increased sharply. Since then, there has generally been an increase (though not entirely consistently) in perceived risk. All three grades showed an increase in 2011, when use showed a decline. For all three grades, the 2011 levels of perceived risk are the highest ever observed. Note the differences in the extent of perceived risk among grade levels. There is a clear age effect, and by the time most youngsters fully appreciate the hazards of smoking, many of their classmates have already initiated the behavior.

Disapproval

Disapproval rates for smoking have been fairly high throughout the study and, unlike perceived risk, are higher in the lower grade levels. Among 12th graders, there was a gradual increase in disapproval of smoking from 1976 to 1986, some erosion over the following five years, and then steeper erosion from the early 1990s through 1997. After 1997, disapproval rose for some years in all three grades, but leveled in grade 12 after 2006 and in the lower grades after 2007. We measure a number of other smoking-related attitudes; these became increasingly negative for some years, but leveled off three to four years ago.

Availability

When the question was first introduced in 1992, availability of cigarettes was reported to be very high by 8th graders (78% saying fairly or very easy to get) and 10th graders (89%). (We do not ask the question of 12th graders, for whom we assume accessibility to be nearly universal.) Since 1996, availability has declined considerably, especially among 8th graders. Some 52% of 8th graders and 74% of 10th graders now say that cigarettes would be easy to get, reflecting declines since 1992 of 26 and 16 percentage points, respectively.

Smokeless and Other Forms of Tobacco

Traditionally, smokeless tobacco has come in two forms: "snuff" and "chew." Snuff is finely ground tobacco usually sold in tins, either loose or in packets. It is held in the mouth between the lip or cheek and the gums. Chew is a leafy form of tobacco, usually sold in pouches. It too is held in the mouth and may, as the name implies, be chewed. In both cases, nicotine is absorbed by the mucous membranes of the mouth. These forms are sometimes called "spit" tobacco because users expectorate the tobacco juices and saliva (stimulated by the tobacco) that accumulate in the mouth. "Snus" (rhymes with goose) is a relatively new variation on smokeless tobacco, as are some other dissolvable tobacco products. Given that snus appears to be gaining in populatity, items regarding the use of snus and dissolvable tobacco were added to the 2011 surveys. *Annual* prevalence among 12th graders were found to be 7.9% for snus and only 1.5% for dissolvable tobacco.

Trends in Use

The use of smokeless tobacco by teens had been decreasing gradually, and 30-day prevalence is now only about half of recent peak levels in the mid-1990s. Among 8th graders, 30-day prevalence dropped from a 1994 peak of 7.7% to a low of 3.2% in 2007. It stands at 3.5% in 2011. Tenth graders' use was down from a 1994 peak of 10.5% to 4.9% in 2004, but has risen some to 6.6% in 2011; and 12th graders' use decreased from a 1995 peak of 12.2% to 6.1% in 2006, before leveling and then rising to 8.3% in 2011. While use had been rising, it did not continue to rise in 2011. Thirty-day prevalence of *daily* use of smokeless tobacco fell gradually, but appreciably, for some years. Daily usage rates in 2011 are 0.8%, 1.7%, and 3.1% in grades 8, 10, and 12, respectively—down substantially from peak levels recorded in the 1990s but, again, the declines in daily use have halted and begun to reverse.

It should be noted that smokeless tobacco use among American young people is almost exclusively a male behavior. For example, among males the 30-day prevalence rates in 2011 are 4.9%, 11.5%, and 14.2% in grades 8, 10, and 12, respectively, versus 1.9%, 1.9%, and 1.8%, respectively, among females. The respective current daily use rates for males are 1.5%, 3.3%, and 6.0% compared to 0.2%, 0.2%, and 0.0% for females.

Perceived Risk

The most recent low point in the level of perceived risk for smokeless tobacco was 1995 in all three grades. For a decade following 1995 there was a gradual but substantial increase in proportions saying that there is a great risk in using smokeless tobacco regularly. It thus appears that one important reason for the appreciable declines in smokeless tobacco use during the latter half of the 1990s was that an increasing proportion of young people were persuaded of the dangers of using it. But the increases in perceived risk ended by 2004, and it declined some in grades 10 and 12 for a couple of years, before leveling. The decline could be due to generational forgetting of the dangers of use, the increased marketing of snus and other smokeless products, and/or public statements about smokeless tobacco use being relatively less dangerous than cigarette smoking.

Disapproval

Only 8th and 10th graders are asked about their personal disapproval of using smokeless tobacco regularly. The most recent low points for disapproval in both grades were 1995 and 1996. After 1996, disapproval rose among 8th graders from 74% to 82% in 2005, about where it remains in 2011 (83%), and from 71% to 82% in 2008 among 10th graders, with a significant decline since 2008 to 79% in 2010. It is 80% in 2011.

Availability

There are no questions on perceived availability of smokeless tobacco.

Hookahs and Small Cigars

Twelfth graders were first asked about smoking small cigars and smoking tobacco using hookahs (waterpipes) in 2010. The *past year* prevalence rate in 2011 was 18.5% for hookah smoking (up from 17.1% in 2010) and 19.5% for small cigars (down significantly from 23.1% in 2010).

Steroids

Unlike all other drugs discussed in this *Overview*, anabolic steroids are not usually taken for their psychoactive effects but rather for muscle and strength development. However, they are similar to most other drugs studied here in two respects: they can have adverse consequences for the user, and they are controlled substances for which there is an illicit market. Questions about steroid use were added to MTF questionnaires beginning in 1989. Respondents are asked: "Steroids, or anabolic steroids, are sometimes prescribed by doctors to promote healing from certain types of injuries. Some athletes, and others, have used them to try to increase muscle development. On how many occasions (if any) have you taken steroids on your own—that is, without a doctor telling you to take them . . . ?" In 2006 the question text was changed slightly in some questionnaire forms—the phrase "to promote healing from certain types of injuries" was replaced by "to treat certain conditions." The resulting data did not show any effect from this rewording. In 2007 the remaining forms were changed in the same manner.

Trends in Use

Anabolic steroids are used predominately by males; therefore, data based on all respondents can mask the higher rates and larger fluctuations that occur among males. (For example, in 2011, annual prevalence rates were 1.0%, 1.4%, and 1.8% for boys in grades 8, 10, and 12, compared with 0.4%, 0.4%, and 0.5% for girls.) Between 1991 and 1998, the overall annual prevalence rate was fairly stable among 8th and 10th graders, ranging between 0.9% and 1.2%. In 1999, however, use jumped from 1.2% to 1.7% in both 8th and 10th grades. (Almost all of that increase occurred among boys increasing from 1.6% in 1998 to 2.5% in 1999 in 8th grade and from 1.9% to 2.8% in 10th grade. Thus, rates among boys increased by about 50% in a single year.) Among all 8th graders, steroid use has declined by about half to 0.7% in 2011. Among 10th graders, use continued to increase, reaching 2.2% in 2002, but then declined by more than half to 0.9% by 2011. In 12th grade there was a different trend story. With data going back to 1989, we can see that steroid use first fell from 1.9% overall in 1989 to 1.1% in 1992—the low point. From 1992 to 1999 there was a more gradual increase in use, reaching 1.7% in 2000. In 2001, use rose significantly among 12th graders to 2.4% (possibly reflecting a cohort effect with the younger, heavier-using cohorts getting older). Their use decreased significantly in 2005 to 1.5%, where it remained in 2010, before falling slightly more to 1.2% in 2011. Use is now down from recent peak levels by 56%, 59%, and 52% among 8th, 10th, and 12th graders, respectively. (The use of androstenedione—a steroid precursor—has also declined sharply since 2001.)

Perceived Risk

Perceived risk and disapproval were asked of 8th and 10th graders for only a few years. All grades seemed to have a peak in perceived risk around 1993. The longer term data from 12th graders show a ten percentage-point drop between 1998 and 2000, and an additional three percentage-point drop by 2003 (to 55%, the lowest point ever). A change this sharp is quite unusual and highly significant, suggesting that some particular event or events in 1998—quite possibly publicity about use of performance-enhancing substances by famous athletes, in particular use of androstenedione by a famous home-run-hitting baseball player—made steroids seem less risky. It seems likely that perceived risk dropped substantially in the lower grades as well, and the sharp upturn in their use that year would be consistent with such a change. By 2011, perceived risk for 12th graders was up to 61%.

Disapproval

Disapproval of steroid use has been quite high for some years. Between 1998 and 2003 there was a modest decrease, though not as dramatic as the drop in perceived risk. From 2003 to 2008, disapproval rose some—as perceived risk rose and use declined—then leveled.

Availability

Perceived availability of steroids was relatively high and increased with grade level; but it has declined appreciably at all grades in recent years. Some steroids were previously sold over-the-counter, but now a number have been scheduled by the DEA. Androstenedione was classified as a Schedule III controlled substance in 2005.

Subgroup Differences

Understanding the important subgroup variations in substance use among the nation's youth allows for more informed considerations of substance use etiology and prevention. In this section, we present a brief overview of some of the major demographic subgroup differences.

Space does not permit a full discussion or documentation of the many subgroup differences on the host of drugs covered in this report. However, *Volume I* in this monograph series—including the one published in 2011 and the one forthcoming in 2012—contains an extensive appendix (Appendix D) with tables giving the subgroup prevalence levels and trends for all of the classes of drugs discussed here. Chapters 4 and 5 in *Volume I* also present a more in-depth discussion and interpretation of those subgroup differences. Comparisons are made by gender, college plans, region of the country, community size, socioeonomic level (as measured by educational level of the parents), and race/ethnicity. In addition, Monitoring the Future Occasional Paper 74—to be succeeded by Occasional Paper 77 (forthcoming)—is available on the MTF Web site (www.monitoringthefuture.org), and provides in chart form the many subgroup trends for all drugs. The reader will probably find the graphic presentations in these occasional papers much easier to comprehend than the tabular material.

Gender

Generally, we have found males to have somewhat higher rates of illicit drug use than females (especially higher rates of *frequent* use), and much higher rates of smokeless tobacco and steroid use. Males have generally had higher rates of heavy drinking; however, in their 30-day prevalence of alcohol use at 8th grade, girls overtook the boys in 2002 and have had higher rates since. At 10th grade, girls caught up to the boys by 2005, but boys have had higher use for the past three years. The genders have had roughly equivalent rates of cigarette smoking in recent years among 8th and 10th graders, at least until the last few years as use by males has begun to exceed that by females. Among 12th graders, the two genders have reversed order twice during the life of the study, but since 1991 males have had slightly higher smoking rates. These gender differences appear to emerge as students grow older. In 8th grade, females actually have higher rates of use for some drugs. Usage rates for the various substances generally tend to move much in parallel across time for both genders, although the absolute differences tend to be largest in the historical periods in which overall prevalence rates are highest.

College Plans

While in high school, those students who are *not* college-bound (a decreasing proportion of the total youth population) are considerably more likely to be at risk for using illicit drugs, drinking heavily, and particularly smoking cigarettes. Again, these differences are largest in periods of highest prevalence. In the lower grades, it was the college-bound who had a greater increase in cigarette smoking in the early to mid-1990s than did their non-college-bound peers.

Region of the Country

The differences associated with region of the country are sufficiently varied and complex that we cannot do justice to them here. In the past, though, the Northeast and West tended to have the highest proportions of students using any illicit drug, and the South the lowest (although these rankings do not apply to many of the specific drugs and do not apply to all grades today). In particular, the cocaine epidemic of the early 1980s was much more pronounced in the West and Northeast than in the other two regions, although the differences decreased as the overall epidemic subsided. While the South and West have generally had lower rates of drinking among students than the Northeast and the Midwest, those differences have narrowed somewhat in recent years. Cigarette smoking rates have generally been lowest in the West. The upsurge of ecstasy use in 1999 occurred primarily in the Northeast, but that drug's newfound popularity then spread to the three other regions of the country.

Population Density

There have not been very large or consistent differences in overall illicit drug use associated with population density since MTF began, helping to demonstrate just how ubiquitous the illicit drug phenomenon has been in this country. Crack and heroin use have generally not been concentrated in urban areas, as is commonly believed, meaning that no parents should assume that their children are immune to these threats simply because they do not live in a city.

Socioeconomic Level

The average level of education of the student's parents, as reported by the student, is used as a proxy for socioeconomic status of the family. For many drugs the differences in use by socioeconomic class are very small, and the trends have been highly parallel. One very interesting difference occurred for cocaine, the use of which was *positively* associated with socioeconomic level in the early 1980s. However, with the advent of crack, which offered cocaine at a lower price, that association nearly disappeared by 1986. Cigarette smoking showed a similar narrowing of class differences, but this time it was a large *negative* association with socioeconomic level that diminished considerably between roughly 1985 and 1993. In more recent years, that negative association has re-emerged in the lower grades as use declined faster among students from more educated families. We believe that the removal of the Joe Camel ad campaign may have played a role in this. Rates of binge drinking are roughly equivalent across the social classes in the upper grades, a pattern that has existed for some time among 12th graders. But, among 10th graders, a negative correlation between social class and binge drinking has begun to develop in the past few years.

Race/Ethnicity

Among the most dramatic and interesting subgroup differences are those found among the three largest racial/ethnic groups—Whites, African Americans, and Hispanics. African-American students have substantially lower rates of use of most licit and illicit drugs than do Whites at all three grade levels. These include any illicit drug use, most of the specific illicit drugs, alcohol, and cigarettes. In fact, African Americans' use of cigarettes has been dramatically lower than Whites' use—a difference that emerged largely during the life of the study (i.e., since 1975).

Hispanic students have rates of use that tend to place them between the other two groups in 12th grade—usually closer to the rates for Whites than for African Americans. Hispanics do have the highest reported rates of use for some drugs in 12th grade—*inhalants, cocaine, crack,* and *crystal methamphetamine.* In 8th grade, they tend to come out highest of the three racial/ethnic groups on nearly all classes of drugs. One possible explanation for this change in ranking between 8th and 12th grade may lie in the considerably higher school dropout rates of Hispanic youth: more of the drug-prone segment of that ethnic group may leave school before 12th grade compared to the other two racial/ethnic groups. Another explanation could be that Hispanics are more precocious in their initiation of these types of behaviors.

Again, we refer the reader to Occasional Paper 77 (forthcoming) at www.monitoringthefuture.org for a much more complete picture of these complex subgroup differences and how they have changed over the years.

Sponsored by—The National Institute on Drug Abuse, National Institutes of Health

This publication was written by the principal investigators and staff of the Monitoring the Future project at the Institute for Social Research, the University of Michigan, under Research Grant No. 3 R01 DA 01411 from the National Institute on Drug Abuse.

The findings and conclusions in this report are those of the authors and do not necessarily represent the views of the sponsor.

Recommended Citation—Johnston, L. D., O'Malley, P. M., Bachman, J. G., & Schulenberg, J. E. (2012). *Monitoring the Future national results on adolescent drug use: Overview of key findings, 2011.* Ann Arbor: Institute for Social Research, The University of Michigan.

Institute for Social Research
The University of Michigan
Ann Arbor, Michigan
Printed February 2012

Notes

1. Prevalence refers to the proportion or percentage of the sample reporting use of the given substance on one or more occasions in a given time interval—e.g., lifetime, past 12 months, or past 30 days. For most drugs, the prevalence of daily use refers to reported use on 20 or more occasions in the past 30 days, except for cigarettes and smokeless tobacco, for which actual daily use is measured, and for binge drinking, defined as having 5+ drinks on at least one occasion in the prior two weeks.

2. The most recent publication in this series is Johnston, L. D., O'Malley, P. M., Bachman, J. G., & Schulenberg, J. E. (2011). *Monitoring the Future national survey results on drug use, 1975–2010: Volume I, Secondary school students.* Ann Arbor: Institute for Social Research, The University of Michigan, 744 pp.

3. The most recent publication in this series is: Johnston, L. D., O'Malley, P. M., Bachman, J. G., & Schulenberg, J. E. (2011). *Monitoring the Future national survey results on drug use, 1975–2010: Volume II, College students & adults ages 19–50.* Ann Arbor: Institute for Social Research, The University of Michigan, 312 pp.

4. The most recent publication in this series is: Johnston, L. D., O'Malley, P. M., Bachman, J. G., & Schulenberg, J. E. (2010). *HIV/AIDS: Risk and protective behaviors among American young adults, 2004–2008* (NIH Publication No. 10-7586). Bethesda, MD: National Institute on Drug Abuse, 52 pp.

5. The term "psychedelics" was replaced with "hallucinogens," and "shrooms" was added to the list of examples, resulting in somewhat more respondents indicating use of this class of drugs. For tranquilizers, Xanax was added to the list of examples given, slightly raising the reported prevalence of use.

6. O'Malley, P. M. & Johnston, L. D. (2003). Unsafe driving by high school seniors: National trends from 1976 to 2001 in tickets and accidents after use of alcohol, marijuana, and other illegal drugs. *Journal of Studies on Alcohol, 64,* 305–312.

Critical Thinking

1. Discuss the changes in adolescent drug use since the 1990s.
2. What drug use do these authors find to be in decline? Why do you think that is?
3. Discuss implications for youth drug use prevention.

Create Central

www.mhhe.com/createcentral

Internet References

Monitoring the Future
www.monitoringthefuture.org
Drug Abuse
www.drugabuse.gov/related-topics/trends-statistics/monitoring-future

---

Article

Prepared by: Mary Maguire, *California State University—Sacramento*
Clifford Garoupa, *Fresno City College*

Transcending the Medical Frontiers

Exploring the Future of Psychedelic Drug Research

DAVID JAY BROWN

Learning Outcomes

After reading this article, you will be able to:

- Discuss the history of psychedelic drug use.

- Discuss the medical benefits of psychedelic drugs.

- Analyze the arguments for and against the medical use of psychedelic drugs.

When I was in graduate school studying behavioral neuroscience I wanted nothing more than to be able to conduct psychedelic drug research. However, in the mid-1980s, this was impossible to do at any academic institution on Earth. There wasn't a single government on the entire planet that legally allowed clinical research with psychedelic drugs. However, this worldwide research ban started to recede in the early 1990s, and we're currently witnessing a renaissance of medical research into psychedelic drugs.

Working with the Multidisciplinary Association for Psychedelic Studies (MAPS) for the past four years as their guest editor has been an extremely exciting and tremendously fruitful endeavor for me. It's a great joy to see how MDMA can help people suffering from posttraumatic stress disorder (PTSD), how LSD can help advanced-stage cancer patients come to peace with the dying process, and how ibogaine can help opiate addicts overcome their addiction. There appears to be enormous potential for the development of psychedelic drugs into effective treatments for a whole range of difficult-to-treat psychiatric disorders.

However, as thrilled as I am by all the new clinical studies exploring the medical potential of psychedelic drugs, I still long for the day when our best minds and resources can be applied to the study of these extraordinary substances with an eye that looks beyond their medical applications, toward their ability to enhance human potential and explore new realities.

This article explores these possibilities. But first, let's take a look at how we got to be where we are.

A Brief History of Time-Dilation Studies

Contemporary Western psychedelic drug research began in 1897, when the German chemist Arthur Heffter first isolated mescaline, the primary psychoactive compound in the peyote cactus. In 1943 Swiss chemist Albert Hofmann discovered the hallucinogenic effects of LSD (lysergic acid diethylamide) at Sandoz Pharmaceuticals in Basel while studying ergot, a fungus that grows on rye. Then, 15 years later, in 1958, he was the first to isolate psilocybin and psilocin—the psychoactive components of the Mexican "magic mushroom," Psilocybe mexicana.

Before 1972, nearly 700 studies with LSD and other psychedelic drugs were conducted. This research suggested that LSD has remarkable medical potential. LSD-assisted psychotherapy was shown to safely reduce the anxiety of terminal cancer patients, alcoholism, and the symptoms of many difficult-to-treat psychiatric illnesses.

Between 1972 and 1990 there were no human studies with psychedelic drugs. Their disappearance was the result of a political backlash that followed the promotion of these drugs by the 1960s counterculture. This reaction not only made these substances illegal for personal use, but also made it extremely difficult for researchers to get government approval to study them.

The New Wave of Psychedelic Drug Research

The political climate began to change in 1990, with the approval of Rick Strassman's DMT study at the University of New Mexico. According to public policy expert and MAPS president Rick Doblin this change occurred because, "open-minded regulators at the FDA decided to put science before politics when it came to psychedelic and medical marijuana research. FDA openness to research is really the key factor. Also, senior researchers who were influenced by psychedelics in the sixties now are speaking up before they retire and have earned credibility."

The past 18 years have seen a bold resurgence of psychedelic drug research, as scientists all over the world have come to recognize the long-underappreciated potential of these drugs. In the past few years, a growing number of studies using human volunteers have begun to explore the possible therapeutic benefits of drugs such as LSD, psilocybin, DMT, MDMA, ibogaine, and ketamine.

Current studies are focusing on psychedelic treatments for cluster headaches, PTSD, depression, obsessive-compulsive disorder (OCD), severe anxiety in terminal cancer patients, alcoholism, and opiate addiction. The results so far look quite promising, and more studies are being planned by MAPS and other private psychedelic research organizations, with the eventual goal of turning MDMA, LSD, psilocybin, and other psychedelics into legally available prescription drugs.

As excited as I am that psychedelic drugs are finally being studied for their medical and healing potential, I'm eagerly anticipating the day when psychedelic drug research can really take off, and move beyond its therapeutic applications in medicine. I look forward to the day when researchers can explore the potential of psychedelics as advanced learning tools, relationship builders, creativity enhancers, pleasure magnifiers, vehicles for self-improvement, reliable catalysts for spiritual or mystical experiences, a stimulus for telepathy and other psychic abilities, windows into other dimensions, and for their ability to possibly shed light on the reality of parallel universes and nonhuman entity contact.

Let's take a look at some of these exciting possibilities.

The Science of Pleasure

Almost all medical research to date has been focused on curing diseases and treating illnesses, while little attention has been paid to increasing human potential, let alone to the enhancement of pleasure. However, one can envision a time in the not-too-distant future when we will have cured all of our most challenging physical ailments and have more time and resources on our hands to explore post-survival activities. It's likely that we'll then focus our research efforts on discovering new ways to improve our physical and mental performance.

A science devoted purely to enhancing pleasure might come next, and psychedelics could play a major role in this new field. Maverick physicist Nick Herbert's "Pleasure Dome" project seeks to explore this possibility, and although this is little more than an idea at this point, it may be the first step toward turning the enhancement of pleasure into a true science.

According to surveys done by the U.S. National Institute of Drug Abuse, the number one reason why people do LSD is because "it's fun." Tim Leary helped to popularize the use of LSD with the help of the word "ecstasy," and sex expert Annie Sprinkle has been outspoken about the ecstatic possibilities available from combining sex and psychedelics. Countless psychedelic trip reports have described long periods of appreciating extraordinary beauty and savoring ecstatic bliss, experiences that were many orders of magnitude more intense than the subjects previously thought possible.

With all the current research emphasis on the medical applications and therapeutic potential of psychedelics, the unspoken and obvious truth about these extraordinary substances is that, when done properly, they're generally safe and healthy ways to have an enormous amount of fun. There's good reason why, they're so popular recreationally, despite their illegality.

When psychedelic research begins to integrate with applied neuroscience and advanced nanotechnology in the future, we can begin to establish a serious science of pleasure and fun. Most likely this would begin with a study of sensory enhancement and time dilation, which are two of the primary effects that psychedelics reliably produce.

Perhaps one day our brightest researchers and best resources will be devoted to finding new ways to enhance sexual, auditory, visual, olfactory, gustatory, and tactile sensations, and create undreamed of new pleasures and truly unearthly delights. Scientific studies could explore ways to improve sexual performance and enhance sensory sensitivity, elongate and intensify our orgasms, enlarge the spectrum of our perceptions, and deepen every dimension of our experience. Massage therapy, Tantra, music, culinary crafting, and other pleasure-producing techniques could be systematically explored with psychedelics, and universities could have applied research centers devoted to the study of ecstasy, tickling, and laughter.

The neurochemistry of aesthetic appreciation, happiness, humor, euphoria, and bliss could be carefully explored with an eye toward improvement. Serious research and development could be used to create new drugs, and integrate neurochemically heightened states with enhanced environments, such as technologically advanced amusement parks and extraordinary virtual realities. In this area of research, it seems that psychedelics may prove to be extremely useful, and countless new psychedelic drugs are just waiting to be discovered.

In addition to enhancing pleasure, psychedelics also stimulate the imagination in extraordinary ways.

Creativity Problem-Solving

A number of early studies suggest that psychedelic drugs may stimulate creativity and improve problem-solving abilities. In 1955, Louis Berlin investigated the effects of mescaline and LSD on the painting abilities of four nationally recognized graphic artists. Although the study showed that there was some impairment of technical ability among the artists, a panel of independent art critics judged the experimental paintings as having "greater aesthetic value" than the artists' usual work.

In 1959, Los Angeles psychiatrist Oscar Janiger asked sixty prominent artists to paint a Native American doll before taking LSD and then again while under its influence. A panel of independent art critics and historians then evaluated these 120 paintings. As with Berlin's study, there was a general agreement by the judges that the craftsmanship of the LSD paintings suffered; however, many received higher marks for imagination than the pre-LSD paintings.

In 1965, at San Francisco State College, James Fadiman and Willis Harman administered mescaline to professional workers in various fields to explore its creative problem-solving abilities. The subjects were instructed to bring a professional problem requiring a creative solution to their sessions. After some psychological preparation, subjects worked individually on their problem throughout their mescaline session. The creative output of each subject was evaluated by psychological tests, subjective reports, and the eventual industrial or commercial validation and acceptance of the finished product or final solution. Virtually all subjects produced solutions judged highly creative and satisfactory by these standards.

In addition to the scientific studies that have been conducted there are also a number of compelling anecdotal examples that suggest a link between creativity and psychedelic drugs. For example, architect Kyosho Izumi's LSD-inspired design of the ideal psychiatric hospital won him a commendation for outstanding achievement from the American Psychiatric Association, and Apple cofounder Steve Jobs attributes some of the insights which lead to the development of the personal computer to his use of LSD. Additionally, a number of renowned scientists have personally attributed their breakthrough scientific insights to their use of psychedelic drugs—including Nobel Prize winners Francis Crick and Kary Mullis.

There hasn't been a formal creativity study with psychedelics since 1965, although there are countless anecdotal reports of artists, writers, musicians, filmmakers, and other people who attribute a portion of their creativity and inspiration to their use of psychedelics. This is an area that is more than ripe for study. Anecdotal reports suggest that very low doses of LSD—threshold level doses, around 20 micrograms—are especially effective as creativity enhancers. For example, Francis Crick was reported to be using low doses of LSD when he discovered the double-helix structure of the DNA molecule.

I'd love to see a whole series of new studies exploring how cannabis, LSD, psilocybin, and mescaline can enhance the imagination, improve problem-solving abilities, and stimulate creativity. As advances in robotics automates more of our activities, I suspect that creativity will eventually become the most valuable commodity of all. Much of the creativity in Hollywood and Silicon Valley is already fueled by psychedelics and research into how these extraordinary tools could enhance creativity even more effectively may become a booming enterprise in the not-too-distant future.

However, creativity isn't the only valuable psychological ability that psychedelics appear to enhance.

ESP Psychic Phenomena

Few people are aware that there have been numerous, carefully controlled scientific experiments with telepathy, psychokinesis, remote viewing, and other types of psychic phenomena, which have consistently produced compelling, statistically significant results that conventional science is at a loss to explain. Even most scientists are currently unaware of the vast abundance of compelling scientific evidence for psychic phenomena, which has resulted from over a century of parapsychological research. Hundreds of carefully controlled studies—in which psi researchers continuously redesigned experiments to address the comments from their critics—have produced results that demonstrate small, but statistically

significant effects for psi phenomena, such as telepathy, precognition, and psychokinesis.

According to Dean Radin, a meta-analysis of this research demonstrates that the positive results from these studies are significant with odds in the order of many billions to one. Princeton University, the Stanford Research Institute, Duke University, the Institute of Noetic Science, the U.S. and Russian governments, and many other respectable institutions, have spent years researching these mysterious phenomena, and conventional science is at a loss to explain the results. This research is summarized in Radin's remarkable book *The Conscious Universe*.

Just as fascinating as the research into psychic phenomena is the controversy that surrounds it. In my own experience researching the possibility of telepathy in animals, and other unexplained phenomena with British biologist Rupert Sheldrake, I discovered that many people are eager to share personal anecdotes about psychic events in their life—such as remarkable coincidences, uncanny premonitions, precognitive dreams, and seemingly telepathic communications. In these cases, the scientific studies simply confirm life experiences. Yet many scientists that I've spoken with haven't reviewed the evidence and remain doubtful that there is any reality to psychic phenomenon. However, surveys conducted by British biologist Rupert Sheldrake and myself reveal that around 78% of the population has had unexplainable "psychic" experiences, and the scientific evidence supports the validity of these experiences.

It's also interesting to note that many people have reported experiencing meaningful psychic experiences with psychedelics—not to mention a wide range of paranormal events and synchronicities, which seem extremely difficult to explain by means of conventional reasoning.

A questionnaire study conducted by psychologist Charles Tart, PhD. of 150 experienced marijuana users found that 76% believed in extrasensory perception (ESP), with frequent reports of experiences while intoxicated that were interpreted as psychic. Psychiatrist Stanislav Grof, M.D., and psychologist Stanley Krippner, PhD., have collected numerous anecdotes about psychic phenomena that were reported by people under the influence of psychedelics, and several small scientific studies have looked at how LSD, psilocybin, and mescaline might effect telepathy and remote viewing.

For example, according to psychologist Jean Millay, PhD., in 1997, students at the University of Amsterdam in the Netherlands did research to establish whether the use of psilocybin could influence remote viewing. This was a small experiment, with only 12 test-subjects, but the results of the study indicated that those subjects who were under the influence of psilocybin achieved a success rate of 58.3 percent, which was statistically significant.

A great review article by Krippner and psychologist David Luke, PhD. that summarizes all of the psychedelic research into psychic phenomena can be found in the Spring, 2011 MAPS Bulletin that I edited about psychedelics and the mind/body connection.

When I conducted the California-based research for two of Sheldrake's books about unexplained phenomena in science,

Dogs That Know When Their Owners Are Coming Home and *The Sense of Being Stared At*, one of the experiments that I ran involved testing blindfolded subjects to see if they could sense being stared at from behind. One of the subjects that I worked with reported an unusually high number of correct trials while under the influence of MDMA. I'd love to run a whole study to see if MDMA-sensitized subjects are more aware of when they're being stared at.

It is especially common for people to report experiences with telepathy, clairvoyance, precognition, remote viewing, and psychokinesis while using ayahuasca, the potent hallucinogenic jungle juice from the Amazon. There have only been several studies with ayahuasca which demonstrate health benefits, but this is an area that is just crying out to be explored carefully and in depth. Future studies could examine ayahuasca's potential and accuracy as a catalyst for psychic phenomena, and all of the traditional studies that have been done with psychic phenomena, which generated positive results, could be redone with subjects dosed with different psychedelics to see if test scores can be improved.

Increasing our psychic abilities may open up the human mind to new, unimagined possibilities—and if you think that harnessing telepathic and clairvoyant abilities is pretty wild, then hold on to your hats for what's likely to come next.

Higher Dimensions and Nonhuman Entity Contact

A primary ingredient in ayahuasca is DMT, and users claim that this remarkable substance has the extraordinary power to open up an interdimensional portal into another universe. Some of the most fascinating psychedelic research has been done with this incredible compound.

DMT is a mystery. One of the strangest puzzles in all of nature—in the same league as questions like "What existed before the Big Bang?" and "How did life begin?"—revolves around the fact that the unusually powerful psychedelic DMT is naturally found in the human body, as well as in many species of animals and plants, and nobody knows what it does, or what function it might serve, in any of these places.

Because natural DMT levels tend to rise while we're asleep at night, it has been suggested that it may have a role in dreaming. But this is pure speculation, and even if true, it may do much more. Because of its endogenous status and unusually potent effects, many people have considered DMT to be the quintessential psychedelic. DMT has effects of such strength and magnitude that it easily dwarfs the titanic quality of even the most powerful LSD trips, and it appears to transport one into an entirely new world—a world that seems more bizarre than our wildest imaginings, yet, somehow, is also strangely familiar.

Psychiatric researcher Rick Strassman, PhD., who conducted a five year study with DMT at the University of New Mexico, has suggested that naturally elevated DMT levels in the brain may be responsible for such unexplained mental phenomena as spontaneous mystical experiences, near-death experiences, nonhuman entity contact, and schizophrenia. Strassman and

others have even gone so far as to speculate about the possibility that elevated DMT levels in the brain might be responsible for ushering the soul into the body before birth, and out of the body after death.

But perhaps what's most interesting about DMT is that, with great consistency, it appears to allow human beings to communicate with other intelligent life forms. When I interviewed Strassman, I asked him if he thought that there was an objective reality to the worlds visited by people when they're under the influence of DMT, and if he thought that the entities that so many people have encountered on DMT actually have an independent existence or not. Rick replied:

> I myself think so. My colleagues think I've gone woolly brained over this, but I think it's as good a working hypothesis as any other. I tried all other hypotheses with our volunteers, and with myself. The "this is your brain on drugs" model; the Freudian "this is your unconscious playing out repressed wishes and fears;" the Jungian "these are archetypal images symbolizing your unmet potential;" the "this is a dream;" etc. Volunteers had powerful objections to all of these explanatory models—and they were a very sophisticated group of volunteers, with decades of psychotherapy, spiritual practice, and previous psychedelic experiences. I tried a thought-experiment, asking myself, "What if these were real worlds and real entities? Where would they reside, and why would they care to interact with us?" This led me to some interesting speculations about parallel universes, dark matter, etc. All because we can't prove these ideas right now (lacking the proper technology) doesn't mean they should be dismissed out of hand as incorrect.

A 2006 scientific paper by computer scientist Marko A. Rodriguez called "A Methodology for Studying Various Interpretations of the N,N-dimethyltryptamine-Induced Alternate Reality" explores how to possibly determine if the entities experienced by people on DMT are indeed independently existing intelligent beings or just projections of our hallucinating brains. Rodriguez suggests a test that involves asking the entities to perform a complex mathematical task involving prime numbers to verify their independent existence. While it seems like a long shot that this method could lead to fruitful results, I think that any serious speculation about establishing communication channels with these mysterious beings is constructive.

Strassman's work could represent the very beginning of a scientific field that systematically explores the possibility of communicating with higher dimensional entities, and this might prove to be a more fruitful endeavor for establishing extraterrestrial contact than the SETI project. What they can teach us, we can only imagine.

My own experiences with DMT lead me to suspect that Strassman's studies would have yielded far more fruitful results had the subjects been dosed with harmaline prior to receiving their DMT injections. Harmaline is an MAO-inhibiting enzyme that is found in a number of plants. It's found in the famous South American vine known as Banisteriopsis cappi, which composes half of the mixture in the sacred hallucinogenic jungle juice ayahuasca, which has been used for healing purposes by indigenous peoples in the Amazon basin for thousands of years. Harmaline is widely known as the chemical that allows the DMT in other plants, like Psychotria viridis, to become orally active.

Orally consumed DMT is destroyed in the stomach by an enzyme called monoamine oxidase (MAO), which harmaline inhibits. However, it does much more than just make the DMT orally active. I've discovered that drinking a tea made from Syrian rue seeds—which also contain harmaline—two hours prior to smoking DMT dramatically alters the experience. Harmaline has interesting psychoactive properties of its own that are somewhat psychedelic, and it slows down the speed of the DMT experience considerably, rendering it more comprehensible, less frightening, and easier to understand. For thousands of years indigenous peoples in the Amazon jungles combined harmaline and DMT, and this long history has cultivated a powerful synergism between how the two molecules react in our body.

In future studies harmaline could be used in conjunction with DMT, to more accurately simulate the ayahuasca experience that strikes such a powerful primordial chord in our species. This would allow for the experience to become much more comprehensible, and last for a greater duration of time, which would allow for more ability to examine the phenomenon of nonhuman entity communication.

Some readers may have noticed that this article has loosely followed a Christian theological progression, from the ego death and bodily resurrection of the medical studies with psychedelics, to the paradisiacal pleasures of Heaven, where we discovered our godlike powers and met with the angels. Ultimately, it appears, this research will lead us to the source of divinity itself.

The Study of Divine Intelligence

Perhaps the most vital function of psychedelics is their ability to reliably produce spiritual or mystical experiences. These transpersonal experiences of inseparability often result in an increased sense of ecological awareness, a greater sense of interconnection, a transcendence of the fear of death, a sense of the sacred or divine, and identification with something much larger than one's body or personal life.

Many people suspect that this experience lies at the heart of the healing potential of psychedelics—and they believe that making this experience available to people is essential for the survival of our species. I agree that we need a compassionate vision of our interconnection with the biosphere to guide our technological evolution and without it we might destroy ourselves.

In his book *The Physics of Immortality*, physicist Frank Tipler introduces the idea that if a conscious designing intelligence is genuinely a part of this universe, then ultimately religion—or the study of this designer intelligence—will become a branch of physics. Psychedelic drug research may offer one pathway toward establishing this future science.

Recent studies by Roland Griffiths and colleagues at Johns Hopkins have confirmed that psilocybin can indeed cause religious experiences that are indistinguishable from religious experiences reported by mystics throughout the ages—and that substantial health benefits can result from these experiences.

These new studies echo the findings of an earlier study done in 1962 by Walter Pahnke of the Harvard Divinity School, and it's certainly not news to anyone who has had a full-blown psychedelic experience. R.U. Sirius responded to this seemingly redundant research by saying that "Wow! Scientists Discover Ass Not Elbow!" Nonetheless, this may represent the beginning of a whole new field of academic inquiry, which explores those realms that have been previously declared off-limits to science.

It appears that the integration of science and spirituality could be the next event horizon—our next adventure as a species. Our future evolution may depend on it. Without a transpersonal perspective of interconnection to guide our evolutionary direction, we seem to be firmly set on a path toward inevitable self-destruction. I personally believe psychedelics can help us get back on track, and help us heal the damage that we've done to ourselves and to the Earth. This is why I believe so strongly in psychedelic drug research.

There isn't much time left before our biosphere starts to unravel, and we may only have a small window of opportunity to save our fragile world. I think that MAPS—and sister organizations, like the Beckley Foundation and the Heffter Research Institute—are industrialized society's best hope for transforming the planet's ancient shamanic plants into the respectable scientific medicines of tomorrows and, in so doing, bring psychedelic therapy to all who need it. This may not only help to heal a number of difficult-to-treat medical disorders and increase ecological harmony on the planet, but it may also open up a doorway to untold and unimagined new worlds of possibility.

Critical Thinking

1. Discuss the benefits and the challenges in the use of psychedelic drugs.

2. Provide an argument for or against legalizing psychedelics for medical reasons.

Create Central

www.mhhe.com/createcentral

Internet References

Drug Policy
www.drugpolicy.org/drug-facts/psychedelics-facts

Science Daily
www.sciencedaily.com/news/mind_brain/psychedelic_drugs

Article   Prepared by: Mary Maguire, *California State University—Sacramento*
Clifford Garoupa, *Fresno City College*

Energy Drink Abuse Worries Health Pros

MICHAEL MCCARTHY

Learning Outcomes

After reading this article, you will be able to:

• Identify the ingredients in a typical energy drink.

• Describe the risks associated with energy drinks.

• Discuss possible means to educate the public about dangers of overuse of energy drinks.

Health experts are sounding the alarm over the possible effects on young athletes of popular energy drinks such as Red Bull, the leading brand in a growing market.

High school and college athletes are increasingly consuming large quantities of these caffeine-loaded drinks to boost athletic performance or lose weight, said a dozen health experts at the SUNY Youth Sports Institute's first national symposium on energy drinks here this week.

But athletes who consume too many energy drinks could suffer from dehydration, tremors, heatstroke or heart attacks, the experts warned. Instead, they say, teen and adolescent athletes should drink water while training and playing, especially during hot and humid summer months.

Some experts called for the U.S. Food and Drug Administration, which treats energy drinks as dietary supplements, to require warning labels on the hundreds of energy drinks on the market.

FDA spokeswoman Susan Cruzan said Wednesday that the agency does not have the authority to do that.

"We have no guidance or regulations that govern the formulation of energy drinks," Cruzan said in an e-mail. "Under current law, the manufacturer is responsible for ensuring that its products are safe and such products do not require FDA pre-market review or approval."

Researchers at Johns Hopkins University are seeking interviews with children and adolescents 8 to 21 years old who have become sick or experienced unpleasant aftereffects from energy drinks.

"There's a tremendous amount of caffeine in these drinks," Jeanna Marraffa, a clinical toxicologist at the Upstate New York Poison Center, told *USA Today* during the conference Tuesday.

"I would say: know what's in these products, have a sense of how much you're consuming and realize they are not safe. Certainly you can have toxic effects from them."

Kathleen Miller, a research scientist at the University at Buffalo's Research Institute on Addictions, said the bitter orange found in some energy drinks is very closely related to ephedra. Because of a number of deaths, the FDA banned the sale of ephedra-containing dietary supplements in 2004.

"In most energy drinks, they're relatively small quantities, so they're probably not doing any harm. But we really don't know," Miller said. "And there's no requirement whatsoever for the manufacturers to moderate the amount that they're putting in."

Eric Small of the Mount Sinai Medical Center in Manhattan told of treating a 17-year-old female runner suffering from chest pains and fatigue. She collapsed at the finish line of a race and was rushed to an emergency room. It turned out she liked to skip breakfast in favor of drinking two or three cans of Red Bull each morning, Small said. More youngsters are substituting protein bars and shakes for real food, he added.

"They think being lighter and eating less and drinking less will improve their performance," Small said.

Kate Zanot, a track and field coach at Harrison High School in Westchester County, N.Y., who attended the conference, said many students don't know the difference between energy drinks such as Red Bull and sports drinks such as Gatorade, so they consume the drinks interchangeably.

"It's a huge concern," she said.

Patrice Radden, a spokeswoman for Red Bull, said via e-mail Wednesday that the company is confident in the safety of its products and does not see the need for warning labels.

"Red Bull is a functional drink and not a thirst quencher or hydrator," she wrote. "Red Bull encourages people who are engaged in a sport or other physical activity and drinking Red Bull to drink lots of water before, during and after the activity."

Rebecca Chang, a Columbia University graduate student who attended the symposium, said the federal government should do more to regulate energy drinks. But, she noted, thrill- or edge-seeking athletes in their teens and 20s might be more attracted to the drinks if they have the added danger of a warning label.

Critical Thinking

1. Discuss the attraction to energy drinks.
2. Analyze the risks associated with regular use and reliance on energy drinks.
3. Develop a plan to mitigate the risks of over-use of energy drinks.

Create Central

www.mhhe.com/createcentral

Internet References

Mayo Clinic
www.mayoclinic.com/health/energy-drinks/AN01303

Brown University Health Education
http://brown.edu/Student_Services/Health_Services/Health_Education/alcohol,_tobacco,_&_other_drugs/energy_drinks.php

Unit 4

Prepared by: Mary Maguire, *California State University—Sacramento*
Clifford Garoupa, *Fresno City College*

UNIT

Other Trends in Drug Use

Rarely do drug-related patterns and trends lend themselves to precise definition. Identification, measurement, and prediction of the consequence of these trends is an inexact science, to say the least. It is, nevertheless, a very important process. One of the most valuable uses of drug-related trend analysis is the identification of subpopulations whose vulnerability to certain drug phenomena is greater than that of the wider population. These identifications may forewarn of the implications for the general population. Trend analysis may produce specific information that may otherwise be lost or obscured by general statistical indications. For example, tobacco is probably the most prominent of gateway drugs, with repeated findings pointing to the correlation between the initial use of tobacco and the use of other drugs.

The analysis of specific trends related to drug use is very important, as it provides a threshold from which educators, health-care professionals, parents, and policymakers may respond to significant drug-related health threats and issues. Over 20 million Americans report the use of illegal drugs. The current rate of illicit drug use is similar to the rates of the past three years. Marijuana remains as the most commonly used illicit drug with more than 14 million current users. Historically, popular depressant and stimulant drugs—such as alcohol, tobacco, heroin, and cocaine—produce statistics that identify the most visible and sometimes the most constant use patterns. Other drugs such as marijuana, LSD, ecstasy, and other "club drugs" often produce patterns widely interpreted to be associated with cultural phenomena such as youth attitudes, popular music trends, and political climate.

Two other continuing trends are those that involve the abuse of prescription drugs and those that involve the use of methamphetamine. Americans are abusing prescription drugs more than ever before with the most frequently mentioned offenders being oxycodone and hydrocodone. Currently, more than 5 million persons use prescription pain relievers for nonmedical reasons. Of those who used pain relievers for nonmedical reasons, 56 percent obtained them for free from a friend or relative. As more and more drugs get prescribed within the population, a steady trend, more and more drugs become easily accessible. The National Institute of Drug Abuse reports that 20 percent of the U.S. population over 12 has used

prescription drugs for nonmedical reasons. Currently, prescription drug abuse among youth ranks second behind only marijuana. The good news is that drug use by youth has declined or leveled off in several important categories such as those associated with marijuana, alcohol, and methamphetamine. And although methamphetamine use is down, it is reported by local and state officials in the West and Midwest as the number one illegal-drug problem.

Although the federal government has modified its survey methods to more accurately identify the number of meth users, many worry that the meth problem is still understated and greatly outweighs those problems associated with other illegal drugs in the West, Southwest, and Midwest. Information concerning drug-use patterns and trends obtained from a number of different investigative methods is available from a variety of sources. On the national level, the more prominent sources are the Substance Abuse and Mental Health Services Administration, the National Institute on Drug Abuse, the Drug Abuse Warning Network, the national Centers for Disease Control, the Justice Department, the Office of National Drug Control Policy, the surgeon general, and the DEA. On the state level, various justice departments, including attorneys general offices, the courts, state departments of social services, state universities and colleges, and public health offices maintain data and conduct research. On local levels, criminal justice agencies, social service departments, public hospitals, and health departments provide information. On a private level, various research institutes and universities, professional organizations such as the American Medical Association and the American Cancer Society, hospitals, and treatment centers, as well as private corporations, are tracking drug-related trends. Surveys abound with no apparent lack of available data. As a result, the need for examination of research methods and findings for reliability and accuracy is self-evident. The articles in this unit provide information about some drug-related trends occurring within certain subpopulations of Americans. While reading the articles, it is interesting to consider how the trends and patterns described are dispersed through various subpopulations of Americans and specific geographical areas. Additionally, much information about drugs and drug trends can be located quickly by referring to the list of websites in the front section of this book.

Article

Prepared by: Mary Maguire, *California State University—Sacramento*
Clifford Garoupa, *Fresno City College*

'Legal Highs' Prevalence Makes Ban Policy 'Ridiculous'

Prohibition approach is 'irrational' say experts as one new synthetic psychoactive substance appears every week.

MARK TOWNSEND

Learning Outcomes

After reading this article, you will be able to:

- Understand how drugs of abuse are increasing in number.
- Understand why the number of abusable drugs continues to rise.
- Identify what type of abusable drugs are most in demand.

"Legal highs" such as mephedrone and naphyrone have been banned, but experts believe UK drugs policy is irrational.

New "legal highs" are being discovered at the rate of one a week, outstripping attempts to control their availability and exposing what some experts claim is the "ridiculous and irrational" government policy of prohibition.

Officials monitoring the European *drugs* market identified 20 new synthetic psychoactive substances in the first four months of this year, according to Paolo Deluca, co-principal investigator at the Psychonaut Research Project, an EU-funded organisation based at King's College London, which studies trends in drug use. He said officials at the European Monitoring Centre for Drugs and Drug Addiction (EMCDDA), an early-warning unit, had detected 20 new substances for sale by May this year. In 2010 the agency had noted 41 new psychoactive substances, a record number, many of which were synthetic cathinone derivatives that can imitate the effects of cocaine, ecstasy or amphetamines.

Deluca said that, given the plethora of new substances, the government's attempts to ban legal highs is not a "feasible" solution. "It's also becoming very difficult to know exactly how many new compounds there are, because you have all these brand names and when you test the batch they are different from the following one." The UK, according to his reasearch, remains Europe's largest market for legal highs and synthetic compounds.

Campaigners at the Transform *Drugs Policy* Foundation (TDPF), a charity, said the unprecedented speed at which new drugs are appearing highlights the government's "unsustainable" strategy of banning each one, as well as a basic lack of understanding of how the drugs market functions.

Last year the government unveiled plans to introduce temporary 12-month bans on "legal highs", while the Advisory Council on the Misuse of Drugs considered a possible permanent ban. So far two substances have received a complete ban—*mephedrone,* the former legal high known as "meow meow", and naphyrone, otherwise known as "NRG1". Another two, phenazepam and Ivory Wave, have also received an import ban, which means the UK Border Agency can seize and destroy shipments following safety concerns.

The government's continued emphasis on banning illegal compounds flies in the face of growing calls for a fresh approach to tackling drugs. Earlier this year prominent public figures, including former heads of MI5 and the Crown Prosecution Service, said the "war on drugs" had failed and should be abandoned in favour of evidence-based policies that treat addiction as a health problem and avoid criminalising users.

Steve Rolles, senior policy analyst at TDPF, said attempts to ban one new substance after another was "like a cat chasing its tail". He added: "Each time they ban one, another emerges. It seems to show a blindness to the basic market dynamic, effectively creating a void for backstreet chemists to create another product." The group is one of many urging the government to adopt a regulatory position between total prohibition or an "internet-free-for all".

Deluca cites the case of mephedrone, which despite being banned last year remains as popular as cocaine among teenagers and young adults, according to official figures released in July. Home Office data from the British Crime Survey estimate that around 300,000 16- to 24-year-olds used mephedrone in the previous 12 months, a similar level of popularity to the use of cocaine among the same age bracket. Deluca added: "The legality of the compounds will not stop potential users, only the quality."

The EMCDDA favours generic bans that would cover entire groups of structurally related synthetic compounds, or chemical families, therefore removing the need to ban individual substances as they appear on the market. Deluca said: "It is impossible to implement a ban for every single new compound."

Rolles said legal highs should be investigated and regulated using the same model as conventional pharmaceuticals. "It's just ridiculous, irrational really. If you're not looking at the regulatory options, then you're not following an evidence-based approach—you are following a political mandate."

Critical Thinking

1. How often are new psychoactive drugs being produced?
2. How many new psychoactive drugs were produced in the year 2010?
3. How many Britons used mephedrone in the year 2010?

Create Central

www.mhhe.com/createcentral

Internet References

Monitoring the Future
www.monitoringthefuture.org

SAMHSA
www.drugabusestatistics.samhsa.gov/trends.htm

Townsend, Mark. From *The Guardian*, September 4, 2011. Copyright © 2011 by Guardian News & Media Ltd. Reprinted by permission.

Article

Prepared by: Mary Maguire, *California State University—Sacramento*
Clifford Garoupa, *Fresno City College*

Alcoholism Isn't What It Used to Be

"NIAAA's goal now and for the foreseeable future is to develop and disseminate research-based resources for each stage of the alcohol use disorder continuum, from primary prevention to disease management," according to acting NIAAA director Ken Warren, PhD.

Learning Outcomes

After reading this article, you will be able to:

- Understand how alcohol abuse/alcohol use has changed.

- Define alcoholism.

- Discuss the extent of alcohol abuse and dependence in the United States.

The realization dawned gradually as researchers analyzed data from NIAAA's 2001–2002 National Epidemiologic Survey on Alcohol and Related Conditions (NESARC). In most persons affected, alcohol dependence (commonly known as alcoholism) looks less like Nicolas Cage in *Leaving Las Vegas* than it does your party-hardy college roommate or that hard-driving colleague in the next cubicle.

"We knew from the 1991–1992 National Longitudinal Alcohol Epidemiologic Study that alcohol dependence is most prevalent among younger adults aged 18 to 29," says Bridget Grant, PhD, chief of NIAAA's Laboratory Epidemiology and Biometry. "However, it was not until we examined the NESARC data that we pinpointed age 22 as the mean age of alcohol dependence onset." Subsequent analysis by Ralph Hingson, Sc.D., director, Division of Epidemiology and Prevention Research, showed that nearly half of people who become alcohol dependent do so by age 21 and two-thirds by age 25.

The NESARC surveyed more than 43,000 individuals representative of the U.S. adult population using questions based on criteria in the *Diagnostic and Statistical Manual of Mental Disorders, Fourth Edition* (DSM-IV) of the American Psychiatric Association (APA). Published in 1994, DSM-IV recognizes alcohol dependence by preoccupation with drinking, impaired control over drinking, compulsive drinking, drinking despite physical or psychological problems caused or made worse by drinking, and tolerance and/or withdrawal symptoms.

Meanwhile, findings continue to accumulate to challenge past perceptions of the nature, course, and outcome of alcoholism. Among those findings:

- Many heavy drinkers do not have alcohol dependence. For example, even in people who have 5 or more drinks a day (the equivalent of a bottle of wine) the rate of developing dependence is less than 7 percent per year.

- Most persons who develop alcohol dependence have mild to moderate disorder, in which they primarily experience impaired control. For example, they set limits and go over them or find it difficult to quit or cut down. In general, these people do not have severe alcohol-related relationship, health, vocational or legal problems.

- About 70 percent of affected persons have a single episode of less than 4 years. The remainder experience an average of five episodes. Thus, it appears that there are two forms of alcohol dependence: time-limited, and recurrent or chronic.

- Although 22 is the average age when alcohol dependence begins, the onset varies from the mid-teens to middle age.

- Twenty years after onset of alcohol dependence, about three-fourths of individuals are in full recovery; more than half of those who have fully recovered drink at low-risk levels without symptoms of alcohol dependence.

- About 75 percent of persons who recover from alcohol dependence do so without seeking any kind of help, including specialty alcohol (rehab) programs and AA. Only 13 percent of people with alcohol dependence ever receive specialty alcohol treatment.

"These and other recent findings turn on its head much of what we thought we knew about alcoholism," according to Mark Willenbring, MD, director of NIAAA's Division of Treatment and Recovery Research. "As is so often true in medicine, researchers have studied the patients seen in hospitals and clinics most intensively. This can greatly skew understanding of a disorder, especially in the alcohol field, where most people neither seek nor receive treatment and those who seek it do so well into the course of disease. Longitudinal, general population studies such as the NESARC permit us to see the entire disease continuum from before onset to late-stage disease."

To Willenbring, these realizations call for a public health approach that targets at-risk drinkers and persons with mild alcohol disorder to prevent or arrest problems before they progress. NIAAA is addressing this need with tools to expand risk awareness (http://rethinkingdrinking.niaaa.nih.gov) and inform secondary prevention and primary care screening (www.niaaa.nih.gov/guide).

New criteria to guide clinicians in diagnosis and treatment await decisions by the DSM-V committee, expected about 2012. Both Dr. Grant and Howard Moss, MD, associate director for clinical and translational research, represent NIAAA on that committee.

"NIAAA's goal now and for the foreseeable future is to develop and disseminate research-based resources for each stage of the alcohol use disorder continuum, from primary prevention to disease management," according to acting NIAAA director Ken Warren, PhD.

Critical Thinking

1. What age group is alcohol dependence most prevalent in?
2. Are all heavy drinkers alcoholic and/or alcohol dependent?
3. What is the average age when alcohol dependence begins?

Create Central

www.mhhe.com/createcentral

Internet References

The National Institute on Alcoholism and Alcohol Abuse
www.niaaa.nih.gov
SAMHSA
www.drugabusestatistics.samhsa.gov/trends.htm

Article

Prepared by: Mary Maguire, *California State University—Sacramento*
Clifford Garoupa, *Fresno City College*

Diagnosis: Human

TED GUP

Learning Outcomes

After reading this article, you will be able to:

- Understand what attention deficit hyperactivity disorder (ADHD) is.
- Explain the drug Adderall and what it is used for.
- Discuss how ADHD drugs are abused.

The news that 11 percent of school-age children now receive a diagnosis of attention deficit hyperactivity disorder—some 6.4 million—gave me a chill. My son David was one of those who received that diagnosis.

In his case, he was in the first grade. Indeed, there were psychiatrists who prescribed medication for him even before they met him. One psychiatrist said he would not even see him until he was medicated. For a year I refused to fill the prescription at the pharmacy. Finally, I relented. And so David went on Ritalin, then Adderall, and other drugs that were said to be helpful in combating the condition.

In another age, David might have been called "rambunctious." His battery was a little too large for his body. And so he would leap over the couch, spring to reach the ceiling and show an exuberance for life that came in brilliant microbursts.

As a 21-year-old college senior, he was found on the floor of his room, dead from a fatal mix of alcohol and drugs. The date was Oct. 18, 2011.

No one made him take the heroin and alcohol, and yet I cannot help but hold myself and others to account. I had unknowingly colluded with a system that devalues talking therapy and rushes to medicate, inadvertently sending a message that self-medication, too, is perfectly acceptable.

My son was no angel (though he was to us) and he was known to trade in Adderall, to create a submarket in the drug among his classmates who were themselves all too eager to get their hands on it. What he did cannot be excused, but it should be understood. What he did was to create a market that perfectly mirrored the society in which he grew up, a culture where Big Pharma itself prospers from the off-label uses of drugs, often not tested in children and not approved for the many uses to which they are put.

And so a generation of students, raised in an environment that encourages medication, are emulating the professionals by using drugs in the classroom as performance enhancers.

And we wonder why it is that they use drugs with such abandon. As all parents learn—at times to their chagrin—our children go to school not only in the classroom but also at home, and the culture they construct for themselves as teenagers and young adults is but a tiny village imitating that to which they were introduced as children.

The issue of permissive drug use and over-diagnosis goes well beyond hyperactivity. In May, the American Psychiatric Association will publish its D.S.M. 5, the Diagnostic and Statistical Manual of Mental Disorders. It is called the bible of the profession. Its latest iteration, like those before, is not merely a window on the profession but on the culture it serves, both reflecting and shaping societal norms. (For instance, until the 1970s, it categorized homosexuality as a mental illness.)

One of the new, more controversial provisions expands depression to include some forms of grief. On its face it makes sense. The grieving often display all the common indicators of depression—loss of interest in life, loss of appetite, irregular sleep patterns, low functionality, etc. But as others have observed, those same symptoms are the very hallmarks of grief itself.

Ours is an age in which the airwaves and media are one large drug emporium that claims to fix everything from sleep to sex. I fear that being human is itself fast becoming a condition. It's as if we are trying to contain grief, and the absolute pain of a loss like mine. We have become increasingly disassociated and estranged from the patterns of life and death, uncomfortable with the messiness of our own humanity, aging and, ultimately, mortality.

Challenge and hardship have become pathologized and monetized. Instead of enhancing our coping skills, we undermine them and seek shortcuts where there are none, eroding the resilience upon which each of us, at some point in our lives, must rely. Diagnosing grief as a part of depression runs the very real risk of delegitimizing that which is most human—the bonds of our love and attachment to one another. The new entry in the D.S.M. cannot tame grief by giving it a name or a subsection, nor render it less frightening or more manageable.

The D.S.M. would do well to recognize that a broken heart is not a medical condition, and that medication is ill-suited to repair some tears. Time does not heal all wounds, closure is a fiction, and so too is the notion that God never asks of us more than we can bear. Enduring the unbearable is sometimes exactly what life asks of us.

But there is a sweetness even to the intensity of this pain I feel. It is the thing that holds me still to my son. And yes, there is a balm even in the pain. I shall let it go when it is time, without reference to the D.S.M., and without the aid of a pill.

Critical Thinking

1. What percentage of school-age children are on ADHD medications?
2. What is ADHD?
3. What is "off label" use of a drug?

Create Central

www.mhhe.com/createcentral

Internet References

National Institute of Mental Health Attention Deficit Hyperactivity Disorder
www.nimh.nih.gov

Centers for Disease Control
www.cdc.gov/ncbddd/adhd

TED GUP is an author and fellow of the Edmond J. Safra Center for Ethics at Harvard University.

Article

Prepared by: Mary Maguire, *California State University—Sacramento*
Clifford Garoupa, *Fresno City College*

Why I Changed My Mind on Weed

Sanjay Gupta

Learning Outcomes

After reading this article, you will be able to:

- Understand the medical uses of marijuana.

- Describe what government funded research on marijuana results have been.

- Explain how long medical marijuana research has been conducted.

Dr. Sanjay Gupta: I've Tried Marijuana

Over the last year, I have been working on a new documentary called "Weed." The title "Weed" may sound cavalier, but the content is not.

I traveled around the world to interview medical leaders, experts, growers and patients. I spoke candidly to them, asking tough questions. What I found was stunning.

Long before I began this project, I had steadily reviewed the scientific literature on medical marijuana from the United States and thought it was fairly unimpressive. Reading these papers five years ago, it was hard to make a case for medicinal marijuana. I even wrote about this in a *Time* magazine article, back in 2009, titled "Why I would Vote No on Pot."

Well, I am here to apologize.

I apologize because I didn't look hard enough, until now. I didn't look far enough. I didn't review papers from smaller labs in other countries doing some remarkable research, and I was too dismissive of the loud chorus of legitimate patients whose symptoms improved on cannabis.

Instead, I lumped them with the high-visibility malingerers, just looking to get high. I mistakenly believed the Drug Enforcement Agency listed marijuana as a schedule 1 substance because of sound scientific proof. Surely, they must have quality reasoning as to why marijuana is in the category of the most dangerous drugs that have "no accepted medicinal use and a high potential for abuse."

They didn't have the science to support that claim, and I now know that when it comes to marijuana neither of those things are true. It doesn't have a high potential for abuse, and there are very legitimate medical applications. In fact, sometimes marijuana is the only thing that works. Take the case of Charlotte

Figi, who I met in Colorado. She started having seizures soon after birth. By age 3, she was having 300 a week, despite being on seven different medications. Medical marijuana has calmed her brain, limiting her seizures to 2 or 3 per month.

I have seen more patients like Charlotte first hand, spent time with them and come to the realization that it is irresponsible not to provide the best care we can as a medical community, care that could involve marijuana.

We have been terribly and systematically misled for nearly 70 years in the United States, and I apologize for my own role in that.

I hope this article and upcoming documentary will help set the record straight.

On August 14, 1970, the Assistant Secretary of Health, Dr. Roger O. Egeberg wrote a letter recommending the plant, marijuana, be classified as a schedule 1 substance, and it has remained that way for nearly 45 years. My research started with a careful reading of that decades old letter. What I found was unsettling. Egeberg had carefully chosen his words:

"Since there is still a considerable void in our knowledge of the plant and effects of the active drug contained in it, our recommendation is that marijuana be retained within schedule 1 at least until the completion of certain studies now underway to resolve the issue."

Not because of sound science, but because of its absence, marijuana was classified as a schedule 1 substance. Again, the year was 1970. Egeberg mentions studies that are underway, but many were never completed. As my investigation continued, however, I realized Egeberg did in fact have important research already available to him, some of it from more than 25 years earlier.

High Risk of Abuse

In 1944, New York Mayor Fiorello LaGuardia commissioned research to be performed by the New York Academy of Science. Among their conclusions: they found marijuana did not lead to significant addiction in the medical sense of the word. They also did not find any evidence marijuana led to morphine, heroin or cocaine addiction.

We now know that while estimates vary, marijuana leads to dependence in around 9 to 10% of its adult users. By comparison, cocaine, a schedule 2 substance "with less abuse potential than schedule 1 drugs" hooks 20% of those who use it. Around 25% of heroin users become addicted.

The worst is tobacco, where the number is closer to 30% of smokers, many of whom go on to die because of their addiction.

There is clear evidence that in some people marijuana use can lead to withdrawal symptoms, including insomnia, anxiety and nausea. Even considering this, it is hard to make a case that it has a high potential for abuse. The physical symptoms of marijuana addiction are nothing like those of the other drugs I've mentioned. I have seen the withdrawal from alcohol, and it can be life threatening.

I do want to mention a concern that I think about as a father. Young, developing brains are likely more susceptible to harm from marijuana than adult brains. Some recent studies suggest that regular use in teenage years leads to a permanent decrease in IQ. Other research hints at a possible heightened risk of developing psychosis.

Much in the same way I wouldn't let my own children drink alcohol, I wouldn't permit marijuana until they are adults. If they are adamant about trying marijuana, I will urge them to wait until they're in their mid-20s when their brains are fully developed.

Medical Benefit

While investigating, I realized something else quite important. Medical marijuana is not new, and the medical community has been writing about it for a long time. There were in fact hundreds of journal articles, mostly documenting the benefits. Most of those papers, however, were written between the years 1840 and 1930. The papers described the use of medical marijuana to treat "neuralgia, convulsive disorders, emaciation," among other things.

A search through the U.S. National Library of Medicine this past year pulled up nearly 20,000 more recent papers. But the majority were research into the harm of marijuana, such as "Bad trip due to anticholinergic effect of cannabis," or "Cannabis induced pancreatitis" and "Marijuana use and risk of lung cancer."

In my quick running of the numbers, I calculated about 6% of the current U.S. marijuana studies investigate the benefits of medical marijuana. The rest are designed to investigate harm. That imbalance paints a highly distorted picture.

The Challenges of Marijuana Research

To do studies on marijuana in the United States today, you need two important things.

First of all, you need marijuana. And marijuana is illegal. You see the problem. Scientists can get research marijuana from a special farm in Mississippi, which is astonishingly located in the middle of the Ole Miss campus, but it is challenging. When I visited this year, there was no marijuana being grown.

The second thing you need is approval, and the scientists I interviewed kept reminding me how tedious that can be. While a cancer study may first be evaluated by the National Cancer Institute, or a pain study may go through the National Institute for Neurological Disorders, there is one more approval required for marijuana: NIDA, the National Institute on Drug Abuse. It is an organization that has a core mission of studying drug abuse, as opposed to benefit.

Stuck in the middle are the legitimate patients who depend on marijuana as a medicine, oftentimes as their only good option.

Keep in mind that up until 1943, marijuana was part of the United States drug pharmacopeia. One of the conditions for which it was prescribed was neuropathic pain. It is a miserable pain that's tough to treat. My own patients have described it as "lancinating, burning and a barrage of pins and needles." While marijuana has long been documented to be effective for this awful pain, the most common medications prescribed today come from the poppy plant, including morphine, oxycodone and dilaudid.

Here is the problem. Most of these medications don't work very well for this kind of pain, and tolerance is a real problem.

Most frightening to me is that someone dies in the United States every 19 minutes from a prescription drug overdose, mostly accidental. Every 19 minutes. It is a horrifying statistic. As much as I searched, I could not find a documented case of death from marijuana overdose.

It is perhaps no surprise then that 76% of physicians recently surveyed said they would approve the use of marijuana to help ease a woman's pain from breast cancer.

When marijuana became a schedule 1 substance, there was a request to fill a "void in our knowledge." In the United States, that has been challenging because of the infrastructure surrounding the study of an illegal substance, with a drug abuse organization at the heart of the approval process. And yet, despite the hurdles, we have made considerable progress that continues today.

Looking forward, I am especially intrigued by studies like those in Spain and Israel looking at the anti-cancer effects of marijuana and its components. I'm intrigued by the neuroprotective study by Lev Meschoulam in Israel, and research in Israel and the United States on whether the drug might help alleviate symptoms of PTSD. I promise to do my part to help, genuinely and honestly, fill the remaining void in our knowledge.

Citizens in 20 states and the District of Columbia have now voted to approve marijuana for medical applications, and more states will be making that choice soon. As for Dr. Roger Egeberg, who wrote that letter in 1970, he passed away 16 years ago.

I wonder what he would think if he were alive today.

Critical Thinking

1. Does marijuana have a high clinical potential for abuse?
2. What diseases and disorders is marijuana effective in treating?
3. What did the LaGuardia commission conclude about the medical use of marijuana?

Create Central

www.mhhe.com/createcentral

Internet References

Cable News Network
    www.cnn.com
Medical Use—norml.org
    www.norml.org

Unit 5

UNIT

Prepared by: Mary Maguire, *California State University—Sacramento*
Clifford Garoupa, *Fresno City College*

Measuring the Social Costs of Drugs

The most devastating effect of drug abuse in America is the magnitude with which it affects the way we live. Much of its influence is not measurable. What is the cost of a son or daughter lost, a parent imprisoned, a life lived in a constant state of fear? The emotional costs alone are incomprehensible. The social legacy of this country's drug crisis could easily be the subject of this entire book. The purpose here, however, can only be a cursory portrayal of drugs' tremendous costs. More than one U.S. president has stated that drug use threatens our national security and personal well-being. The financial costs of maintaining the federal apparatus devoted to drug interdiction, enforcement, and treatment are staggering. Although yearly expenditures vary due to changes in political influence, strategy, and tactics, examples of the tremendous effects of drugs on government and the economy abound. The federal budget for drug control exceeds $14 billion and includes almost $1.5 billion dedicated to drug fighting in Mexico and Central America under the Merida Initiative. Mexican criminal syndicates and paramilitaries who control trafficking across the U.S. southern border threaten the virtual sovereignty of the Mexican government. Many argue that the situation in Mexico is as dangerous to the United States as the current situation in Afghanistan.

Since 9/11, the restructuring of federal, state, and local law enforcement apparatus in response to terrorism has significantly influenced the nature and extent of drug trafficking in the United States. Huge transnational investigative, intelligence, and enforcement coalitions have formed between the United States and its allies in the war against terrorism. One significant impact of these coalitions has been a tightening of border access and a decreased availability of international trafficking routes. Although drugs are believed to still pour in from Mexico, drug shortages, increased street prices, and a decrease in purity are occurring. Powder heroin is not widely available in the West, and many major U.S. cities are reporting major street declines in the availability of cocaine.

Still, drugs exist, in association with terrorism, as the business of the criminal justice system. Approximately 80 percent of the people behind bars in the country had a problem with drugs or alcohol prior to their incarceration—more of its citizens than almost any other comparable society, and the financial costs are staggering. Doing drugs and serving time produces an inescapable nexus, and it doesn't end with prison. Almost 29 percent of persons on supervised parole or probation abuse drugs. Some argue that these numbers represent the fact that Americans have come to rely on the criminal justice system in an unprecedented way to solve problems of drug abuse. Regardless of the way one chooses to view various relationships, the resulting picture is numbing.

In addition to the highly visible criminal justice-related costs, numerous other institutions are affected. Housing, welfare, education, and health care provide excellent examples of critical institutions struggling to overcome the strain of drug-related impacts. In addition, annual loss of productivity in the workplace exceeds well over a $160 billion per year. Alcoholism alone causes 500 million lost workdays each year. Add to this demographic shifts caused by people fleeing drug-impacted neighborhoods, schools, and businesses, and one soon realizes that there is no victimless public or private institution. Last year, almost 4 million Americans received some kind of treatment related to the abuse of alcohol or other drugs. Almost 23 million Americans need treatment for an illicit drug or alcohol problem. Fetal Alcohol Syndrome is the leading cause of mental retardation in the United States, and still, survey data continue to report that over 11 percent of pregnant women drink alcohol. Add to this injured, drug-related accident and crime victims, along with demands produced by a growing population of intravenous drug users infected with AIDS, and a frighteningly-overwhelmed health-care system comes to the fore. Health-care costs from drug-related ills are staggering. Drug abuse continues to cost the economy more than $13 billion annually in health-care costs alone. Approximately 71 million Americans over 12 are current users of a tobacco product.

It should be emphasized that the social costs exacted by drug use infiltrate every aspect of public and private life. The implications for thousands of families struggling with the adverse effects of drug-related woes may prove the greatest and most tragic of social costs. Children who lack emotional support, self-esteem, role models, a safe and secure environment, economic opportunity, and an education because of a parent on drugs suggest costs that are difficult to comprehend or measure. In some jurisdictions in California and Oregon, as many as 50 percent of child welfare placements are precipitated by methamphetamine abuse.

When reading this unit of this book, consider the diversity of costs associated with the abuse of both legal and illegal drugs. As you read the following articles, consider the historical progressions of social costs produced by drug abuse over the past century. How are the problems of the past replicating themselves and how have science, medicine, and social policy changed in an attempt to mitigate these impacts? Ample evidence informs us that there is no single approach to mitigate the diverse nature of drug-related social impacts. Further, some of the most astounding scientific discoveries about how addiction develops remain mysterious when compared to the reality of the lives of millions who find drugs an end in themselves. Some have argued that the roots of drug-related problems today seem even more elusive, complicated, and desperate. Good progress has been made in treating drug addiction, but only moderate progress has been made in preventing it in the first place. What are the disproportionate ways in which some populations of Americans are harmed by drugs? Are there epidemics within epidemics? How is drug abuse expressed within different populations of Americans? How do the implications for Native American families and culture differ from those for other racial and ethnic groups? What are the reasons for these disparities and how should they be addressed?

Prepared by: Mary Maguire, *California State University—Sacramento*
Clifford Garoupa, *Fresno City College*

Article

Drugs 'R' Us

Drugs are a part of our lives in ways we can't come to grips with.

STANTON PEELE

Learning Outcomes

After reading this article, you will be able to:

• Understand how widespread the use of psychoactive drugs is.

• Discuss any ineffectiveness of our drug control policies.

• Discuss why people use drugs to alter their consciousness.

W hat do these *New York Times* headlines appearing in the last month have in common?

June 10: Candidates in Mexico Signal a New Tack in the Drug War

Candidates for the Mexican presidency indicate they are no longer willing to suffer the domestic losses required to staunch the flow of drugs into the United States.

June 9: Risky Rise of the Good-Grade Pill

Use of A.D.H.D. stimulants like Adderall by high school and college students is an accepted method for enhancing school performance. The alternate *Times* title for this article: Seeking Academic Edge, Teenagers Abuse Stimulants.

June 9: Parents Created This Problem, and Must Address It

Parental pressures on children have generated the "widespread abuse of stimulants like Ritalin and Adderall by teenagers and college students."

June 8: Global Soccer: Unrelenting Pressure to Mask the Pain

Use of painkillers is commonplace among World Cup soccer players.

June 8: Prescription Drug Overdoses Plague New Mexico

"For years now, New Mexico has wrestled with high rates of poverty, drunken-driving deaths and substance abuse— particularly heroin addiction, which has been passed down through generations in the state's northern, rural reaches. But over the past few years, a new affliction has hammered New Mexico: prescription drug overdoses."

June 4: In Hockey Enforcer's Descent, a Flood of Prescription Drugs

"In his final three seasons playing in the National Hockey League, before dying last year at 28 of an accidental overdose of narcotic painkillers and alcohol, Derek Boogaard received more than 100 prescriptions for thousands of pills from more than a dozen team doctors."

May 11: Diagnosing the D.S.M.

The American Psychiatric Association's new diagnostic manual (D.S.M.-5) is "proceeding with other suggestions that could potentially expand the boundaries of psychiatry to define as mentally ill tens of millions of people now considered normal."

May 11: Addiction Diagnoses May Rise Under Guideline Changes

The D.S.M.'s expansion of the definition of addiction indicates that more people will be treated for it. " 'The ties between the D.S.M. panel members and the pharmaceutical industry are so extensive that there is the real risk of corrupting the public health mission of the manual,' said Dr. Lisa Cosgrove, a fellow at the Edmond J. Safra Center for Ethics at Harvard, who published a study in March that said two-thirds of the manual's advisory task force members reported ties to the pharmaceutical industry or other financial conflicts of interest."

Five things are going on here:

1. Privileged students and their parents seek every advantage they can to get ahead in life, including use of stimulant prescription drugs thought to enhance academic performance.

2. America's endless taste for illicit substances has overwhelmed the resources of Mexico and other Latin American countries, despite—or because of—all of our pressure on these countries to stem the flow of drugs into the U.S.

3. Athletes rely on drugs to deal with the everpresent pain that can sideline them and their careers, often leading to permanent injuries and drug dependence.

4. In poorer, rural regions, and not only these, prescription medications have replaced illicit substances as the primary source of drug abuse.

5. The medicalization and pharmaceuticalization of mental, emotional, and addiction problems is expanding, perhaps beyond our ability to grasp.

American life is suffused with drugs—there is no escaping them. Remember when Congress held hearings on steroid use by major-league baseball players, and the players fell into two groups—those who admitted their use of steroids and those who lied and denied it? Such drug use by baseball players (and football players, cyclists, boxers, track athletes, et al.), like students' use of amphetamines, is for the purpose of performance enhancement. At the same time, the model of humans as fundamentally flawed and requiring constant administration of drugs to remedy their deficits is so integral to our thinking that we can't begin to question it. And, of course, the recreational use of drugs continues apace.

We can bemoan this new reality, but we can't reverse it. We need a new strategy to deal with the ubiquity of drugs in our lives. If people can't manage such experiences, it is hard to see how they can cope in the 21st century. Nor will our society be able to function without a reconceptualization of drug use.

Critical Thinking

1. What drugs are high school and college students using to enhance their academic performance?

2. How prevalent is prescription drug abuse in professional hockey?

3. The American Psychiatric Association is expected to expand diagnostic criteria for addictive disorders in 2013. What effect, if any do you think this will have?

Create Central

www.mhhe.com/createcentral

Internet References

Drug Policy Alliance
  www.drugpolicy.org
The November Coalition
  www.november.org

Article

Prepared by: Mary Maguire, *California State University—Sacramento*
Clifford Garoupa, *Fresno City College*

OxyContin Abuse Spreads from Appalachia across United States

BILL ESTEP, DORI HJALMARSON, AND HALIMAH ABDULLAH

Learning Outcomes

After reading this article, you will be able to:

- Explain what OxyContin is.
- Understand OxyContin abuse and dependence.
- Explain how current patterns of OxyContin abuse and dependence got started.

Shawn Clusky has seen every side of Kentucky's battle with pain pill addiction over the past 10 years.

Clusky first tried OxyContin at age 17 with his school buddies, shortly after the high-powered narcotic painkiller went on the market. He was an occasional user and seller until about age 21, when he became fully addicted.

When he was 25, he got arrested at a Lexington gas station for selling $15,000 worth of pills. Clusky received probation, but was still using until he was sent to the WestCare rehabilitation center in eastern Kentucky.

He now works there as a counselor.

"A lot of times people believe a drug addict comes from poverty," he said. Not true. "Nine out of 10 of the guys I partied with came from millionaire families; their parents didn't use, they had good families."

Ten years ago, Kentucky learned it had a major drug problem.

OxyContin, a powerful prescription painkiller, was being abused at alarming rates in the Appalachian areas of eastern and southern Kentucky. A decade later, the level of pain pill abuse throughout the state and across the country is at epic levels, officials say.

Despite some successes—including several high-profile drug arrests across the country, increased treatment programs and the adoption of prescription drug monitoring programs in 43 states—the problem is now so entrenched that the cheap flights and van rentals drug traffickers use to travel from Florida to Kentucky and other states to peddle "hillbilly heroin" are nicknamed the "OxyContin Express."

The sheer scope of the problem is a key reason.

Kentucky often ranks at or near the top in U.S. measures of the level of prescription pain pill abuse.

According to a study by the Substance Abuse and Mental Health Services Administration, there was a fourfold increase nationally in treatment admissions for prescription pain pill abuse during the past decade. The increase spans every age, gender, race, ethnicity, education, employment level and region.

The study also shows a tripling of pain pill abuse among patients who needed treatment for dependence on opioids—prescription narcotics.

The rate of overdose-related deaths more than doubled among men and tripled among women in Kentucky from 2000 to 2009, according the state Cabinet for Health and Family Services.

Nearly every family in eastern Kentucky has been touched by prescription-drug addiction and death.

In the late 1990s, it was easier to find OxyContin—pure oxycodone with a time release—in Kentucky. The pill's maker, Purdue Pharma, was selling it "hand over fist" to doctors in eastern Kentucky, rich with coal mine injuries and government health care cards, Clusky said.

Clusky said a high school friend who worked at a pharmacy would steal the pills for his friends, so "It didn't cost any of us anything."

When many of the eastern Kentucky pill sources dried up after law enforcement raids in 2001, Clusky said, the trade moved to Mexico, where oxycodone could be bought for pennies over the counter and sold for as much as $100 a pill in the rural U.S. Clusky began making trips to Nuevo Laredo, driving back home with thousands of pills. By this time, heroin was his drug of choice. He often traveled to larger cities, where heroin could be found more cheaply.

"Five hundred dollars worth of heroin would last me a week. Five hundred dollars worth of oxy would last me one day," Clusky said.

Clusky lived part time in Ohio, sometimes making three doctor-shopping trips a day from Lexington to Dayton. He did a few stints in rehab, at one point trying methadone and Suboxone to treat his opiate addiction. It didn't work.

"I was as useless to society on methadone as I was on heroin," he said.

Nationally, prescription drug abuse has become a front-burner issue. There are more recovery options available now than a decade ago, but many states still don't have enough treatment available for all who need it.

Though Kentucky was no stranger to the abuse of prescription drugs long before federal regulators approved OxyContin in 1996, so many people in rural areas, including Appalachia, started abusing OxyContin in the late 1990s, it earned the nickname "hillbilly heroin."

Many chronic pain sufferers said the drug helped them immensely.

But abusers figured out they could crush a pill and snort or inject it, destroying the time-release function to get a whopping 12 hours' worth of the drug in one rush.

OxyContin quickly became the drug of choice in eastern Kentucky.

"You could leave a bag of cocaine on the street and no one would touch it, but leave one OxyContin in the back of an armored car and they'll blow it up to get at it," U.S. Attorney Joseph Famularo said at the February 2001 news conference announcing the first major roundup involving the drug.

By 2002, a quarter of the overdose deaths in the nation linked to OxyContin were in eastern Kentucky, authorities said.

Police, regulators and elected officials charged that Purdue Pharma, the Connecticut-based maker of OxyContin, marketed the drug too aggressively, feeding an oversupply and diversion onto the illicit market.

Purdue Pharma denied that, but the company and three top officials ultimately pleaded guilty in 2007 to misleading the public about the drug's risk of addiction and paid $634.5 million in fines.

Authorities had begun pushing back long before that against growing abuse of OxyContin and other prescription drugs, but addicts and traffickers kept finding ways to get pills.

"Law enforcement adjusts, and the criminals adjust," said Frank Rapier, the head of the Appalachia High Intensity Drug Trafficking Area, which includes 68 counties in Kentucky, Tennessee and West Virginia.

Kentucky Rep. Hal Rogers' voice grows tight with frustration whenever he talks about the prescription drug epidemic that's gripped Appalachia for more than a decade.

"Crook doctors operating these pill mills" in Florida are running rampant and are fueling the flow of illegally obtained prescription drugs to states such as Kentucky, Rogers, the chairman of the House Appropriations Committee, told Attorney General Eric Holder during a recent hearing. "My people are dying."

The White House "has got to act," Rogers said. "We've got more people dying of prescription drug overdoses than car accidents."

The Obama administration counters that it's the first to publicly call the prescription drug abuse problem an epidemic, has stepped up drug arrests and has directed millions in funding to state monitoring programs. The administration says it also has focused efforts on the Appalachia High Intensity Drug Trafficking Area.

In the meantime, Rogers hopes legislation he's co-sponsoring with Rep. Vern Buchanan, a Florida Republican, calling for a tougher federal crackdown on so-called "pill mills"—pain clinics that dispense prescription drugs—will help stem the flow of drugs across state lines.

The measure includes provisions to support state-based prescription drug monitoring programs; to use the money from seized illicit operations for drug treatment; to strengthen prescription standards for certain addictive pain drugs; and to toughen prison terms and fines for pill mill operators.

The bill comes on the heels of Florida Republican Gov. Rick Scott's calls to repeal a monitoring program modeled after Kentucky's and designed to stem interstate prescription drug trafficking—a move lawmakers from Florida and Kentucky and White House officials oppose.

Scott has cited concerns about costs and patient privacy rights. He's turned down a $1 million donation by Purdue Pharma to help pay for a prescription database.

(Estep and Hjalmarson, of the Lexington Herald-Leader, reported from Lexington. Abdullah reported from Washington.)

Critical Thinking

1. What kind of drug is OxyContin? Why is it prescribed?
2. Nationally, how much did OxyContin use increase between 2000–2009?
3. What state ranks at or near the top for prescription painkiller abuse?

Create Central

www.mhhe.com/createcentral

Internet References

National Drug Control Policy
www.ncjrs.org
Trac DEA Site
http://trac.syr.edu/tracdea

Article

Prepared by: Mary Maguire, *California State University—Sacramento*
Clifford Garoupa, *Fresno City College*

Cannabis: Colorado's Budding Industry

Dispensaries selling cannabis bath salts, 'bud-tenders' advising on blends, even a marijuana university. As Colorado gears up for legalisation, we get the dope on Denver's 'green rush.'

Jenny Kleeman

Learning Outcomes

After reading this article, you will be able to:

- Understand how marijuana laws have changed in the state of Colorado.

- Identify what those changes actually are.

- Understand how these changes conflict with federal marijuana laws.

I'm being driven around Denver by America's first professional stoner. William Breathes is the marijuana critic for the award-winning local paper *Westword*. Every week for the past three years, his boss has been paying for his weed.

"I don't really drink wine, so if this reference is a bit off, please forgive me, but if you really like merlots, you know what a merlot should taste like," he says, drumming the steering wheel for emphasis. "A lot of marijuana strains are like that. If I'm offered Sour Diesel, and it doesn't look or smell like it should, I know it."

This morning, like every morning, Breathes woke up and got stoned. Now he's driving me through a snowstorm.

Getting stoned in Denver is as unexceptional as getting a cup of coffee or a beer. In some ways, it's easier: there are more marijuana dispensaries in Denver than liquor stores or branches of Starbucks. In the shadow of the Rocky Mountains, Denver has become America's highest city.

Marijuana has been legal for medical use in Colorado since 2000 and, last November, Colorado and Washington became the first U.S. states to legalise recreational use. Coloradans are allowed to have six cannabis plants at home and an ounce in their pocket. In January next year, the first specially regulated retail stores will open to sell marijuana to anyone aged over 21.

Denver was founded as a mining town during the 19th-century gold rush, and the reversal of state marijuana laws has sparked what people here call a green rush. Everyone wants a slice of the pie, selling plants and resin, marijuana-laced gourmet food, pipes, growing equipment, cultivation courses, balms, you name it. Businesses are opening every week. No longer the drug of choice for the drop-out or the slacker, weed is where the consultants, critics and entrepreneurs are focusing their energies.

Breathes is giving me a tour of South Broadway, known locally as Broadsterdam, because of the profusion of marijuana dispensaries. The area used to be full of empty properties until the industry breathed new life into it. Every two or three doors there's another green neon sign.

"Evergreen Apothecary—that's a pretty clean shop," Breathes says. "They feel really corporate. The Wellspring Collective—they're good, they've dropped their prices down to compete with other shops, like Ganja Gourmet, right here. There's The Kind Room—not that great, a small mom-and-pop shop. The Herbal Center right here, not too great, but the shop right behind it, I can't remember its name, was good. Walking Raven, that's the first place I ever reviewed." He catches his breath and smiles. "You can see how saturated this market is."

The 500 licensed dispensaries in Colorado generated $186m in sales last year, and $5.4m in sales tax. At present, they can sell only to the 110,000 card-carrying medical marijuana users referred by their doctors for symptoms such as chronic weight loss, pain and nausea, but they will be first in line to get retail licences to sell to recreational users once the new law comes into effect in 2014. Within the next five years, the governor's office expects the industry to grow to as much as five times its current size. The state will be able collect tax of up to 15%, with the first $40m already earmarked to build public schools across Colorado.

Amendment 64, which legalises marijuana for recreational use in Colorado, has been a massive headache for the state's government, and governor John Hickenlooper had been vocally against legalisation. It came about through a "citizens' initiative": if enough people sign a petition asking for a constitutional amendment in Colorado, it can be put to the vote. The Amendment 64 ballot took place on the same day as last year's presidential election, and more Coloradans voted for marijuana than for Obama. It passed with 53% of the vote, catching the state off guard.

The rest of the U.S. is watching Colorado carefully. Twenty-five million Americans consume 14,000 tonnes of pot annually, and economist Stephen Easton estimates legal marijuana could be a $45bn–$100bn industry nationwide. Inmates incarcerated on marijuana-related charges cost U.S. prisons $1bn every year. And, according to a paper endorsed by 300 economists, the U.S. government would save an estimated $13.7bn on prohibition-enforcement costs and tax revenue by legalising marijuana.

But marijuana remains federally illegal, and no one is sure what the U.S. attorney general is going to do about Amendment 64. In theory, the federal government could sue Colorado. Hickenlooper has appealed to the White House for guidance, but hasn't yet heard back.

Breathes's desk at *Westword* HQ is a classic American office cubicle, sober and businesslike, even though the shelves around his computer are filled with cigarette papers and joint holders. A former local reporter with a journalism degree, Breathes, 32, beat 350 candidates to bag his job in 2009. Wearing socks festooned with blue marijuana leaves, he's as evangelical as the next pothead, but with articulacy, ethics and punctuation to impress any of his journalist peers.

"You have to take it seriously," he says. "When I'm testing, I'll do my strains separately, and I'll smoke them on different days to get the feel for them. I've got a recorder, and I talk to myself"—he puts on a voice like a wine aficionado—' "Hmm, very rubbery. A little tart—there's some strawberry in there.' I'll talk about how it popped and sizzled, taking notes between taking hits. And I try not to write my reviews when I'm really, really stoned." Does he meet his deadlines? He smiles, sheepishly. "Not all the time."

He may be Denver's most famous pothead, but William Breathes isn't his real name. As a registered medical marijuana patient—for a chronic stomach condition—he has to show ID every time he goes into a dispensary, and fears he'd get special treatment if the "budtenders" knew they were serving the influential critic. "I know what would happen in an industry like this, where everyone is trying to get a leg up."

In a market this competitive, it takes a lot for a dispensary to stand out. "If the cannabis is good, none of the decor matters. But ambience means a lot to me. I don't know who's reading my reviews. For younger people, it's cool to go into a dispensary with Bob Marley playing and young budtenders, whereas if my grandmother was sick and I was telling her to go to a dispensary, she probably wouldn't like the same one I go to."

Breathes's grandmother would probably like Denver Relief. With its fat leather sofas, potted palms and water cooler, the reception could be a dentist's waiting room were it not for the waft of cannabis that hits you as soon as you walk through the door. (This comes from the plants alone, not from marijuana smoke—lighting up in a dispensary is illegal.) I hand over my driving licence to a receptionist behind bulletproof glass and browse through volumes of an expensive-looking coffee-table book called The Cannabible: glossy photographs of different marijuana strains, richly shot and glistening under studio lights, with names such as Early Queen and Blue Stupor.

The dispensary's owners, Ean Seeb, 37, and Kayvan Khalatbari, 29, are two smokers not apparently devoid of ambition. As well as owning the Denver Relief dispensary and employing 12 full-time staff, they're CEOs of Denver Relief Consulting, advising 70 clients around the country on how to operate within the marijuana industry. They're also founder members of the National Cannabis Industry Association, a political lobby group fighting for the industry in Washington. No one knows for sure what Denver Relief is worth—there's no reliable industry data—but Seeb and Khalatbari say $5m–$10m is a conservative estimate. They pay $100,000 annually in sales tax, "enough to cover at least one city council member's entire budget for the year", Seeb says with a smile.

Seeb and Khalatbari are wearing matching black caps and polo shirts, branded with the sober green cross that is Denver Relief Consulting's logo. They hand me their business cards and take me through a locked door into the dispensary.

"We would consider ourselves businessmen, without a doubt," says Khalatbari, a former engineer who also owns a chain of pizzerias. "Our first interest is to change the perception of the industry. We want it to evolve into something a little better."

The "medicine room" looks like a cross between a whole-food store and a bank. The counter is split into individual stalls, separated by wooden barriers. "It allows us to have one-on-one, discreet communication between the patient and the budtender," Seeb explains. Behind is a wall of exposed brick, with shelves filled with huge jars of marijuana, priced from $10 to $335 a gram—not the cheapest in town, but less expensive than street prices where marijuana is illegal. Can't Buy Me Love plays gently from a large speaker in the corner.

"We have a more professional clientele than other places, because we offer higher quality and more discretion," Khalatbari says. "It's fair to make comparisons with beer—there are craft beers people are willing to spend more money on because they're higher quality."

The shelves in the middle of the room look like a sweet shop. The cannabis-infused products include lollipops, gummy sweets, cookies, brownies, cartons of grape, mango and cherry juice, and chocolate bars in foil packets with exotic flavours such as banana and walnut. They range in size, potency and price. There's a tiny bar, the size of a minute square of chocolate, that's seriously strong and costs $23. For the older customer—sorry, patient—with a less sweet tooth, there are sprays, topical salves and even bath salts.

The corporate meeting room two floors above the dispensary is bare except for a few branded Denver Relief pens on the table and a banner reading "Denver Relief Consulting—Pioneers of the Industry". Seeb and Khalatbari advise many of their product manufacturers, writing marketing reports on their branding, package design and product quality. They also help other dispensaries to get a licence to operate and find reliable staff.

The industry needs consultants, the pair say, because navigating it is a nightmare. Seeb slams a copy of their licence application on the table—it's well over an inch thick. "They took photos of all of my tattoos and scars," Khalatbari says. Licensing costs $12,000 at state level and $5,000 for the city of Denver, renewable every two years. The number of dispensaries in Denver has actually fallen since 2010, when tougher regulation came in.

Most challenging of all, you aren't allowed to get a bank loan, accept credit cards or even have a bank account. American banks are subject to federal law, and they fear losing their insurance if they allow a federally illegal business as a customer. That means the Colorado cannabis industry is purely cash-based: staff are paid in cash, customers pay in cash and businesses pay their taxes in cash in person at the department of revenue.

Colorado repealed alcohol prohibition in 1932, a year before it was repealed nationwide. Seeb and Khalatbari believe the state is now blazing a trail for the rest of the country. Denver's most senior official, on the other hand, doesn't want his city to be America's guinea pig. "We're not proud of it," says mayor Michael Hancock, sternly. "It creates some real challenges for Denver. You've got a lot of businesspeople walking around here with a lot of cash in their pockets or in their facilities, which makes them a target. There are some environmental impacts that we have to be considerate of. It's a very pungent operation—it stinks. And we can't measure what it means to be high. Right now, I can tell you when you're drunk, but I can't tell if you're high. We don't have the standard set within law enforcement to say you are illegally operating a vehicle."

While lawmakers debate how much THC (the psychoactive component in marijuana) a person can have in their blood before they're a danger on the road, Colorado's policemen have to rely on field sobriety tests.

Legalisation also worries officials in neighbouring states. Colorado is expecting a tourism boom as soon as the recreational shops open, and while the amount non-residents can buy in each transaction will be limited, there's nothing to stop tourists going to 100 dispensaries and buying 100 small amounts. No one patrols the state borders. Many in the Mormon state of Utah next door are horrified.

It's certainly true that marijuana stinks. The Denver Relief growing facility is in a vast, grey unmarked warehouse, but I can smell it from across the street. The snow is blowing horizontally on the industrial estate, but once I'm inside the door, there's tropical heat, bright blueish lights, and Smells Like Teen Spirit is playing on the radio.

"Come on in," head grower Nick Hice says. He takes me into the vegetation room, one of three 1,000 sq ft spaces filled with cannabis. There are 1,000 plants in this room alone, and every one is tagged and labelled. "All the 'moms' are here," he says. "We take cuttings off these big gals; they get potted up and repotted as they grow." There are 35 strains in the warehouse, some fat and spiky, others thin and spindly. They look beautiful and exotic, but the immaculately clean room, with its white walls and giant whirring fans, has the atmosphere of a hospital or a laboratory.

Cannabis is notoriously difficult to cultivate, and an operation this intensive requires serious investment. In every room, 10,300 watts-worth of lights shine 24 hours a day, generating a $5,000-a-month electricity bill. The warehouse gets through 14,000 litres of water a week. A grow technician is surveying every leaf with a magnifying glass, looking for mites. "There are bugs that love cannabis," Hice says. "If we had a catastrophic crop loss in this one room, it would cost us anywhere from $200,000 to $300,000." Even so, the Denver Relief grow site is only moderately sized by Colorado standards. Across the state, 45 tonnes of marijuana was cultivated last year.

Knowing how to grow cannabis is a lucrative business, as the brains behind THC University are finding out. Matt Jones, 25, and Freeman LaFleur, 26, run what they call "the nation's premier cannabis training destination", teaching keen amateurs and budding businessmen how to make the most of the six plants they're allowed to grow at home. They've been entrepreneurs since they were teenagers. The night Amendment 64 passed, they started talking about how they could get into the marijuana industry.

We meet at the Karmaceuticals dispensary, where Jones, LaFleur and head instructor Ted Smith are having promotional shots taken for their website. Around 50 people have so far signed up to take one of their 14 classes, which range from the best-selling Growing Marijuana 101 to Hash and Oils, Pests and Disease, Cooking and Infusion, and Marijuana Law and Business. "We're teaching total plant husbandry," Smith says.

This expertise doesn't come cheap. The classes cost $100 each online, or $200 in their rented university classroom on Auraria campus. Students get accreditation for attending a certain number of classes: "budtenders" have been to five, "certified indoor growers" 10, and "masters" to all 14. Doing the full course costs close to $1,500. But Jones and LaFleur say it's worth it—they're going to create an industry-standard qualification, and are applying to be a state-certified occupational school.

It's not the first marijuana business idea Jones has come up with. In 2010 he set up CannaCoups, a kind of Groupon for medical marijuana discounts. "It was really before its time. Now Toke Daily Deals are doing it. It's really popular," he shakes his head.

THC University, too, appears to be ahead of the curve. "The green rush isn't at full steam yet, but it's building," LaFleur says. "In five years it's going to be a very different landscape." Jones is more emphatic: "In five years, we'll see federal decriminalisation, at least."

The rise of the marijuana industry in Denver certainly appears unstoppable. Too many people want a piece of the action, and there are too many customers willing to part with their money for it.

Breathes has been smoking cannabis for more than half his life, but he has no nostalgia for the old days, no regrets about the industry becoming commercialised. "People are fighting for customers," he says. "From a consumer standpoint, it's great.

I have no problems with the commercialisation of it, because that equates with normalisation in America. In Colorado, it's really very normal."

Critical Thinking

1. How have marijuana laws changed in the state of Colorado?
2. How do these state laws conflict with federal drug laws?
3. How did the changes in marijuana laws in Colorado come about?

Create Central

www.mhhe.com/createcentral

Internet References

Laws and regulations—Colorado.gov
www.colorado.gov

The Denver Post
www.denverpost.com/marijuana

Article

Prepared by: Mary Maguire, *California State University—Sacramento*
Clifford Garoupa, *Fresno City College*

When Booze Comes Off the Battlefield

Editors' note: This post follows one on Thursday that discussed alcohol use and regulation in combat zones. Alcohol clearly looms large in the minds of some service members in the wake of the killing of Afghan civilians in the Panjwai district of Kandahar Province and accusations that the man accused in the shootings, Staff Sgt. Robert Bales had been drinking.

STEVE GRIFFIN

Learning Outcomes

After reading this article, you will be able to:

- Understand alcohol use and its impact upon the military.

- Describe how the military deals with alcohol use.

- Discuss the problems that result from alcohol use in the military.

It is Sunday, Day 2 of Reintegration—the Army's program to socialize soldiers back into society after a year's worth of combat. I am sitting in a large auditorium listening to some civilian—who is probably not a veteran, or at least not a combat veteran—drone on about substance abuse and how bad it is. It is not the first time I have heard this speech. To my right, a buck sergeant sitting two seats down from me, is passed out in his chair, drooling all over himself. I stand up and walk outside to check on one of my soldiers who is on all fours vomiting in the grass six feet from the front door. I take it that he has decided to be nice and not mess up the toilets for everyone else.

Fast-forward two months. All the canned briefings are over, our 30-day post-deployment leave has passed, and some sort of normalcy has returned to garrison life in the Army. It is a Saturday night, and I am sitting down to a nice dinner with my wife at a local restaurant. As I take my seat, my battalion sergeant major sees me from across the room and runs over to tell me the big news. He asks me if I heard what happened to one of my staff officers, a captain, the night before. I cringe in anticipation as I see the letters slowly roll off his tongue, "D . . . U . . . I."

What is the obvious common denominator here? Alcohol. The powerful, dangerous, yet legal substance, obtainable in so many ways, that contributes to some of the worst disciplinary problems for units returning from combat. Drunken driving, battery, domestic violence, sexual assault, and suicide are just some of the more common alcohol-induced episodes that are seen on almost a weekly basis. Yet, so many soldiers, sailors, airmen, and Marines continue to partake at levels far beyond what is considered normal.

In full disclosure, yes, I drink, and I drank while I was a soldier. The military has a long history of alcohol use, dating back long before my time. Some might say it is part of the tradition, part of the culture, or just part of being a soldier. Serving in our military is a hard way of life, and this perpetual hardship contributes to a "work hard, party hard" mentality that resonates throughout the force at all ranks and echelons.

But contrary to some opinions, drinking is not all bad. The fact remains that alcohol acts as sort of a "social lubricant," helping hard-working soldiers decompress after a long week of training. Make no mistake, free booze is a surefire way to get everyone in a unit together after hours. It breaks down the barriers of rank and formality, enabling those who would not otherwise converse during the duty day to have what civilians call a "normal" conversation. The crux is that these alcohol-induced social functions facilitate the building of a team, and teamwork is the linchpin of an effective fighting force. After-hours bacchanalian romps accomplish something that hard training alone cannot achieve—the building of camaraderie.

As a young platoon leader, I remember seeing Facebook photos of my soldiers having these parties in their barrack's rooms on Friday and Saturday nights. Crushed beer cans and empty Jack Daniels bottles sprawled out over every inch of countertop, it was obvious by the smiles on their faces that this was when the bonding was done. It was their chance to leave rank at the door, kick back with their fellow platoon mates, talk about better times, and bask in the glory of being a soldier. No officers or senior noncommissioned officers were invited. And when outsiders want to know where the drive to run head-on into enemy fire during combat to pull a fellow soldier to safety comes from, they need not look much further than this.

All of this drinking, however, often comes at a steep price. Most binge drinking is done immediately following a long combat deployment. During these tours, General Order No. 1 is placed into effect, a resolute ban on the consumption of any alcoholic beverage. So when service members finally reach "freedom" again, overindulgence is the name of the game. It is typically in some kind of celebratory manner or in an earnest effort to "make up for lost time." Many careers are ruined during these critically vulnerable few months as soldiers try to drink vast quantities of alcohol on a tolerance that has not been tested in over a year. In my brigade alone, we were averaging almost one alcohol-related episode a day for the first month back from combat, with most incidents being D.U.I.'s or "drunk and disorderly" charges. I once had a soldier arrested for D.U.I. while driving his car the quarter of a mile from his barracks building to the nearest gas station one night. He and his buddies had run out of beer and were on a mission to acquire more. A quarter mile. He could have walked there faster.

Post-Traumatic Stress Disorder, or P.T.S.D., is the other common culprit in excessive drinking. The recent case of Staff Sgt. Robert Bales of the Army, who is charged in the killing of 17 Afghans while ostensibly drinking one night, is an excellent example of what these two powerful elements can produce when mixed.

Most people think that soldiers, especially combat soldiers, drink heavily because of the horrific things that they witness in battle. From someone who has experienced this firsthand, I can tell you that such theories are not always the case. The truth is that combat is such an adrenaline rush that soldiers come home still seeking that thrill. When they cannot find it in their banal garrison routine, they turn to drinking as a quick and easy substitute. Most combat soldiers do not drink because they are trying to forget the bad stuff; they drink because they miss the good stuff.

Meanwhile, efforts to counteract excessive drinking within the military are numerous, albeit somewhat disingenuous. Substance-abuse briefings during reintegration, safety briefings every Friday afternoon, one-on-one counseling, and even direct threats to one's career are just some of the efforts to staunch this practice. But many are treated as merely "check-the-box" exercises, and, as seen above, sometimes leaders can be the worst perpetrators of all. They are the ones who will give a safety briefing on a Friday afternoon, only to turn around and immediately go on an all-night bender.

The military often tends to contradict itself, too. On the one hand, drinking and driving is explicitly discouraged, but attendance at Friday afternoon "beer calls" is exhorted. These events, which are end-of-the-week gatherings held at a post's club, are centered on drinking and socializing with fellow unit members. The only problem is that most people who attend are required to drive home afterward. "Dining outs," another popular, yet formal social event filled with military traditions and courtesies, are similarly conducive to hard drinking. As tradition has it, after the commander leaves for the night, the gloves are allowed to come off. My last dining out in the Army ended in several field-grade officers lighting their bow ties on fire in an indecorous drunken stupor at the bar.

With nearly one in every four soldiers identified as having a drinking problem, the Army has most recently tried to take further action to curtail this epidemic. In 2009, a pilot program to offer confidential treatment to soldiers was started but has since fizzled. The program, created because current policy requires a soldier's commander to be notified if substance-abuse counseling is sought, attempted to offer an outlet to those who wanted help but feared for their careers as a result of seeking it. Consequently, those soldiers still have nowhere to turn to today. Advocates of the program maintain that this is a huge mistake and a contributing factor to the continuing issue.

Unfortunately, this is not a problem that will simply go away when the war in Afghanistan finally winds down. Alcohol is deeply rooted in military culture, and just as in American society, as long as it is available, soldiers will continue to abuse it. I like to kick back and drink a cold beer as much as the next guy or gal, but binge drinking is not something that our armed forces can afford to ignore any longer. Some leaders believe that our military should adopt the policies of many of our European allies during combat—that of two beers a day. The hope is that having a little something now might quell one's desire to have a lot of something later. You typically don't miss what you can have every day. The Navy, in an attempt to control drinking within its ranks, has recently introduced random breathalyzer tests for its sailors. The British Army uses this same practice, but even takes it a step further—those who are determined to be on a "higher" state of readiness are allowed to drink less alcohol. The amount authorized for consumption is set by each unit's commander, who then enforces this policy through random breathalyzer tests for both on-duty and off-duty soldiers. Anyone found in violation is subject to court-martial.

These are just some of the options available to military leaders today to try to control this pandemic. Pessimists, on the other hand, think such policies are merely treating symptoms of the issue and not the real problem. In the end, until leaders can come together, and until alcohol abuse is made both an individual and a unit problem, my guess is we will continue to see our men and women in uniform struggle with this very difficult challenge in the post-war years to come.

Critical Thinking

1. What kinds of problems have resulted from the use of alcohol by members of the military?
2. How does the military deal with alcohol use?
3. How common is alcohol use by members of the armed forces?

Create Central

www.mhhe.com/createcentral

Internet References

National Institutes of Alcoholism and Alcohol Abuse
www.pubs.niaaa.nih.gov

Military Mental Health
www.militarymentalhealth.org

STEVE GRIFFIN spent five years as an Army officer. He served two tours in Iraq as a tank and rifle platoon leader in 2006 and as a civil military officer in 2008. Today he is a program manager for a military contractor in Florida. He is also a member and advocate for Team Red, White, and Blue, a nonprofit organization that provides support in conjunction with the Department of Veterans Affairs for wounded veterans.

Article

Prepared by: Mary Maguire, *California State University—Sacramento*
Clifford Garoupa, *Fresno City College*

Did Cocaine Use by Bankers Cause the Global Financial Crisis?

Coked-up bankers caused the credit crunch, according to the former drug tsar David Nutt. One former City worker can well believe it.

GERAINT ANDERSON

Learning Outcomes

After reading this article, you will be able to:

- Understand the nature of drug use by investment bankers.

- Understand the effect of cocaine use upon decision making.

- Decide whether drug use played a role in the great recession.

"Wall Street got drunk" was George W Bush's typically incisive take on the main cause of the emerging financial crisis in July 2008. Two years later the governor of the Bank of England, Mervyn King, explained in his Mansion House speech that "the role of a central bank in monetary policy is to take the punch bowl away just as the party gets going" (something that he admitted had not occurred). But perhaps the wrong intoxicant was being blamed. The controversial former drug tsar David Nutt told the *Sunday Times* this weekend that cocaine-using bankers with their "culture of excitement and drive and more and more and more . . . got us into this terrible mess".

I'm inclined to agree. Cocaine is (I'm reliably informed) a drug that results in intense bouts of over-exuberance as well as a tendency to talk extremely convincingly about stuff you know nothing about. Everyone accepts that a credit bubble occurred in the mid-noughties and that it was a direct result of what the former US Federal Reserve chief Alan Greenspan has referred to as "irrational exuberance". It could also be argued that traders would be better able to sell absurdly complicated financial weapons of mass destruction after taking a confidence-boosting narcotic such as cocaine. Furthermore, surely only cocaine-ravaged buffoons would actually buy billions of dollars worth of mortgage-backed securities when they were so clearly doomed to explode the minute the property boom stalled.

I certainly saw my fair share of sniffly noses and gurning jaws at City bars every Thursday night. I also heard overconfident gibberish being spouted by brash wide-boys throughout my 12-year banking career. There were also lots of stories about some of the big swingers in New York enjoying a line or 10 of an evening. Bernie Madoff's office was apparently known as "the North Pole" such were the gargantuan quantities of "snow" to be found there and most bankers are aware of the published allegations that Jimmy Cayne (former CEO of Bear Stearns) had an anti-acid medication bottle that was filled with cocaine.

Dr Chris Luke, an A&E specialist based at Cork University Hospital, Ireland, who has studied the effects of cocaine on bankers, has stated that "prominent figures in financial and political circles made irrational decisions as a result of megalomania brought on by cocaine usage". He concludes that "people were making insane decisions and thinking they were 110% right . . . which led to the current chaos".

Greed, selfishness, ignorance and ruthlessness also played their part, of course, but I think it would be foolish not to see the role that the drug played in creating the bubble. Herd mentality, which thrives during times of uncertainty, is certainly much more explicable when you factor in the trembling insecurity and depleted discernment that go hand in hand with a coke habit.

There is, I'm pleased to say, a happy ending to this sorry tale: my ex-colleagues and clients who still work in the Square Mile tell me that many City boys are now too scared to keep snorting the Bolivian marching powder. This may mean bankers are having less fun but, surely, it can only lead to a more restrained and sensible financial system.

Critical Thinking

1. How did President George Bush describe Wall Street and its role in the 2008 recession?

2. How common was cocaine use by investment bankers before the great recession?

3. Who was Bernie Madoff? What is he most noted for?

Create Central

www.mhhe.com/createcentral

Internet References

Cable News Business Network
www.cnbc.com/ld/100650821

United Press International
www.upi.com

Anderson, Geraint. From *The Guardian*, April 15, 2013. Copyright © 2013 by Guardian News & Media Ltd. Reprinted by permission.

Article

Prepared by: Mary Maguire, *California State University—Sacramento*
Clifford Garoupa, *Fresno City College*

Secret U.S. Drug Agency Unit Passing Surveillance Information to Authorities

Wiretaps and telephone records are being funnelled across the country to launch criminal investigations of Americans.

Learning Outcomes

After reading this article, you will be able to:

- Understand the role of wiretaps in drug investigations and drug law enforcement.

- Explain what the "special operations division" of the drug enforcement administration is.

- Understand how antiterrorism efforts impact drug law enforcement.

A secretive U.S. Drug Enforcement Administration unit is funneling information from intelligence intercepts, wiretaps, informants and a massive database of telephone records to authorities across the nation to help them launch criminal investigations of Americans.

Although these cases rarely involve national security issues, documents reviewed by Reuters show that law enforcement agents have been directed to conceal how such investigations truly begin—not only from defense lawyers but also sometimes from prosecutors and judges.

The undated documents show that federal agents are trained to "recreate" the investigative trail to effectively cover up where the information originated, a practice that some experts say violates a defendant's constitutional right to a fair trial. If defendants don't know how an investigation began, they cannot know to ask to review potential sources of exculpatory evidence—information that could reveal entrapment, mistakes or biased witnesses.

"I have never heard of anything like this at all," said Nancy Gertner, a Harvard Law School professor who served as a federal judge from 1994 to 2011. Gertner and other legal experts said the program sounds more troubling than recent disclosures that the National Security Agency has been collecting domestic phone records. The NSA effort is geared toward stopping terrorists; the DEA program targets common criminals, primarily drug dealers.

"It is one thing to create special rules for national security," Gertner said. "Ordinary crime is entirely different. It sounds like they are phonying up investigations."

The Special Operations Division

The unit of the DEA that distributes the information is called the Special Operations Division, or SOD. Two dozen partner agencies comprise the unit, including the FBI, CIA, NSA, Internal Revenue Service and the Department of Homeland Security. It was created in 1994 to combat Latin American drug cartels and has grown from several dozen employees to several hundred.

Today, much of the SOD's work is classified, and officials asked that its precise location in Virginia not be revealed. The documents reviewed by Reuters are marked "Law Enforcement Sensitive", a government categorization that is meant to keep them confidential.

"Remember that the utilization of SOD cannot be revealed or discussed in any investigative function," a document presented to agents reads. The document specifically directs agents to omit the SOD's involvement from investigative reports, affidavits, discussions with prosecutors and courtroom testimony. Agents are instructed to then use "normal investigative techniques to recreate the information provided by SOD."

A spokesman with the Department of Justice, which oversees the DEA, declined to comment.

But two senior DEA officials defended the program, and said trying to "recreate" an investigative trail is not only legal but a technique that is used almost daily.

A former federal agent in the northeastern United States who received such tips from SOD described the process. "You'd be told only, 'Be at a certain truck stop at a certain time and look for a certain vehicle.' And so we'd alert the state police to find an excuse to stop that vehicle, and then have a drug dog search it," the agent said.

'Parallel Construction'

After an arrest was made, agents then pretended that their investigation began with the traffic stop, not with the SOD tip, the former agent said. The training document reviewed by Reuters refers to this process as "parallel construction".

The two senior DEA officials, who spoke on behalf of the agency but only on condition of anonymity, said the process is kept secret to protect sources and investigative methods. "Parallel construction is a law enforcement technique we use every day," one official said. "It's decades old, a bedrock concept."

A dozen current or former federal agents interviewed by Reuters confirmed they had used parallel construction during their careers. Most defended the practice; some said they understood why those outside law enforcement might be concerned.

"It's just like laundering money—you work it backwards to make it clean," said Finn Selander, a DEA agent from 1991 to 2008 and now a member of a group called Law Enforcement Against Prohibition, which advocates legalizing and regulating narcotics.

Some defense lawyers and former prosecutors said that using "parallel construction" may be legal to establish probable cause for an arrest. But they said employing the practice as a means of disguising how an investigation began may violate pretrial discovery rules by burying evidence that could prove useful to criminal defendants.

A Question of Constitutionality

"That's outrageous," said Tampa attorney James Felman, a vice-chairman of the criminal justice section of the American Bar Association. "It strikes me as indefensible."

Lawrence Lustberg, a New Jersey defense lawyer, said any systematic government effort to conceal the circumstances under which cases begin "would not only be alarming but pretty blatantly unconstitutional".

Lustberg and others said the government's use of the SOD program skirts established court procedures by which judges privately examine sensitive information, such as an informant's identity or classified evidence, to determine whether the information is relevant to the defense.

"You can't game the system," said former federal prosecutor Henry E Hockeimer Jr. "You can't create this subterfuge. These are drug crimes, not national security cases. If you don't draw the line here, where do you draw it?"

Some lawyers say there can be legitimate reasons for not revealing sources. Robert Spelke, a former prosecutor who spent seven years as a senior DEA lawyer, said some sources are classified. But he also said there are few reasons why unclassified evidence should be concealed at trial.

"It's a balancing act, and they've been doing it this way for years," Spelke said. "Do I think it's a good way to do it? No, because now that I'm a defense lawyer, I see how difficult it is to challenge."

Concealing a Tip

One current federal prosecutor learned how agents were using SOD tips after a drug agent misled him, the prosecutor told Reuters. In a Florida drug case he was handling, the prosecutor said, a DEA agent told him the investigation of a US citizen began with a tip from an informant. When the prosecutor pressed for more information, he said, a DEA supervisor intervened and revealed that the tip had actually come through the SOD and from an NSA intercept.

"I was pissed," the prosecutor said. "Lying about where the information came from is a bad start if you're trying to comply with the law because it can lead to all kinds of problems with discovery and candor to the court." The prosecutor never filed charges in the case because he lost confidence in the investigation, he said.

A senior DEA official said he was not aware of the case but said the agent should not have misled the prosecutor. How often such misdirection occurs is unknown, even to the government; the DEA official said the agency does not track what happens with tips after the SOD sends them to agents in the field.

The SOD's role providing information to agents isn't itself a secret. It is briefly mentioned by the DEA in budget documents, albeit without any reference to how that information is used or represented when cases go to court.

The DEA has long publicly touted the SOD's role in multi-jurisdictional and international investigations, connecting agents in separate cities who may be unwittingly investigating the same target and making sure undercover agents don't accidentally try to arrest each other.

SOD's Big Successes

The unit also played a major role in a 2008 DEA sting in Thailand against Russian arms dealer Viktor Bout; he was sentenced in 2011 to 25 years in prison on charges of conspiring to sell weapons to the Colombian rebel group FARC. The SOD also recently coordinated Project Synergy, a crackdown against manufacturers, wholesalers and retailers of synthetic designer drugs that spanned 35 states and resulted in 227 arrests.

Since its inception, the SOD's mandate has expanded to include narco-terrorism, organized crime and gangs. A DEA spokesman declined to comment on the unit's annual budget. A recent LinkedIn posting on the personal page of a senior SOD official estimated it to be $125m.

Today, the SOD offers at least three services to federal, state and local law enforcement agents: coordinating international investigations such as the Bout case; distributing tips from overseas NSA intercepts, informants, foreign law enforcement partners and domestic wiretaps; and circulating tips from a massive database known as Dice.

The Dice database contains about 1bn records, the senior DEA officials said. The majority of the records consist of phone log and Internet data gathered legally by the DEA through subpoenas, arrests and search warrants nationwide. Records are kept for about a year and then purged, the DEA officials said.

About 10,000 federal, state and local law enforcement agents have access to the Dice database, records show. They can query it to try to link otherwise disparate clues. Recently, one of the DEA officials said, Dice linked a man who tried to smuggle $100,000 over the US south-west border to a major drug case on the east coast.

"We use it to connect the dots," the official said.

'An Amazing Tool'

Wiretap tips forwarded by the SOD usually come from foreign governments, US intelligence agencies or court-authorized domestic phone recordings. Because warrantless eavesdropping on Americans is illegal, tips from intelligence agencies are generally not forwarded to the SOD until a caller's citizenship can be verified, according to one senior law enforcement official and one former US military intelligence analyst.

"They do a pretty good job of screening, but it can be a struggle to know for sure whether the person on a wiretap is American," the senior law enforcement official said.

Tips from domestic wiretaps typically occur when agents use information gleaned from a court-ordered wiretap in one case to start a second investigation.

As a practical matter, law enforcement agents said they usually don't worry that SOD's involvement will be exposed in court. That's because most drug-trafficking defendants plead guilty before trial and therefore never request to see the evidence against them. If cases did go to trial, current and former agents said, charges were sometimes dropped to avoid the risk of exposing SOD involvement.

Current and former federal agents said SOD tips aren't always helpful—one estimated their accuracy at 60%. But current and former agents said tips have enabled them to catch drug smugglers who might have gotten away.

"It was an amazing tool," said one recently retired federal agent. "Our big fear was that it wouldn't stay secret."

DEA officials said that the SOD process has been reviewed internally. They declined to provide Reuters with a copy of their most recent review.

Critical Thinking

1. What types of information does the DEA gather?
2. How is this information obtained and used?
3. Is this information commonly divulged and shared with the legal system?

Create Central

www.mhhe.com/createcentral

Internet References

United States Drug Enforcement Administration
   www.justice.gov/dea
The American Civil Liberties Union
   www.aclu.org

Unit 6

UNIT

Prepared by: Mary Maguire, *California State University—Sacramento*
Clifford Garoupa, *Fresno City College*

Creating and Sustaining Effective Drug Control Policy

The drug problem consistently competes with all major public policy issues, including the wars in Iraq and Afghanistan, the economy, education, and foreign policy. Drug abuse is a serious national medical issue with profound social and legal consequences. Formulating and implementing effective drug control policy is a troublesome task. Some would argue that the consequences of policy failures have been worse than the problems that the policies were attempting to address. Others would argue that although the world of shaping drug policy is an imperfect one, the process has worked generally as well as could be expected. The majority of Americans believe that failures and breakdowns in the fight against drug abuse have occurred in spite of various drug policies, not because of them. Although the last few years have produced softening attitudes and alternatives for adjudicating cases of simple possession and use, the get-tough, stay-tough enforcement policies directed at illegal drug trafficking remain firmly in place and widely supported. Policy formulation is not a process of aimless wandering.

Various levels of government have responsibility for responding to problems of drug abuse. At the center of most policy debate is the premise that the manufacture, possession, use, and distribution of psychoactive drugs without government authorization is illegal. The federal posture of prohibition is an important emphasis on state and local policymaking. Federal drug policy is, however, significantly linked to state-by-state data, which suggests that illicit drug, alcohol, and tobacco use vary substantially among states and regions. The current federal drug strategy began in 2001 and set the goals of reducing drug use by young persons by 25 percent over five years. In 2008, President Bush announced that drug use by the population in this age group was down by 24 percent. President Obama has continued the basic strategic constructs of the Bush policy. Core priorities of the overall plan continue to be to stop drug use before it starts, heal America's drug users, and disrupt the illegal market. These three core goals are re-enforced by objectives outlined in a policy statement produced by the White House Office of Drug Control Policy. All three goals reflect budget expenditures related to meeting goals of the overall policy. The current drug control policy, in terms of budget allocations, continues to provide for over $1.5 billion to prevent use before it starts, largely through education campaigns, which encourage a cultural shift away from drugs, and more than $3.4 billion to heal America's users. Each year produces modifications to the plan as a result of analysis of trends and strategy impacts. Allocations for interdiction, largely a result of the attempt to secure the borders and frustrate alliances between drug traffickers and terrorists, remain the most significant component of the budget at $10 billion dollars.

One exception to prevailing views that generally support drug prohibition is the softening of attitudes regarding criminal sanctions that historically applied to cases of simple possession and use of drugs. There is much public consensus that incarcerating persons for these offenses is unjustified unless they are related to other criminal conduct. The federal funding of drug court programs remains a priority with more than $38 million dedicated to state and local operation. Drug courts provide alternatives to incarceration by using the coercive power of the court to force abstinence and alter behavior through a process of escalating sanctions, mandatory drug testing, and outpatient programs. Successful rehabilitation accompanies the re-entry to society as a citizen, not a felon. The drug court program exists as one important example of policy directed at treating users and deterring them from further involvement in the criminal justice system. Drug courts are now in place in all 50 states.

The majority of Americans express the view that legalizing, and in some cases even decriminalizing, dangerous drugs is a bad idea. The fear of increased crime, increased drug use, and the potential threat to children are the most often stated reasons. Citing the devastating consequences of alcohol and tobacco use, most Americans question society's ability to use any addictive, mind-altering drug responsibly. Currently, the public favors supply reduction, demand reduction, and an increased emphasis on prevention, treatment, and rehabilitation as effective strategies in combating the drug problem. Shaping public policy is a critical function that greatly relies upon public input. The policymaking apparatus is influenced by public opinion, and public opinion is in turn influenced by public policy. When the president refers to drugs as threats to national security, the impact on public opinion is tremendous. Currently, record amounts of opium are being produced in Afghanistan, and the implications for its providing support for the Taliban and terrorism are clear. Opium production in Southwest Asia, an entrenched staple in the region's overall economic product, continues as a priority of U.S. national security. The resulting implications for sustaining enforcement-oriented U.S. drug policy are also clear; and in the minds of most Americans, they are absolutely necessary. The U.S. Department of State alone will receive $336 million for alternative crop production, diplomacy, interdiction, and enforcement.

Although the prevailing characteristic of most current drug policy still reflects a punitive, "get tough" approach to control, an added emphasis on treating and rehabilitating offenders is visible in policy changes occurring over the past 10 years. Correctional systems are reflecting with greater consistency the view that drug treatment made available to inmates is a critical component of rehabilitation. The California Department of Corrections, the largest in the nation, was recently renamed the California Department of Corrections and Rehabilitation. A prisoner with a history of drug abuse, who receives no drug treatment while in custody, is finally being recognized as a virtual guarantee to reoffend. In 2006, the National Institute of Drug Abuse published the first federal guidelines for administering drug treatment to criminal justice populations.

Another complicated aspect of creating national as well as local drug policy is consideration of the growing body of research on the subject. The past 20 years have produced numerous public and private investigations, surveys, and conclusions relative to the dynamics of drug use in U.S. society. Although an historical assessment of the influence of research on policy produces indirect relationships, policy decisions of the last few years can be directly related to evidence-based research findings and not just political views. One example is the consistently increasing commitment to treatment. This commitment comes as a direct result of research related to progress achieved in treating and rehabilitating users. Treatment, in terms of dollars spent, can compete with all other components of drug control policy.

One important issue affecting and sometimes complicating the research/policymaking relationship is that the policymaking community, at all levels of government, is largely composed of persons of diverse backgrounds, professional capacities, and political interests. Some are elected officials, others are civil servants, and many are private citizens from the medical, educational, and research communities. In some cases, such as with alcohol and tobacco, powerful industry players assert a tremendous influence on policy. As you read on, consider the new research-related applications for drug policy, such as those related to the rehabilitation of incarcerated drug offenders.

Article

Prepared by: Mary Maguire, *California State University—Sacramento*
Clifford Garoupa, *Fresno City College*

Do the United States and Mexico Really Want the Drug War to Succeed?

Robert Joe Stout

Learning Outcomes

After reading this article, you will be able to:

- Discuss the history of the narco-war on the Mexico–United States border.

- Discuss the contributing factors and barriers to ending the "war on drugs."

- Discuss policy reforms that affect the current state of drug trafficking.

Until 1914 laudanum and morphine were legally sold and distributed in the United States, heroin was prescribed as a cough medicine, and coca and cocaine were mixed with wine and cola drinks. Although most of the opium came from the Orient, Chinese settlers on Mexico's west coast, particularly in the state of Sinaloa, began cultivating adormidera (opium gum) during the 1870s and gradually developed an export trade.

Even after the use of opium-based products was declared illegal in the United States the exportations from Sinaloa continued; prosecution of offenders, if it happened at all, was benign. The adormidera crossed into the United States through places like Tijuana, a dusty little frontier town until the mid-twentieth century; San Luis Rio Colorado, across the border from Yuma, Arizona; Nogales, also on the Arizona border; and Ojinaga, across the Rio Grande River from Presidio in Texas's isolated Big Bend country. Customs agents on both sides of the border, but particularly in Mexico, cooperated with the exporters and the flow of drugs, though not large by 1960s or '70s standards, went through virtually unimpeded.

The majority of those involved were locals who spent the cash they acquired in the areas in which they operated. They hired local residents for construction, transportation, ranching, and other sidelines in which they invested their earnings. As far as most of their neighbors were concerned they were good citizens whose business was no better or worse from that of any other.

Prohibition changed this genial and basically cooperative landscape. Large amounts of liquor were harder to conceal than adormidera or marijuana, making it necessary for exporters to bribe—or form partnerships—with those in charge of customs. Politicians ranging from local councilmen to state governors became involved, forcing the local exporters either to join them or evade them as well as evade law enforcement.

The end of Prohibition wounded but did not slay the golden calf of liquor exportation. The politically connected entrepreneurs that controlled the aduanas (customs inspection stations) also controlled prostitution and a percentage of drug exportations. They financed the construction and operation of luxurious night clubs, gourmet restaurants, and gambling activities that attracted large numbers of U.S. residents. Both politically affiliated and independent drug exporters invested in these enterprises as Tijuana, Ciudad Juárez, and other border cities became brightly lit tourist meccas surrounded by desolate slums packed with new arrivals, deportees, addicts, beggars, and petty criminals.

By 1948 the volume of Sinaloa adormidera crossing the border triggered harsh recriminations from representatives of the U.S. federal government. Mexico's Attorney General responded with equally acerbic suggestions that officials north of the border deal with those who were purchasing the drugs since the market attracting the exports was in the United States. Mexican federal and state law enforcement did arrest a few farmers and mulas (mules, i.e., those hired to transport contraband) but did not prosecute any leading political or business figures.

Despite cinema and television depictions of drug runners as gun-toting, Pancho Villa-like gangsters, the truth was that many well-attired and well-educated governors, bankers, and businessmen considered the business of growing and exporting adormidera as natural (and as profitable) as growing cotton or corn. The income from drug exportations filtered through the economies of the states involved and was attributed to "sale of agricultural products" if the source was questioned.

As marijuana and cocaine use increased exponentially during the 1960s in the United States, Sinaloa drug exporters expanded into other areas, particularly Tamaulipas in northeastern Mexico, where they clashed with exporters who had greater access to delivery points across the border. They also competed for connections with the major Colombian "cartels."

By the 1970s importing Colombian cocaine and getting it into the United States had become an increasingly complex business. The socalled "cartels" or drug corporations included accountants, lawyers, chemists, legislators, and entire corps of police departmentalized into individual functions which included marketing, investment, press relations, and militarized units, most of which were led by experienced former Mexican Army and Navy officers. (The term "cartel" is erroneous since the drug organizations have nothing to do with medieval trade unions; instead they function like private corporations.)

As these organizations grew they brought more elements of Mexican society into their operations, particularly for laundering profits and transporting drugs. Tourists and businessmen and women—well-dressed, affable, polite—crossed the border with false-bottomed luggage filled with cocaine. Soccer balls and balloons contained packets of powder. Brassieres that made small-breasted women seem much more amply endowed were padded with cocaine sewed into the garments. According to retired U.S. Air Force journalist James McGee, importers in El Paso brought thousands of colorful Mexican piñatas across the border—piñatas that never were retailed but ripped open and discarded after the cocaine packed inside them had been removed.

As happens with most corporations, junior operatives (executives) began to break away and form smaller organizations of their own. Murders and assassinations between rival bands increased as they vied for portions of the lucrative trade. Breakaway groups unable to chisel a large enough portion for themselves branched into people smuggling, counterfeiting, business shakedowns, prostitution, auto theft, and kidnapping. Others paid their bribes and expenses with "merchandise" (i.e., cocaine or heroin) or, unable to push it into the United States, increased distribution in Mexico, where profits were lower but easier to obtain. Gradually—first along the frontier with the United States, then in cities throughout the country—more and more Mexican nationals, especially those under thirty years of age, became habitual drug users.

Gradually the principal criminal organizations gobbled up smaller local operatives. ("Join us or join those in the cemetery," was the ultimatum usually given.) The smaller criminal bands paid monthly "quotas" to be allowed to operate. The dominant corporations paid quotas to government officials, business executives, and military commanders, while also purchasing legitimate businesses like major sports franchises and investing in the stock market.

The financial fluidity of these rapidly expanding corporations enabled them to establish "nations within the nation" that were functionally self-governing and absorbed or supplanted many social and communal activities. The kingpin was Juan García-Ábrego; his so-called "Cartel del Golfo" transferred thousands of tons of cocaine that had been flown from Colombia to clandestine landing strips in Quintana Roo and the Yucatán for smuggling into the United States.

When Mexican authorities arrested and extradited García-Ábrego to the United States in 1996 his organization foundered and its new leaders temporarily allied themselves with the Sinaloa group. Such "marriages" and subsequent breakups occurred frequently throughout the 1980s and '90s depending upon arrests, betrayals, governmental changes, and business opportunities. But although the names and faces changed the business continued unabated.

In many aspects (investment, trade, communication, transportation, defense) the "nations within the nation" that the drug corporations formed paralleled the structure of Mexico's federal government. Many who operated within the corporate systems functioned in similar capacities within federal and state law enforcement and financial entities. The capos contributed to local and regional political campaigns, thus assuring themselves of being able to extract needed favors and permissions from the many officeholders in their debt. According to a retired state employee named Pedro Enrique Martinez who chauffeured a number of Sinaloa politicians:

The capos (drug lords) realized it wasn't cost effective to have to keep bribing those who held higher offices so they started recruiting young local candidates, helping finance them to win elections. Soon every city, every municipio (county), every state bureaucracy was infiltrated. Sometimes the capos would go years and not require anything then one day they'd say "We need this bill passed" or "We need this shipment to go through" and they'd get what they wanted.

What the leader of the so-called "Sinaloa cartel" Joaquin ("El Chapo") Guzman wanted, he informed the government of Mexican president Felipe Calderón, was to be allowed to run his business without interference from the military. Some members of the bureaucracy and Senate and House of Deputies quietly supported this concept, harking back to the presidency of the PRI's Carlos Salinas de Gortari between 1988 and 1994, when drug exportations enriched participating politicians without arousing bloody criminal confrontations. Nonetheless, Calderón and his administration remained committed to U.S. financed policies of militarized action.

Although Calderón and his inner circle were loath to admit it the militarization provoked greater violence and bloodshed without diminishing the flow of drugs northward (and rapidly increasing narcotics use and addiction in Mexico). As proof of the success of the military operations Calderón cited increases in the street price of cocaine in the United States, but he did not mention how much those increases stimulated importers and producers to greater activity.

Addiction and crime associated with drug users became a major problem in the United States but the vast majority of users—like the vast majority of persons who buy and use alcoholic beverages—are not addicts. Bankers, politicians, athletes, university professors, insurance salespersons, construction workers, and thousands of others indulge only on weekends or at parties or as sexual provokers. They purchase the cocaine and marijuana from other athletes, salespersons, or bankers who have regular suppliers, most of whom they have been doing business with for years. All are far removed from street warfare between mafiosos and armed military and they are a primary reason that the "War on Drugs" has not reduced the demand for cocaine, marijuana, and other narcotics in the United States.

In her "Americas Program" column on September 3, 2009, entitled "Drug War Doublespeak," Laura Carlsen insisted: "Drug-war doublespeak pervades and defines the United

States–Mexico relationship today. The discourse aims not to win the war on drugs, but to assure funding and public support for the military model of combating illegal drug trafficking, despite the losses and overwhelming evidence that current strategies are not working."

According to Mexican national security specialist Ghaleb Krame the narcotraficantes developed a sophisticated counter-intelligence system and utilized highly mobile guerrilla groups that constantly changed their bases and personnel while the Mexican army, bogged down by traditional channels of protocol and information, was unable to effectively counter these maneuvers. As a consequence the Mexican government expanded its dependence on paramilitaries to do what the police and military could not do legally.

Undercover operations are not confined to infiltrating and investigating drug corporation activities but like the brigadasblancas of the 1960s and '70s guara sucia ("dirty war") they disrupted social protest movements and sequestered and sometimes tortured those defending ecological, communal, or union rights. Human rights advocates and journalists like Miguel Badillo insist that the "War on Drugs" is "a simulation whose real objective is to stomp out growing social discontent" in the country.

Other forces primarily formed of former military and police personnel became private "armies" contracted by individual entrepreneurs. They escort dignitaries and their families, guard business and industrial sites, and—like the drug organization paramilitaries—serve as armed couriers. As a Oaxaca self-employed contractor, Ali Jiménez, told me, "It's come to the point that the government lets these guys (entrepreneurs) surround themselves with gunmen since nobody can trust the police and there's no public security." A former Chihuahua journalist who left the profession because of death threats told me, "The War on Drugs is like a football [soccer] game without coaches or referees, soldiers and narcos charging this way and that, doing more harm to the spectators than to each other."

The drug corporations have infiltrated all levels of government and their payrolls include thousands of lookouts, messengers, farmers, and truck drivers. However, the federal government and the inexperienced Mexican military seem to lack cohesive intelligence reports or effective plans for doing anything more than random searches and seizures. Often they respond to misleading or false information they acquire from informants, many of whom are paid by the drug organizations to finger competitors or businesses whose only connection with the mafiosos is having failed to pay adequate protection money.

Drug corporations like the "Cartel del Golfo" were even able to seduce high-ranking members of Mexico's top organized crime-fighting agency, SIEDO (Sub-Prosecutor General of Special Investigations into Organized Crime). The PGR (Prosecutor General of the Republic, Mexico's Attorney General's office), which had its own problems with infiltrators in its ranks, investigated high-ranking SIEDO functionaries in 2008—investigations that were hampered because SIEDO informants, some of whom were receiving more than $450,000 a month, informed the "Cartel del Golfo" of every step that the PGR was taking. Finally, through a former Cartel del Golfo member

who testified against the organization as a protected witness, the PGR arrested Sub-Prosecutor Noé Ramírez-Mandujano and Miguel Colorado, SIEDO's Coordinator of Intelligence, for their connections with organized crime.

The drug corporations retaliated. In May 2007 gunmen assassinated José Lugo, Mexico's coordinator of information of the Center for Planning and Analysis to Combat Organized Crime. Others ambushed and shot Edgar Millán, acting head of Mexico's federal police, later that same year. In November 2008 a drug organization hit squad abducted and executed Army General Mauro Tello a few days after he assumed the post of anti-drug czar in Cancun, Quintana Roo. In 2009 they executed government-protected witness Edgar Enrique Bayardo-del Villar while he was breakfasting in a Mexico City *Starbucks*.

Although Calderón's government tried to squelch rumors that the fatal crash of a Lear jet carrying Government Secretary Juan Camilo Mouriño was not the result of pilot error, journalists and commentators throughout the country insisted that government version was a cover up and the aircraft had been sabotaged by El Chapo Guzman's corporation in retaliation for the arrest and imprisoning of one of his top aides.

As competition among the major drug organizations increased, with assassinations of rival leaders commonplace, the militarized "Zetas" emerged as an elite armed force, first aligned with the Beltrán-Leyva Gulf Cartel, but later an independent corporation functioning on both Mexico's northern and southern borders. The Zetas were tightly disciplined (their leaders were deserters from Mexico's Special Forces and many had been trained by the U.S. School of the Americas and/ or the Kaibilies in Guatemala) and brazenly recruited active duty militaries.

Although the Zetas occasionally openly confronted police and military units they focused primarily on intimidating and extracting quotas from growers and transporters as well as those engaged in legitimate businesses, including cattle ranchers, merchants, local entrepreneurs, bar and nightclub owners, farmers, polleros (people smugglers), and truckers. They dealt harshly with those who tried to circumvent or reduce these obligations—kidnapping, torturing, and often decapitating those who were delinquent in their payments.

By 2008 Mexico had committed some 50,000 troops to the "War on Drugs." Because the Mexican military had been a peacetime force primarily involving garrison duty (and, since 1994, containment controls around the Zapatista autonomous communities in Chiapas) it offered relatively few benefits and minimal salaries to enlisted personnel. Recruiting was focused on marginal residents of city slums where life was hazardous, and in poverty-wracked rural areas that offered no other hopes of employment. Theoretically recruits needed to have completed junior high school to enter the military but proof seldom was required and criminal behavior, if confined to misdemeanors, often was overlooked.

These poverty-bred soldiers, many just out of basic training, adhere to medieval practices of supplementing their meager salaries with what they acquire during cateos (searches and seizures of property) and shakedowns. Victims accuse soldiers of stealing money and stripping personnel property from persons stopped at highway checkpoints. Federal authorities derail prosecution of soldiers accused of abuses by insisting that those levying the charges "are politically motivated" and that the accusations are exaggerated or falsified.

The drug corporations also recruit from marginal areas. Although they promise "guns, money, cars, and women" to potential deserters many of the hundreds of thousands they hire do not carry weapons and primarily act as lookouts, messengers, decoys, and money handlers. Like many legitimate corporations the drug organizations have established salary scales, usually beginning with the equivalent of US$800 per month, a figure that doubles after a set number of months or year of service. (Schoolteachers in southern Mexico receive the equivalent of $800–$1,100 per month and most workers are paid less, thus vaulting a newly recruited drug corporation lookout or messenger into the upper 10 percent of money earners in his or her community.)

To tens of thousands of young people employment with a drug corporation "at least offers something," as a seventeen-year-old high school dropout told me after a friend offered to connect him with a recruiter. Aljazeera quoted a drug organization member: "I could never go back to making ten dollars a day. At least here I get paid and I have some opportunity to rise up. In other jobs I will always be at the bottom." That most of these newly recruited members have no criminal records and intermingle with the general population created an environment "like those old science-fiction movies about androids, you never know who's on your side and who isn't," as an editor from a Mexican daily exclaimed during a Mexico City news conference.

Drug-associated killings became so frequent that by 2008 Mexican newspapers like *La Jornada* grouped daily execution and assassination reports under a single back page headline. During the first eight months of 2009 they reported an average of twenty-one killings a day. By 2010 the average number of drug-associated deaths averaged nearly forty a day.

Because President Calderón needed—or thought he needed (or his ultra-conservative National Action Party thought that he needed)—the support of governors alleged to have connections with various drug organizations he shunted aside revelations about their narco-business contacts. Prosecution of commerce in cocaine, marijuana, and other drugs occurred in a patchwork pattern, with political alliances given priority over enforcement. Many governors, high-ranking politicians, business impresarios, and generals remained immune even when military raids or PGR investigations targeted their agencies.

Only when "the structure of power that those controlling the politics of the nation have maintained as accomplices and members of this series of criminal organizations has collapsed" will real solutions to the internal warfare among the "nations within a nation" be possible, Guillermo Garduño-*Valero,* a specialist in national security analysis from Mexico's Metropolitan University (UAM), told *La Jornada.* The drug corporations have become so powerful politically, he argued, that both the federal and state governments have become subservient to them and the occasional arrests and assaults on organization leaders have little or no impact on the lucrative trade.

Both the governments of Mexico and the United States have demonstrated a need to justify military actions and to portray the "War on Drugs" as a battle between good and evil with no gray areas in between. To make the rhetoric effective it has been necessary to villainize the perpetrators of the "evil" and to ignore the dominant reasons that the evil exists: unabated drug consumption in the United States. Also overlooked has been drug associated violence in the United States, particularly in city ghettos where gang warfare involving drug distribution has existed since the 1960s.

Until late in the twentieth century heroin and cocaine addiction in Mexico was not considered a major problem. Narcotics filtered to Mexican buyers as a spin off from smuggling, but most production and distribution was focused on getting the narcotics to consumers north of the border who would pay ten or more times what the drugs sold for in Mexico. Governmental sources in both countries consistently denied that U.S. military intervention into Mexican territory was being planned; nevertheless several governors of states on the U.S. side of the border have requested permanent military "protection," including armed patrols and battle-ready commandos.

Many of the groups that distribute narcotics in the United States are linked to specific Mexican corporations just as U.S. auto, livestock, cosmetics, and computer exporters are linked with importers in Mexico. Gangs in the United States clash primarily over obtaining drugs for street sales, but the majority of imported narcotics passes into the hands of white-collar distributors with regular clients who can afford the prices established for purchasing cocaine and other drugs.

Although many journalists and editors would like to deny it, newspapers and television which rely financially on readers, viewers, and advertisers profit more from graphic reports about beheadings, drug raids, and highspeed chases than they do from features about controlled or casual use of narcotics. Attitudes towards drug use in both countries run a gamut between "drugs are a sin" to "I enjoy them, why not?" That they can be detrimental to one's health, just as the consumption of alcoholic beverages, cigarette smoking, overeating, driving a car at excessive speeds, or longterm exposure to direct sunlight can be detrimental, is grounded in fact.

Unfortunately facts and politics do not go hand in glove. Nor do facts and marketing. Newspaper wire services and television reports designed to stimulate interest and sell sponsors' products (and/or comply with ownership political biases) influence public opinion and public opinion influences the decisions of legislators and Congressmen. As Laura Carlson insists: "These claims and others like them, although unsubstantiated, accumulate into a critical mass to push a public consensus on implementing dangerous and delusional policies. . . . Like the model it mimics—the Bush war on terror—the drug war in Mexico is being mounted on the back of hype, half-truths, omissions and outright falsehoods."

Unfortunately, major questions that need to be answered are shunted aside by policymakers on both sides of the border and preference is given to partisan stances that have less to do with the drug trade or the war against it than they have to do with maintaining economic and political power. Neither government seems capable of asking: Can Mexico really afford to end the production and exportation of heroin, cocaine, marijuana, amphetamines, and designer drugs without its U.S. dependent economy collapsing?

In many respects, the drug organizations operating in Mexico exemplify what "free enterprise" is about: developing and marketing a product that satisfies willing consumers. Their armed components make their competition deadlier than competitors in other industries, but their methods of operation duplicate those of legitimate corporations: they seek (or buy) government support, network a well-organized retail trade, and invest their profits in condominiums, the stock market, and high-visibility consumer items. Their corporate structures, divided into distinct operations and with well-defined chains of command, enable them to replace any executive who is arrested or killed without that materially affecting production or sales.

The money they bring into Mexico, unlike money brought in by legitimate corporations, does not require government investment and consequently is untaxed and unreported (which prevents it from benefiting the nearly 80 percent of the population with inadequate and/or poverty level incomes). Nevertheless, what the mafiosos spend on purchases, construction, and salaries circulates throughout the economy. The owner of a Michoacán taquería reflected the viewpoint of many Mexican residents: "They have lana [literally wool, but popularly used to describe money], they eat well; I now have five locations instead of just one."

Proposals to decriminalize the possession of small amounts of marijuana, as various states in the United States have done, came under discussion during the early years of President Vicente Fox's administration but evoked a vehemently negative response, particularly from the Catholic Church hierarchy and those influenced by Church doctrine. Calderón's PAN government seemed more inclined to reinstitute the Salinas de Gortari era of tacit coordination with a single dominant drug corporation, a process that could not be discussed openly and would involve purging local, state, and federal governments of alignments with everyone except the chosen affiliate (which many sources in Mexico insist is El Chapo's "Sinaloa Cartel").

As long as the assassinations, beheadings, cáteos, and the majority of the corruption of government officials remain south of the border the United States can maintain its pro-military stance, send money and arms to Mexico's conservative government, and focus on more demanding issues. Mexico, in contrast, rejecting any form of legalization, remains bound to its U.S. appeasing commitment to continue a bloody confrontation that seems to have no end.

Although legalization would re-channel importation and sales and make addiction, overdoses, and side effects a public health problem instead of strictly a law-enforcement concern, drug-related crimes would continue to exist, just as alcohol-related crimes continued to make headlines and fill jails after the repeal of Prohibition. Taxes on importation and sales could finance rehabilitation and other government programs; corporations handling importation and sales could be effectively audited but social, ethical, and religious conflicts over morality and behavior would continue.

Nor would legalization magically resolve the economic issues that gave rise to the complex business of drug exportation and use, and it would have to occur in both Mexico and the United States to be effective. Restricting or controlling the financing of drug operations would not be possible without breaking up the distribution and investment chains that involve not only the two governments, but also entrepreneurs and legalized businesses. But it can hardly be denied that legalization is a necessary first step toward any decent, or even tolerable, outcome.

The nationalism exhibited by the governments of both the United States and Mexico has impeded dealing rationally with drug cultivation and distribution. Coupled with the lack of accurate information—and/or falsification of the information available—it has created a paradigm where the solution has preceded analysis and wrenched fact and fiction into a definition that fits the solution, rather than the solution being the culmination of analysis. In much the same way that trying to solve the "illegal immigration problem" by constructing walls and making arrests puts the cart (solution) before the horse (employers), trying to curb the importation of cocaine, marijuana, heroin, and other drugs by militarized procedures is doomed to fail because it does not recognize or deal with the undiminished demand for the products involved.

Critical Thinking

1. What do you believe were the most important turning points in the history of United States drug policy?

2. What do you believe were the most important turning points in the history of Mexican drug policy?

3. Discuss the current barriers to resolution for the shared United States–Mexico drug war.

Create Central

www.mhhe.com/createcentral

Internet References

Drug Sense Map
www.drugsense.org/cms/wodclock
PBS Thirty Years of America's Drug War
www.pbs.org/wgbh/pages/frontline/shows/drugs/cron

ROBERT JOE STOUT (mexicoconamor@yahoo.com) lives in Oaxaca, Mexico, and his articles and essays have appeared recently in *America*, *Conscience*, *The American Scholar*, and *Monthly Review*. His most recent book is *Why Immigrants Come to America* (Praeger Publishers, 2007). Copyright *Monthly Review Press*, Jan 2012.

Stout, Robert Joe. From *Monthly Review*, vol. 63, no. 8, January 2012, pp. 34–44. Copyright © 2012 by Monthly Review Foundation. Reprinted by permission.

Article

Prepared by: Mary Maguire, *California State University—Sacramento*
Clifford Garoupa, *Fresno City College*

Engaging Communities to Prevent Underage Drinking

ABIGAIL A. FAGAN, J. DAVID HAWKINS, AND RICHARD F. CATALANO

Learning Outcomes

After reading this article, you will be able to:

- Identify the risk factors for underage drinking.
- Describe at least two programs for the prevention of underage drinking.
- Discuss factors that lead to successful prevention programs for underage drinking.

Community-based efforts offer broad potential for achieving population-level reductions in alcohol misuse among youth and young adults. A common feature of successful community strategies is reliance on local coalitions to select and fully implement preventive interventions that have been shown to be effective in changing factors that influence risk of youth engaging in alcohol use, including both proximal influences and structural and/or environmental factors related to alcohol use. Inclusion of a universal, school-based prevention curriculum in the larger community-based effort is associated with the reduction of alcohol use by youth younger than 18 years of age and can help reach large numbers of youth with effective alcohol misuse prevention.

Research has identified multiple risk factors that increase the likelihood of alcohol use among youth and young adults. These conditions or experiences include individual characteristics (e.g., displaying aggression at a young age or believing that alcohol use is not harmful), peer influences (e.g., having friends who use alcohol or who believe that alcohol use is acceptable), family experiences (e.g., heavy alcohol use by parents or siblings, or inadequate parental supervision), school factors (e.g., academic failure, or having a low commitment to school or education), and neighborhood experiences (e.g., availability of alcohol to youth, or community norms that are permissive of youth alcohol use) (Durlak 1998; Hawkins et al. 1992; Pentz 1998). Protective or promotive factors that ameliorate the negative influences of risk factors or directly reduce the likelihood of alcohol use among young people also exist in all areas of people's lives. They include, for example,

being attached to others who do not abuse alcohol, having a resilient temperament, or holding clear standards against the use of alcohol before one is of legal age (Pollard et al. 1999; Werner 1993).

Prevention efforts aimed at reducing rates of alcohol use typically do so by seeking to minimize the target population's exposure to harmful risk factors and/or enhance protective/promotive factors (Coie et al. 1993; Munoz et al. 1996). Focusing prevention efforts on youth offers particularly great potential, because the early onset of drinking has been associated with an increased likelihood of alcohol dependence later in life (Hingson et al. 2006). Although many prevention efforts have been found to reduce tobacco, alcohol, and other drug use (Hawkins et al. 1995; National Research Council and Institute of Medicine 2009; Spoth et al. 2008), these strategies often are limited by addressing risk and protective factors in just one socialization domain. Thus, most of these efforts focus only on the most direct (i.e., proximal) causes of alcohol use, such as the availability of alcohol or peer or family influences, rather than targeting the complex contexts in which youth and young adults live. This narrow focus may reduce the overall impact and long-term effectiveness of alcohol-abuse prevention strategies, both because multiple factors affect alcohol use and because the effectiveness of any intervention likely is compromised if the environment in which people live is unfavorable to or does not support intervention goals and activities (Flay 2000; Wagenaar and Perry 1994).

One at least equally promising strategy for affecting rates of alcohol use, abuse, and dependence (not just among youth and young adults) centers on community-based efforts. Such approaches rely on multiple strategies intended to change a variety of factors that place individuals at risk for engaging in alcohol misuse (Pentz 1998; Wandersman and Florin 2003). Most of these efforts seek to alter not only proximal influences, but also the long-term, structural, and environmental influences associated with alcohol abuse and dependence, which increases their potential to make a significant and long-lasting impact (Wagenaar et al. 1994). By saturating the environment with prevention strategies and messages, community-based efforts aim to reach many individuals, which may allow them to achieve population-level reductions in alcohol misuse.

Another potential advantage of community-based strategies is their reliance on members of the local community to plan, implement, and monitor prevention activities, usually via coalitions made up of stakeholders from diverse organizations and backgrounds. By actively involving the community in the prevention effort, these approaches may enhance community buy-in for prevention activities and may help to ensure that services are a good fit with local needs, resources, and norms (Hawkins et al. 2002; Stevenson and Mitchell, 2003; Wandersman et al. 2003; Woolf 2008). The levels of risk and protective/promotive factors vary across communities, and measures most needed in one community to reduce youth alcohol use may not be needed in another community (Hawkins et al. 2002; Reiss and Price 1996). Thus, prevention efforts that are based upon assessing local needs (i.e., risk and protective/promotive factors faced by those in the community) and implementing prevention strategies that are best suited to address these needs may be more effective than implementing a single prevention program across many communities. Community mobilization also may allow for effective pooling of information and resources across agencies and individuals, minimizing duplication of services, and potentially offering more cost-effective services that can be implemented better and are more likely to be sustained.

After defining what exactly community mobilization implies, this article explores what community-based strategies work to reduce alcohol use and misuse among youth and the role of school-based interventions in the context of community-level efforts. Finally, the article looks at the challenges associated with the successful implementation of community-based programs to prevent youth alcohol use.

What Is Community Mobilization to Prevent Alcohol Misuse?

Existing community-based alcohol abuse prevention efforts are tailored to local circumstances, which makes it difficult to identify the specific components that define this type of approach. Nonetheless, community mobilization efforts have in common the goal of reducing alcohol misuse by changing the larger environment, using approaches that are owned and operated by the local community (Wandersman et al. 2003). Most programs rely on coalitions of community stakeholders to collaboratively plan and coordinate prevention activities. In some cases, coalitions focus on implementing, in a coordinated fashion, multiple, discrete prevention programs and practices that seek to decrease elevated risk factors and enhance depressed protective/promotive factors related to alcohol use (Hawkins et al. 2002). Other efforts specifically focus on transforming the environment via changes in local ordinances, norms, and policies related to alcohol. These latter efforts target a more limited number of risk factors, particularly community norms and laws related to alcohol use, the availability of alcohol, and individual attitudes favorable to alcohol use (Pentz 2000). Some community-based efforts rely on a combination of these strategies.

What Community-Based Strategies Work to Reduce Alcohol Misuse Among Youth?

The findings presented in this article are based upon a comprehensive review of evaluations conducted in the United States that involved the implementation of a substantial, community-based prevention initiative aimed at reducing alcohol and other drug (AOD) use among minors (i.e., adolescents and young adults age 20 or younger). Projects were included in the review if they met the following criteria:

- They were evaluated using a well-conducted quasi-experimental or true experimental design that involved, at a minimum, one intervention group (implementing the strategy) and one comparison group.
- Data on alcohol use outcomes were collected at least twice during the research project (e.g., before and after the intervention was conducted).
- There were no significant threats to the validity and reliability of the study, as determined by the first two authors of this review.

Although many studies were reviewed, only nine community-based initiatives demonstrated reduced rates of alcohol use or alcohol availability among youth and young adults according to the above criteria (see the table). It is notable that several of these strategies affected not only alcohol use but also the use of tobacco and, in some cases, other illicit drugs. The table briefly describes each program, the population in which the intervention was evaluated, and the program's significant effects in reducing AOD use.

The findings allow the following conclusions. First, a common feature of successful community-based prevention approaches is reliance on local coalitions to select effective preventive interventions and implement them with fidelity. Second, the inclusion of a universal, school-based drug prevention curriculum as part of the larger community initiative is associated with reductions in alcohol use among middle- and high-school students. Third, environmental strategies focused on changing local laws, norms, and policies related to alcohol access and use do not appear to reduce alcohol use among adolescents younger than age 18 when implemented independently of other community-based strategies. However, they have been part of successful multicomponent interventions and, when implemented on their own, have reduced the availability of alcohol in communities and lowered the rate of drunk-driving arrests among young adults.

Reliance on Community Coalitions

All of the community-based initiatives listed in the table relied on local coalitions to plan and implement prevention activities. This observation indicates that to be successful, community efforts must ensure the presence of active, broad-based groups of

Table Community Mobilization Strategies with Evidence of Effectiveness in Reducing the Use and/or Availability of Alcohol for Minors

Study	Description	Study Population	Significant Effects
Kentucky Incentives for Prevention (Collins et al. 2007)	Coalition-based prevention strategy targeting risk and protective factors related to drug use with effective programs conducted in schools and other community agencies	19 coalitions in Kentucky; 25,032 students in grades 8 and 10	Reduced smoking, drinking, and binge drinking among 10th graders
Communities That Care (CTC) (Hawkins et al. 2009)	Coalition-based prevention strategy targeting elevated risk and depressed protective factors related to drug use with effective programs conducted in schools and other community agencies for peer review	24 communities in 7 states; 4,407 students in grade 5	Reduced the initiation of smokeless tobacco, smoking, and alcohol Reduced past-month use of smokeless tobacco, alcohol, and binge drinking
Midwestern Prevention Project (Pentz et al. 1989)	Combines coalition-led community mobilization strategies with the implementation of school-based prevention curricula	42 schools in Kansas City; 5,065 students in grades 6 and 7	Reduced past-month smoking and drinking
Project SixTeen (Biglan et al. 2000)	Combines coalition-led community mobilization strategies with the implementation of school-based prevention curricula	16 communities in Oregon; 4,438 students in grades 7 and 9	Reduced smoking, drinking, and marijuana use
Project Northland (Perry et al. 2002)	Combines coalition-led community mobilization strategies with the implementation of school-based prevention curricula	24 school districts in Minnesota; 2,953 students in grade 6	Reduced binge drinking and alcohol sales to minors
Native American Project (Schinke et al. 2000)	Combines coalition-led community mobilization strategies with the implementation of school-based prevention curricula	27 tribal and public schools in the Midwest; 1,396 students in grades 3–5	Reduced smokeless tobacco, alcohol, and marijuana use
DARE Plus (Perry, Komro, Veblen-Mortenson et al. 2003)	Combines coalition-led community mobilization strategies with the implementation of school-based prevention curricula	24 schools in Minnesota; 7,261 students in grade 7	Reduced past-year and past-month smoking and drinking for boys and having ever been drunk for girls
Communities Mobilizing for Change on Alcohol (Wagenaar et al. 2000a, b)	Coalition-led activities seeking changes to community policies, practices, and norms related to alcohol use	15 school districts in Minnesota and Wisconsin; 4,506 students in grade 12, and 3,095 18- to 20-year-olds	Reduced the provision of alcohol to minors and arrests for drunk driving reported by 18- to 20-year-olds
Community Trials Project (Grube 1997; Holder et al. 2000)	Coalition-led activities seeking changes to community policies, practices, and norms related to alcohol use	6 communities in California and South Carolina	Reduced heavy drinking among adults, alcohol sales to minors, and alcohol-related car crashes

individuals who believe it is possible to prevent youth AOD use and who are willing to engage in collaborative prevention activities. Although coalitions vary in their structures, sizes, goals, and activities, a defining feature of such groups is their focus on facilitating desired changes through collaborative action. Although the specific members of a coalition may vary depending on the focus of the group, coalitions usually seek to be broad based and to unite diverse stakeholders and key leaders from key agencies and sectors of the community. For example, coalitions focused on preventing alcohol use by youth may include representatives from law enforcement, local government, schools, health and human service agencies, youth service groups, business, religious groups, youth, and parents. The coalitions typically are formed around a common vision that inspires and motivates their actions. By working together to bring about change, they allow intervention approaches to be tailored to local needs, as identified by coalition members. They also increase political alliances, foster communication among community members, and coordinate human and financial resources (Hawkins et al. 2002; Pentz 2000; Wandersman et al. 2003).

Although coalitions are a common element of effective community-based prevention, not all coalition efforts have produced significant changes in alcohol use. Some coalition initiatives have failed to reduce rates of AOD use among youth and adolescents, even when they were well funded and members were well intentioned and willing to make changes. Evaluations of two coalition efforts—the Fighting Back (Hallfors and Godette 2002) and Community Partnership (Yin et al. 1997) initiatives—found that both failed to bring about changes in youth AOD use. The evaluations indicated that the coalitions involved in these projects had insufficient guidance in how to enact prevention strategies, varied widely in the nature and amount of prevention services provided, and largely relied on locally created prevention strategies that likely had not been previously evaluated for effectiveness in reducing AOD use. These studies suggest that the mere presence of an active, well-intentioned coalition is not enough to prevent AOD use. In other words, simply gathering local stakeholders and asking them to collaborate to do their best to solve local drug problems or prevent underage drinking does not produce desired changes.

Instead, the evidence suggests that in order to be successful, coalitions must ensure the following (Hallfors et al. 2002):

- They must have clearly defined, focused, and manageable goals;
- They must have adequate planning time;
- Prevention decisions must be based on empirical data about what needs to change in the community and on evidence from scientifically valid studies of what has worked to address those needs;
- They must implement prevention policies, practices, and programs that have been tested and shown to be effective; and
- They must carefully monitor prevention activities to ensure implementation quality.

One prevention system that exemplifies these principles is Communities That Care (CTC), which has been found to reduce the initiation and prevalence of youth alcohol use community-wide (Feinberg et al. 2007; Hawkins et al. 2009). CTC provides proactive training and technical assistance to community coalitions to ensure that they select and implement prevention strategies that previously have been demonstrated to be effective in reducing youth AOD use. The CTC model involves a structured and guided intervention process involving five phases in which coalitions (1) assess community readiness to undertake collaborative prevention efforts, (2) form a diverse and representative prevention coalition, (3) use epidemiologic data to assess prevention needs, (4) select evidence-based prevention policies and programs that target these needs, and (5) implement the new policies and programs with monitoring to ensure fidelity and evaluation to ensure that goals are being met. The coalitions are structured, ideally with a chair person, cochairs, and workgroups; employ at least a half-time coordinator; and are broad based. The prevention activities chosen and implemented can take place in a variety of settings and may target individual, family, school, peer, and/or community risk and protective/promotive factors related to youth AOD use. They are selected by the community coalitions from a menu of options that only includes policies and programs that have been shown in at least

one study using a high-quality research design to significantly change risk and protective factors and reduce rates of AOD use (Hawkins and Catalano 1992; Hawkins et al. 2002).

Several evaluations of the CTC coalition model have been conducted, including a randomized trial involving 24 communities in 7 states that were randomly assigned to either implement the CTC system (n = 12) or serve as control communities (n = 12) (Hawkins et al. 2008). The intervention sites received training in the CTC model, proactive and intensive technical assistance, and funding for 5 years to plan and implement their chosen prevention strategies. This study found that after 4 years of the intervention, students in the CTC communities had lower rates of AOD use compared with students in control communities. They were less likely to initiate cigarette, alcohol, and smokeless tobacco use as well as delinquent behavior by the eighth grade. In addition, eighth-grade students in the intervention communities reported significantly lower rates of drinking, binge drinking, and smokeless tobacco use in the past month, as well as delinquent behavior in the past year, compared with students in the control communities (Hawkins et al. 2009).

These results indicate that when local community coalitions are provided with proactive training and technical assistance, have clear goals and guidelines, and ensure effective implementation of prevention strategies that have prior evidence of effectiveness, they have the potential to significantly reduce alcohol and tobacco use as well as delinquent behavior community-wide. Moreover, the findings indicate that coalitions may enact a variety of prevention policies and programs targeting a range of different risk and protective factors and still be successful, as long as their efforts focus on using methods that have been demonstrated to be effective and ensure that prevention activities are carefully implemented, monitored, and coordinated.

Inclusion of School-Based Curricula in Community-Based Efforts

Implementation of universal, school-based drug prevention curricula as part of the larger community effort appears to predict reduced rates of AOD use among middle- and high-school students. All of the initiatives listed in the table that were effective in preventing or reducing alcohol use among those younger than age 18 involved the implementation of a school-based curriculum. Although neither the CTC prevention system nor the Kentucky Incentives for Prevention initiative (Collins et al. 2007) requires the use of school-based curricula, all of the coalitions involved in the randomized CTC evaluation (Hawkins et al. 2009), and all but one of the 19 coalitions evaluated in Kentucky, implemented a school curriculum to target particular risk factors whose influence in the community was considered too high or protective factors whose influence was considered too low by local coalitions.

The other community-based prevention initiatives listed in the table that reduced alcohol use among those younger than age 18 involved implementation of a particular school curriculum offered to students in conjunction with coalition-led efforts to change community-level risk factors related to drug use. The latter efforts typically attempted to change community norms and local ordinances related to alcohol use and availability. An evaluation of the Project Northland Program in Minnesota (Perry et al. 2002), for example, demonstrated reduced rates of alcohol use in communities that implemented a multiyear school curriculum and modified local policies and practices associated with youth alcohol use. The school program focused on altering student views regarding the acceptability of alcohol use, improving student skills in refusing drug offers, and fostering parent/child communication about alcohol use through homework assignments and information mailed to parents. Environmentally focused strategies included increased identification checks by retail liquor establishments and legal consequences for selling alcohol to minors. The evaluation of Project Northland found that after receiving services in both middle and high school, students in the intervention communities had lower rates of binge drinking (i.e., drinking five or more alcoholic beverages on one occasion) compared with students in control communities. In addition, retail establishments were less likely to sell alcohol to minors in intervention than in control communities (Perry et al. 2002).

A similar combination of activities was advocated in the Midwestern Prevention Project (MPP). This program involved the implementation of a 2-year middle-school curriculum to promote students' drug resistance skills, along with parent education, media campaigns to reinforce antidrug messages throughout the community, and local policy changes to reduce demand and supply of drugs. When implemented in schools in Kansas City, the MPP demonstrated reductions in past-month smoking and alcohol use for students receiving the intervention compared with students in control schools (Pentz et al. 1989).

In Project SixTeen, small communities in Oregon implemented a five-session, school-based program aimed at reducing youth tobacco use, along with media campaigns and responsible beverage training for alcohol retail outlets. The evaluation showed a significant reduction in past-week smoking and marijuana use for seventh- and ninth-grade students in intervention communities compared with control communities; similarly, alcohol use was reduced among ninth graders (Biglan et al. 2000).

These studies indicate that the inclusion of school-based prevention programs in comprehensive, coalition-led, community-based initiatives can contribute to reductions in alcohol use among adolescents. Currently, most schools in the United States provide some type of drug-prevention programming to students. However, not all school districts implement strategies that have evidence of effectiveness, even though the Safe and Drug-Free School (SDFS) legislation mandates the use of effective substance-use prevention curricula. Inclusion of school-based programs in larger community prevention initiatives provides multiple advantages, including the ability to reach a large proportion of the youth population and thus increase the potential of achieving community-level changes in desired outcomes. Community coalitions can help school districts fulfill the SDFS mandate by helping them identify and adopt effective strategies and by helping to ensure that the new programs are well suited to addressing the needs of local students. In addition, coalitions can partner with schools to find the needed resources to initiate and sustain new effective prevention strategies and can help oversee the implementation of new strategies to ensure quality. To promote successful partnerships, coalitions should ensure that

school personnel, including administrators (e.g., superintendents and principals) and staff (e.g., teachers and counselors), are actively involved in the decisionmaking process and prevention efforts from the beginning of the initiative (Fagan et al. 2009).

Targeting Environmental Risk Factors for Substance Use

The initiatives just described combined the implementation of school curricula with community mobilization efforts that target environmental risk factors in order to reduce the availability of and demand for alcohol. Such efforts include changes in community-level policies, practices, and norms, such as increasing alcohol pricing, creating drug-free zones, limiting alcohol sales in venues easily accessible to youth, requiring keg registrations, and increasing the use or severity of community laws related to alcohol use by minors or adults (Pentz 2000; Wagenaar et al. 1994). Changes in community practices also may involve responsible beverage service training—that is, educating merchants about the negative consequences of providing alcohol to minors or serving intoxicated patrons, encouraging identification checks, and ensuring that merchants who violate rules are appropriately sanctioned (Holder 2000). Media campaigns may also be used in conjunction with these activities to educate the public about the negative effects of alcohol use, increase support for drug prevention, and counter norms favorable to alcohol use. Such media campaigns increase public awareness by saturating the community with print, radio, and television advertisements; mailing informational fliers to businesses or homes; or holding community forums to discuss alcohol-use issues.

Evidence is mixed regarding the effectiveness of these types of environmentally focused prevention strategies. As discussed in the previous section, when offered in conjunction with school-based prevention curricula, these prevention strategies seem to be effective in reducing rates of adolescent alcohol use. However, efforts that focus exclusively on changing environmental risk factors at the local level, without also targeting more proximal risk factors related to alcohol use, have not been associated with reductions in alcohol use among youth under age 18. An evaluation of Communities Mobilizing for Change on Alcohol (CMCA) found no statistically significant changes (i.e., $p < .05$ using two-tailed test of significance) in alcohol or drug use among 12th-grade students or 18- to 20-year-olds in communities implementing CMCA compared with those in control communities (Wagenaar et al. 2000b). In this project, community coalitions coordinated a variety of activities aimed at limiting alcohol sales to minors, increasing enforcement of underage drinking laws, and changing alcohol policies at community events, as well as increasing public attention about problems associated with underage drinking. Although rates of alcohol use by youth were not significantly changed by the intervention, the evaluation did show that 18- to 20-year-olds from intervention sites were significantly less likely to provide alcohol to minors (Wagenaar et al. 2000a, b).

The Community Trials Project used similar environmentally focused prevention strategies to reduce alcohol use and related risky behaviors. A quasi-experimental evaluation of this program in six communities indicated significantly fewer alcohol-related automobile crashes in intervention communities than in control communities (Holder et al. 2000). Among adults (those age 18 or older), a greater proportion of those in communities implementing the program reported having one or more drinks in the past year versus those in comparison communities. However, among those who reported any drinking, adults in intervention sites had lower rates of self-reported heavy drinking and drunk driving (Holder et al. 2000). Although there were fewer sales to minors by alcohol sales establishments in intervention versus comparison sites (Grube 1997), none of the evaluations of the Community Trials Project have found significant reductions in drinking among youth under age 18 in intervention versus comparison sites.

The available evidence indicates that these types of community-based, environmentally focused strategies are effective in reducing alcohol use among those under age 18 only when offered in conjunction with effective school curricula. However, few evaluations have been conducted of community-based prevention efforts that rely solely on changing community policies, practices, and norms, and more research is needed to assess the impact of environmental strategies when used independently and when combined with other types of prevention strategies.

Challenges Associated With Community Mobilization Efforts

There is much public support for community mobilization efforts that seek to reduce substance use, particularly by youth and young adults, and many communities have coalitions in place to coordinate local prevention strategies. However, implementing, evaluating, and sustaining such efforts can be challenging. For example, it often is difficult to recruit, engage, and ensure collaboration among community members from diverse backgrounds who may have different skills, needs, resources, and ideas about what is needed to prevent AOD use (Merzel and D'Afflitti 2003; Quinby et al. 2008; Stith et al. 2006). Furthermore, compared with single prevention programs, community-level strategies likely are costlier to implement and evaluate because they entail more components and require longer-term interventions to achieve community-wide outcomes (Merzel et al. 2003). It also can be difficult to define community boundaries, gain support for participation in a research study from key leaders and stakeholders, and measure processes and outcomes that may vary across communities (Stith et al. 2006; Wandersman et al. 2003). Finally, community-based prevention strategies are intended to be owned and operated by the community, which can create tension between local practitioners and scientists who may differ in their ideas about what is most needed to prevent alcohol misuse (Holder et al. 1997; Hyndman et al. 1992; Merzel et al. 2003).

The many challenges related to the implementation of community-based prevention efforts likely are responsible for the relatively small number of interventions that have demonstrated evidence of success (see the table). In addition, evaluations of some community prevention programs have failed to demonstrate significant effects on alcohol use, sometimes because of problems related to program implementation and intensity. For example, the initial evaluation of Project Northland in Minnesota indicated that the original 3-year intervention, which was implemented in middle schools, was insufficient to lead to sustained effects on alcohol use. Therefore, additional services were added in high schools, which reduced rates of alcohol use through grade 12 (Perry et al. 2002). A replication of this extended program in Chicago, Illinois, however, failed to produce positive effects, which led the evaluators to recommend that in lower-income, urban populations, where problems other than youth alcohol use (e.g., gangs, violence, and housing) may take precedence, longer-term and more intense community-based strategies may be needed to bring about change (Komro et al. 2008).

The Project Northland replication in Chicago and other evaluations have noted that implementation challenges, such as difficulties in engaging community members in the initiative and challenges in moving from planning to action, may compromise the ability of community-based efforts to produce significant effects. On the other hand, evaluations of the CTC prevention system have shown that communities can successfully mobilize volunteers, create high-functioning and goal-driven coalitions, and ensure high-quality implementation of prevention strategies that target salient risk and protective factors (Quinby et al. 2008). One factor that increases the likelihood of success is the provision of proactive and high-quality training and technical assistance from system developers to the community coalitions (Feinberg et al. 2008). In the absence of such training and technical assistance, common implementation challenges are likely to threaten implementation and the likelihood of realizing desired reductions in youth alcohol use.

Research also has indicated that communities that rely on prevention-focused coalitions, as in the CTC model, can successfully sustain the implementation of tested and effective programs, despite the human and financial costs associated with these efforts. An evaluation of 110 CTC coalitions in Pennsylvania (Feinberg et al. 2008) indicated that nearly all coalitions (91 percent), which still were operating after the State discontinued funding for CTC activities, continued to implement effective programs. In fact, on average, the coalitions were able to fund their program and coalition activities at levels exceeding those initially provided by the State. Funding success was positively associated with having a well-functioning coalition, adhering to the CTC model, and planning for sustainability. These findings reinforce the importance of utilizing broad-based coalitions to plan, implement, and sustain prevention activities in communities.

Identifying the cost-effectiveness of community-based prevention initiatives also is important. Although the review presented here identified nine community-based strategies with evidence of effectiveness in reducing alcohol use and availability among minors, only two of these interventions have been rigorously evaluated for cost-effectiveness. In both cases, the analyses demonstrated fiscal savings. According to the Washington State Institute for Public Policy (Aos et al. 2004), every dollar spent on Project Northland in Minnesota resulted in savings of $2.45 in later treatment, morbidity, mortality, and criminal justice costs; similarly, the MPP produced savings of $1.27 per dollar spent. Because cost is a major factor influencing community decisions to adopt new programs, information on financial benefits may help to increase the dissemination of community-based prevention strategies, their long-term sustainability, and ultimately their potential to substantially reduce rates of alcohol use among young people.

In summary, this review clearly has shown that community-based efforts can reduce alcohol use and misuse among youth. A common feature of successful community strategies is reliance on local coalitions to select and fully implement preventive interventions that have prior evidence of effectiveness in changing risk and protective or promotive factors related to alcohol use. Inclusion of a universal, school-based prevention curriculum in the larger community-based effort is associated with lower rates of drinking, binge drinking, and other drug use by those younger than 18. Focusing community-based prevention efforts on youth offers particularly great potential, because it not only lowers rates of alcohol use among minors but also reduces the likelihood of alcohol misuse and dependence later in life (Hingson et al. 2006).

References

Aos, S.; Lieb, R.; Mayfield, J.; et al. Benefits and Costs of Prevention and Early Intervention Programs for Youth. Olympia, WA: Washington State Institute for Public Policy, 2004.

Biglan, A.; Ary, D.V.; Smolkowski, K.; et al. A randomised controlled trial of a community intervention to prevent adolescent tobacco use. Tobacco Control 9:24–32, 2000. PMID: 10691755

Coie, J.D.; Watt, N.F.; West, S.G.; et al. The science of prevention: A conceptual framework and some directions for a national research program. American Psychologist 48:1013–1022, 1993. PMID: 8256874

Collins, D.; Johnson, K.; and Becker, B.J. A meta-analysis of direct and mediating effects of community coalitions that implemented science-based substance abuse prevention interventions. Substance Use and Misuse 42:985–1007, 2007. PMID: 17613959

Durlak, J.A. Common risk and protective factors in successful prevention programs. American Journal of Orthopsychiatry 68:512–520, 1998. PMID: 9809111

Fagan, A.A.; Brooke-Weiss, B.; Cady, R.; and Hawkins, J.D. If at first you don't succeed . . . keep trying: Strategies to enhance coalition/school partnerships to implement school-based prevention programming. Australian & New Zealand Journal of Criminology 42:387–405, 2009. PMID: 20582326

Feinberg, M.E.; Bontempo, D.E.; and Greenberg, M.T. Predictors and level of sustainability of community prevention coalitions. American Journal of Preventive Medicine 34:495–501, 2008. PMID: 18471585

Feinberg, M.E.; Greenberg, M.T.; Osgood, D.W.; et al. Effects of the Communities That Care model in Pennsylvania on youth risk and problem behaviors. Prevention Science 8:261–270, 2007. PMID: 17713856

Feinberg, M.E.; Ridenour, T.A.; and Greenberg, M.T. The longitudinal effect of technical assistance dosage on the functioning of Communities That Care prevention boards in Pennsylvania. Journal of Primary Prevention 29:145–165, 2008. PMID: 18365313

Flay, B.R. Approaches to substance use prevention utilizing school curriculum plus social environment change. Addictive Behaviors 25:861–885, 2000. PMID: 11125776

Grube, J.W. Preventing sales of alcohol to minors: Results from a community trial. Addiction 92(Suppl):S251–S260, 1997. PMID: 9231448

Hallfors, D., and Godette, D. Will the "principles of effectiveness" improve prevention practice? Early findings from a diffusion study. Health Education Research 17:461–470, 2002.

Hallfors, D.; Cho, H.; Livert, D.; and Kadushin, C. Fighting back against substance use: Are community coalitions winning? American Journal of Preventive Medicine 23:237–245, 2002. PMID: 12406477

Hawkins, J.D., and Catalano, R.F. Communities That Care: Action for Drug Abuse Prevention. San Francisco, CA: Jossey-Bass, 1992.

Hawkins, J.D.; Arthur, M.W.; and Catalano, R.F. Preventing substance abuse. In: Tonry, M., and Farrington, D.P. (Eds.) Crime and Justice: A Review of Research. Building a Safer Society: Strategic Approaches to Crime Prevention. Volume 19. Chicago, IL: University of Chicago Press, 1995, pp. 343–427.

Hawkins, J.D.; Catalano, R.F.; and Arthur, M.W. Promoting science-based prevention in communities. Addictive Behaviors 27: 951–976, 2002. PMID: 12369478

Hawkins, J.D.; Catalano, R.F.; Arthur, M.W.; et al. Testing Communities That Care: The rationale, design and behavioral baseline equivalence of the Community Youth Development Study. Prevention Science 9:178–190, 2008. PMID: 18516681

Hawkins, J.D.; Catalano, R.F.; and Miller, J.Y. Risk and protective factors for alcohol and other drug problems in adolescence and early adulthood: Implications for substance abuse prevention. Psychological Bulletin 112:64–105, 1992. PMID : 1529040

Hawkins, J.D.; Oesterle, S.; Brown, E.C.; et al. Results of a type 2 translational research trial to prevent adolescent drug use and delinquency: A test of Communities That Care. Archives of Pediatrics & Adolescent Medicine 163:789–798, 2009. PMID: 19736331

Hingson, R.W.; Heeren, T.; and Winter, M.R. Age at drinking onset and alcohol dependence: Age at onset, duration, and severity. Archives of Pediatrics & Adolescent Medicine 160:739–746, 2006. PMID: 16818840

Holder, H.D. Community prevention of alcohol problems. Addictive Behaviors 25:843–859, 2000. PMID: 11125775

Holder, H.D.; Gruenewald, P.J.; Ponicki, W.R.; et al. Effect of community-based interventions on high-risk drinking and alcohol-related injuries. JAMA: Journal of the American Medical Association 284:2341–2347, 2000. PMID: 11066184

Holder, H.D.; Saltz, R.F.; Grube, J.W.; et al. Summing up: Lessons from a comprehensive community prevention trial. Addiction 92(Suppl 2):S293–S301, 1997. PMID: 9231452

Hyndman, B.; Giesbrecht, N.; Bernardi, D.R.; et al. Preventing substance abuse through multicomponent community action research projects: Lessons learned from past experiences and challenges for future initiatives. Contemporary Drug Problems 19:133–164, 1992.

Komro, K.A.; Perry, C.L.; Veblen-Mortenson, S.; et al. Outcomes from a randomized controlled trial of a multi-component alcohol use preventive intervention for urban youth: Project Northland Chicago. Addiction 103:606–618, 2008. PMID: 18261193

Merzel, C., and D'Afflitti, J. Reconsidering community-based health promotion: Promise, performance, and potential. American Journal of Public Health 93:557–574, 2003. PMID: 12660197

Munoz, R.F.; Mrazek, P.J.; and Haggerty, R.J. Institute of Medicine report on prevention of mental disorders: Summary and commentary. American Psychologist 51:1116–1122, 1996. PMID: 8937259

National Research Council and Institute of Medicine. Preventing Mental, Emotional, and Behavioral Disorders Among Young People: Progress and Possibilities. Committee on the Prevention of Mental Disorders and Substance Abuse Among Children, Youth, and Young Adults: Research Advances and Promising Interventions. Washington, DC: Board on Children, Youth, and Families, Division of Behavioral and Social Sciences and Education, National Academies Press, 2009.

Pentz, M.A. Preventing drug abuse through the community: Multicomponent programs make the difference. In: Sloboda, Z., and Hansen, W.B. (Eds.) Putting Research to Work for the Community. NIDA Research Monograph. Rockville, MD: National Institute on Drug Abuse, 1998, pp. 73–86.

Pentz, M.A. Institutionalizing community-based prevention through policy change. Journal of Community Psychology 28:257–270, 2000.

Pentz, M.A.; Dwyer, J.H.; MacKinnon, D.P.; et al. A multicommunity trial for primary prevention of adolescent drug abuse: Effects on drug use prevalence. JAMA: Journal of the American Medical Association 261:3259–3266, 1989. PMID: 2785610

Perry, C.L.; Komro, K.; Veblen-Mortenson, S.; et al. A randomized controlled trial of the middle and junior high school D.A.R.E. and D.A.R.E. Plus programs. Archives of Pediatrics & Adolescent Medicine 157:178–184, 2003. PMID: 12580689

Perry, C.L.; Williams, C.L.; Komro, K.A.; et al. Project Northland: Long-term outcomes of community action to reduce adolescent alcohol use. Health Education Research 17:117–132, 2002. PMID: 11888042

Pollard, J.A.; Hawkins, J.D.; and Arthur, M.W. Risk and protection: Are both necessary to understand diverse behavioral outcomes in adolescence? Social Work Research 23:145–158, 1999.

Quinby, R.; Fagan, A.A.; Hanson, K.; et al. Installing the Communities That Care prevention system: Implementation progress and fidelity in a randomized controlled trial. Journal of Community Psychology 36:313–332, 2008.

Reiss, D., and Price, R.H. National research agenda for prevention research: The National Institute of Mental Health report. American Psychologist 51:1109–1115, 1996. PMID: 8937258

Schinke, S.P.; Tepavac, L.; and Cole, K.C. Preventing substance use among Native American youth: Three-year results. Addictive Behaviors 25:387–397, 2000. PMID: 10890292

Spoth, R.L.; Greenberg, M.T.; and Turrisi, R. Preventive interventions addressing underage drinking: State of the evidence and steps towards public health impact. Pediatrics 121(Suppl 4):S311–S336, 2008. PMID: 18381496

Stevenson, J.F., and Mitchell, R.E. Community-level collaboration for substance abuse prevention. Journal of Primary Prevention 23:371–404, 2003.

Stith, S.; Pruitt, I.; Dees, J.E.; et al. Implementing community-based prevention programming: A review of the literature. Journal of Primary Prevention 27:599–617, 2006. PMID: 17051431

Wagenaar, A.C., and Perry, C.L. Community strategies for the reduction of youth drinking: Theory and application. Journal of Research on Adolescence 4:319–345, 1994

Wagenaar, A.C.; Murray, D.M.; and Toomey, T.L. Communities Mobilizing for Change on Alcohol (CMCA): Effects of a randomized trial on arrests and traffic crashes. Addiction 95:209–217, 2000a. PMID: 10723849

Wagenaar, A.C.; Murray, D.M.; Gehan, J.P.; et al. Communities Mobilizing for Change on Alcohol: Outcomes from a randomized community trial. Journal of Studies on Alcohol 61:85–94, 2000b. PMID: 10627101

Wandersman, A., and Florin, P. Community intervention and effective prevention. American Psychologist 58:441–448, 2003. PMID: 12971190

Werner, E.E. Risk, resilience, and recovery: Perspectives from the Kauai longitudinal study. Development and Psychopathology 5:503–515, 1993.

Woolf, S.H. The power of prevention and what it requires. JAMA: Journal of the American Medical Association 299:2437–2439, 2008. PMID: 18505953

Yin, R.K.; Kaftarian, S.J.; Yu, P.; and Jansen, M.A. Outcomes from CSAP's Community Partnership Program: Findings from the national cross-site evaluation. Evaluation and Program Planning 20:345–355, 1997.

Critical Thinking

1. Describe one common feature in successful community strategies that address substance abuse.

2. Discuss the most salient risk factors for adolescent alcohol abuse.

3. Analyze what works for prevention of adolescent alcohol abuse.

Create Central

www.mhhe.com/createcentral

Internet References

SAMHSA
www.samhsa.gov/underagedrinking

Stop Alcohol Abuse
www.stopalcoholabuse.gov/prevention.aspx

ABIGAIL A. FAGAN, PHD, is an assistant professor in the Department of Criminology and Criminal Justice, University of South Carolina, Columbia, South Carolina. **J. DAVID HAWKINS, PHD,** is Endowed Professor of Prevention, and **RICHARD F. CATALANO, PHD,** is Bartley Dobb Professor for the Study and Prevention of Violence and director of the Social Development Research Group, School of Social Work, University of Washington, Seattle, Washington.

Acknowledgments—This work was supported by a research grant from the National Institute on Drug Abuse (R01 DA015183–03), with co-funding from the National Cancer Institute, the National Institute of Child Health and Human Development, the National Institute of Mental Health, the Center for Substance Abuse Prevention, and the National Institute on Alcohol Abuse and Alcoholism. The content of this paper is solely the responsibility of the authors and does not necessarily represent the official views of the funding agencies.

Financial Disclosure—The authors declare that they have no competing financial interests.

Article

Prepared by: Mary Maguire, *California State University—Sacramento*
Clifford Garoupa, *Fresno City College*

Do No Harm

Sensible Goals for International Drug Policy

PETER REUTER

Learning Outcomes

After reading this article, you will be able to:

- Discuss the need for an international drug policy.
- Discuss the barriers and competing stakeholders in the development of international drug policy.
- Identify and discuss at least one sensible international drug policy.

D rug policy has been an inconvenient issue for the national security apparatus of the United States, whether run by a Democratic or Republican administration. Even after 35 years of some sort of domestic "war on drugs", forcefully articulated by every President since Ronald Reagan, the international dimension of the issue remains distasteful to diplomats. It often involves dealing with law enforcement in corrupt countries and complicates many a U.S. Ambassador's life. The contending lobbies that care about it are loud, moralistic and well informed. If that were not enough, most of our principal allies, particularly in Europe, think there is a certain madness in the American belief that international interventions against the drug trade can accomplish much good.

Mere inconvenience is an insufficient reason to abandon a policy, of course, but in this case there are stronger arguments for change. The Obama Administration has an opportunity before it, for both history and argument show that U.S. international efforts to control drug production and trafficking cannot do much more than affect where and how coca and opium poppies are grown. The quantity produced is minimally affected, since suppression of production in one country almost invariably leads to expansion in another.

More important, control efforts often cause damage. Not only are such programs as spraying poppy and coca fields themselves harmful, but forcing the drug trade to move from one country to another may hurt the new producer country more than it helps the old one. Hence, the U.S. government should no longer push for "global containment", as the policy has been defined. Rather, it should focus attention and resources on supporting the few states both willing and able to do something about production or trafficking in their countries. Unfortunately, Afghanistan, the center of attention right now, is not one of those countries.

American Bull in the China Shop

The United States has been the principal driver of international drug control efforts since 1909, when it convened a meeting of the International Opium Commission (primarily aimed at helping China cut its opium consumption). The United States then pushed for the creation of a web of prohibitionist international treaties under the auspices first of the League of Nations and then the United Nations. Its voice is the dominant one at the annual meetings of the UN Commission on Narcotic Drugs. In that forum it has stood firm against any softening of existing policies. Most prominently, the United States has denounced in recent years "harm reduction" interventions such as needle-distribution programs aimed at reducing the spread of HIV.

Nor does it hesitate to scold even its closest neighbors for deviating from its hard-line, prohibitionist stance. In 2003, U.S. drug czar John Walters accused Canada of poisoning American youth when Ottawa proposed decriminalizing marijuana possession, a policy similar to that of a dozen U.S. states. The United States has even proven willing to barter specific foreign policy interests to influence other nations' drug policies. In the Clinton Administration senior State Department officials told Australia that trade negotiations would be dragged out if Canberra went ahead with a planned experiment in which the most troubled heroin addicts might be supplied with the drug (a program now routine in Switzerland and the Netherlands). Though not a lot of money (by the standards of the overall U.S. drug policy budget) is spent on overseas drug control, Plan Colombia ($5 billion since 2001) is by far the largest U.S. foreign assistance program in Latin America, making Colombia the fourth largest recipient of U.S. aid.

These interventions have real consequences for U.S. foreign policy. Tensions with NATO allies in Afghanistan have been exacerbated by disagreements over how aggressively to act against opium production. Plan Colombia, which funds the civil rights-abusing Colombian military, causes much unease among neighboring countries. From 1986 until 2001, relations with Mexico were roiled by Mexican indignation at the U.S. annual "certification", in which the world's largest drug consumer decided whether its neighbors had done enough to reduce its own importation of drugs.

What these policies and programs seem not to have done is to reduce either the American or the global drug problems. That is not the consequence of badly designed programs or administrative incompetence, though there are plenty of both. Rather, it is a result of the fact that international programs like eradication or interdiction simply cannot make much of a difference because they aim at the wrong part of the problem: production and trafficking in source countries. The right part of the problem to aim at is demand in importing countries, including our own. But, of course, that is a difficult and uncertain task, and even successful programs take a long time to have much effect.[1]

It would not be wise to close up shop altogether. After all, there are some connections between the illicit drug trade and terrorist financing that Americans would be foolish to ignore, and there may occasionally be promising opportunities to help specific countries. But we should adopt more limited, common sense goals for U.S. international drug policy.

Heroin and Cocaine

Today's mass market in illegal heroin is a new phenomenon. Before 1965, the drug was a niche product and one of declining popularity in the United States. Poppies were refined into opium and mostly consumed in Asia. However, between 1965 and 1995 heroin epidemics erupted in many rich industrialized countries from Australia to Norway. The loosening of social and economic controls in China in the late 1980s and the break-up of the Soviet Union in the early 1990s added a few more countries to the list of those with heroin problems. Iran, Pakistan, Thailand and other traditional opium producers also became heroin-consuming countries, partly as a consequence of Western pressures to crack down on opium distribution. Heroin use can't be found everywhere in the world these days, but it is certainly no longer just a niche problem. So serious is the challenge that there have even been times when the United States, Iran and Russia have quietly made common cause to deal with it.

While heroin use was spreading, heroin production became more concentrated. By the 1980s, Afghanistan and Burma had come to dominate production, accounting for more than 90 percent of the total each year. Since 2002, Afghanistan has been the dominant producer: In 2007, with a new record output, it produced roughly 93 percent of the world total, about 8,000 tons. (Before the Taliban banned opium production in 2000, production had only once exceeded 4,000 tons.)

Why do Afghanistan and Burma dominate? It's not because either is particularly well suited in terms of land or climate. Opium has been produced in many countries; Australia and France are two big producers for the contemporary legal market, while Thailand and Macedonia were major producers in the past. So what accounts for the current situation?

Afghanistan was not historically a large opium producer, but three major events combined to change that. The overthrow of the Shah in 1979 led to the installation of an Iranian regime much more concerned with drugs as a moral issue. The Islamic Republic promptly cracked down on opium production in Iran. Willing to execute producers and growers after only minimal due process, Iran quickly eliminated domestic opium poppy cultivation. However, it was much less successful in reducing demand, and the result was a new market for Afghan exports. This happened at roughly the same time that the Soviet Union invaded Afghanistan, which eroded central government authority and led to the rise of warlords for whom opium production was a major source of income. The civil war that broke out following the exit of the Soviet troops exacerbated the situation and made Afghanistan still more attractive for opium growing and heroin refining.

For Burma the shaping events took place over an even longer period. Those events relate partly to the political history of China. When the Communists took the Chinese Mainland in 1949, some Kuomintang army units retreated south into up-country Burma. Now forced to support themselves, they put their military and organization skills to work in the opium industry. Then, in the 1970s, the Burmese Communist Party, cut off from Chinese government finance as China attempted to improve relationships with its neighbors, turned to the heroin trade as a way to finance its activities. Thus Chinese anti-communists and Burmese communists alike helped raise Burma's heroin production profile—proof of how deeply the drug trade is embedded in larger geopolitical processes. Drug production cannot be treated as just another industry, responding primarily to economic influences. The Burmese and Afghan cases also illustrate how easily the location of production can shift. There are many corrupt and poor countries available for production if for some reason Afghanistan should cut its production.

Cocaine lacks the global reach of heroin; it's still mostly a rich nation's drug (though, of course, not mostly rich people in those nations use it). What seemed in the 1980s a uniquely American problem has now spread to Europe. Britain and Spain clearly have substantial cocaine problems and others are vulnerable as well. Eastern Europe is also catching up in heretofore Western vices as its productivity and politics approach Western levels.

The production story here is straightforward. Bolivia, Colombia and Peru are the only commercial producers of cocaine for the illegal market. Whereas in the 1980s Colombia was the third most important producer of coca leaves, for the past ten years it has accounted for about two thirds of the total, as well as the vast majority of refining. The shift of coca growing from Peru and Bolivia to Colombia is probably the result both of massive rural flight in Colombia and tougher policies in the other two countries. The violent conflict in Colombia's established rural areas has forced farmers to frontiers within the country where there is little infrastructure for legitimate agriculture, and coca growing is very attractive in part because these areas are difficult to monitor or police. Despite a massive eradication campaign, production levels for the Andes as a whole have been fairly stable over the past decade.

Ties to Terrorism

That U.S. policies over several decades now have not appreciably affected the overall level of heroin and cocaine on the market is a cause for some frustration. One reason it vexes U.S. policymakers is that illegal drugs are funding some terrorist organizations—though it would be counterproductive to exaggerate the extent of this funding. In 2003, the Office of National Drug Control Policy attracted considerable derision with its Super Bowl ads tying drug use to the promotion of international terrorism. Since most U.S. drug use is limited to marijuana, much of it produced domestically or in Canada, the connection seemed flimsy. The ads disappeared quickly.

That said, the problem is not imaginary. Before it banned opium production in 2000, the Taliban taxed it, though no more than it taxed other agricultural products. Since it didn't provide much in the way of government services, the estimated $30 million the Taliban got from opium taxes was the second largest source of revenue, after its taxation of consumer goods smuggled into Pakistan. Al-Qaeda's sources of revenue are a matter of mystery, at least in the unclassified literature, but it certainly has earned some money from trafficking opium or heroin over the years. Nowadays its involvement in protecting (i.e., taxing) opium production in Afghanistan may be an important activity. Secretary of Defense Robert Gates has asserted that al-Qaeda receives $80–100 million annually from the heroin trade. (Like all such figures, this one has no known provenance and should be treated with some skepticism.)

Many other terrorist groups have known ties to drug trafficking. The FARC in Colombia taxes coca growing, the Kurdistan People's Party in Turkey has some connection to drug traffickers among the Kurdish diaspora in Europe, and the Tamil Tigers have been caught smuggling heroin. None of these groups are particularly important in the global drug trade, but the trade may be particularly important to them.

For policymakers the relevant question is whether attacking the drug trade is an efficient method for cutting terrorist finance. Given the fact that there are few successful examples of policies that generate large-scale reductions in drug revenues, the answer is generally no. While there might be specific opportunities in which, say, moving the drug trade from one route to another could help reduce the flow of funds to terrorists, in general these criminal problems are hardly twins joined at the hip. The drug trade is just one of many illegal activities for which terrorist organizations have some useful organizational assets. In short, we would not cripple terrorist financing even if we were successful in international drug policy efforts. But this is merely an academic point, for experience shows us why we cannot be successful.

Cutting Drug Exports

The United States has pushed three types of programs to cut source country production: eradication, alternative development and in-country enforcement. Eradication, usually involving aerial spraying, aims literally to limit the quantity of the drug available in the United States, raise the costs of those drugs, or otherwise discourage farmers from producing them. Alternative development is the soft version of the same basic idea. It encourages farmers growing coca or poppies to switch to legitimate crops by increasing earnings from these other products—for example, by introducing new and more productive strains of traditional crops, better transportation to get the crops to market or some form of marketing scheme. Finally, the United States pushes other countries to pursue traffickers and refiners more vigorously. None of the three methods has worked all that well.

Few countries are willing to allow aerial eradication, which may cause environmental damage. It is also politically unattractive because it targets peasant farmers, who are among the poorest citizens even when growing coca or poppy. Colombia and Mexico, neither one traditional producers of drugs, have been the producer countries most willing to allow spraying. Most others allow only manual eradication, a slow and cumbersome method.

The fundamental problem of source-country interventions aimed at producers of coca and poppy is easily described. These programs have always had a peculiar glamor and occupy a large share of the headlines about drug policy. But the fact that the actual production costs of coca or opium account for a trivial share of the retail price of cocaine or heroin dooms source-country interventions as ways of controlling the problem.

It costs approximately $300 to purchase enough coca leaves to produce a kilogram of cocaine, which retails for about $100,000 in the United States when sold in one-gram, two-thirds pure units for $70 per unit. The modest share of the agricultural costs associated with cocaine production is easily explained: Production involves cheap land and labor in poor countries, and it requires no expensive specialized inputs. (Even Bolivia, the smallest of the three producer countries, has more than 500,000 square miles of territory—much of it opaque to surveillance.) Assume that eradication efforts lead to a doubling of the price of coca leaf, so that cocaine refiners now must pay $600 for enough leaf to produce one kilogram of cocaine. Even if the full cost increase is passed along, the change in retail price will still be negligible. Indeed, leaf prices have varied enormously over the past decade, while the retail price of cocaine has fallen almost throughout the same period. If retail prices do not rise, then total consumption in the United States will not decline as a consequence of eradication. In this scenario, there will be no reduction in total production—just more land torn up in more places to plant an environmentally damaging crop.

There is, of course, a less harsh option for policy in the source country: alternative development. Offer the farmers the opportunity to earn more money growing pineapples than coca, and they will move to the legal crop, the argument goes.

Quite aside from the time and money it takes to implement a successful alternative-crop program, the argument, alas, is subject to the same economic illogic as that for eradication. It assumes that the price of coca leaf will not increase enough to tempt the peasants back to coca growing. But as long as the price of leaf is so small compared to the street price of cocaine in Chicago, refiners will offer a high enough price to get back the land and labor needed to meet the needs of the cocaine market. Peasants will be better off than before the alternative development, but only because they will make more money growing coca. Mexican peasants are substantially better off than those in Bolivia, but that has not kept them out of the drug business. Indeed, the same can be said for Kentucky corn farmers, who are prominent in the marijuana trade in the United States.

Three Countries, Three Problems

For the United States the international drug problem is dominated by three countries: Afghanistan, Colombia and Mexico. Each presents a different problem, both to the United States and to the producing country. But all three show why the elimination/interdiction approach to source country supply doesn't work.

The United States is trying to create an effective democratic state in Afghanistan and is demonstrably failing. Further, despite the presence of 60,000 NATO and U.S. troops, Afghanistan's output of opium has increased massively over the seven years since the Taliban fell. That has provided important funding for the Taliban and al-Qaeda as well as for warlords independent of the central government. It has also worsened the country's deep-seated corruption. According to the former coordinator of U.S. counter-narcotics efforts in Afghanistan, there was much conflict within the Bush Administration about pursuing aggressive counter-narcotics efforts. Insiders argued over whether these efforts were needed to establish a strong state or, on the contrary, whether they would threaten the very existence of the Karzai government.[2]

The drug hawks have usually won the rhetorical battles, but they have lost the programmatic wars. In October 2008, Defense Secretary Gates declared that the U.S. military will go after traffickers and warlords but will not eradicate farmers' poppy fields. Given the relative invisibility of trafficking, this is effectively a truce. But better a truce than a "war" against poppies that cannot be won and might be counterproductive politically if it were won.

Colombia, unlike Afghanistan, is a principal producer of drugs for the United States, most prominently cocaine but also heroin. The United States has tried to strengthen a Colombian government long beleaguered by guerrilla conflict, and in this it has succeeded reasonably well. But the primary goal of its assistance has been to reduce the flow of Colombian-produced cocaine into the United States, and in that task it has largely failed.

Mexico, occasionally described as a natural smuggling platform for the United States, has been the principal drug transshipment country into the United States for two decades. The bulk of America's imports of cocaine, heroin, marijuana and methamphetamine all come through Mexico. In the past two years the level of violence associated with the U.S.-destined drug trade has skyrocketed. More than 5,000 people were killed in drug-related violence in 2008; that included systematic terror killings of innocent individuals, honest police and reporters. This has happened partly because of changes in the trade itself and partly as a consequence of government efforts

to control the violence. The new U.S. program to help Mexico—$400 million for training police and military—may ostensibly be aimed at cutting down the flow of drugs to the United States, but such low levels of funding are not likely to achieve much. The money is more properly viewed as reparations: Mexico is suffering from the consequences of our continued appetite for illegal drugs, so the United States has an obligation to help ameliorate those problems regardless of whether it cuts U.S. drug imports.

Strategic Consequences of the Balloon Effect

There is almost universal skepticism that international efforts by rich countries can reduce global production of cocaine and heroin. It is hard to find anyone outside of the State Department, the White House or Congress who argues otherwise. But efforts to curb production in specific places have had some effect. We noted previously that targeting Bolivian and Peruvian smuggling into Colombia helped make Colombia the dominant producer of coca. The Chinese government since about 1998 has pushed the United Wa State Army to successfully (and brutally) cut Burma's production of heroin. Spraying in Mexico in the 1970s shifted opium production from a five-state region in the north to a much more dispersed set of states around the country.

Interdiction can also affect the routing of the trade. In the early 1980s then-Vice President George H.W. Bush led the South Florida Task Force that successfully reduced smuggling through the Caribbean. The traffic then shifted to Mexico, but the effort did help several Caribbean governments. Similarly, more heroin may now be flowing through Pakistan because the Iranian government has intensified its border control.

In recent years this kind of interaction has been most conspicuous with respect to cocaine trafficking. The Netherlands Antilles is conveniently located for Colombian traffickers shipping to Europe, as there are many direct flights from Curaçao to Amsterdam's Schiphol airport, one of the busiest in Europe. In response to evidence of growing cocaine trafficking to Amsterdam, the Dutch government implemented a 100 percent search policy for airline passengers from Curaçao in March 2004. Whereas cocaine seizures in the Netherlands Antilles had not exceeded 1.3 tons before 2003, in 2004 they reached nine tons, a remarkable figure for a jurisdiction with fewer than 200,000 inhabitants. (The United States seizes only about 150 tons per year.) Shipments through Schiphol airport have since fallen sharply.

Probably as a consequence, new trafficking routes have opened up from South America to Europe via West Africa. For example, Guinea-Bissau is impoverished and small, it has no military or police capacity to deal with smugglers, and its government is easily corrupted. Smugglers have begun using landing strips there for large shipments. In 2007, there was one seizure of three-quarters of a ton, and it is believed that an even larger quantity from that shipment made it out of the country.

Ghana, a larger nation but one with fragile institutions, has also seen a sudden influx of cocaine traffickers. In 2005, flights from

Accra accounted for more seized cocaine at London's Heathrow airport than from flights from any other city. There are now regular reports of multi-kilo seizures of the drug either in Ghana itself or at airports receiving flights from Ghana.

Assuming that Ghana and Guinea-Bissau are serving as trafficking platforms at least in part because of the effective crackdown on an existing route through Curaçao, is the world better off? Certainly the Netherlands has helped itself. One can hardly be critical of a country making a strong effort to minimize its involvement in the drug trade. However, one can reasonably ask whether, in making these decisions, the Netherlands should take into account the likely effects of its actions on other, more vulnerable countries.

This analysis also applies to Afghanistan, assuming that it will for the foreseeable future be the most attractive location for opium production. The U.S. government continues to press the Karzai Administration to begin eradication activities in the areas it controls. At the same time, the United States emphasizes the importance of opium production to the Taliban. If farmers in government-controlled areas are forced out of business, it is likely that more of the growing activity, and probably more refining as well, will shift to areas controlled by the Taliban. The result may be to increase Taliban strength, both politically and financially—obviously not a result we would ever intend.

Awkward Choices

International drug policy will not be high on the Obama Administration's list of priorities, given that the U.S. drug problem itself is gradually declining. It has indeed not been a major issue for the Bush Administration. Congress was fairly passive on the issue during the past eight years, but those members who have been vocal have all been drug hawks, passionately arguing that this nation has a moral obligation to fight one of the great scourges of modern times on a worldwide scale. The public is apparently indifferent, seeing the drug problem as one for which every measure (tough enforcement, prevention or more treatment slots) is fairly hopeless. This, in turn, has not encouraged liberal members of Congress to take on the issue.

Drug policy is one of many areas of international policy in which the Obama Administration would benefit from adopting a more humble attitude. The arrogance with which U.S. delegations at the annual Commission on Narcotic Drugs lecture the rest of the world would be laughable if it weren't for the fact that many nations are still cowed by the sheer scale of U.S. efforts. There is no evidence that the United States knows how to help reduce the world's drug problems or to affect the ease with which cocaine, heroin and methamphetamine are procured and trafficked. Moreover, the harm that some of our interventions cause is more apparent than their benefits. For example, spraying coca fields in Colombia clearly has adverse environmental consequences if only because it spreads

production further, and it also probably sharpens conflict between the Colombian government and its citizens. Pressing the Karzai government to spray poppy fields increases tensions with our allies. Our attack on drug policy initiatives in other countries exacerbates the U.S. reputation for bullying and disinterestedness in true multilateral collaboration.

Doing less about a problem is rarely an attractive policy recommendation. But for international drug policy it is the only recommendation one can make with confidence. It is perhaps true, as Simone Weil once said, that "it is better to fail than to succeed in doing harm."

Notes

1. See, for example, Jonathan Caulkins and Peter Reuter, "Re-orienting Drug Policy", *Issues in Science and Technology* (Fall 2006); David Boyum and Peter Reuter, *An Analytic Assessment of U.S. Drug Policy* (American Enterprise Institute Press, 2005); and Mark A.R. Kleiman, "Dopey, Boozy, Smoky—and Stupid", *The American Interest* (January/February 2007).

2. Thomas Schweich, "Is Afghanistan a Narco-State?" *New York Times Magazine,* July 27, 2008.

Reference

Reuter, Peter. (2009, March/April). The American Interest: Do No Harm. *Sensible Goals for International Drug Policy,* vol. IV, no. 4, 46–52.

Critical Thinking

1. Should we continue with our current international drug policy? Why?
2. Some argue that current strategies to counter global drug issues are not working. What suggestions would you make?

Create Central

www.mhhe.com/createcentral

Internet References

International Drug Policy Consortium
http://idpc.net

International Centre on Human Rights and Drug Policy
www.humanrightsanddrugs.org/international-law/international-drug-control-law

PETER REUTER is a professor of public policy and criminology at the University of Maryland. He is co-author (with Letizia Paoli and Victoria Greenfield) of the forthcoming *The World Heroin Market: Can Supply Be Cut?* (Oxford University Press).

Article

Prepared by: Mary Maguire, *California State University—Sacramento*
Clifford Garoupa, *Fresno City College*

Turning the Tide on Drug Reform

With state-level victories in November, activists are ready to take the fight to the feds.

KRISTEN GWYNNE

Learning Outcomes

After reading this article, you will be able to:

- Discuss the tension between state and federal drug laws.

- Discuss the success or failure of the "war on drugs."

- Discuss arguments in favor of and against legalizing marijuana.

In *Barack Obama: The Story,* biographer David Maraniss writes that the president spent his youth in Hawaii getting stoned on a paved road up Mount Tantalus, where he took "roof hits" in smoke-filled cars with his friends, the Choom Gang. ("Choom" is Hawaiian slang for smoking marijuana.) Obama loved weed so much, Maraniss writes, he thanked his pot dealer, but not his mother, in his high school yearbook.

Decades later, the Choomer turned president is in a historically unprecedented position when it comes to drug policy in the United States. Marijuana is illegal under the Controlled Substances Act, but two states, Washington and Colorado, voted in November to legalize and regulate its sale and use by adults 21 and older. This conflict with federal law puts all eyes on Obama, who, despite his smoke-filled teenage years, has refused to consider marijuana legalization as an alternative to prohibition. Indeed, drug policy reformers have endured a rocky four years (to put it mildly) in their relationship with the Obama administration. That's why, when the president told Barbara Walters in December that his administration had "bigger fish to fry" than prosecuting recreational users of state-legal pot, legalization advocates took that statement with a grain of salt. The last time Obama said he would allow the states to determine their own policies on medical marijuana, he ended up busting more state-sanctioned dispensaries than George W. Bush.

Ethan Nadelmann, executive director of the Drug Policy Alliance, is confident that the recent state-level legalization victories mark a "turning point" that will inspire more politicians and voters to become curious, even passionate, about marijuana policy. "It's causing lawmakers to rethink this issue," Nadelmann says, adding that political risk is "the same reason

the White House said nothing about the ballot initiatives in Washington and Colorado before the election."

While preparing a response to a possible federal crack-down is a priority for the legalization movement, advocates are hoping for more than just nonintervention from the feds. They would like to see an open conversation about drug policy that will turn more policy-makers into legalization advocates, and more states (red and blue alike) a cannabis-friendly green. For that domino effect to happen, however, they must first craft a message that convinces people that voting for reform or even outright legalization is not a vote for pot, but a vote against the multidimensional disasters of prohibition—a web of mass incarceration and racial injustice, tangled up with everything from foreign policy to public benefits at home.

According to the FBI, in 2011 more than 750,000 Americans were arrested for marijuana-related offenses, accounting for roughly half of all drug crimes in the United States. Eighty-seven percent of marijuana-related arrests were for possession alone—a minor crime that can still cause major problems in one's life.

The good news is that, should the feds decide to crack down on Colorado and Washington, there is no way to force local law enforcement to arrest marijuana users in those two states. They could, however, still go after some large-scale distributors, as they have done with medical marijuana suppliers in California and Montana.

That's why the marijuana legalization movement's first priority, says Paul Armentano, deputy director of the National Organization for the Reform of Marijuana Laws (NORML), is making sure that all goes smoothly in Washington and Colorado. It must ensure that policy-makers follow through on implementing legalization, to avoid situations like the one in Delaware, where a medical marijuana bill was passed in April 2011 but has never taken effect.

At the same time, Armentano says, legalization advocates must make sure that new laws continue to reflect the will of the voters. This means establishing viable and effective guidelines to regulate how marijuana will be sold and consumed, while also looking out for unnecessary regulatory schemes. In effect, Washington and Colorado must create a model that lawmakers from other states won't be afraid to support.

"With drug law reform, it's the states that move federal policy," Armentano adds. "There's going to continue to be increased efforts at the state level to bring about additional reforms—legislative in 2013, or possible citizen initiatives in 2014 or 2016." These will include everything from medical marijuana legalization to decriminalization of possession to full legalization of recreational use and sale.

The Marijuana Policy Project (MPP) tells *The Nation* that the next round of marijuana legalization measures is most likely to come from Alaska, Maine, Oregon, California, Massachusetts, Rhode Island and Nevada. Meanwhile, Armentano is optimistic that, elsewhere, efforts to decriminalize, rather than legalize, pot stand a particularly good chance at success, since they do not invite the same conflict with the feds. (Decriminalization typically reduces the penalties for small amounts of marijuana possession from an arrest to ticket or fine, while legalization removes all penalties for adult possession and sale.)

Texas and New Jersey have already introduced decriminalization bills. In New Hampshire, MPP says, three bills will be introduced this year: one to legalize medical marijuana, one to decriminalize, and one to tax and regulate. "The election of Governor Maggie Hassan, who has expressed support for medical [marijuana], means a medical bill would almost surely be signed," says MPP's Mason Tvert.

Still, Armentano believes that legalization bills will remain on hold until state lawmakers can feel reasonably confident that there will be no federal crackdown. "To be realistic, I don't think that we're going to see a state legalize legislatively in 2013. Most state lawmakers are going to want to take a wait-and-see approach for at least a year, maybe two, to see how this all shakes out in Colorado and Washington."

A year from now, says Rick Steves, a PBS travel show host who co-sponsored the Washington initiative (I-502), residents in that state can expect stores selling pot to open their doors, though under stringent regulations. Indeed, while some in the legalization movement have criticized I-502 for being too strict—a DUI provision has been especially controversial—Steves notes that "we had to seriously consider and address the concerns of the public that does not use marijuana." Part of the goal was to "write a law that is so public-safety-minded that you get local law enforcement endorsing it." That strategy worked: not only did a Seattle sheriff and former prosecutor endorse the initiative, the former prosecutor co-sponsored it.

A much bigger challenge than passing state-level reforms will be convincing Congress to take up the issue. But advocates say they are up to the challenge. "It is a high priority of NORML and other organizations to take the victories of Colorado and Washington and try to translate them into a much more serious and prolific discussion in Congress," Armentano says. He predicts that at the federal level too, "a greater number of elected officials [will be] talking about marijuana-law reform."

As for potential allies in Congress, MPP's director of government relations, Steve Fox, says the reform movement's "biggest supporters are in the Democratic caucus." With Ron Paul and Barney Frank—previously the "biggest players"—gone from Congress, Fox says there's "a lot of younger people coming up, trying to take the mantle." He cites Jared Polis of Colorado, Earl Blumenauer of Oregon and Steve Cohen of Tennessee as leading the charge, adding: "The mood in DC on this issue has completely shifted in light of the recent election."

Representative Diana DeGette of Colorado has already introduced the Respect States' and Citizens' Rights Act of 2012, which would amend the Controlled Substances Act to exempt state marijuana laws from federal control. This kind of legislation, aimed at finally resolving the conflict between state and federal law regarding marijuana, is what Americans can expect to see coming out of Congress over the next four years. (Whether it can garner enough votes to pass is another story.)

The key to that effort is messaging, says Tom Angell, the founder and chair of the group Marijuana Majority, who points to recent polls showing that most Americans do not want the federal government interfering in Washington and Colorado. "Our task now," he adds, "is to show [elected officials] that the voters are way ahead of them, and that they'll be rewarded for speaking up and not punished for it." Bridging that gap between public opinion and policy, however, requires instilling in politicians the confidence necessary to attach their names to marijuana-law reform. Marijuana Majority is dedicated to this work; much of what it does is spread awareness of the broad range of support for marijuana-law reform so that an increasing number of people, politicians and citizens alike, realize that "when you speak out for marijuana reform, you're in good company and won't be attacked and marginalized."

If supporting pro-marijuana legalization is increasingly mainstream, so is the opinion that the drug war as we know it has failed. Even Obama's drug czar, Gil Kerlikowske, head of the Office of National Drug Control Policy, has distanced himself from the "war on drugs," recasting it as a public health issue. "There is some truth to the notion that there's been a shift," Nadelmann says, but he adds that legislators have failed to match their rhetorical shift with a change in funding, and that spending for incarceration still outweighs funds for treatment.

The White House, too, has not lived up to its rhetoric. "I think the Obama administration would be well served to take a page from what the states are doing with respect to incarceration policy in general," says Mary Price, vice president and general counsel for Families Against Mandatory Minimums (FAMM). She adds that while much reform at the state level is driven, at least in part, by budgetary concerns, "it's also driven by a new interest in evidence-based solutions" to criminal justice problems. Harm reduction, rather than incarceration, is one kind of drug policy that would use a public health model to minimize and prevent the harms (such as overdosing) that are often associated with drug use.

Still, while the Obama administration has shown some signs of taking a more public-health-oriented approach (by backing federally funded needle exchange programs, for example), it has been silent on prisons. "What's telling is that Obama has yet to make one powerful comment about the high rate of incarceration in this country, or the fact that we have the highest rate in the world, or the incredible racial disproportion involved," says Nadelmann, who adds that while Obama worked early on to reduce the racially charged sentencing disparity for crack versus powder cocaine (from 100-to-1 to 18-to-1), "there's really been a lack of leadership."

The disconnect is particularly egregious given the outsize role of mandatory minimum sentencing in drug cases. As Price notes, the "stacking" of such mandatory minimums leads to such injustices as the case of Montana medical marijuana provider Chris Williams, who initially faced over eighty years in federal prison for possessing both marijuana and guns—neither of which were illegal under state law at the time. "If a gun is found in connection to the offense, even if it is not directly related, the person is subject to this rather extreme mandatory minimum," says Price, who explained that the first gun charge carries a minimum of five years, followed by a twenty-five-year minimum for every additional charge. (Prosecutors ultimately offered Williams a plea deal that would reduce his sentence to five to ten years.)

With the Sandy Hook tragedy moving Obama and Congress to target guns, Price says she is "somewhat concerned" that the House might push for new mandatory sentencing schemes. But vocal opposition by Senator Patrick Leahy to mandatory minimums gives her confidence they would not pass the Senate.

Coupled with drug reform victories, such progressive stances by elected officials reflect a larger ongoing shift in attitudes toward criminal justice policy, driven by the states. Increasingly, people realize that the country's exorbitantly expensive, excessively harsh prison system has been more costly than it has been successful at making us safe. The question is whether Congress and the White House will recognize this and use their powers to expedite, rather than impede, change.

Critical Thinking

1. Discuss what most marijuana-related arrests are for and the resulting implications of this level of enforcement.

2. Discuss the implications of differences in drug laws on the state and federal level.

3. Develop a critical argument in favor of, or in opposition to, drug law reform related to marijuana.

Create Central

www.mhhe.com/createcentral

Internet References

Coalition for Cannabis Reform
www.cannabispolicyreform.org
Drug Policy Alliance
www.drugpolicy.org/reforming-marijuana-laws

KRISTEN GWYNNE is a New York–based reporter and drug policy editor at AlterNet. Her work has also appeared on Salon and Rolling-Stone.com.

Article

Prepared by: Mary Maguire, *California State University—Sacramento*
Clifford Garoupa, *Fresno City College*

Legalize Drugs—All of Them!

Vanessa Baird

Learning Outcomes

After reading this article, you will be able to:

- Summarize a general understanding of the drug policies of at least one country outside of the United States.

- Define the differences between decriminalization and legalization of drugs.

- Discuss the implications of legalizing drugs in the United States.

We were sitting in a café drinking cola. My two companions, drug enforcement soldiers, kept their guns resting across their knees. Fingers not quite on triggers but close enough for rapid response. They were smiling.

The woman running the café was not. Her face was closed, expressionless. Through the open window we could hear the almost constant sound of light aircraft taking off and landing somewhere in the thick greenery of Peru's Upper Huallaga Valley. When, earlier, I had innocently asked a local mayor whether such planes were carrying drugs, he had smiled and equally innocently replied: 'They are air taxis. That's how people get about here.'

Later I went out with soldiers on patrol. Running through the jungle, we spotted coca plants being grown between generous banana leaves. Finally we came upon a lab for making coca paste. It was a simple affair—two big piles of coca leaves, a trough made out of wood and plastic sheeting, and some cans of kerosene.

'It's been abandoned,' remarked one of the soldiers. He didn't seem surprised or disappointed. 'Will they be back?' I asked.

'Probably not. They won't use this one again if they know we have been here. They will make another lab somewhere else. It's easy.'

This was 27 years ago, early days in the 'war on drugs'. And already then it seemed hopeless.

Steps to Showdown

'They used to laugh at us,' says Danny Kushlick of Transform, a British drug policy reform group.

Today he and his colleagues are regularly called upon to make the case for ending the prohibitionist policy that has dominated the world since the UN Single Convention on Narcotic Drugs was put in place in 1961.

They have been researching other possibilities, including an idea that until recently was pretty much taboo—making all drugs legal.

The list of high-profile figures supporting the cause for reform is growing by the minute, and ranges from Nobel laureate economists and police chiefs to stand-up comedians and drug activists.

Serving politicians have tended to be cautious, fearing voter backlash. Before coming to power, both Barack Obama and David Cameron indicated that they were in favour of reform, including some degree of legalization. Once in high office, they fell silent. Mexico's former leader Vicente Fox, now a leading advocate of 'legalization all the way', waited until he was safely out of office.

But today, even incumbent leaders are sticking their heads above the parapet. 'That's something new,' says Kushlick.

In the past few months, President Juan Manuel Santos of Colombia, for example, has initiated a global taskforce for a total rethink of drug policy. Costa Rica's Laura Chinchilla has said the consumption of drugs should be a matter of health, not law. Guatemalan President Otto Pérez Molina is calling for legalization of the use and sale of drugs. While in Uruguay, President José Mujica has proposed a groundbreaking law that would enable the state to sell marijuana to its people and derive tax revenue from it. 'Someone has to be first,' he commented.

Uruguayan President José Mujica has proposed a law that would enable the state to sell marijuana and derive tax revenue from it. 'Someone has to be first,' he says

The US is not immune to the whiff of drug revolution. In November three states—Washington, Oregon and Colorado—will vote on legalization of marijuana for adult recreational use. This would directly contravene both federal law and the UN

Convention. 'We're heading for a showdown,' says Sanho Tree of the Institute for Policy Studies in Washington. 'It's hard to talk about tipping points but I think we are close to one with regard to cannabis. This is a clear sign that people are looking for a different paradigm.'

War on Drugs

From a country like Mexico, where ever-deepening drug-related violence claims 33 lives a day, the global 'war on drugs' declared by President Nixon 40 years ago can be seen for what it is—a colossal failure. Costing more than a trillion dollars, this 'war' has involved hundreds of thousands of military personnel, customs officers, enforcement agents, crop eradicators, police and prison staff. But still the illegal narcotics trade flourishes—worth about $320 billion a year—and drug use keeps growing.

Drugs have little intrinsic value. It's prohibition that gives an astronomical 'price support' to traffickers. The profits are extreme and so are the violence and corruption needed to protect them.

Worse, the war on drugs has unleashed a deadly set of 'unintended consequences'.

It's 'like trying to put out an electrical fire by dousing it with water,' says Sanho Tree.

Crackdowns on drug cartels have increased the huge profits bestowed by illegality. Violence has surged as rival groups jockey to fill the vacuum left when a major cartel has been hammered by government forces.

The global war is militarizing societies and tearing up democratic rights. It also enables illegal drug money to flow into the coffers of Al Qaeda, the Taliban, and the Colombian FARC, ELN, AUC and others.[1,2] Meanwhile, punishing drug users and sellers has filled prisons and increased addiction.

Something needs to be done.

'It is the biggest, most complex challenge facing us today,' says Mauricio Rodríguez, Colombian ambassador in London and a close ally of President Santos, whose proposed taskforce of global experts is already at work under the auspices of the Inter-American Drug Abuse Control Commission (CICAD), expected to report within 12 months.

Colombians know better than most the cost of the war on drugs. They have been on the frontline of the US-designed Plan Colombia, a $7 billion anti-narcotics and military aid drive also used to tackle leftwing insurgency. In 2002 the conflict was claiming some 28,000 Colombian lives a year.[3]

Today, violence is down by about a third and coca production has declined by 58 per cent. 'But any improvements in Colombia have meant serious deterioration in other parts of Latin America and the world,' says Rodríguez. 'Production has gone to Peru and Bolivia and traffic has gone mostly to Central America, West Africa, and islands of the Caribbean.'

This is the so-called balloon effect, where action taken in one place simply pushes the illegal drug problem into another.

Latin Americans, the ambassador says, are fed up with drug-related violence. 'Why do we have to pay such a price for a problem that is essentially not ours? We are not big consumers; it's unfair that tens of thousands of Mexicans or Colombians or Guatemalans have to lose their lives because of consumption in the US. Who is really responsible? The consumers are and so are those who have created this model of illegality. Either consuming nations need to reduce their consumption or they need to help us to change this model.'

The Damage Done?

Many people in those major consuming nations would agree. In recent months opinion polls have shown remarkable upswings in people supporting legalization of some drugs at least. A survey in Colorado showed 61 per cent of the population supported legalization of cannabis. Polls in Britain, Australia and Canada show similar seismic shifts in public attitude.

The number of people who have never tried an illegal recreational drug is dwindling and with it the hysteria that surrounds narcotics. Psychoactive—mind-altering—substances have always been a part of human experience. And other animal experience too, if you count elephants bingeing on fermenting fruit and goats getting high on coffee beans.

The effects of different drugs and their wider impacts vary enormously. But for many people, current legal classification of drugs seems divorced from the reality they know, especially in relation to cannabis or 'party drugs' like ecstasy.

There is also a growing awareness that some legal drugs—alcohol and tobacco, for example—are much more harmful than many currently illegal ones. Some illicit substances have medically therapeutic benefits, such as cannabis (to alleviate the symptoms of multiple sclerosis) and ecstasy or magic mushrooms (for treating post-traumatic stress disorder), that cannot be properly researched or exploited by medical professionals and patients.

But what about the hard stuff?

Heroin and crack cocaine are high on the scientific list of harmful illegal drugs. The 27 million 'problem drug users' in the world tend to be addicted to these or related substances. The proliferation of drugs like krokodil (a cheaper heroin derivative that gets its name from the skin damage it causes and its flesh-devouring tendencies) in Russia compounds fear of drugs and what they can do.

Andria Efthimiou-Mordaunt is a Harm Reduction activist and former heroin addict living in London. She sees addiction as a disease to be treated. She also thinks that legal regulation and control is the only way to go. 'I don't say it fearlessly though, because I think that, at least temporarily, there will be an increase in drug use. But I don't think that will be sustained.'

In 2001, Portugal embarked on one of the most daring and progressive actions in recent times: it effectively decriminalized the personal use of all drugs, including the hard ones.

The results were interesting. Drug use carried on increasing but at a slower rate than in Spain or France. But, significantly, addiction to hard drugs fell by half, from an estimated 100,000 addicts before decriminalization to 40,000 in 2011. Opiate-related deaths and HIV infection were also down—the latter by 17 per cent.[4,5] This is partly because Portugal coupled decriminalization with a well-funded public health programme to help people get off drugs.

Counter-intuitive as it may seem, the evidence suggests that criminalization does not deter use—but decriminalization does.

It makes perfect sense to Andria Efthimiou-Mordaunt. 'I have now heard thousands of stories of people who have become dependent on heroin, cocaine and so on. Most of us were most interested because these drugs were forbidden.

'Also we were a bit vulnerable, didn't have much love for ourselves, and therefore we put ourselves in danger. We don't care that it's a crime and we could go to jail. We just want to use this drug that we have found is comforting or exciting or pleasurable.'

She explains: 'People aren't wilfully creating havoc: they are doing something that they find will assist them in their lives, even if it's temporary and it gets them into all sorts of other problems. But for the majority of us, it is clear that the prohibitive punitive system has actually been the cause of most of our other problems—like poverty, homelessness, sex work, shoplifting, dealing.'

These problems in turn intensify the need for the drug and make it harder to stop.

'What saddens me is that some of the people who are most punitive and intolerant are those who are directly affected. One of our arguments needs to be that just because you are legalizing the drug does not mean that you are promoting it. You can say: look, we are not changing the laws because we want everyone to take these substances, but because they're currently bloody dangerous because of where you get them from.'

There are many good models for reducing harm, through a combination of *de facto* decriminalization and supportive treatment. 'In Switzerland they found that people would come off heroin faster because there was nothing to fight against any more; they still had their addictions but once the other bits of their lives had been sorted to some degree, there wasn't this huge monster that needed to be medicated every day.'

In Vancouver, Canada, the response to a high level of drug deaths was the creation of a 'consumption room' where users can safely inject legal or illegal drugs. They call it 'the demilitarized zone'. Similar initiatives have been developed in Australia, Spain, Germany, Portugal and the Netherlands.

Decriminalize or Legalize?

So why not go down the Portuguese route and decriminalize the use of all drugs?

It is, to varying degrees, already happening in practice in around 25 countries, mainly in Europe and Latin America, where people found in possession may simply have their drugs confiscated but will not be prosecuted.[5]

However, decriminalization does not deal with the supply side—and the deadly nexus of money and violence.

Drugs have little intrinsic value. It's prohibition that gives an astronomical 'price support' to traffickers. The profits are extreme and so are the violence and corruption needed to protect them. Hence the grotesquely cruel methods used by the gangs, making simple decapitation a blessing.

Only legalization and regulation can break the hold of the criminals. Legal drugs could be taxed. The corrupt network of tax-evading banks and front companies that support the industry by laundering drug money would have to start paying their way. 'The war on drugs I would like to see is the war on laundering drug money,' says ambassador Rodríguez. And some of the criminals might even be caught. It's worth remembering that only when the prohibition of alcohol ended in the US was Al Capone finally apprehended—on a charge of tax evasion in 1933.

Making drugs legal has many potential benefits. It could interrupt the flow of money to warlords, corrupt officials and the Taliban that is ensuring continuing instability in Afghanistan and other parts of the world. This is highlighted in a recent study by the former MI6 director of operations Nigel Inkster and Virginia Comolli, a research analyst at the International Institute of Strategic Studies.[6]

It could dramatically reduce prison populations. The billions the world spends on the global war on drugs could instead go towards health, addiction treatment and prevention, and other socially useful things. It would lower the risk of death by overdose because the strength and quality of drugs would be marked and controlled.

But one of the biggest impacts would be on HIV/AIDS. Contrary to global trends, infection through injecting drug use is on the rise and now accounts for a third of all new HIV infections outside sub-Saharan Africa. Punitive policies are fuelling the AIDS pandemic in the US, Thailand, China and especially the former soviet states. In Russia violent police attacks on drug users are commonplace, opiate substitutes are outlawed, and needle exchange programmes non-existent. 'Refusing to reduce HIV infection and protect people who have a drug problem is criminal,' said entrepreneur Richard Branson at the launch of a hard-hitting report by the Global Commission on Drugs, a collection of ex-drug tsars, former leaders and experts who are calling upon current world leaders to decriminalize drug use and to invest in harm reduction.[7]

In a world where drug taking was not a crime, addicts would be less likely to go underground, less likely to share needles and more likely to test for HIV. Millions of new HIV infections could be averted.

Other human rights abuses generated by prohibition could be reduced, such as capital punishment in Iran. This is mainly used against people found in possession of drugs and is effectively being funded by Britain, Ireland and others through a UN anti-drug smuggling programme.[8]

Finally, legalization would provide a decent living, without fear, for thousands of poppy and coca farmers in some of the world's poorest countries.

What Next?

What happens in the US, the world's premier drugs consumer and also the most ardent guardian of the UN Convention, is critical. In the lead-up to November's elections, President Obama is in ultra-cautious mode. He has said he is

---

To Take It Further . . .

Action and Resources

Organizations

International

The Global Commission on Drug Policy
globalcommissionondrugs.org
International Drug Policy Consortium idpc.net
International Centre for Science in Drug Policy icsdp.org
Transnational Institute tni.org
International HIV/AIDS Alliance aidsalliance.org
International Network of People who Use Drugs
(INPUD) inpud.net

Aotearoa/New Zealand

The Green Party greens.org.nz/druglawreform
Legalise marijuana legalise.org.nz

Australia

Australian Drug Law Reform Foundation adlrf.org.au
Families of Drug Users fds.org.au
Family and Friends for Drug Law Reform ffdlr.org.au

Britain

Transform drug policy foundation tdpf.org.uk
The Beckley Foundation reformdrugpolicy.com
Harm Reduction International ihra.net
The Independent Scientific Committee on Drugs
drugscience.org.uk

Canada

Canadian Harm Reduction Network
canadianharmreduction.com

Canadian Drug Policy Coalition drugpolicy.ca
Canadian Foundation for Drug Policy cfdp.ca

US

Drug Policy Alliance drugpolicy.org
Law Enforcement Against Prohibition (LEAP) leap.cc
Drug Reform Co-ordination Network
stopthedrugwar.org
NORML norml.org
Drug Sense drugsense.org
Drug War Facts drugwarfacts.org

Books

Legalize by Max Rendall, 2011 (*Stacey International*)
After the War on Drugs: Blueprint for Regulation by
Steve Rolles/Transform, 2009 (download at tdpf.org.uk)
Fixing Drugs by Sue Pryce, 2012 (*Palgrave Macmillan*)
Drugs—without the hot air by David Nutt, 2012 (*UIT
Cambridge*)
The Candy Machine by Tom Feiling, 2009 (*Penguin*)
Drug War in Mexico by Peter Watt and Roberto Zepeda,
2012 (*Zed*)
Seeds of Terror by Gretchen Peters, 2009 (*Oneworld*)
Drugs, Insecurity and Failed States by Nigel Inkster and
Virginia Cornolli, 2012 (IISS)

Reports

The Alternative World Drug Report, Transform, June
2012, nin.tl/Mbmuoa
The War on Drugs and HIV/AIDS, Global Commission
on Drugs, June 2012 nin.tl/M3ldEw
World Drug Report, UNODC, June 2012 nin.tl/Mbnqcd

'critical' of legalization but is prepared to consider whether Washington policies are 'doing more harm than good in certain places'.

The US drug warriors in Congress and in the military are entrenched and still have international clout, as Bolivia saw when it tried to legalize production of coca for traditional use.

In theory, the US can act against countries that depart from the UN Convention by blocking loans from financial institutions such as the IMF or the World Bank. But when there is a regional uprising, with one country after another saying they want to legalize, be it Belize or Uruguay or Argentina, it may get harder to do.

In the US itself Sanho Tree reckons that: 'Once we have a regulated model for cannabis, it will show voters that the sky didn't fall, life did not grind to a halt. That will help. On the hard drugs, examples from Europe of successful harm reduction programmes will show people in the US that another way is possible.'

But he adds that the main political work will be in public education. This is because drugs policy is, by its nature, counter-intuitive; being tough is the opposite of being effective.

Prohibition is a simplistic solution to a complex problem that simply does not work. At no time or place in history has it ever worked. Sue Pryce, an academic and mother of a drug addict, observes: 'There is an uncomfortable similarity between the drug addict and those who support drug prohibition. The addict comes to see a fix as the solution to life's problems; the prohibitionists have come to see prohibition as the fix for the drug problems which are also part of life itself.'[9]

Even if the world, or even a part of it, comes to accept that legalization is the way forward, the devil will be in the detail. Pricing, for example, is a tricky issue—too cheap and use may rocket; too expensive and the rationale for a criminal market is re-ignited.

Antonio Maria Costa, former UN drug tsar and a leading prohibitionist, warns that multinational corporations will muscle in if drugs are legalized. Steve Rolles from Transform, however, presents a model that involves considerable state control and a ban on advertising.[10]

In an ideal world the UN would replace the prohibitionist conventions with a new progressive policy that all countries could sign up to together. Perhaps President Santos' global taskforce process will produce a blueprint for such a policy. But it's questionable how radical it will be if it has to have US and Canadian approval. UN-watcher Damon Barrett of Harm Reduction International thinks that real change is more likely to come 'from below'. Social and harm reduction activists, public educators and just ordinary people opening their minds will be the key players in this revolution.

People have and always will take intoxicants that provide pleasure and harm. But there are ways in which we can make that activity safer, less damaging to individuals, to society, to the world.

It may sound paradoxical, but ridding ourselves of prohibition could be the best way of getting a grip.

1. Gretchen Peters, *Seeds of Terror: How heroin is bankrolling the Taliban and Al Qaeda,* Oneworld Publications, 2009. **2.** BBC nin.tl/OqjN6j **3.** *Los Angeles Times* nin.tl/MptbV8 **4.** *Forbes* nin.tl/OqkDQx **5.** Transform, 'The Alternative World Drugs Report', 2012 nin.tl/Oqp0Lf **6.** Nigel Inkster and Virginia Comolli *Drugs, Insecurity and Failed States: the Problems of Prohibition,* IISS, 2012 **7.** Global Commission on Drugs, 'The War on Drugs and HIV/AIDS', globalcommissionondrugs.org **8.** Harm Reduction International, 'Partners in Crime', 2012 nin.tl/MpuQtS **9.** Sue Pryce, *Fixing Drugs: the Politics of Drug Prohibition,* Palgrave Macmillan, 2012. **10.** Intelligence Squared, 'It's time to end the war on drugs', nin.tl/OqvtG5

Critical Thinking

1. Analyze Baird's position on the war on drugs.
2. Describe the key arguments for legalizing drugs.
3. Discuss the comparisons Baird makes between the United States and other countries.

Create Central

www.mhhe.com/createcentral

Internet References

Open Society Foundation
www.opensocietyfoundations.org/reports/drug-policy-portugal-benefits-decriminalizing-drug-use

Drug Policy Alliance
www.drugpolicy.org

Baird, Vanessa. From *New Internationalist,* vol. 455, 2012, pp. 12–17. Copyright © 2012 by New Internationalist. Reprinted by permission.

Prepared by: Mary Maguire, *California State University—Sacramento*
Clifford Garoupa, *Fresno City College*

Article

Moving the Needle

Lance Armstrong toppled, the war on PEDs continues in a new direction with new alliances.

DAVID EPSTEIN AND RICHARD O'BRIEN

Learning Outcomes

After reading this article, you will be able to:

• Discuss the limitations of traditional screening tests for doping.

• Discuss responses to doping by specific sports.

• Discuss the role of the World Anti-Doping Agency in the fight against doping.

Lance Armstrong, the biggest target in sports doping history, has been taken down, his sponsors decamping en masse, his seven Tour de France titles stripped away. So does that signal the beginning of the end of the war on performance-enhancing drugs? Not necessarily.

Consider that one of the most recent positive tests at the World Anti-Doping Agency-accredited laboratory in Montreal was, according to the lab's director, Christiane Ayotte, the result of "total luck."

The urine sample had already passed the screening test, which looks at the ratio of testosterone to epitestosterone, where a 4 to 1 is considered suspiciously high. This sample had a T/E ratio of 1 to 1, exactly normal. But the sample was selected for a second round of testing—isotope ratio mass spectrometry, which looks specifically for synthetic testosterone. To Ayotte's surprise, the IRMS test came back "heavily positive." The athlete, it turned out, was doping with synthetic testosterone but excreted testosterone and epitestosterone in a way that fools the T/E test. The athlete had a biological gift, one that is troublingly common.

In 2006, Swedish scientists found that a variation in a gene allows some people to maintain a low T/E ratio no matter how much testosterone they inject. In that study 9.3% of Swedes and 66.7% of Koreans had the condition. So now, says Ayotte, in addition to those simply "doping below the radar," the lab must contend with athletes blessed with get-out-of-drug-testing-free genes. "It's very frustrating," she says. "I cannot retire before we've found a better probe."

As the U.S. Anti-Doping Agency's recent report on Armstrong made clear, athletes often foil drug tests, by hook or by crook or by saline infusions. Even with massive advances in testing in the last decade, WADA statistics show that, year in and year out, only 1% to 2% of worldwide drug tests are reported as positive—the same as it was 10 years ago. The advances of the dopers and the antidopers, it seems, are in technological lockstep.

As Paul Scott, head of Scott Analytics, which provides testing services in six sports, puts it: "Drug testing has a public reputation that far exceeds its capabilities. . . . With testing, the risk/reward equation is still massively shifted in favor of reward." But another implication of the USADA report is that drug testing is not the only weapon in today's anti-doping battle.

"Marion Jones had more than 160 tests during her career, none of them positive," says David Howman, director general of WADA. "[For] Balco we realized we had to get evidence from other means, so we worked closely with the federal investigators." That realization led WADA to partner with Interpol in 2008. Today WADA has its own chief investigative officer—a former U.S. federal agent—and last year published guidelines for national anti-doping bodies that want to collaborate with law enforcement and customs "to take advantage of the investigative powers of those public authorities, including search and seizure, surveillance and compulsion of testimony under penalties of perjury," the guidelines read.

In its post-Mitchell Report era Major League Baseball has frequently discussed with WADA methods of investigating doping violations that do not rely on testing. MLB now has its own Department of Investigations, which recently helped debunk an excuse that Giants outfielder Melky Cabrera was apparently going to use to appeal his positive drug test. (An associate of Cabrera's purchased a website and created a fake ad for a nonexistent product to make it appear that Cabrera had used a tainted supplement.)

Not that improvements in and implementation of testing technology are unimportant. This season MLB became the first major North American league to introduce blood testing for human growth hormone (year-round in the minors but only in spring training and the off-season in the bigs). "The strides that have been made in baseball are pretty significant," Howman says. "They're getting closer to what the [WADA] code says." In November, when MLB sits down to talk to the players' union, the new HGH biomarker test that has a longer window of detection will be on the table.

The NFL, meanwhile, remains at an impasse over testing for HGH, which former quarterback Boomer Esiason estimated last month is used by 60% to 70% of players. After agreeing to testing last year, the NFLPA challenged the validity of the test that has been in use at the Olympics since 2004, and it was never implemented. If the NFL can get past that stalemate, the next frontier for the pro leagues will be the kind of unannounced off-season testing which Olympians undergo.

In cycling, the development of the biological passport program, which monitors the fluctuation of each rider's blood parameters over a series of tests, must be making some difference: Cyclists have suddenly slowed down, and power outputs on mountain stages of the Tour de France have plummeted. But, says Scott, "the passport has forced athletes to keep these parameters in a narrow range. As a result they aren't doping as effectively as they were before."

Scott does take some comfort in what he considers the greatest weapon against doping: a new emphasis on responsible behavior. In two cycling teams he has worked with—Team Type 1 and Team Slipstream (now Garmin-Sharp-Barracuda)—Scott

saw upper management hammer home the message that part of being a member of a team is "not jeopardizing the lives and careers of the people around you."

"It was to the point," he says, "of making sure that this culture is more important than making sure the team has victories."

Investigations and ethics. Two more weapons in the ongoing war.

Critical Thinking

1. Discuss the contributions to changing pressures on athletes to perform.

2. Discuss the "weapons" against doping in contemporary athletics.

3. Discuss the relative merits of plans by the MLB and the NFL to decrease doping.

Create Central

www.mhhe.com/createcentral

Internet References

United States Anti-Doping Agency
   www.usada.org
UNESCO
   www.unesco.org/new/en/social-and-human-sciences/themes/
   anti-doping

Prepared by: Mary Maguire, *California State University—Sacramento*
Clifford Garoupa, *Fresno City College*

Article

Getting a Fix

Portugal decriminalized drugs a decade ago. What have we learned?

Michael Specter

Learning Outcomes

After reading this article, you will be able to:

- Describe the Portuguese approach to drug addiction.
- Discuss the historical and contemporary patterns of drug use in Portugal.
- Discuss the historical and contemporary patterns of drug use in the United States.

Nuno Miranda has been parking cars for thirteen years, most of them in a lot just below Belém National Palace, the eighteenth-century estate that serves as the official residence of the President of Portugal. Miranda, who is thirty-seven, is a lanky, amiable man, dressed in the style of hipsters the world over: a few layers of untucked shirts and skinny black jeans tucked into well-worn work boots. His dishevelled hair falls just below his collar, and by 11 A.M. one day recently the sun was bouncing off the thin gold chain around his neck. Miranda's "job," like that of the now-banished squeegee men of New York, falls into the poorly defined space between labor and harassment. Nobody is required to pay Miranda, but he rarely earns less than fifty euros a day—a passable sum in one of Europe's poorest countries. There is no fighting for turf, nor have the police ever tried to shoo him away. "I serve a purpose," Miranda told me, waving a metallic-blue Volkswagen Passat into an open slot.

"But I know I am lucky. I could have died long ago."

Miranda is a heroin addict. Fifteen years ago, overwhelmed by depression and anxiety about the future, he turned to drugs. "Everyone did it then," he said. "It was something I had to try. It made my life bearable—it still does. Though it can ruin people, too. I have seen that. When we started, we had no idea of the consequences."

By the nineteen-eighties, drug abuse had become a serious problem in Portugal. The Lisbon government responded in the usual way—increasing sentences for convictions and spending more money on investigations and prosecutions. Matters only grew worse. In 1999, nearly one per cent of the population—a hundred thousand people—were heroin addicts, and Portugal reported the highest rate of drug-related AIDS deaths in the European Union.

In 2001, Portuguese leaders, flailing about and desperate for change, took an unlikely gamble: they passed a law that made Portugal the first country to fully decriminalize personal drug use. (Other nations, such as Italy and the Netherlands, rarely prosecute minor drug offenses, but none have laws that so explicitly declare drugs to be "decriminalized.") "We were out of options," João Goulão told me. Goulão is the president of the Institute on Drugs and Drug Addiction, a department of the Ministry of Health that oversees Portuguese drug laws and policy. "We were spending millions and getting nowhere." For people caught with no more than a ten-day supply of marijuana, heroin, ecstasy, cocaine, or crystal methamphetamine—anything, really—there would be no arrests, no prosecutions, no prison sentences. Dealers are still sent to prison, or fined, or both, but, for the past decade, Portugal has treated drug abuse solely as a public-health issue.

That doesn't mean drugs are legal in Portugal. When caught, people are summoned before an administrative body called the Commission for the Dissuasion of Drug Addiction. Each panel consists of three members—usually a lawyer or a judge, a doctor, and a psychologist or a social worker. The commissioners have three options: recommend treatment, levy a small fine, or do nothing. Counselling is the most common approach, and that is what Nuno Miranda received when he appeared, in 2002, before the commission in Lisbon. "I was using drugs for five or seven years before that law passed," he said. "Since then, everything has changed. Everything."

In most respects, the law seems to have worked: serious drug use is down significantly, particularly among young people; the burden on the criminal-justice system has eased; the number of people seeking treatment has grown; and the rates of drug-related deaths and cases of infectious diseases have fallen. Initial fears that Portugal would become a haven for "drug tourism" have proved groundless. Surprisingly, political opposition has been tepid and there has never been a concerted repeal effort.

Yet there is much to debate about the Portuguese approach to drug addiction. Does it help people to quit, or does it transform them into more docile drug addicts, wards of an indulgent state, with little genuine incentive to alter their behavior? By removing the fear of prosecution, does the government actually encourage addicts to seek treatment? Unfortunately, nothing about substance abuse is simple. For instance, although many people maintain that addiction would decline if drugs were legal in the United States, the misuse of legally sold prescription medications has become a bigger health problem than the sale of narcotics or cocaine. There are questions not only about the best way to address addiction but also about how far any society should go, morally, philosophically, and economically, to placate drug addicts.

For Miranda, however, and for thousands of others who find themselves participating in civil life rather than disrupting it, such questions don't matter. He has a wife and a sixteen-year-old son, and adores them both. "My wife would never let me use heroin at home," he said. "I am not even allowed to smoke cigarettes in the house." With a stable family, a regular dealer, and his spot in the parking lot, Miranda's life has become orderly, almost routine. "This is because of the law," he said. "We are not hunted or scared or looked upon as criminals," he added, referring to the country's addicts. "And that has made it possible to live and to breathe." I asked if he had ever tried to overcome his addiction. He shrugged. "I guess I should," he said. "I know I should. But I'm not sure I can, and it isn't really necessary. I am lucky to live in a society that has accepted the fact that drugs and addiction are part of life."

In 1974, after decades of authoritarian rule, a left-leaning faction of the Portuguese military led a coup that subsequently became known as the Carnation Revolution. Suddenly, a closed society became a boisterous democracy, and Portugal began to face enormous social, economic, and political challenges. As one of its first acts, the new government granted independence to Angola, Mozambique, and other colonies. Hundreds of thousands of Portuguese citizens returned from abroad, adding to the social tumult. "We had a tough regime for forty-eight years and we were a closed society, and this was particularly true for young people," Goulão said as we sat in his airy Lisbon office. Pictures of foreign dignitaries lined the walls. "We were completely isolated from other parts of the world—the hippies in San Francisco, the students in France in the sixties. Faint echoes reached our shores, but nothing really sunk in." In the United States, as in many European countries, the acceptability of drug use—and its consequences—had been debated extensively. But in Portugal, Goulão said, "the issue was never discussed." As international drug traffickers discovered a new market in Lisbon, they also realized that the Iberian Peninsula was an ideal gateway to Europe. Portugal became a transit point for the distribution of cocaine from South America, heroin from Spain, and hashish and marijuana from Morocco and other African countries. (That has not changed. Goulão's institute estimates that seventy-seven per cent of the drugs seized in Portugal are destined for other countries.)

"It spread very fast," Goulão said. "We had an extremely low prevalence of drug use compared with other countries, but then all at once the gap between occasional users and people with a problem began to disappear." By the 1980s, after the initial years of openness and experimentation, the government panicked and began running extremely harsh advertisements on television equating drug use with madness, evil, and crime.

In those days, Goulão ran a clinic in the Algarve. "It was a disaster," he said. "Such widespread heroin abuse fuelled the AIDS epidemic. It was difficult to find a single family without a drug problem."

Every effort to increase drug penalties, to add police officers, or to build neighborhood consensus seemed to end in failure. Prohibition and its enforcement appeared to intensify the harm they were trying to address. (That was most obviously true with the H.I.V. epidemic; H.I.V. spreads rapidly among people who share dirty needles.) In addition, banning some addictive substances while permitting and taxing others has proved difficult to defend, particularly considering the relative impact of the substances involved. There is no country where illegal drugs kill as many people as legal addictive substances. The World Bank estimates that tobacco will kill five hundred million of the present global population.

It has been exactly fifty years since the United Nations adopted the Single Convention on Narcotic Drugs, the first truly international effort to prohibit the growth, production, and sale of narcotics, cannabis, and other illegal substances. Since 1961, however, Western nations have struggled with rising rates of drug abuse. Law-enforcement officials, politicians, and public-health leaders have debated their alternatives frequently—and frequently disagreed about what to do. That debate has never ended, and there are still essentially two approaches to substance abuse: rehabilitation and incarceration. In Portugal, though, a consensus quickly formed, even among law-enforcement officials, that devoting ever-increasing resources to drug interdiction had little or no effect. And neither did relying on the criminal-justice system to address the problem.

Eventually, the Portuguese government moved responsibility for drug-control issues from the Justice Department to the Ministry of Health. It was a striking decision; in other countries, drug abuse has remained primarily a matter for law-enforcement agencies. In the past forty years, American police officers have arrested millions of nonviolent drug offenders, and hundreds of thousands have been prosecuted. Rather than try to eliminate drug abuse, Portugal's approach, commonly known as "harm reduction," attempts to minimize the negative consequences for society. In recent years, those consequences have become both more obvious and more significant.

"The prevailing approach in the rest of the world ignores scientific reality and squanders resources on things that have been shown again and again to fail," said Miguel Vasconcelos, the chief psychiatrist at the Taipas treatment center, the largest in Lisbon, with eighteen hundred patients. When Vasconcelos began working at the clinic, more than twenty years ago, there was no attempt at harm reduction. "The goal was to get people off drugs," he said. "And for many patients that is still the goal. But there are people for whom it is hard and some for whom it is not possible. This is an alternative that does get people off the streets, reduces the rates of H.I.V. infection, and lowers crime. It is humanistic but also pragmatic."

The relationship between crime and addiction has long been clear. In the United States, more than seventy per cent of inmates test positive for illicit drugs when they are arrested; substance abuse is by far the most common reason for parole violations. The attempt to support a habit frequently leads to criminal behavior—drug sales, theft, prostitution. Vasconcelos pointed out that punishment is not a deterrent: "The prisons are full, but that has not helped lower the rate of drug abuse. Our law does not permit drug use; that is important. Harm reduction is like a lure in fishing. It is the thing we can do to talk to people and tell them there is a way to stop."

Statistics associated with drug abuse are not easy to parse. Laws, approaches, and customs vary widely among countries, and they change over the years. In the 1980s, the prevailing trend in most of the world was toward harsher treatment of even casual users. Today, policy officials in many countries are trying to change that pattern, but there are many goals in the war on drugs, and it is hard to choose the most meaningful among them. Is drug use increasing? Has it become socially and economically ruinous? What drugs are being used and by whom? How much violence is associated with drug addiction? How old are those with the biggest problem and why do they have that problem? Poverty is often the answer to the last question, and in 1999, before Portugal introduced the new regimen, the country had a high level of poverty compared with other European nations, many heroin addicts, and a serious problem with H.I.V. Thirty-seven per cent of injecting drug users were receiving methadone to manage their addiction; ten years later, that figure was sixty-seven per cent. The number of people convicted of drug offenses fell from forty-four per cent of the prison population, in 2000, to twenty-one per cent, in 2005; the percentage of people using heroin in prison also fell sharply.

"I used to be the biggest believer in locking up the bad guys," João Figueira, the chief inspector of the Judicial Police crime squad and its drug division in Lisbon, said. He told me that he was unhappy when the law was introduced, and he struggled with it morally. Within a year, he had changed his mind. "In the last years before the law, consumers were arrested by police," he continued. "They were fingerprinted and made statements and took mug photos and were presented to court. And always, always, always released. It was a waste of everyone's time. It didn't stop drug use or slow down the dealers. So the idea that somehow people are getting away with what they did not get away with before is silly."

Elisabete Moutinho, a clinical psychologist, who works for one of the drug outreach programs funded by the Ministry of Health, stood on a cobblestone plateau above the slope that leads to what was once the center of Lisbon's Casal Ventoso neighborhood. She looked across a nearby highway at a housing development of the type that often seems to rise along the ring roads that circle the world's capitals. It was utilitarian, and utterly lacking in charm. "That must be a dull place to live," I said. She smiled and replied, "There are worse things than dull. In this area, dull is an improvement." Twenty-five years ago, Casal Ventoso was essentially a giant shooting gallery, and, every day, thousands of people would line up to buy heroin, then they would fade into the dense warren of homes and kiosks that covered a series of connected hills. Walking through the squalid neighborhood meant weaving around piles of used, often bloody needles and, on occasion, stepping over a dead body. Casal Ventoso was a daily catalogue of human misery. In

1998, the government brought in a fleet of bulldozers and razed the neighborhood.

Moutinho, who is thirty, is a charismatic and idealistic woman with a demeanor that invites people to tell her their problems. "We are not here to judge or scold," she said. "This is purely a public-health initiative. We want these people in the system, unafraid, able to come to us if they are in need. And in turn we test them for diseases, treat them when they are sick. This is a better outcome for them than taking them to the hospital or the morgue. And it is a better outcome for the people of this country."

She and her team had arrived in a station wagon filled with drug paraphernalia: tinfoil, for people who smoke heroin rather than shoot it (which is often the only way for longtime addicts to get their fix, since years of injections have ruined their veins), and stacks of clean syringes, sterile wipes, and other accessories required to inject heroin safely. The exchange policy is simple: bring in a used needle and get a new one. "There is no limit," Moutinho said, as a man approached clutching nine syringes in his fist. She chatted with him as he deposited the needles, one by one, into a container she had placed in the center of the platform. "How is your arm?" she asked, noticing what appeared to be significant ulcerations along the inner part of his left arm. He shrugged and told her that he had been at the doctor's office two days earlier; in order to receive methadone, people must agree to periodic checkups and blood tests. When the man had deposited the last of his refuse, Moutinho counted out nine new pouches for fixing heroin, along with nine syringes, and handed them over. He nodded and moved on.

As people straggled up to the team, Moutinho explained, "We are here the same time every day, and people can count on that." I asked if she had any qualms about aiding people in their quest to satisfy addictions. "That is the wrong way to think about what we do," she said. "Of course, you can come here and still buy heroin. The dealers know where we are and when we are here. People exchange syringes and then go buy drugs.

"I know that is not easy for everyone to accept," she continued. "But they don't get AIDS from a dirty needle, or hepatitis. They are not beaten by gangs or arrested or put in jail. There is no police corruption, because there is nothing to get rich from. It is a program that reduces harm, and I don't see a better approach."

Later that afternoon, in the Alcântara section of Lisbon, I visited the Centro de Acolhimento, a short-term residency for drug addicts who need a place to begin new lives. The building, near the docks, is on both the seedy side of town and the cool side, and could easily have been the headquarters of an adventurous industrial designer. The floors—unbroken expanses of concrete—and the soaring windows made the room feel accessible and spacious. A few dozen people sat quietly eating at picnic-style tables arranged in the middle of the room. Francisco Chaves, the psychologist who has run the center since it opened, in 2009, admitted that he had mixed feelings about Portugal's approach to drug addiction. He is a religious activist who believes in rehabilitation and moral tenacity. To him, "harm reduction" offers little of that. "This law takes away all pressure to stop using drugs," he said. "Nobody stops without pressure. That's not the way humans are built. When you promise methadone to anyone who wants it, you are going to get people who say there is no reason to stop. This idea that everybody has a right to take drugs is wrong. Morally, I don't agree. I worry because are we not simply creating a society that is completely socially dependent?"

That view is echoed by Manuel Pinto Coelho, a physician who has treated addicts for many years, and is the president of the Association for a Drug Free Portugal. He has emerged as perhaps the most vigorous Portuguese critic of decriminalization, and when we met, in Lisbon, Pinto Coelho had just returned from Vienna, where, before the United Nations Office on Drugs and Crime, he had spoken passionately against easing drug penalties. "Medicalization of this deviant behavior has provided powerful support to the idea of expanding the concept of addiction as a disease," he told me. "That convinces most addicts that they have to remain dependent on methadone rather than struggle to become independent. It is a service neither to them nor to society." He is particularly offended by the notion that supporting human rights implies supporting greater investment in harm reduction: "Is it really a human right to remain in chemical chains?" Pinto Coelho argues that the system has been tilted in favor of those who don't even try to quit. "I have treated many addicts in my life," he said. "It is very hard to quit, and some people fail. But many succeed, and society should reward their success, not make a statement that the effort is unnecessary. We shouldn't be making life easier for people who decide to use drugs—we should make it more difficult."

Richard Nixon declared a "war on drugs" in 1971. For the next fifteen years, though, instead of battles there were mostly minor skirmishes. Then, in 1986, Ronald Reagan signed National Security Directive 221, which turned the war into a national-security priority. The reasons were clear: cocaine from South America, where drug cartels fought openly, had displaced Southeast Asian heroin as the major drug threat to the United States, and violence associated with drug sales escalated rapidly. Federal spending on drug control rose just as sharply, from $1.5 billion, in 1980, to $6.7 billion, in 1990. The number of arrests for drug offenses nearly quadrupled, to more than four hundred thousand per year. According to the United Nations Office on Drugs and Crime, by the mid-1990s trafficking and sales of illegal drugs had become a four-hundred-billion-dollar-a-year industry—ranking it with the oil companies and the worldwide (and legal) arms trade. In the United States, tough words on drugs became a required part of any politician's rhetoric. In 1996, President Bill Clinton named Army General Barry McCaffrey as director of the Office of National Drug Control Policy and increased its staff significantly. Later that year, Clinton announced a new National Drug Control Strategy. The first priority, according to the president, was "to get young people to reject drugs." The problem had become acute, and many policymakers wanted to solve it no matter the cost.

By June, 1998, the sense of urgency had reached the United Nations. That month, delegates gathered in New York for a special session devoted to the world's growing drug problem. The session even had a slogan, "A Drug-Free World: We Can Do It." The purpose was to produce a plan that the international community could use to fight, and win, the global war on drugs. The United States took the lead in writing early drafts of the proposal, which called for a complete end to illicit drug use by 2008. Later, after lobbying from Latin-American delegates, who were more realistic, the wording was amended to include the phrase "eliminating or significantly reducing."

Nobody questioned the severity of the crisis, but many politicians, scientists, and criminal-justice officials doubted that relying so heavily on law enforcement—and abolition—would work. There was already strong evidence that drug addiction was a biologically and psychologically complex illness—one far more amenable to preventive efforts and medical care than to punishment. On the first day of the special session, hundreds of the world's leading statesmen and political officials published an open letter to Secretary-General Kofi Annan in *The New York Times*. The signatories included former U.N. Secretary-General Javier Pérez de Cuéllar, former Secretary of State George Shultz, Walter Cronkite, former Attorney General Nicholas Katzenbach, many Nobel Prize winners, and elected officials from around the world. "We believe that the global war on drugs is now causing more harm than drug abuse itself," the letter began, and pointed out that U.N. conventions, focussed largely on crime and punishment, made it difficult for countries to devise effective local solutions. Despite increasingly harsh sanctions, the drug industry "has empowered organized criminals, corrupted governments at all levels, eroded internal security, stimulated violence, and distorted both economic markets and moral values." The letter concluded by warning that "realistic proposals to reduce drug-related crime, disease and death are abandoned in favor of rhetorical proposals to create drug-free societies."

The leadership at the United Nations ignored the message completely. But conservatives, who objected to any shift from punishment to rehabilitation, responded sharply. In the Times, A. M. Rosenthal, the paper's former executive editor, praised the U.N. meeting and described harm reduction as nothing more than the first step on the slippery slope to legalization. Bill Clinton seemed to agree. In 1993, his Surgeon General, Joycelyn Elders, had been quoted on the subject of prosecuting drug users. "I do feel we would markedly reduce our crime rate if drugs were legalized," she said. "But I don't know all the ramifications of this. I do feel that we need to do some studies." Elders never advocated legalization or even the removal of criminal sanctions; she wanted more research. The White House had other ideas. "The President is firmly against legalizing drugs," Clinton's press secretary said at the time. "And he is not inclined in this case to even study the issue." Attitudes under George W. Bush were no different.

"This is an extremely complex issue involving producers, suppliers, distributors, local salespeople, and consumers, and we are into absolute simplicity," said Alan Leshner, the chief executive officer of the American Association for the Advancement of Science and a former director of the National Institute on Drug Abuse. He added that Americans tend to see these issues in stark terms; people are either for legalization or against it. "Those kinds of positions help no one," he said. "We need to use law enforcement. But, if there is one thing about this issue I can promise you, it is that we are not going to arrest ourselves out of this problem.

"Yet we live in an ideologically fraught society," he continued, "a society that can pretend that drug use will go away if we just fight hard enough, if we 'just say no.' What politician will vote to reduce funds dedicated to the war on drugs?"

In the United States, the penalty for using a particular drug has rarely had any relationship to its inherent danger. As Arthur Benavie pointed out in "Drugs, America's Holy War," in 2009, the American approach to illegal substances has as much to do with who takes the drugs as it does with the drugs' putative effects on people or society. In the late nineteenth century, doctors often prescribed opiates with abandon—"The typical opiate addict was a chronically ailing middle- or upper-class woman who had been addicted by her doctor," Benavie wrote. Mary Tyrone, a character in Eugene O'Neill's "Long Day's Journey Into Night," believed to be modelled on his mother, was that kind of addict. Most cocaine addicts were doctors. Nobody talked about sending them to prison.

By 1915, however, the demographics of addiction had changed and so had American attitudes toward drug users. Cocaine had come to be seen as a drug taken by lower-class, urban men, who were often looked upon with fear and disdain. Opium had been tolerated in the United States for more than a century—until Chinese laborers began to compete with Americans for jobs. Since then, the more directly a drug has been perceived to be associated with minorities and the poor, the graver the danger it is seen as posing to society. Until last year, when President Obama signed the Fair Sentencing Act, penalties for possessing or selling crack cocaine, used heavily by minorities, were a hundred times more severe than those for powder cocaine, a form of the drug often consumed by prosperous white people.

"There has been, since the dawn of man, the desire to get high," Thomas McLellan, a longtime expert on addiction, told me not long ago. "Some of the first crops raised by humans were not meant to eat or to feed livestock. They were for fermentation. To drink." McLellan recently returned to academia after serving for two years as the deputy director of the Office of National Drug Control Policy. He has taught at the University of Pennsylvania Medical School for thirty years and runs the Center for Substance Abuse Solutions, in Philadelphia, which promotes science-driven reform of substance-abuse policy. He had never served in the government until he was appointed the Administration's leading spokesman on prevention and treatment options. McLellan said that he wasn't eager to accept the job, but did so for personal reasons. In 2008, a few months before he assumed his position, McLellan's youngest son, who was thirty, died of an overdose of anti-anxiety medication mixed with alcohol. McLellan's wife is a former cocaine addict. "My entire family is in recovery," he said. "I thought, maybe there's a way where what I know plus what I feel could make a difference." Together with Gil Kerlikowske, the U.S. drug czar, who is a former Seattle police chief, the Office of

National Drug Control Policy has attempted to shift the focus in the war on drugs from combat to treatment.

Under Kerlikowske and McLellan, the Obama Administration has placed a new emphasis on medical solutions to drug abuse. The Affordable Care Act, passed last year, requires for the first time that substance abuse be considered a chronic disease, like diabetes or hypertension. Beginning in 2014, insurers may no longer deny coverage based on known substance-abuse problems. "For approximately twenty-three million Americans, substance use progresses to the point that they require treatment," McLellan told Congress last year. "This is roughly the same number of American adults who suffer from diabetes. In the U.S., the only disease that affects more people is heart disease." Yet currently available medicine is rarely relied upon in drug programs. The Obama Administration has pushed for wider adoption of treatments that help manage withdrawal symptoms as well as those which reduce cravings for drugs. The drug-control office has also initiated programs that help health-care workers spot problems early.

"I think for some folks radical change will be their only measure of success," Kerlikowske has said. "I don't think we'll see that. I think we'll make a lot of progress, we'll slow the freighter down and start turning it in the direction of the more balanced view." Federal health officials have estimated that every dollar spent on substance-abuse treatment saves the United States seven dollars that would be spent on prison, police, and courts. "I understand the desire to wring somebody's neck when you find out they are using drugs," McLellan told me. "If you imagine that addiction is the willful act of an antisocial person who needs to learn his lesson, you ought to lock him up. But we have tried that and I don't see many people learning their lesson."

Nonetheless, McLellan does not favor a Portuguese approach for the United States. "It's not an ideology with me," he said. "If you make any attractive commodity available at lower cost, you will have more users. Anything like legalizing drugs is preposterous—no less ridiculous than trying to lock up every offender." As evidence, he points to the epidemic of prescription-drug abuse. "These drugs are created, controlled, and distributed in the most careful possible way," he said. "It doesn't prevent abuse."

Many people argue that because nobody is forced to take drugs the burden of addiction should not be borne by society. "It is true that you don't have to start," McLellan said. "But once you do, and once you become an addict, then a certain series of biological changes take place and you are no longer able to simply stop." Nearly all addicts believe they can overcome their dependence without help. The overwhelming majority do not succeed. Research has shown that long-term drug abuse results in changes in the brain that persist after a person stops taking drugs. Often, the first time somebody abuses drugs, he experiences particularly intense feelings of pleasure. The brain has activated circuits that make him feel good, and that message is carried by the neurotransmitter dopamine. As the brain starts to become used to those pleasures and demand them, neurons, sensing a surplus, begin to make less dopamine. The chemical begins to lose its ability to activate the pleasure circuits. As that happens, people start to need drugs just to bring dopamine levels back to normal. To feel good, or to get high, requires more and more dopamine—which requires more and more drugs.

"Addiction is a disease you have for which there is no cure, and which fits the model of chronic illness," McLellan said. "It will be a problem for the rest of your life. So you don't want a thirty-day program. It won't help. There are no thirty-day diabetes programs or twelve-visit hypertension clinics. The name for that is malpractice.

"Imagine we had an insurance program for diabetics along the lines of the programs we have had for substance abuse," he went on, noting the American inclination to treat chronic diseases after they have already caused irreparable harm. "Do you want to tell people who ate too many doughnuts that the American health-care system can't accommodate their illnesses? It is nobody's idea of the best use of a forty-two-thousand-dollar cell to house a person who has committed a minor crime or a parole violation associated with drug abuse. We all know that. And we are a better country than that."

Nobody can say with certainty whether Portugal's decriminalization program is helping persuade people to seek treatment, since those facilities became far more accessible just as the new law was passed. There are also questions about whether the benefits that Portugal has seen since 2001 reflect evolving patterns in European life and not the success of its program. Between 1998 and 2008, even though the number of addicts in Portugal enrolled in treatment jumped by sixty-three per cent—from twenty-three thousand to more than thirty-eight thousand—that could have potentially happened, critics say, without decriminalization or the expansion of clinics. "We know Portugal decriminalized drugs," said John Carnevale, a former director of planning, budget, and research at the Office of National Drug Control Policy under Presidents Reagan, Bush, and Clinton. "But we don't know the effects of that decriminalization." People who favor policy reform say that Portugal's experiment shows, if nothing else, that decriminalization has permitted the Portuguese criminal-justice system to focus on more significant criminals and more dangerous crimes. But what works in a small seaside nation in Southern Europe is not necessarily likely to work in a place that is larger, richer, and more heavily plagued by drug abuse. And, though about half of American adults believe that marijuana use should be legalized, there has been no serious discussion of making all drugs legal in the U.S.—or in any other country. Still, if prison were no longer a common penalty, there would clearly be more money available for treatment programs. And, if the Portuguese pattern held true, there would be fewer crimes to punish.

"It is never easy to draw a lesson from complex experience," Brendan Hughes, of the European Monitoring Centre for Drugs and Drug Addiction, in Lisbon, said. "But here we are in Lisbon thirteen years after the U.N. vowed to abolish illicit drugs in a decade. Has anybody here seen a drug-free world?" he said, noting that the annual United Nations World Drug Report usually runs to about three hundred pages. During the ten years following the 1998 declaration, when eradication was supposed to have been accomplished, the number of people using opiates throughout the world grew by thirty-five per cent; the number of cocaine users grew by nearly thirty per cent.

Expenditures, particularly those associated with the criminal prosecution of drug abusers, have also risen dramatically, as has the size of the correctional system in the United States. Since the late 1980s, most of that growth can be attributed directly to drug abuse. The cost of running the state-prison systems has grown by four hundred per cent, and it is expected to grow even more rapidly in the next decade. According to the National Center on Addiction and Substance Abuse, those costs represent at least ten times the amount of money spent on treatment, prevention, and research. In Portugal, where drug control is funded in part by lottery receipts and money seized from traffickers, the ratio is the opposite: more than ninety per cent of costs are now devoted to treatment, not punishment.

Before I left his office, Hughes suggested that I take a close look at the 2009 World Drug Report, in part because it was issued by the same agency that, little more than a decade before, had called for the worldwide elimination of drugs. It, too, expressed the need for a radical reassessment of the war on drugs.

Perhaps the strongest case against the current system of drug control has less to do with its costs, or even its effectiveness in reducing the availability of drugs, than with the violence and corruption associated with the black market. The prevailing approach has had the perverse effect of enriching criminals who kill and bribe their way from the countries where drugs are produced to the countries where drugs are consumed.

It is common in the U.S. to judge drug addiction morally rather than medically, and most policy flows from that approach. By now, however, the data showing that the war on drugs has failed are not in dispute; Obama Administration officials do not even use the phrase. Yet one has only to look at the American health-care system to be reminded that neither science nor evidence necessarily drives public-policy decisions. More money, per capita, and a greater percentage of income, is spent on health care in the United States than in any other nation. Nevertheless, the U.S. lags behind most of the rest of the Western world in health outcomes. If anything, the war on drugs is more complex; while it is clear that a purely punitive approach cannot succeed, it is far less obvious what might. While it would make no sense to base American policy on a decade-long Portuguese experiment, it seems even more foolish to ignore results that call so clearly for an increased focus on treatment, not jail time.

"You started by asking if I thought Portugal was on the right track," Hughes said. "That's not really a question I feel competent to answer. But if you look at enough of these reports, and study the data behind them, you can't help but feel that the country can't be on more of a wrong track than the rest of the world."

Night had begun to fall at the underpass near Lisbon's Praça de Espanha metro station. Two methadone vans, which cruise the city with the eerie regularity of ice-cream trucks, pulled into a cul-de-sac under the motorway. People were starting to gather for their daily doses. An outreach team arrives every day at 6 P.M. and stays for an hour and a half, and often another van appears, carrying a doctor who is available to conduct check-ups. "This is a strategic location," one of the physicians told me. "People need to take their methadone every day, and this place is near the metro and just off the roadway. If you are in a car, you can stop off without being conspicuous. If you need to get here on the metro, we are easy to find." This van serves about six hundred people a day, and the economic status of the clients is not always easy to determine. Several people drove up in Fiats, but a couple of Mercedes sedans were also parked at the side of the road. A nurse sat with a laptop, a bottle of metha-done, and a few hundred Dixie cups. Each person presented an I.D., and the nurse checked his or her dosage on a database, then gave the person a cup and a bottle of spring water to wash it down. Several cops walked by and smiled. The vans make five stops a day between 8:30 A.M. and 7:30 P.M. Everyone does his business briskly and walks away. There are no chats or knots of people who hang around at the methadone truck after work. It was a ghostly assembly, an effect no doubt enhanced by the failing light. You don't see a lot of smiles or laughter in lines like these. You don't sense a lot of promise, either. I told the doctor I was with that the entire program seemed strangely methodical.

He laughed and replied, "Thank you. We like methodical. It is better than frantic, or desperate, or dangerous. I admire these people exactly because they are methodical. They are trying. Every day, they get up and try. The main complaint about our approach, as far as I can tell, is that they ought to try for some-thing harder. They all ought to stop using drugs."

"I think what's hard is to acknowledge reality," he continued. "These people are living in the real world. If they are boring, or live with narrowed vision or limited ambition, I am happy. I am proud. Because I know what the other side looks like. It is ugly. Perhaps it is a national failing, but I prefer moderate hope and some likelihood of success to the dream of perfection and the promise of failure."

Critical Thinking

1. Develop an argument for either why the Portuguese approach to drug addiction helps drug addicts or hinders drug users.

2. Discuss whether U.S. drug policy is morally or medically motivated.

3. Develop a plan for U.S. drug policy reform.

Create Central

www.mhhe.com/createcentral

Internet References

ACLU
    www.aclu.org/blog/tag/drug-law-reform
The White House
    www.whitehouse.gov/ondcp/drugpolicyreform

Unit 7

Prepared by: Mary Maguire, *California State University—Sacramento*
Clifford Garoupa, *Fresno City College*

UNIT

Prevention, Treatment, and Education

There are no magic bullets for preventing drug abuse and treating drug-dependent persons. Currently, more than 22 million Americans are classified as drug dependent on illicit drugs and/or alcohol. Males continue to be twice as likely to be classified as drug dependent as females. Research continues to establish and strengthen the role of treatment as a critical component in the fight against drug abuse. Some drug treatment programs have been shown to dramatically reduce the costs associated with high-risk populations of users. For example, recidivism associated with drug-related criminal justice populations has been shown to decrease by 50 percent after treatment. Treatment is a critical component in the fight against drug abuse but it is not a panacea. Society cannot "treat" drug abuse away just as it cannot "arrest" it away.

Drug prevention and treatment philosophies subscribe to a multitude of modalities. Everything seems to work a little and nothing seems to work completely. The articles in this unit illustrate the diversity of methods utilized in prevention and treatment programs. Special emphasis is given to treating the drug problems of those who are under the supervision of the criminal justice system. All education, prevention, and treatment programs compete for local, state, and federal resources. Current treatment efforts at all public and private levels are struggling to meet the demands for service due to the impacts from the U.S. economic crisis of the past few years.

Education: One critical component of drug education is the ability to rapidly translate research findings into practice, and today's drug policy continues to emphasize this in its overall budget allocations. Funding for educational research and grants is generally strong with the trend being toward administering funds to local communities and schools to fund local proposals. For example, in 2011 more than $50 million was again made available to schools for research-based assistance for drug prevention and school safety programs. Another example is the refunding of the $120 million National Youth Media Campaign designed to help coach parents in processes of early recognition and intervention. Encouraging successful parenting is one primary emphasis in current federal drug policy. Other significant research efforts continue to support important education, prevention, and treatment programs such as The National Prevention Research Initiative, Interventions and Treatment for Current Drug Users Who Are Not Yet Addicted, the National Drug Abuse Treatment Clinical Trial Network, and Research Based Treatment Approaches for Drug Abusing Criminal Offenders. In 2011, federal research-related grants totaling almost $100 million were made available to local and state school jurisdictions.

Prevention: A primary strategy of drug prevention programs is to prevent and/or delay initial drug use. A secondary strategy is to discourage use by persons minimally involved with drugs. Both strategies include (1) educating users and potential users; (2) teaching adolescents how to resist peer pressure; (3) addressing problems associated with drug abuse such as teen pregnancy, failure in school, and lawbreaking; (4) creating community support and involvement for prevention activities; and (5) involving parents in deterring drug use by children. Prevention and education programs are administered through a variety of mechanisms, typically amidst controversy relative to what works best. Schools have been an important delivery apparatus. Funding for school prevention programs is an important emphasis within the efforts to reduce the demand for drugs. Subsequently, an increase in federal money was dedicated to expanding the number of high school programs that implement student drug testing. Drug testing in high schools, authorized by the Supreme Court in a 2002 court decision, has produced a positive and measurable deterrent to drug use. Despite its controversy, school drug testing is expanding as a positive way to reinforce actions of parents to educate and deter their children from use. The testing program provides for subsequent assessment, referral, and intervention process in situations where parents and educators deem it necessary.

In addition, in 2011, approximately $90 million in grant funds were again dedicated to support the federal Drug-Free Communities Program, which provides funds at the community level to anti-drug coalitions working to prevent substance abuse among young people and in local neighborhoods. There are currently more than 700 local community coalitions working under this program nationwide. Also, there are community-based drug prevention programs sponsored by civic organizations, church groups, and private corporations. All programs pursue funding through public grants and private endowments. Federal grants to local, state, and private programs are critical components to program solvency. The multifaceted nature of prevention programs makes them difficult to assess categorically. School programs that emphasize the development of skills to resist social and peer pressure generally produce varying degrees of positive results. Research continues to make more evident the need to focus prevention programs with specific populations in mind.

Treatment: Like prevention programs, drug treatment programs enlist a variety of methods to treat persons dependent upon legal and illegal drugs. There is no single-pronged approach to treatment for drug abuse. Treatment modality may differ radically from one user to the other. The user's background, physical and mental health, personal motivation, and support structure all have serious implications for treatment type. Lumping together the diverse needs of chemically dependent persons for purposes of applying a generic treatment process does not work. In addition, most persons needing and seeking treatment have problems with more than one drug—polydrug use. Current research also correlates drug use with serious mental illness (SMI). Current research by the federal Substance Abuse and Mental Health Services Administration (SAMHSA) reports that adults with a drug problem are three times more likely to suffer from a serious mental illness. The existing harmful drug use and mental health nexus is exacerbated by the fact that using certain powerful drugs such as methamphetamine push otherwise functioning persons into the dysfunctional realm of mental illness. Although treatment programs differ in methods, most provide a combination of key services. These include drug counseling, drug education, pharmacological therapy, psychotherapy, relapse prevention, and assistance with support structures. Treatment programs may be outpatient oriented or residential in nature. Residential programs require patients to live at the facility for a prescribed period of time. These residential programs, often described as therapeutic communities, emphasize the development of social, vocational, and educational skills. The current trend is to increase the availability of treatment programs. One key component of federal drug strategy is to continue to fund and expand the Access to Recovery treatment initiative that began in 2004. This program uses a voucher system to fund drug treatment for individuals otherwise unable to obtain it. This program, now operational in 14 states and one Native American community, allows dependent persons to personally choose care providers, including faith-based care providers. It is hoped that this program will encourage states to provide a wider array of treatment and recovery options. As one example, the state of Missouri has transformed all public drug treatment within the state to an "Access to Recovery-Like" program in which involved persons choose their providers and pay with state vouchers. It is hoped that this and similar programs will allow a more flexible delivery of services that will target large populations of dependent persons who are not reached through other treatment efforts.

Prepared by: Mary Maguire, *California State University—Sacramento*
Clifford Garoupa, *Fresno City College*

Article

Old Habits Die Hard for Ageing Addicts

The number of older drug users is rising. But what health and care challenges do they face as they age, and is the system prepared to deal with them?

MATTHEW FORD

Learning Outcomes

After reading this article, you will be able to:

- Understand the challenges ageing addicts present to society.
- Understand the extent of drug addiction in the ageing population.
- Discuss how the Netherlands is addressing the problem of ageing drug addicts.

Maggie Jones receives a regular dose of methadone from her GP and dreads the thought of having to go into a care home with her dependency.

"I know I'm lucky: I've got a great GP who will arrange things and make sure I get my methadone if I have to go into hospital. But the idea of being stuck in a bed somewhere and not having your [prescription], that's very scary.

"As for the thought of going into an old people's home, that's absolutely terrifying. Or what if you get infirm and get stuck at home and can't get to the chemist to get your prescription?

"Getting old is worrying for many people, I know that. But if you're an addict then there is this consuming fear of being powerless."

Jones (not her real name) is not alone in contemplating her dotage with a long-standing addiction. Although an early death is a reality for many addicts, methadone prescriptions and the success of harm-reduction programmes now mean that large numbers of people who began using drugs in the 1960s and 1970s are living longer. Figures from the National Treatment Agency for Substance Misuse show that there were more than 1,300 addicts over the age of 60 in treatment in England in 2009. In 1998, just 8 percent of drug users were aged 40–49, but by 2006, a quarter were in this age bracket. Caryl Beynon, reader in substance use epidemiology at the centre for public health, Liverpool John Moores University, calculates that there are now around 70,000–75,000 addicts aged over 40 in the UK.

Older drug users face a grim catalogue of serious health problems as they age. "What we are seeing is that users in their 40s frequently have many of the health issues of someone in their 60s or even 70s," says Beynon. "There is also some evidence that addicts are more prone to early onset dementia."

But public services are not geared up for older addicts. Society just does not expect older people to be addicts, and drugs remain firmly linked with youth behaviour. As a result, treatment is still focused on the needs of the young, but that will need to change. "There's definitely a gap in service provision for older users," says Michael Simpson, communications officer at the charity DrugScope.

Of particular concern are the health problems facing people who have been using intravenously for many years. "I've seen horrendous injuries that have gone untreated," says Erin O'Mara, editor of *Black Poppy*, a magazine for heroin users, whose co-founder, Chris Drouet, died of an overdose last year, aged 60.

"There are ulcers, amputations, repeated heart problems, abscesses, breaks that aren't healed properly. Often, when people do seek help, the care they get is so lackadaisical. Many people have said to me that medical staff treat addicts like scumbags, and so they just won't go to the doctor's," O'Mara adds.

Jones agrees that health issues are worse for those still using intravenously. "Drug use takes a hefty toll: they've got Hepatitis C, HIV, bronchial problems, depression."

Reluctance to seek treatment almost cost Andrew O'Malley, 48, a recovering addict, his hand. "It was badly infected in the bone, but I felt too ashamed to get treatment. Every day I was covering it up and trying to get along," he says. "In the end I went to hospital, but I've lost most of the movement in my hand."

Older addicts also find it harder to cope with pain than elderly people who do not take drugs. "Inadequate pain relief is a real concern," says Beynon. "If someone has been on opiates for years, their tolerance will be higher and they will need higher doses to achieve an analgesic effect. But some doctors don't realise that.

"Another big problem is that as people age they inevitably need to take more medicine, particularly if they have health issues. Helping addicts to keep track of complicated regimes can be hard. They just don't remember to take their pills."

There is also mounting evidence that overdoses can be more likely as users get older—despite the false confidence many might feel after surviving decades using a particular substance.

"General problems of ageing may well make it harder to fight an overdose, putting long-standing users at greater risk," says Simpson. In particular, emphysema, bronchitis and other lung problems—smoking cigarettes as well as illegal substances is common among addicts—can result in chronic obstructive pulmonary disease, which can in turn heighten the risk of overdose.

Some addicts and those who work with them believe that the culture of methadone prescriptions has exacerbated the problem, as for decades treatment has focused on stabilising addicts, leaving many "parked up" at home.

"They just sit there waiting for the dole to turn up," says Lewis Ward, 55, a service user involvement worker in Castleford, west Yorkshire, for the social enterprise Turning Point. He was addicted to heroin for 20 years until he quit five years ago. "Although I was always working, I know how they feel. I thought I couldn't give up for years and years because I was raising a family and I couldn't afford the six-month disruption of getting clean."

Under the coalition government's drug strategy, every addict should be helped off all drugs, including methadone. But there are concerns that it will be much harder for older users to get clean than younger addicts, who have not been using drugs for as long. "We need to be really sensitive about how we do this," says O'Mara. "It's very different dealing with a 20-year-old who might have been on heroin for a short time and someone who's been an addict for 30–40 years. A lot of people are thinking: 'I'm 60. How am I going to do this?' "

She also believes that there needs to be some acknowledgment that, for some, it will be too late to change. "Most people don't want to be an addict forever. But at the same time we need to recognise that for some people they just can't live any other way. They've been on opiates their whole lives and we can't just start poking them with a stick and saying: 'Get up. Get a job.' "

Ultimately, there will come a point for many ageing addicts when they can no longer look after themselves at home, and then there is huge uncertainty about what to do.

In Rotterdam, this apprehension is being allayed. Seniorepand is a semi-private medical foundation billed as the world's first retirement home for drug users. In the Netherlands, addicts receive free healthcare and methadone, and while residents at Seniorepand are encouraged to use fewer drugs, its aim is to provide a place for them to live out their last days in dignity.

Could such a facility work in the UK? "There are no plans to introduce similar specialist facilities in England," says Paul Hayes, chief executive of the National Treatment Agency for Substance Misuse.

But representatives of the care industry remain concerned that it is not fully prepared for rising numbers of addicts and that care homes for older people cannot at present meet drug users' needs.

"[Managing people with addictions] will be an enormous challenge," says Martin Green, chief executive of the English Community Care Home Association. Care homes are not paid to look after addicts and do not have the requisite expertise to manage people with significant drug or indeed alcohol problems.

"This is an issue that will increase in prevalence and the health and social care system needs to start planning for it. The government should acknowledge this issue and re-direct some of the money currently in rehab services to care providers," says Green.

But a spokesman for the Department of Health insists the system is ready: "Before a person is admitted to a care home, the local authority social services department should assess their health and personal care needs, including any addictions, and arrange care to meet those needs that fall within its eligibility criteria."

Either way, Jones is not reassured: "Can you imagine being an addict in a regular old people's home? You wouldn't be able to move without being glared at. It would be terrible.

"With the way things are I'd rather be dependent on drugs than other people," she says.

Critical Thinking

1. Why are addicts living longer?
2. What are some of the serious health problems that addicts confront as they are age?
3. What is Seniorepand? What do they do?

Create Central

www.mhhe.com/createcentral

Internet References

Drug Watch International
 www.drugwatch.org

The Drug Reform Coordination Network (DRC)
 www.drcnet.org

Article   Prepared by: Mary Maguire, *California State University—Sacramento*
                                                       Clifford Garoupa, *Fresno City College*

Addiction Diagnoses May Rise Under Guideline Changes

Ian Urbina

Learning Outcomes

After reading this article, you will be able to:

- Describe what the D.S.M is.

- Explain how the D.S.M defines drug addiction.

- Explain how the latest edition of the D.S.M has changed the criteria used to define drug addiction and dependence.

In what could prove to be one of their most far-reaching decisions, psychiatrists and other specialists who are rewriting the manual that serves as the nation's arbiter of mental illness have agreed to revise the definition of addiction, which could result in millions more people being diagnosed as addicts and pose huge consequences for health insurers and taxpayers.

The revision to the manual, known as the Diagnostic and Statistical Manual of Mental Disorders, or D.S.M., would expand the list of recognized symptoms for drug and alcohol addiction, while also reducing the number of symptoms required for a diagnosis, according to proposed changes posted on the website of the American Psychiatric Association, which produces the book.

In addition, the manual for the first time would include gambling as an addiction, and it might introduce a catchall category—"behavioral addiction—not otherwise specified"—that some public health experts warn would be too readily used by doctors, despite a dearth of research, to diagnose addictions to shopping, sex, using the Internet or playing video games.

Part medical guidebook, part legal reference, the manual has long been embraced by government and industry. It dictates whether insurers, including Medicare and Medicaid, will pay for treatment, and whether schools will expand financing for certain special-education services. Courts use it to assess whether a criminal defendant is mentally impaired, and pharmaceutical companies rely on it to guide their research.

The broader language involving addiction, which was debated this week at the association's annual conference, is intended to promote more accurate diagnoses, earlier intervention and better outcomes, the association said. "The biggest problem in all of psychiatry is untreated illness, and that has huge social costs," said Dr. James H. Scully Jr., chief executive of the group.

But the addiction revisions in the manual, scheduled for release in May 2013, have already provoked controversy similar to concerns previously raised about proposals on autism, depression and other conditions. Critics worry that changes to the definitions of these conditions would also sharply alter the number of people with diagnoses.

While the association says that the addiction definition changes would lead to health care savings in the long run, some economists say that 20 million substance abusers could be newly categorized as addicts, costing hundreds of millions of dollars in additional expenses.

"The chances of getting a diagnosis are going to be much greater, and this will artificially inflate the statistics considerably," said Thomas F. Babor, a psychiatric epidemiologist at the University of Connecticut who is an editor of the international journal *Addiction*. Many of those who get addiction diagnoses under the new guidelines would have only a mild problem, he said, and scarce resources for drug treatment in schools, prisons and health care settings would be misdirected.

"These sorts of diagnoses could be a real embarrassment," Dr. Babor added.

The scientific review panel of the psychiatric association has demanded more evidence to support the revisions on addiction, but several researchers involved with the manual have said that the panel is not likely to change its proposal significantly.

The controversies about the revisions have highlighted the outsize influence of the manual, which brings in more than $5 million annually to the association and is written by a group of 162 specialists in relative secrecy. Besieged from all sides, the association has received about 25,000 comments on the proposed changes from treatment centers, hospital representatives, government agencies, advocates for patient groups and researchers. The organization has declined to make these comments public.

While other medical specialties rely on similar diagnostic manuals, none have such influence. "The D.S.M. is distinct from all other diagnostic manuals because it has an enormous, perhaps too large, impact on society and millions of people's lives," said Dr. Allen J. Frances, a professor of psychiatry and behavioral sciences at Duke, who oversaw the writing of the current version of the manual and worked on previous editions. "Unlike many other fields, psychiatric illnesses have no clear biological gold standard for diagnosing them. They present in different ways, and illnesses often overlap with each other."

Dr. Frances has been one of the most outspoken critics of the new draft version, saying that overly broad and vaguely worded definitions will create more "false epidemics" and "medicalization of everyday behavior." Like some others, he has also questioned whether a private association, whose members stand to gain from treating more patients, should be writing the manual, rather than an independent group or a federal agency.

Under the new criteria, people who often drink more than intended and crave alcohol may be considered mild addicts. Under the old criteria, more serious symptoms, like repeatedly missing work or school, being arrested or driving under the influence, were required before a person could receive a diagnosis as an alcohol abuser.

Dr. George E. Woody, a professor of psychiatry at the University of Pennsylvania School of Medicine, said that by describing addiction as a spectrum, the manual would reflect more accurately the distinction between occasional drug users and full-blown addicts. Currently, only about 2 million of the nation's more than 22 million addicts get treatment, partly because many of them lack health insurance.

Dr. Keith Humphreys, a psychology professor at Stanford who specializes in health care policy and who served as a drug control policy adviser to the White House from 2009 to 2010, predicted that as many as 20 million people who were previously not recognized as having a substance abuse problem would probably be included under the new definition, with the biggest increase among people who are unhealthy users, rather than severe abusers, of drugs.

"This represents the single biggest expansion in the quality and quantity of addiction treatment this country has seen in 40 years," Dr. Humphreys said, adding that the new federal health care law may allow an additional 30 million people who abuse drugs or alcohol to gain insurance coverage and access to treatment. Some economists have said that the number could be much lower, though, because many insurers will avoid or limit coverage of addiction treatment.

The savings from early intervention usually show up within a year, Dr. Humphreys said, and most patients with a new diagnosis would get consultations with nurses, doctors or therapists, rather than expensive prescriptions for medicines typically reserved for more severe abusers.

Many scholars believe that the new manual will increase addiction rates. A study by Australian researchers found, for example, that about 60 percent more people would be considered addicted to alcohol under the new manual's standards. Association officials expressed doubt, however, that the expanded addiction definitions would sharply increase the number of new patients, and they said that identifying abusers sooner could prevent serious complications and expensive hospitalizations.

"We can treat them earlier," said Dr. Charles P. O'Brien, a professor of psychiatry at the University of Pennsylvania and the head of the group of researchers devising the manual's new addiction standards. "And we can stop them from getting to the point where they're going to need really expensive stuff like liver transplants."

Some critics of the new manual have said that it has been tainted by researchers' ties to pharmaceutical companies.

"The ties between the D.S.M. panel members and the pharmaceutical industry are so extensive that there is the real risk of corrupting the public health mission of the manual," said Dr. Lisa Cosgrove, a fellow at the Edmond J. Safra Center for Ethics at Harvard, who published a study in March that said two-thirds of the manual's advisory task force members reported ties to the pharmaceutical industry or other financial conflicts of interest.

Dr. Scully, the association's chief, said the group had required researchers involved with writing the manual to disclose more about financial conflicts of interest than was previously required.

Dr. O'Brien, who led the addiction working group, has been a consultant for several pharmaceutical companies, including Pfizer, GlaxoSmithKline and Sanofi-Aventis, all of which make drugs marketed to combat addiction.

He has also worked extensively as a paid consultant for Alkermes, a pharmaceutical company, studying a drug, Vivitrol, that combats alcohol and heroin addiction by preventing craving. He was the driving force behind adding "craving" to the new manual's list of recognized symptoms of addiction.

"I'm quite proud to have played a role, because I know that craving plays such an important role in addiction," Dr. O'Brien said, adding that he had never made any money from the sale of drugs that treat craving.

Dr. Howard B. Moss, associate director for clinical and translational research at the National Institute on Alcohol Abuse and Alcoholism, in Bethesda, Md., described opposition from many researchers to adding "craving" as a symptom of addiction. He added that he quit the group working on the addiction chapter partly out of frustration with what he described as a lack of scientific basis in the decision making.

"The more people diagnosed with cravings," Dr. Moss said, "the more sales of anticraving drugs like Vivitrol or naltrexone."

Critical Thinking

1. What exactly is the Diagnostic and Statistical Manual of Mental Disorders?
2. What is a "behavioral addiction"?
3. Who is responsible for writing and publishing the D.S.M?

Create Central

www.mhhe.com/createcentral

Internet References

Home/APA DSM-5
   www.dsm5.org
Psychiatry Online
   psychiatryonline.org

Article

Prepared by: Mary Maguire, *California State University—Sacramento*
Clifford Garoupa, *Fresno City College*

California Prisons Spend Big on Anti-Psychotic Drugs

DON THOMPSON

Learning Outcomes

After reading this article, you will be able to:

- Understand what anti-psychotic drugs are.
- Understand why anti-psychotic drugs are widely used in correctional facilities.
- Discuss how much the use of these drugs cost the California prison system.

Under federal court oversight, California's prison mental health system has been spending far more on anti-psychotic drugs than other states with large prison systems, raising questions about whether patients are receiving proper treatment.

Figures compiled by the Associated Press show that California has been spending a far greater percentage on anti-psychotic medication for inmates than other states with large prison systems. While the amount has been decreasing in recent years, anti-psychotics still account for nearly $1 of every $5 spent on pharmaceuticals purchased for the state prison system.

Questions about the spending have been raised by the state budget analyst and by the court-appointed authority in charge of buying prison pharmaceuticals, who concluded that California's inmate mental health professionals appear to over-medicate their patients. Even a former top prison mental health administrator acknowledged that fear of lawsuits often drove the decisions about inmates' treatment.

Nearly 20 percent of the $144.5 million California spent on all prison pharmaceuticals last year went for anti-psychotic drugs, according to the AP's figures, which were obtained through requests under the state Public Records Act.

"Why are all these people on meds? A lot of it, I think, we overprescribe on mental health. Anybody who comes in on mental health (referrals), we put on a psychotropic," said J. Clark Kelso, the federal court-appointed receiver who controls prison medical care.

His office buys psychiatric drugs for the prison system, but he is not in charge of prison mental health care and thus has no say over how often the pharmaceuticals are used.

Kelso raised an alarm with prison mental health officials internally three years ago when he identified what he thought was an extraordinary use of anti-psychotics, which in 2008 accounted for 34 percent of all prison pharmaceuticals spending. Spending on anti-psychotics has since fallen from about 26 percent of all prescription spending in 2009–2011 to 19 percent last year.

When he raised concerns, Kelso said he was told that "we have a substantial reliance on drug treatment programs, more so than in other states around the country."

The comparatively high use of the drugs in California is feeding a debate between doctors and the attorneys representing inmates over whether mentally ill prisoners receive too much medication or not enough. California's poor treatment of inmates with mental health problems prompted a federal court takeover of that operation and persuaded federal judges to order the prison population sharply reduced to improve prisoner care.

A federal judge recently decided to maintain court oversight of the mental health system, finding that the state continues to violate constitutional standards. More than 32,000 of California's nearly 133,000 inmates are receiving mental health treatment.

Psychotropic drugs include anti-psychotics, as well as sedatives, antidepressants, stimulants and tranquillizers. Anti-psychotics are generally used to treat schizophrenia and bipolar disorder.

California's use of the anti-psychotic medications stands out among the nation's large prison systems, according to comparison figures compiled by the AP.

New York's prison department spent about 17 percent of its prescription drug budget on all psychotropic drugs at the same time California was spending 26 percent of its budget on anti-psychotics alone.

Texas, which has a unique method of buying low-cost drugs, spent 6 percent of its prison pharmaceutical budget on psychotropic drugs, including anti-psychotics last year, while just 3 percent of Florida prisons' prescription drug spending is going for psychotropics this fiscal year.

In a report published last year, the independent Legislative Analyst's Office said California spent about $1,500 annually on psychiatric drugs for each inmate in a mental health program, compared to an average $610 a year per inmate in Florida, Georgia, New Jersey, Ohio and Pennsylvania.

Budget analyst Aaron Edwards, who compiled the report, said his figures included spending on mentally ill inmates by all state agencies and private contractors so the state-by-state spending comparisons would be as direct as possible.

California corrections officials said they have no reason to believe that anti-psychotics are overprescribed to inmates.

Yet Sharon Aungst, formerly the chief deputy secretary for the department's Division of Health Care Services, said the treatments given inmates are largely driven by lawsuits, federal court orders and the court-appointed special master overseeing a long-running legal settlement that governs virtually every aspect of inmate mental health care.

Aungst said there was a tendency for prison health care workers to practice "defensive medicine" for fear of triggering a lawsuit or violating federal court orders.

"One of the concerns that our staff always have, if we take someone off the caseload because we don't think they ought to be on there anymore, and anything goes wrong, then we get clobbered," Aungst said shortly before she left the department in 2011, at a time when anti-psychotics accounted for one quarter of prison pharmaceutical spending. "So we are playing defensive medicine quite a bit, and so it's much safer for our staff, because they're risk-averse, to keep them on the caseload and continue to treat even if we're not so sure that that's absolutely necessary."

She spoke at the time on behalf of the department, with the department's chief psychiatrist, assistant chief legal counsel and a department spokesman sitting in on the interview. The court-appointed special master overseeing prison mental health treatment, Rhode Island attorney Matthew A Lopes Jr., did not return repeated telephone messages for this story.

Dr. Karen Higgins, the chief psychiatrist for the state corrections department, said about 64 percent of inmates diagnosed with serious mental illness are prescribed some form of psychotropic medication, a class that includes anti-psychotics.

"While we do not have data to support the assertion of over-prescribing as an indication of defensive medicine, it is a possibility that we must guard against with appropriate checks and balances," Higgins said in an emailed response to questions.

She said the department has set up drug-use guidelines and a list of preferred drugs that doctors and mental health workers can prescribe, as well as a computer program to help providers choose the right medication.

The department also tracks doctors' prescribing practices and requires them to justify their reasons for using more expensive medications that are not on the preferred list. A bill signed into law in 2011 requires that state prison inmates not be given psychotropic medications without their informed consent.

That same year, attorney Ken Karan won a court order prohibiting the department from forcing one of his inmate clients from taking psychotropic medication against his will.

"My feeling is it's being used as a disciplinary measure, as a way to control people who are not institutional type of people," said Karan, who is based in the San Diego County community of Carlsbad. "One way to make them comply is to pump them up with dangerous drugs."

He said he had not seen evidence of that for inmates other than his client because the scope of his lawsuit was narrow.

In another case, the family of Joseph Sullivan won a lawsuit and a $475,000 settlement against the state corrections department in 2009, three years after Sullivan was found hanging by a bed sheet in Chuckawalla Valley State Prison, located in the Southern California desert along the Arizona border.

Experts who reviewed his case as part of the family's investigation said the 26-year-old was a victim of mind-altering drugs he didn't need but that were still prescribed by a prison doctor. Sullivan had been prescribed the anti-psychotic drug olanzapine, which goes by the trade name, Zyprexa.

"Joseph was put on psychotropic drugs for no good reason," said David Springfield, one of the Sullivan family's attorneys.

An autopsy showed Sullivan had nearly double the maximum therapeutic amount of Zyprexa in his system. The combination of the drug and the isolation and high temperatures within the prison cell likely drove him "to hopelessness and despair," the autopsy said.

Fellow inmates and a medical expert hired by the family said he had not demonstrated signs of being suicidal before he started taking the drug.

His father, Daniel Sullivan, said a letter from his son arrived a day after his death, in which the younger man said he was looking forward to being transferred to a prison closer to home. In the letter, the son promised, "We're going to have a new life together. I want to pick up and go forward."

Critical Thinking

1. How much of California's prison budget is spent on psychiatric medications?
2. What are these medications used for?
3. Can inmates be forced to take psychiatric medications?

Create Central

www.mhhe.com/createcentral

Internet References

California Department of Corrections
www.cdcn.ca.gov

The College of Family Physicians of Canada
www.wcbi.nim.nih.gov

Prepared by: Mary Maguire, *California State University—Sacramento*
Clifford Garoupa, *Fresno City College*

Article

Understanding Recovery Barriers

Youth Perceptions about Substance Use Relapse

Objective: To qualitatively explore how treatment-involved youth retrospectively contextualize relapse from substance use. *Methods:* Fourteen focus groups were conducted with 118 youth (78.3% male; 66.1% Latino) enrolled in participating substance abuse treatment programs (4 young adult and 10 adolescent) throughout Los Angeles County. Transcripts were analyzed for relapse perception themes. *Results:* Dominant relapse themes include emotional reasons (90%), life stressors (85%), cognitive factors (75%), socialization processes (65%), and environmental issues (55%). *Conclusions:* Youth perceptions about relapse during treatment should be used to better inform clinical approaches and shape early-intervention recovery agendas for substance-abusing youth.

RACHEL GONZALES ET AL.

Learning Outcomes

After reading this article, you will be able to:

- Understand what challenges are present in trying to prevent relapse in drug dependent youth.

- Discuss the types of drugs youths are using.

- Understand some of the reasons why young people become dependent on drugs.

Substance use problems among youth under 25 represent one of the major prevention and treatment issues in the United States: nearly 70% of all youth mortality (ages 15–24) has been attributed to unintended injuries, homicide, and suicide,[1] all of which are highly correlated with substance use behaviors.[2,3] Moreover, statistics from general population US-based prevalence surveys, national treatment admission data, and juvenile justice drug offense cases support the extent of the problem. National (US) survey studies show that illicit substance use and binge drinking trends for youth are up from previous years: 10.0% of 12- to 17-year-olds and 21.2% of 18- to 25-year-olds report past-month use of illicit substances, and past-month binge drinking rates were 8.8% and 41.7% for 12- to 17- and 18- to -25-year-olds, respectively.[4] Publicly funded treatment admissions are also high: 7.6% of admissions are under 18 and increase to 21.6% for those 18–25.[5] Substance use-related juvenile/criminal court cases are common as well:

44.2% of all cases ages 10–24 were for drug offenses, 15.1% for juveniles 10–17 years of age.[6]

Given such public health complexities, much of the attention regarding addressing substance use issues among youth has been directed at interrupting drug use through treatment settings, where the main goals are to "effectively reduce substance use behaviors and improve critical areas of life functioning that are expected to be positively influenced by treatment."[7] Large-scale treatment outcome studies with youth demonstrate that treatment (in general) produces positive changes in substance use and other psychosocial outcomes;[8–11] however, treatment benefits tend to diminish over time.[12] Substance use "relapse" is of primary concern, which is typically about 65% in the first 90 days after treatment and increases to rates of about 85% during the post-year follow-up period.[11,13–20]

Relapse has been contextualized both as a "discrete outcome" or "a process."[21] Definitions of relapse also differ and typically have been either operationalized as "a return to any use" or "a return to original problematic use" before treatment.[22,23] There have been several attempts to establish specific conceptual models for relapse among adult populations.[23–33]

To date, conceptual models tend to categorize relapse using 4 major precursors/antecedents,[34,35] including the specific drug (agent), characteristics of the user (personal), characteristics of the user's social relationships/setting (interpersonal), and environmental (situational) factors. Relapse precursors that have received the most support include negative affective emotional states,[34,36,37] cognitive-behavioral factors including self-efficacy/confidence,[38] outcome expectancies,[39] urges/temptations,[40] coping,[41,42] and motivation/readiness to change.[34,44,45]

Interpersonal determinants include relationship conflict,[46-48] social pressures,[49] social support, and life stressors.[50-53] Environmental determinants include cue-situational exposures and geographic disadvantage, ie, high availability of drugs, crime and poverty.[27,54-57] Despite these findings, many studies conclude that relapse is often random, complex, and dynamic,[58-60] determined by an interaction of diverse physiological, individual, and situational factors,[32,61] and cannot be solely captured by a single process model.[62]

Research on substance use relapse among youth is less extensive. Existing youth-based studies have identified similar relapse determinants as are found among adult samples;[63-66] however, it is considered to be particularly more complex for several reasons: adolescents are still undergoing brain maturation and are in the midst of greater cognitive and social-emotional development processes;[67-69] have higher co-occurring mental health and psychosocial dysfunctions within family, school, and legal settings;[70-73] have greater influence from social agents/events;[74-76] have different clinical courses of substance use severity/diagnosis[77-80] and lower levels of treatment motivation.[80,81]

Although the literature is growing in the area of substance use relapse among youth populations, retrospective accounts of the relapse process are limited, and many substantive questions remain. This study employed a qualitative approach to examine the following research questions: (1) How do youth in treatment perceive their risk for substance use after treatment? (2) What are some major factors that are associated with relapse risk among treatment-involved youth? This study seeks to address these questions to identify some of the early warning signals indicating potential relapse for youth 24 years and younger to better inform clinical approaches to better meet the needs of substance-abusing youth as well as shape early-intervention recovery agendas.

Methods

A convenience sample of youth aged 12–24 was drawn from participating substance abuse treatment programs (10 adolescent specific and 4 adult) in diverse Los Angeles areas (San Gabriel Valley, North Hollywood, West Los Angeles, San Fernando Valley, and Antelope Valley). Unlike the adolescent-specific programs used, this sample does not include young adult-specific programs, but rather a select set of participating adult programs that had designated young adult groups to capture youth 18–24. Hence, due to the participating treatment sites availability of young adults, there are fewer young adults groups available. Research procedures were approved by the Institutional Review Board of the University of California Los Angeles.

Participants

One-hundred eighteen youth between 12 and 24 constitute the study sample: average age was 17.4 ± 2.9 years; 78.3% male; 66.1% Latino and 25.2% white (25.2%); 69.5% were in outpatient treatment; and most reported marijuana (40.9%) or methamphetamine (30.4%) as their primary substances of abuse. Sample characteristics are representative of youth based on wide-scale California treatment evalautions: average age of youth admissions is 17, 68% male, and 59% Latino.[84]

Procedure

A total of 14 focus groups were conducted with 118 youth in participating substance abuse treatment programs between September 2010 and December 2010. Focus groups were 90 minutes in length and digitally audio-recorded. Each participant received a $10 gift card for incentive. The principal investigator (PI) moderated each group using scripted questions.[34] A research assistant (RA) trained in focus group procedures assisted with moderating the focus groups.

The scripted questions covered youth perceptions and attitudes around substance use behaviors, substance use relapse, and substance use recovery. The focus group leader (PI) used a standardized script to discuss the relapse concept and provide a common level of understanding of relapse. For this, participants were asked to think about life after treatment and consider the most common situations or reasons that caused them to relapse ([defined as both (1) using any alcohol or drugs again and (2) reverting back to their pretreatment pattern of drug use]). Using the following scenario: "Jane/John went through treatment for substance use problems. After treatment (within the next 3 months), he/she relapsed. Finish my statement: 'He/she relapsed because . . . ?'" After general responses to the relapse scenario were noted (ie, stress), specific reasons related to each response were assessed (ie, family, school, legal, etc). In addition to participating in the focus group discussion, all participants anonymously completed a demographic questionnaire collecting age, gender, race/ethnicity, primary substances used, and treatment history information for descriptive purposes.

Data Analysis

Audio recordings for 14 focus groups were transcribed by 2 research assistants and edited and re-reviewed by the research team for accuracy and fidelity. Transcripts were coded using a systematic set of procedures based on grounded theory[84] to inductively develop themes around relapse perceptions among youth. To ensure completeness and accuracy, 2 reviewers coded each transcript, and a third coder was used to resolve any discrepant coding by a consensus approach with the research team.[85] Using ATLAS.Ti, a qualitative statistical software program for content and text analysis,[86] focus group responses from all youth participants (N = 118; 92 adolescents and 24 young adults) were assessed to obtain overall percentages for each theme identified and unique responses per theme by age-group. Responses to the brief demographic questionnaire were quantitatively analyzed using SPSS, version 18; however, because of the assured anonymity, demographic questionnaire data could not be linked to focus group responses; hence, these results are presented descriptively. Overall, themes reported in results are based on analysis of open-ended responses to focus group scripted questions. Where appropriate, focus group (age) differences (ie, adolescent versus young adult) are reported.

Table 1 General Themes of Substance Use Relapse Among Youth 12–24 (N = 118)

	% Overall Group Response
Emotional Reasons	90%
Life Stressors	85%
Cognitive Factors	75%
Socialization Processes	65%
Environmental Issues	55%

Table 2 Combined Qualitative Youth (12–24) Statements of "Emotional Reasons"

"To cope or take the edge off of problems"

"To feel better about all the drama in our life"

"To cope with negative feelings, anger, sadness, loneliness, guilt, fear, pain, and anxiety"

"To escape or just to get away from reality"

"They don't want to face their fears"

"They know there is a better feeling than being sober where life sucks"

"Because it helps you break those internal barriers"

Results

Table 1 provides 5 major themes that emerged in response to qualitative youth responses to the relapse scenario "He/She Relapsed Because . . . " This table is followed by examples of youth statements supporting each theme. It is important to note that some youth (from 10 adolescent focus groups, n = 92) did not even know what *relapse* meant (10%). For these youth, they were asked to consider responding to the questions based on the definitions of relapse used in the field [defined as (1) using any alcohol or drugs again or (2) reverting back to their pre-treatment pattern of drug use].

Emotional Reasons

The dominant relapse theme for youth, including both adolescents (ages 12 through 17) and young adults (ages 18 through 24) was emotional reasons (90%), feeling unable to cope with negative emotions without drugs. Table 2 displays combined statements from youth supporting this theme.

Life Stressors

The second theme identified was life stressors (85%) for both adolescent and young adults as supported by statements such

as "To take the stress away," "To get away from life stressors," "Because life and everything that comes with it—sucks." However, when questioned more deeply about the reasons for stress, responses greatly differed for adolescent and young adult participants worth noting. For adolescents (12–17), stress was referred to more so because of parents (criticizing, nagging, mistrust, conflict, put-downs, no faith/confidence in us, not being around), school (failing classes, getting in trouble), and peer pressure (fitting in); whereas older-aged youth (18–24) were more likely express stress in terms of realities of life that had to do with intimate relationships (commitment), financial responsibility (debt, employment issues) and housing stress (rent and bills). Table 3 displays statements from both youth groups supporting this theme.

Cognitive Factors

The third theme in response to "He/She Relapsed Because . . . " was cognitive (75%), with the dominant reasons for both adolescents and young adults alike being poor motivation, craving/urges, and low confidence. Table 4 displays combined statements from youth supporting this theme.

Table 3 Qualitative Statements of Life Stressors by Youth Group

Adolescents (12–17)

"Still, after treatment, parents continue to just criticize us all the time and put us down . . . we're no good, failures. They constantly complain and nag about how we do everything wrong. They don't trust us, where we go, who we talk to. Basically they have no faith or confidence in us."

"School is hard, all the homework, tests, and class things you have to keep up with . . . it never ends."

"Relapsing has to do with the stress of hanging out with your friends and fitting in." "Using starts as a social thing, and then after a while, it becomes all you do with your friends . . . You wouldn't know what else to do."

Young Adults (18–24)

"Well coming out of treatment you're on a pink cloud, telling everyone you're gonna do hella f'ing well. . . . And then life kicks in . . . just reality is a bitch . . . the stress is overwhelming and makes me feel, like stuck. Cuz I've gotten myself in a hole and that makes me want to use you know."

"Relapse happens because relationships go bad, break-ups and being lonely, sex becomes an issue, or just commitment issues."

"Drugs and alcohol become an easy solution for fears about your financial and life stressors . . . having a job or a place to live."

Table 4   Combined Qualitative Youth (12–24) Statements of Cognitive Factors

Poor Motivation

"They weren't ready or willing to do what it takes to stay clean"

"There are some who choose to be here, but most are here because of parents or court-ordered, so they're gonna relapse because they have to want to stop on their own"

"Because motivation is the biggest issue for most of us—and it's not mere . . . everything told to us in treatment just comes in one ear and out the other"

"No more testing, they're finally out of treatment"

Cravings/Urges

"Having positive feelings that make you want to celebrate—have a drink or use"

"They had cravings because you are either in the presence of drugs or alcohol, drug or alcohol users, or at places where you used or bought drugs before"

"Because that's what typically happens after treatment—we all go back to craving or chasing that first high"

Low Confidence (Self-efficacy)

"Because they were scared to take on the challenge of quitting . . . they didn't have the strength to not use again"

"Not having confidence to manage their life on their own"

Socialization Processes

The fourth theme had to do with socialization processes (65%); however, responses regarding the type of social processes differed between adolescents and young adults. Specifically, adolescents were more likely to note peer pressure and media influence whereas young adults discussed issues related to social networks and social norms. Table 5 displays statements from both youth groups supporting this theme.

Environmental Issues

The final theme identified among both youth groups was environmental issues (55%), which included responses about access/availability and cues/triggers (55%). Table 6 displays statements from both youth groups supporting this theme.

Discussion

Considering the relapse ecology of youth, our data highlight 5 major reasons for youth relapse: negative emotions, stress, cognitive factors, socialization processes, and environmental

Table 5   Qualitative Statements of Socialization Processes by Youth Group

Adolescents (12–17)

Peer Pressure

"Because my friends are negative influences . . . they keep asking—you want to get high"

"For me, it's not really about the place or situation—like a party, but about the people there—friends have a strong influence on what we do—they can turn any place into a bad place"

Media Influence

"Because they saw it glorified on TV or heard about how fun it is on the radio, so it reminds them of how it feels and how it's good, and how happy they will feel"

"I think because of the media influence. All types, TV, radio, film, internet, video games show alcohol, cigarettes, marijuana, prescription pills, other drugs, in a positive light and make using/drinking normal. So we start to believe it and think it's a normal part of life"

Young Adults (12–24)

Social Networks

"They continued to want to party and connect with old drug use networks"

Social Norms

"Like seriously? Like if you've never tried pot. Like, I mean, you don't have to be a black tar heroin user, but I mean it's just what's in our social culture and expected"

"Because of the social standards or whatever you want to call them about using alcohol and drugs in our age group—young people just use a lot of drugs . . . and they think it's normal and being sober is not normal"

Table 6   Combined Qualitative Youth (12–24) Statements of Environmental Issues

Access/Availability

"We just have to walk down the street in our neighborhood . . . dope dealers and drugs are everywhere."

Cues/Triggers

"Just triggers—the day-to-day things we hear, see, do."

"It's always around—in your face . . . and when you see it or smell it you're like damn, pass that—you might contemplate it little bit, but in the end, you just say, ok."

---

issues. Although this study contributes a qualitative assessment of the relapse process among treatment-involved youth, there is still significant complexity in understanding the developmental pathways to relapse.

As supported by our results, such pathways are best conceptualized as multifactorial,[87,88] which fall into 3 general theoretical streams of influences: individual-level factors, socialization influences, and broader environmental influences. Specifically, individual-level influences included negative emotions, stress, and cognitive factors; socialization influences included peer pressure, social network/social norms, and media influence; and broader environmental influences included access/availability and cues/triggers, which merit separate discussions for each. It is important to note that, as discussed in the introduction, these relapse determinants are fairly similar to relapse factors observed among adult samples;[63–66] however, such relapse processes have more emphasis around social-emotional and environmental development processes, rather than personal clinical orientations around substance use severity.

Negative Emotions

Research supports that the majority of youth with substance use problems also have one or more co-occurring problems such as depression, anxiety, traumatic stress, self-mutilation or suicidal thoughts, hyperactivity and conduct disorder, criminal or violent tendencies, etc. Prevailing beliefs under the psychoanalytic framework is that drug use is a symptom of an underlying psychological disorder.[89] Accordingly, substance use is a secondary condition caused by underlying mental disturbances, known as the self-medication model, whereby individuals use drugs to self-medicate or relieve symptoms of psychological distress.[90] Because relapse is likely to occur if these symptoms are not adequately addressed during treatment, a major goal of treatment programs is to include care and services (counseling interventions) that uncover and treat the underlying psychopathology feeding drug abuse behaviors.[91,92] Although treatment programs are working to effectively address such multiple problems simultaneously (eg, standardized assessment for other problems and provision/coordination of case management services),[16] extending these efforts beyond formal treatment is not a common practice.[95] It is possible that the positive outcomes

observed in treatment could be better sustained if posttreatment recovery maintenance services (ie, continuing care models) included emotion regulation and coping skills for dealing with negative emotions.

Stress

Stress has been well established as a significant risk factor for relapse.[96–101] We found developmental differences in relapse-associated stress that support the conceptualization of stress "as a relationship between an individual and his/her environment."[102] For adolescents, parental issues, peer pressure, and school problems were dominant stressors, whereas for young adults, stress was described more in terms of life circumstances, emerging adult responsibilities, and interpersonal romantic relationships that coincide with their current developmental period: "gaining greater independence" and "leaving the parent nest or family environment."[103] Many studies consistently show that parents, peers, and school serve as major socialization factors in predicting the initiation, maintenance, and exacerbation of substance abuse in adolescents; and the stress-related findings specific to young adults are similar to what is typically found with older adults in treatment, which is linked to pretreatment problems of legal issues, relationships, job loss, and financial debt.[104,105] From a clinical and recovery support perspective, these results highlight the importance of integrating stress management efforts into programs rather than simply focusing on parental, school, or employment problems specifically as is done in most programs.[76,106,107]

Cognitive Factors

Three important cognitive factors warrant further consideration in terms of understanding relapse among youth: motivation, cravings/urges, and confidence, ie, self-efficacy. As other studies have found, relapse or continued use of alcohol and drugs, is related to the fact that few youth with substance use problems are motivated to be in treatment as they rarely express desires to quit or any strong commitments to maintain abstinence.[81,108,109] Further, most youth presenting for treatment are not self-referred. Instead, they are coerced by a parent, juvenile justice system official (judge, probation or parole officer), school official, child welfare worker, or representative of some other community institution.[8,10] These findings highlight the need for relapse prevention models in both clinical and recovery support settings to take into account the extent to which youth are motivated or ready to change their substance use behaviors.[44,110] Future research on youth relapse needs to consider the potential differences in perceptions among youth mandated to treatment versus youth voluntarily in treatment. By ignoring motivation at treatment admission, assessments of outcomes become complicated and often limit interpretation of relapse prevention models.

Confidence (self-efficacy) was also cited as an important cognitive factor related to relapse as has been found in other studies.[111] However, the confidence expressed by youth had more to do with one's ability to abstain from drugs in the face of life stressors or internal/social cues/triggers, such as the stress of fitting in, rather than on peer pressure associated with being "forced" to use drugs.

This result highlights the importance of integrating stress management skills (in addition to peer resistance skills) into youth relapse-prevention models. Lastly, an interesting area of research worthy of further inquiry has to do with continued substance use after treatment that is not related to one's primary drug of choice, particularly tobacco use. As others have noted, a major issue facing individuals in treatment (in general) is a drug-use recovery environment that far too often facilitates tobacco use.[112]

Socialization Processes

All youth support the view that relapse is a byproduct or function of socialization processes that influence developmental vulnerability for relapse. Although we observed differences in socialization processes between adolescent and young adults, the circumstances and extent to which relapse occurs is largely regulated by peer/social norms, customs, traditions, and standards.[113] In general, adolescents reported friendships and peer pressure along with media influence as important relapse triggers; whereas young adults tended to highlight social networks and social norms as dominant features of their social surrounding that influenced relapse.

Numerous studies have established that peer-group and social norm processes are strong influencers of drug use behaviors,[86,115,116] as they foster positive expectancies about drug use and create prosocial norms, and both serve to encourage drug use behavior.[117,118] It is important to point out that for most adolescents, cliques or friendship bonds are an important and a common feature during social/emotional development contributing to substance use risk behaviors.[114,115,120,121] However, as our data indicate, the peer/friendship clique might not be as important for young adults as they have "developed and matured" over time into a web of social relationships and social networks more associated with larger social processes operating.[122]

Moreover, although not as apparent for older youth, media depictions of drugs were noted as important determinants of relapse by many adolescents. Other research supports this view, such that the tobacco and alcohol industries alone spend billions of dollars each year aggressively marketing their products to adolescents through depicting images of glamour, success, and independence—all highly esteemed social values within American society.[123] Such marketing strategies have paid off as noted by several studies showing a positive impact on youth decisions to smoke or drink.[124,125] Overall, such socialization processes that youth experience are complex issues that create obstacles for those attempting to develop a drug-free recovery lifestyle (ie, break free from peer pressure and extant social norms that promote and normalize substance use).

Environmental Issues

As reflected by our data, environmental factors of access/availability and cues/triggers also play a critical role in facilitating relapse for youth. According to most, drugs are readily available and accessible to them. National survey data from Monitoring the Future highlight the importance of the positive relationship between perceived availability of drugs and trends in use among adolescent youth.[126]

To date, most attention on relapse determinants has been directed at individual-level factors, promoting the view that the responsibility for one's relapse ultimately falls on oneself and shifting attention away from larger environmental forces that also may be influencing relapse behavior. However, such environmental influences on relapse are important to consider as "the individual cannot be conceptualized as an autonomous actor making self-governing decisions in a social vacuum."[129] For clinical and recovery support programs to be effective, they must also address such structural influences.

Limitations

The present study must be considered in light of its limitations. The accuracy of relapse descriptions or circumstances among this clinical sample must be questioned as they are retrospectively providing aggregate perceptions of relapse rather than any specific experiences. Also, the data were from a single time point, thereby limiting conclusions regarding the process of posttreatment relapse. Additionally, the results cannot be overgeneralized to treatment-involved youth in other treatment settings given the variability between the treatment sites used to conduct the qualitative work as well as the nature of the sample used (convenience). Finally, focus group thematic results are only presented descriptively. Although it may be that the general risk for substance use relapse among youth as a whole may be similar, with some general differences noted among age-groups, there may be important gender or other differences in relapse risk factors among treatment-involved youth that this study did not consider due to confidentiality limitations associated with anonymous data collection. Further research should find procedures to remedy such deficiencies.

Conclusion

This study contributes to the extant literature on relapse specific to youth populations. Results add clarity to the dynamic process of relapse in youth as they explicate the actual experiences and perceptions of treatment-involved youth. Overall, there is no single variable sufficient to predict relapse among youth alone. Although individual(personal)-level factors have been shown to account for much of the variance explaining proneness to youth initiation and maintenance of substance use,[84,108] there is still a wide array of social and environmental forces that contribute to the progression of substance use behavior.[128,129] Hence, the interrelations among key individual, socialization, and broader environmental variables are likely to be of increasing importance for understanding the developmental relapse trajectories of treatment-involved youth.

Furthermore, because treatment for substance use and related problems tends to be treated acutely and for a relatively short period (less than 3 months),[130] a systems issue to consider is the need for ongoing interventions (continuing care) to promote the necessary skills acquired during treatment, as they may not carry over or be sustainable posttreatment. It needs to be recognized that most treatment-involved youth are in a structured clinical environment and when it is removed they struggle with the loss of structure as they transition into a less unstructured world. In the transition they continue to experience co-occurring issues that can hijack emotions, be exposed to drug using friends, encounter repeated life stressors, face competing social norms that reinforce drug use, enter into a broader environment where drugs and alcohol are frequently available, and continue to be triggered or cued to drug use. To minimize adverse effects, continuing care models must be developed addressing such complex, interrelated issues.

References

1. Centers for Disease Control and Prevention. (2009) Youth Risk Behavior Survey. Available at: www.cdc.gov/yrbss. Accessed March 10, 2011.

2. American Academy of Pediatrics. Practicing adolescent medicine: Priority health behaviors in adolescents: Health promotion in the clinical setting. Adolescent Health Update. 3(2). 1991. Available at: www.aap.org. Accessed March 10, 2011

3. Robert Wood Johnson Foundation. Reclaiming Futures: Quick Facts. Retrieved Available at: www.reclaimingfutures.org/quickfacts.asp. Accessed February 12, 2004.

4. Substance Abuse and Mental Health Services Administration. (2010a). Results from the 2009 National Survey on Drug Use and Health: Volume I. Summary of National Findings (Office of Applied Studies, NSDUH Series H-38A, HHS Publication No. SMA 10-4586 Findings). Rockville, MD. Available at: www.cdc.gov/nchs/data/hus/hus10.pdf#061

5. Substance Abuse and Mental Health Services Administration, Office of Applied Studies. Treatment Episode Data Set (TEDS). Rockville, MD: U.S. Department of Health and Human Services; 2010.

6. U.S. Department of Justice, Federal Bureau of Investigation. Crime in the United States. Available at: www2.fbi.gov/ucr/cius2008/data/table_38.html. Accessed September 16, 2009.

7. McLellan AT, Chalk M, Bartlett J. Outcomes, performance, and quality—What's the difference? *J Subst Abuse Treat.* 2007; 32:331–340.

8. Dennis ML. Global Appraisal of Individual Needs Manual: Administration, Scoring and Interpretation. Bloomington, IL: Lighthouse; 1998.

9. Brown SA, D'Amicio EJ, McCarthy DM, et al. Four-year outcomes from adolescent alcohol and drug treatment. *J Stud Alcohol.* 2001; 62:381–388.

10. Hser YI, Grella CE, Hubbard RL, et al. An evaluation of drug treatments for adolescents in 4 cities. *Arch Gen Psychiatry.* 2001; 58:689–695.

11. Winters KC, Stinchfield RD, Opland E, et al. The effectiveness of the Minnesota Model approach in the treatment of adolescent drug abusers. *Addiction.* 2000; 95:601–612.

12. Brown SA, Vik PW, Creamer VA. Characteristics of relapse following adolescent substance abuse treatment. *Addict Behav.* 1989; 14:291–300.

13. Brown SA, Mott M, Myers MG. Adolescent alcohol and drug treatment outcome. In Watson RR, ed. Drug and Alcohol Abuse Prevention. Totowa, NJ: Humana Press; 1990.

14. Brown SA, Gleghorn A, Schuckit MA, et al. Conduct disorder among adolescent alcohol and drug abusers. *J Stud Alcohol.* 1996; 57:314–324.

15. Williams RJ, Chang SY, Addiction Centre Adolescent Research Group. A comprehensive and comparative review of adolescent substance abuse treatment outcome. *Clin Psychol: Sci Prac.* 2000; 7:138–166.

16. Kaminer Y, Burleson JA, Burke RH. Efficacy of outpatient aftercare for adolescents with alcohol use disorders: a randomized controlled study. *J Am Acad Child Adolesc Psychiatry.* 2008; 47:1405–1412.

17. Brown S, Tapert S, Granholm E, et al. Neurocognitive functioning of adolescents: effects of protracted alcohol use. *Alcohol Clin Exp Res.* 2000; 24(2):164–171.

18. Lewis RA, Piercy FP, Sprenkle DH, et al. Family-based interventions for helping drug abusing adolescents. *J Adolesc Res.* 1990; 50:82–95.

19. Dennis M, Godley SH, Diamond G, et al. The Cannabis Youth Treatment (CYT) Study: main findings from two randomized trials. *J Subst Abuse Treat.* 2004; 27:197–213.

20. Cornelius JR, Maisto SA, Pollock NK, et al. Rapid relapse generally follows treatment for substance use disorders among adolescents. *Addict Behav.* 2003; 28:381–386.

21. Milkman H, Weiner SE, Sunderwirth S. Addiction relapse. *Adv Alcohol Subst Abuse.* 1984; 3:119–134.

22. Polivy J, Herman CP. If at first you don't succeed: false hopes of self-change. *Am Psychol.* 2002; 57(9):677–689.

23. Marlatt GA, Gordon JR. Determinants of relapse: Implications for the maintenance of behavior change. In PO Davidson & SM Davidson, eds, Behavioral Medicine: Changing Health Lifestyles. Elmsford, NY: Pergamon; 1980: 410–452.

24. Abrams DB, Niaura RS, Carey KB, et al. Understanding relapse and recovery in alcohol abuse. *Ann Behav Med.* 1986; 8:27–32.

25. Witkiewitz K, Marlatt GA. Relapse prevention for alcohol and drug problems: that was Zen, this is Tao. *Am Psychologist.* 2004; 59:224–235.

26. Davis JR, Tunks E. Environments and addiction: a proposed taxonomy. *Int J Addict* 1990; 25:805–826.

27. Tucker JA, Vuchinich RE, Gladsjo JA. Environmental influences on relapse in substance use disorders. *Int J Addict.* 1991; 25(7A/8A):017–1050.

28. Dielman TE, Butchart AT, Shope JT, et al. Environmental correlates of adolescent substance use and misuse: implications for prevention programs. *Int J Addict.* 1991; 25:855–880.

29. Rosenhow DJ, Niaura RS, Childress AR, et al. Cue reactivity in addictive behaviors: theoretical and treatment implications. *Int J Addict.* 1991; 25:957–994.

30. Simpson DD, Joe GW, Brown BS. Treatment retention and follow-up outcomes in the Drug Abuse Treatment Outcome Study (DATOS). *Psychol Addict Behav.* 1997; 11:294–307.

31. Gifford R, Hine DW. Substance misuse and the physical environment: the early action of a newly completed field. *Int J Addict.* 1991; 25:827–853.

32. Brownell KD, Marlatt GA, Lichtenstein E, et al. Understanding and preventing relapse. *Am Psychologist.* 1986; 41:765–785.

33. Marlatt GA, Baer JS, Quigley LA. Self-efficacy and addictive behaviour. In Banura A, ed, Self-efficacy in Changing Societies. New York, NY: Cambridge University Press; 1995: 289–315.

34. Miller WR, Westerberg VS, Harris RJ, et al. What predicts relapse? Prospective testing of antecedent models. *Addiction.* 2002; 91(12s1):155–172.

35. Miller WR, Carroll K. Rethinking Substance Abuse: What the Science Shows, and What We Should Do About it. New York, NY: Guilford Press; 2006.

36. De Leon G. Integrative recovery: a stage paradigm. *Subst Abuse.* 1996; 17:15–63.

37. Cornelius JR, Maisto SA, Wood DS, et al. Major depression associated with earlier alcohol relapse in treated teens with alcohol use disorder. *Addict Behav.* 2004; 29:1035–1038.

38. McKay JR, Rutherford MJ, Alterman AI, et al. An examination of the cocaine relapse process. *Drug Alcohol Depend.* 1995; 38:35–43.

39. Jones BT, Corbin W, Fromme K. A review of expectancy theory and alcohol consumption. *Addiction.* 2001; 96:57–72.

40. Niaura R. Cognitive social learning and related perspectives on drug craving. *Addiction.* 2000; 95:155–163.

41. Moos RH. Coping Responses Inventory. Odessa, FL: Psychological Assessment Resources; 1993.

42. Drummond DC, Litten RZ, Lowman C, et al. Craving research: future directions. *Addiction.* 2000; 95(Suppl 2):247–255.

43. Burke BL, Arkowitz H, Menchola M. The efficacy of motivational interviewing: a meta-analysis of controlled clinical trials. *J Consult Clin Psychol.* 2003; 71(5):843–861.

44. Simpson DD, Curry SJ. Drug abuse treatment outcome studies. *Psychol Addict Behav.* 1997; 11:211–337.

45. Joe GW, Simpson DD, Sells SB. Treatment process and relapse to opioid use during methadone maintenance. *Am J Drug Alcohol Use.* 1994; 20:173–197.

46. Dobkin PL, Civita M, Paraherakis A, et al. The role of functional social support in treatment retention and outcomes among outpatient adult substance abusers. *Addiction.* 2002; 97(3):347–356.

47. Anderson KG, Frissell KC, Brown SA. Contexts of post-treatment use for substance abusing adolescents with comorbid psychopathology. *J Child Adolesc Subst Abuse.* 2007; 17:65–82.

48. Ulrich RS, Simons RF, Losito BD, et al. Stress recovery during exposure to natural and urban environments. *J Environment Psychol.* 1991; 11:201–230.

49. Ennett ST, Flewelling RL, Lindrooth RC, et al. School and neighborhood characteristics associated with school rates of alcohol, cigarette, and marijuana use. *J Health Social Beh.* 1997; 38:55–71.

50. Anglin MD, Hser Y-I. Treatment of Drug Abuse Drugs & Crime, eds. M Tonry, JQ Wilson. Chicago, IL: The University of Chicago Press; 1990.

51. Beattie MC, Longabaugh R. General and alcohol specific social support following treatment. *Addict Behav.* 1999; 24(5):593–606.

52. Moos RH, Finney JW, Cronkite RC. Alcoholism Treatment: Context, Process and Outcome. New York, NY: Oxford University Press; 1990.

53. Lang MA, Belenko S. Predicting retention in a residential drug treatment alternative to prison program. *J Subst Abuse Treat.* 2000; 19:145–160.

54. De Leon G, Hawke J, Jainchill N, et al. Therapeutic communities enhancing retention in treatment using "senior professor" staff. *J Subst Abuse Treat.* 2000; 19:375–382.

55. Lillie-Blanton M, Anthony JC, Schuster CR. Probing the meaning of racial/ethnic group comparisons in crack cocaine smoking. *JAMA.* 1993; 269:993–997.

56. Agnew JA, Duncan JS. The Power of Place, Boston, MA: Unwin Hyman; 1989.

57. Boardman JD, Finch BK, Ellison CG, et al. Neighborhood disadvantage, stress, and drug use among adults. *J Health Soc Behav.* 2001; 42:151–165.

58. Buhringer G. Testing CBT mechanisms of action: humans behave in a more complex way than our treatment studies would predict. *Addiction.* 2000; 95(11):1715–1716.

59. Dononvan DM. Marlatt's classification of replase precipitants: is the emperor still wearing clothes? *Addiction.* 1996; 91(Suppl):131–137.

60. Longabaugh R, Rubin A, Stout RL, et al. The reliability of Marlatt's taxonomy for classifying relapses. *Addiction.* 1996; 91(Suppl):73–88.

61. Carroll KM. Relapse prevention as a psycho-social treatment: a review of controlled clinical trials. *Exp Clin Psychopharmacol.* 1996; 4:46–54.

62. Irvin JE, Bowers CA, Dunn ME, et al. Efficacy of relapse prevention: a meta-analytic review. *J Consult Clin Psychol.* 1999; 67(4):563–570.

63. Brown SA, D'Amico EA. Outcomes of alcohol treatment for adolescents. In Galanter M, ed. Recent Developments in Alcoholism, vol. 16. New York, NY: Kluwer Academic/Plenum; 2003: 289–312.

64. Myers RJ, Smith JE. Clincal Guide to Alcohol Treatment: The Community Reinforcement Approach. New York, NY: Guilford Press; 1995.

65. Brown SA, Vik PW, Craemer VA. Characteristics of relapse following adolescent substance abuse treatment. *Addict Behav.* 1989; 14:291–300.

66. Brown SA. Measuring youth outcomes from alcohol and drug treatment. *Addiction.* 2004; 99(Suppl 2):38–46.

67. Labouvie EW, Bates M. Reasons for alcohol use in young adulthood: validation of a three-dimensional measure. *J Stud Alcohol.* 2002; 63:145–155.

68. Millman RB, Botvin GJ. Substance use, abuse, and dependence. In: Levine M, Carey NB, Crocker AC, Gross RT, eds. Developmental-behavioral Pediatrics. New York, NY: W. B. Saunders; 1992:451–467.

69. McNeal RB, Hansen WB. Developmental patterns associated with the onset of drug use: changes in postulated mediators during adolescence. *J Drug Issues.* 1999; 29(2):381–400.

70. Jessor RS, Chase JD, Donovan JE. Psychosocial correlates of marijuana use and problem drinking in a national sample of adolescents. *Am J Public Health.* 1980; 70:604–613.

71. Grella CE, Hser Y, Joshi V, Rounds-Bryant J. Drug treatment outcomes for adolescents with comorbid mental and substance use disorders. *J Nerv Ment Dis.* 2001; 189:384–392.

72. Morral AR, McCaffrey DF, Ridgeway G. Effectiveness of community-based treatment for substance-abusing adolescents: 12-month outcomes of youths entering Phoenix Academy or alternative probation dispositions. *Addict Behav.* 2004; 18(3):257–268.

73. Stein JA, Newcombe MD, Bentler PM. An 8-year study of multiple influences on drug use and drug use consequences. *JPers Soc Psychol.* 1987; 53:1094–1105.

74. Oetting ER, Donnermyer JF. Primary socialization theory: the etiology of drug use and deviance I. *Subst Use Misuse.* 1998; 33(4):995–1026.

75. Jessor R. Risk behavior in adolescence: a psychosocial framework for understanding and action. *J Adolesc Health.* 1991; 12:597–605.

76. Sameroff AJ, Seifer R, Bartko WT. Environmental perspectives on adaptation during childhood and adolescence. In Luthar SS, Burak JA, Cicchetti D, et al., eds, Developmental Psychopathology: Perspectives on Adjustment, Risk, and Disorder. New York, NY: Cambridge University Press; 1997: 507–526.

77. Liddle H, Rowe C, eds. Treating Adolescent Substance Abuse: State of the Science. Cambridge, UK: Cambridge University Press; 2006.

78. Oetting ER. Primary socialization theory. Developmental stages, spirituality, government institutions, sensation seeking, and theoretical implications V. *Subst Use Misuse.* 1999; 34(7):947–82.

79. Waldron HB, Slesnick N, Brody JL, et al. Treatment outcomes for adolescent substance abuse at 4- and 7-month assessments. *J Consult Clin Psychol.* 2001; 69:802–813.

80. Maisto SA, Martin CS, Pollock NK, et al. Non-problem drinking outcomes in adolescents treated for alcohol use disorders. *Exp Clin Psychopharmacol.* 2002; 10:324–331.

81. Ramo, DE, Anderson KG, Tate SR, et al. Characteristics of relapse to substance use in comorbid adolescents. *Addict Behav.* 2005; 30:1811–1823.

82. Rawson RA, Gonzales R, 2009. CalOMS. Evaluation of the Substance Abuse Treatment System. Los Angeles: UCLA Integr. Subst. Abuse Progr. Available at: www.uclaisap.org/caloms/documents/CalOMSEvaluationReport.pdf. Accessed March 4, 2011.

83. Huba GJ. Bentler PM. A developmental theory of drug use: derivation and assessment of a causal modeling approach. In Baltes PB, Brim Jr OG Jr., eds, Lifespan Development and Behavior. New York: Academic Press, 1982; 4:47–203.

84. McNeal RB, Hansen WB. Developmental patterns associated with the onset of drug use: changes in postulated mediators during adolescence. *J Drug Issues.* 1999; 29(2):381–400.

85. Krueger RA. Moderating Focus Groups. Thousand Oaks, CA: Sage; 1998.

86. Miles MB, Huberman AM. Qualitative Data Analysis: An Expanded Sourcebook. 2nd ed. Thousand Oaks, CA: Sage; 1994.

87. Alexander BK. What can professional psychotherapists do about heroin addiction? *Medicine and Law.* 1986; 5(4):323–330.

88. Hawkins JD, Catalano RF, Miller JY. Risk and protective factors for alcohol and other drug problems in adolescence and early adulthood. Implications for substance abuse prevention. *Psychol Bull.* 1992; 112:64–105.

89. Khantzian EJ. The self-medication hypothesis of addictive disorders: focus on heroin and cocaine dependence. *Am J Psychiatry.* 1985; 142:1259–1264.

90. Hwang S. Utilizing qualitative data analysis software: a review of Atlas.ti. *Social Science Computer Review.* 2008; 26(4):519–527.

91. Aarons GA, Brown SA, Hough RL, et al. Prevalence of adolescent substance use disorders across five sectors of care. *J Am Acad Child Adolesc Psychi.* 2001; 40:419–426.

92. Kaminer Y, Napolitano C. Dial for therapy: aftercare for adolescent substance use disorders. *J Am Academy Child Adolesc Psychiatry.* 2004; 43:1171–1174.

93. Dennis ML, Titus JC, Diamond G, et al. The Cannabis Youth Treatment (CYT) experiment: Rationale, study design and analysis plans. *Addiction.* 2002; 97(Suppl 1):84–97.

94. Kaminer Y, Napolitano C. Dial for therapy: aftercare for adolescent substance use disorders. *J Am Academy Child Adolesc Psychiatry.* 2004; 43:1171–1174.

95. Godley MD, Kahn JH, Dennis ML, et al. The stability and impact of environmental factors on substance use and problems after adolescent outpatient treatment for cannabis abuse or dependence. *Psychol Addict Behav.* 2005; 19:62–70.

96. Preston KL, Epstein DH. Stress in the daily lives of cocaine and heroin users: relationship to mood, craving, relapse triggers, and cocaine use. (Published online ahead of print 12 February 2011). *Psychopharmacol (Berl).* 2011. Available at: www.springerlink.com/content/j82465x38 5448145/. Accessed March 6, 2011.

97. Goeders NE. The impact of stress on addiction. *European Neuropsychopharmacol.* 2003; 13:435–441.

98. Goeders NE. Stress and cocaine addiction. *J Pharmacol Exp Ther.* 2002; 301:785–789.

99. Sinha R, Fuse T, Aubin LR, et al. Psychological stress, drug-related cues and cocaine craving. *Psychopharmacol.* 2000; 152:140–148.

100. Sinha R. How does stress increase risk of drug abuse and relapse? *Psychopharmacol.* 2001; 158:343–359.

101. Wills TA. Stress, coping, tobacco and alcohol use in early adolescence. In: Shiffman S, Wills TA, eds. Coping and Substance Use. New York, NY: Academic Press; 1986.

102. Lazarus RS, Folkman S. Stress, Appraisal, and Coping. New York, NY: Springer; 1984.

103. Wilks J. The relative importance of parents and friends in adolescent decision making. *J Youth Adolescence.* 1986; 15:323–334.

104. Chassin L, Presson CC, Sherman SJ, et al. Changes in peer and parental influence during adolescence: longitudinal versus cross-sectional perspectives on smoking initiation. *Dev Psychol.* 1986; 22:327–334.

105. Whiston SC. The relationship among family interaction patterns and career indecision and career decision-making self-efficacy. *J Career Dev.* 1996; 23:137–149.

106. Jessor R, Donovan JE, Costa FM. Beyond Adolescence: Problem Behavior and Young Adult Development. New York, NY: Cambridge University Press; 1991.

107. King KM, Chassin L. Mediating and moderated effects of adolescent behavioral under control and parenting in the prediction of drug use disorders in emerging adulthood. *Psychol Addict Behav.* 2004; 18(3):239–249.

108. Cornelius JR, Maisto SA, Pollock NK, et al. Rapid relapse generally follows treatment for substance use disorders among adolescents. *Addict Beh.* 2003; 28:381–386.

109. Chung T, Maisto SA. Review and reconsideration of relapse as a change point in clinical course in treated adolescents. *Clin Psychol Rev.* 2006; 26:149–161.

110. Godley SH, Godley MD, Dennis ML. The assertive aftercare protocol for adolescent substance abusers. In: Wagner E, Waldron H, eds. Innovations in Adolescent Substance Abuse Interventions. Elsevier Science; New York: 2001.

111. Bobo JK, Slade J, Hoffman AL. Nicotine addiction counseling for chemically dependent patients. *Psychiatr Svcs.* 1995; 46:945–947.

112. Burleson JA, Kaminer Y. Self-efficacy as a predictor of treatment outcome in adolescent substance use disorders. *Addict Behav.* 2005; 30:1751–1764.

113. Berkowitz AD. The Social Norms Approach: Theory, Research, and Annotated Bibliography. Newton, MA: Higher Education Center for Alcohol and Other Drug Prevention; 2001.

114. Dishion TJ. Cross-setting consistency in early adolescent psychopathology: deviant friendships and problem behavior sequelae. *J Pers.* 2000; 68(6):1109–1126.

115. Vandell DL. Parents, peer groups, and other socializing influences. *Dev Psychol.* 2000; 36(6):699–710.

116. Clapp JD, McDonnell AL. The relationship of perceptions of alcohol promotion and peer drinking norms to alcohol problems reported by college students. *J Coll Stud Dev.* 2000; 41:19–26.

117. Dishion TJ, Capaldi DM, Spracklen KM, Li F. Peer ecology of male adolescent drug use. *Dev Psychopathol.* 1995; 7:803–824.

118. Duncan TE, Duncan SC, Hops H. The effects of family cohesiveness and peer encouragement on the development of adolescent alcohol use: a cohort sequential approach to the analysis of longitudinal data. *J Stud Alcohol.* 1994; 55:588–599.

119. Hartup WW. The company they keep: Friendships and their developmental significance. *Child Dev.* 1996; 67:1–13.

120. Elliot D, Huizinga D, Ageton S. Explaining Delinquency and Drug Use. Newbury Park, California: Sage Publications, Inc; 1985.

121. Kandel DB. Processes of peer influence in adolescence: In: Silberstein, R.K., Eyferth, K. & Rudinger, G. (Eds.). Development as Action in Context: Problem Behavior and Normal Youth Development. New York, NY: Springer-Verlag; 1986: 203–227.

122. Perry CL, Baranowski T, Parcel GS. How Individual, Environments, and Health Behavior Interact: Social Learning Theory. San Francisco: Jossey-Bass; 1997.

123. Arnett J. Adolescents' uses of media for self-socialization. *J Youth Adolesc.* 1995; 24(5):519–533.

124. Kelly K, Donohew L. Media and primary socialization theory. *Subst Use Misuse.* 1999; 34(7):1033–1045.

125. Moore DJ, Williams JD, Qualls WJ. Target marketing of tobacco and alcohol-related products to ethnic minority groups in the United States. *Ethn Dis.* 1996; 6(12):83–98.

126. Johnston LD, O'Malley PM, Bachman JG, et al. Monitoring the Future National Results on Adolescent Drug Use: Overview of Key Findings, 2005. (NIH Publication No. 06–5882). Bethesda, MD: National Institute on Drug Abuse: 2006.

127. Thombs DL, Wolcott BJ, Farkash LG. Social context, perceived norms and drinking behavior in young people. *J Subst Abuse.* 1997; 9:257–267.

128. Sussman S, Dent CW, Galaif ER. The Correlates of substance abuse and dependence among adolescents at high risk for drug abuse. *J Subst Abuse.* 1997; 9:241–255.

129. Oetting ER, Donnermyer JF, Deffenbacher JL. Primary socialization theory: the influence of the community on drug use and deviance III. *Subst Use Misuse.* 1998; 33(8): 1629–1665.

130. Becker SJ, Curry JF. Outpatient interventions for adolescent substance abuse: a quality of evidence review. *J Consult Clin Psychol.* 2008; 76:531–543.

Critical Thinking

1. Discuss the reasons youth report they relapse from drug treatment.

2. What is one limitation of the study described in this article?

3. Discuss possible approaches to reducing the barriers to youth treatment success.

Create Central

www.mhhe.com/createcentral

Internet References

Join Together
www.jointogether.org

D.A.R.E.
www.dare-america.com

RACHEL GONZALES, Research Psychologist; M. Douglas Anglin, Professor in Residence, Associate Director; Rebecca Beattie, Staff Research Associate; Chris Angelo Ong, Staff Research Associate, Integrated Substance Abuse Programs, University of California, Los Angeles, CA, Semel Institute for Neuroscience and Human Behavior, David Geffen School of Medicine at UCLA, Los Angeles, CA. Deborah C. Glik, Professor, School of Public Health, University of California, Los Angeles, CA.

Acknowledgments—The authors would like to thank the administrative and treatment staff at the participating treatment programs for their support. This study was supported by a grant provided by the National Institute on Drug Abuse (NIDA), grant number DA027754-01A1.

Contact Dr Gonzales; rachelmg@ucla.edu

Article

Prepared by: Mary Maguire, *California State University—Sacramento*
Clifford Garoupa, *Fresno City College*

High-Risk Offenders Participating in Court-Supervised Substance Abuse Treatment

Characteristics, Treatment Received, and Factors Associated with Recidivism

Elizabeth Evans, David Huang, and Yih-Ing Hser

Learning Outcomes

After reading this article, you will be able to:

- Understand the nature of court ordered drug treatment.
- Discuss the challenges of drug treatment within the criminal justice system.
- Discuss whether or not court ordered drug treatment is effective.

Introduction

Since 2001, California's voter-initiated Substance Abuse and Crime Prevention Act, more commonly known as Proposition 36 (Prop 36), has been providing community-based treatment to eligible drug offenders. Under Prop 36, adults convicted of nonviolent drug possession offenses can choose to receive drug treatment in the community in lieu of incarceration. Offenders on probation or parole who commit nonviolent drug possession offenses or who violate drug-related conditions of probation or parole can also opt to receive treatment. The intent of the Prop 36 program is to preserve jail and prison beds for serious and violent offenders, enhance public safety by reducing drug-related crime, and improve public health by reducing drug abuse through proven and effective treatment strategies.[1] From a broader perspective, Prop 36 is one example of the trend in the USA and several other countries toward use of alternative sentencing policies to rehabilitate drug offenders in lieu of imprisonment, and lessons learned from California's experiences with treating high- and low-risk drug offenders have implications for other similar types of programs.

The Prop 36 program has resulted in taxpayer savings, primarily due to reduced use of incarceration, and savings are highest among offenders who complete drug treatment.[2] Despite these gains, however, California's state budget crisis worsened in recent years, and Prop 36 stakeholders have struggled to maintain the integrity of the program in the context of increasing fiscal constraints.[3] At the same time, legislators charged with deciding funding amounts for the continuation of Prop 36 have called for strategies for making the program more cost-effective.[4]

It was in this context that evaluation reports identified a subgroup of Prop 36 offenders that comprised only 25 percent of all offenders in the program but that accounted for 80 percent of the re-arrests and costs that occurred over the 30 months following program entry.[2] The new crimes committed by these "high-risk, high-cost" offenders are eroding the savings and other benefits reaped by the Prop 36 program thus far and risk undermining the public safety that the Prop 36 law intends to protect. High-risk, high-cost offenders have been primarily characterized as having five or more prior convictions at program entry, and compared to other Prop 36 offenders, more are male and younger, their arrest and conviction costs after Prop 36 program entry are 26 times higher, and their treatment completion rates are significantly lower.[2] Prop 36's high-risk offenders have been identified only recently as one area for targeting program improvement efforts, and it follows that relatively little is known about this subgroup. For example, no study has examined the impact of drug treatment "dose" or other program and offender-level factors, such as offender motivation level and urine testing during treatment, that prior research on Prop 36 has identified as being associated with outcomes.[5,6] Outside of the Prop 36 arena, the topic of high-risk

High-Risk Offenders Participating in Court-Supervised Substance Abuse Treatment by Elizabeth Evans, David Huang, and Yih-Ing Hser

191

drug offenders and how best to address their addiction and criminal behavior in community-based treatment settings has been the focus of research for some time.

Much of the research on drug treatment for offenders proposes that outcomes are enhanced when risk of criminal recidivism is factored into choosing the appropriate level of care and that it is most effective to intensify treatment based on criminogenic factors in addition to need for services.[7,8] Furthermore, although challenging at times,[9] an integrated approach that combines close judicial supervision with high-intensity treatment has been found to be particularly effective for high-risk offenders.[10–13] Among non-criminal justice samples, better outcomes for individuals with more severe substance abuse or psychiatric problems have also been associated with providing more intensive treatment.[14–17] However, in two major studies of alcoholics (i.e., Project MATCH and the US Department of Veterans Affair Effectiveness Study), matching treatment to patient attributes was shown to only minimally enhance outcomes (see[18] for a summary of study findings). More recent analyses found that while treatment matching was beneficial but not essential to achieving good outcomes, mismatches had serious consequences, and this effect was magnified with multiple mismatches.[19] The potentially iatrogenic effects of treatment mismatching were also reported by a study of offenders which found that residential treatment decreased recidivism rates among higher risk offenders but increased recidivism rates among lower risk offenders.[20]

Aside from documenting the additive value of receipt of appropriate drug treatment intensity by risk level, the literature on treatment for offenders also highlights how there is no general consensus on how best to define "high risk." Risk classification has included the use of individual items such as history of involvement with the criminal justice system, diagnostic criteria for antisocial personality disorder, and history of prior drug abuse treatment,[12,13] as well as the use of risk screening tools that combine information on a variety of behaviors such as prior criminal and substance abuse history, psychological health, education level, and employment status.[7,8,20] Among Prop 36 offenders, five or more prior convictions was identified as a strong predictor of later recidivism, and research showed that average crime costs increased as the number of convictions prior to program entry increased.[2]

It has been recommended that high-risk offenders be made ineligible for Prop 36 program participation or, to better manage these offenders, more intense treatment and supervision is needed.[2] While it is clear that high-risk offenders are a costly component of the Prop 36 program and that strategies are needed to improve their outcomes, very little else is known about this group. Furthermore, analysis of an early cohort of Prop 36 offenders revealed that compared to clients referred to treatment through other means, Prop 36 offenders with severe drug problems were significantly less likely to be treated in a residential treatment setting, that is, high drug severity Prop 36 offenders tended to be "undertreated".[21] Although there is variation in the operation and performance of Prop 36 by county,[22] reports have confirmed that across California, Prop 36 resulted in an expansion of mostly outpatient treatment capacity,[23] that most Prop 36 offenders are treated in outpatient settings,

and that very few Prop 36 offenders receive residential treatment,[24] a treatment setting that some research indicates more commonly provides wraparound services for offenders.[25] Public policy discussions on what to do with high-risk Prop 36 offenders—provide more intense supervision or make them ineligible for Prop 36 program participation—require information on whether some high-risk offenders can demonstrate successful outcomes after program participation and whether the provision of more intensive treatment can be effective with this population.

To better understand the characteristics of high-risk offenders in Prop 36, their treatment experiences, recidivism rates, and impact of providing more treatment on recidivism, the following research questions were examined: (1) How are high-risk offenders different from low-risk offenders in characteristics at assessment for treatment and in experiences during drug treatment? (2) What offender characteristics and treatment factors predict more re-arrests over 12 months and over 30 months after assessment for treatment? (3) Does offender risk level interact with the amount of treatment received to impact the number of re-arrests?

It was hypothesized that high-risk offenders would exhibit more severe problems at intake assessment than their low-risk counterparts and that few would receive intensive treatment. Also, it was expected that the re-arrest rate would be higher among high-risk offenders but that more treatment would decrease recidivism.

Methods
Data Source
Data analyzed in this study were derived from "Treatment System Impact and Outcomes of Proposition 36 (TSI)," a NIDA-funded multisite prospective treatment outcome study designed to assess the impact of Prop 36 on California's drug treatment delivery system and evaluate the effectiveness of the services delivered. Thirty treatment assessment sites in five counties were selected for participation based on geographic location, population size, and diversity of Prop 36 implementation strategy (see[26] for additional information). County assessment center or treatment program staff collected data from all Prop 36 participants assessed for treatment in the selected counties. Of participants who had completed the intake assessment in 2004 ($n = 2,636$), a sample of 1,588 was randomly selected for telephone follow-up by UCLA-trained interviewers at 3 and 12 months post-intake. Participants were paid US $10 and $15, respectively. Additionally, administrative data were acquired on all participants on arrest histories from the California Department of Justice (DOJ) and on mental health services utilization from the California Department of Mental Health (DMH). Data linking procedures and quality of data linkage are described elsewhere.[27] The Institutional Review Boards at UCLA and at the California Health and Human Services Agency approved all study procedures.

Subjects and Recruitment
Of the 1,588 targeted, 1,465 completed the 3-month follow-up interview (48 were incarcerated, 3 were deceased, 6 refused, and the remainder was not found or was unable to complete the

interview) and 1,290 completed the 12-month follow-up interview (73 were incarcerated, 12 were deceased, 9 refused, and the remainder was not found or was unable to complete the interview). Excluding the deceased and incarcerated from the interview pool, the follow-up interview completion rates were 95 percent and 86 percent, respectively. Comparisons between those who did and did not complete the interview revealed no statistically significant differences in all variables examined (county, treatment modality, age, race/ethnicity, marital status, education, employment, lifetime arrest, and primary drug problem) except for gender. More females (30 percent vs. 20 percent) were in the follow-up completion group than in the non-completion group.

Of the total sample, mean age was 36.8 years, 29.1 percent were women, 50.6 percent were White, 24.8 percent were Hispanic, 18.1 percent were African American, 6.3 percent were other race/ethnic group, mean years of education was 11.7, 51.4 percent reported methamphetamine as their primary drug, and more than one third was employed full- or part-time (38.6 percent).

This analysis focuses on 1,087 Prop 36 offenders in TSI who completed the 3-month follow-up interview and also had a criminal history record on file with the California DOJ. Examination of the 378 who were omitted from analysis [because of missing 3-month follow-up variables ($n = 6$) or a missing DOJ record ($n = 372$)] showed that this group was different from the 1,087 who were included in analysis on gender only; slightly more males were in the study sample than in the non-study sample (72 percent vs. 66 percent). Missing DOJ records may have resulted from several factors such as data entry error, record expungement, commission of probation or parole violations that made an offender eligible for the Prop 36 program but did not result in a new arrest, deliberate falsification of personal information, and inaccuracies in the personal identifiers needed to link data. Of note is that this study applied a deterministic method to link records, and a combination of personal identifiers (including offender name, Social Security number, and date of birth) served as the primary linking variables. Only those cases that completely fulfilled the matching criteria were treated as a match. For this reason, underlinkage of data was expected, but this concern was outweighed by the high certainty of linkage associated with the deterministic method and the corresponding level of confidence in resulting findings.

Eligibility for the Prop 36 program is determined based on the offender's current offense and past criminal history, with special attention paid to convictions that occurred during the 5-year period prior to the offender's current offense.[28] For example, not eligible are drug offenders with a prior serious or violent felony conviction, unless the associated prison time has been served and the individual has been living in the community for 5 years with no felony or violent misdemeanor conviction. If eligible, offenders are offered treatment in lieu of routine criminal justice processing, and offenders who choose to participate complete a treatment assessment. Assessment entails a systematic review of offender drug problem severity and other service needs followed by a decision regarding appropriate treatment placement. Offenders are required to report to their assigned treatment program promptly, typically within 3–7 days after assessment.

To replicate prior analyses,[2] DOJ conviction data were analyzed; offenders with five or more convictions in the 5 years prior to their Prop 36 treatment assessment date were coded as "high-risk" ($n = 78$) and offenders with fewer than five convictions coded as "low-risk" ($n = 1,009$). Convictions over the 5-year pre-period were examined by offense type. For both groups, most convictions were for drug-related offenses, but compared to low-risk offenders, high-risk offenders had significantly greater numbers of convictions ($p < 0.001$) for all offense types, including drug offenses (e.g., drug possession or use; 2.6 vs. 0.9 convictions); property offenses (e.g., theft, burglary; 1.4 vs. 0.2 convictions); violent offenses (e.g., homicide, rape, robbery; 0.3 vs. <0.1 convictions); and other offenses (e.g., prostitution, vandalism; 1.6 vs. 0.4 convictions, data not shown). Analysis of lifetime adult conviction data revealed similar patterns, with significantly more high-risk offenders having been convicted of offenses related to drugs (97.4 percent vs. 86.6 percent), property (74.4 percent vs. 44.7 percent), violence (29.5 percent vs. 14.5 percent), and other crimes (88.5 percent vs. 56.8 percent, data not shown).

Instruments and Measures
At assessment for treatment

The baseline assessment included the Addiction Severity Index (ASI), a semi-structured interview instrument that captures *demographic information* and also assesses *problem severity* in seven areas: alcohol and drug use, employment, family and social relationships, legal, psychological, and medical status.[29,30] A composite score can be computed for each scale to indicate severity in that area; scores range from 0 to 1, with higher scores indicating greater severity. Distinguished by excellent inter-rater and test–retest reliability as well as high discriminant and concurrent validity,[31,32] the ASI is widely used in the addictions field.[33]

Motivation for treatment was also measured at baseline using the Stages of Change Readiness and Treatment Eagerness Scale (SOCRATES) 8D, a 19-item questionnaire which assesses readiness for change among drug and alcohol abusers. Responses are captured using a 1–5 Likert scale. A variable was constructed by summing all responses to measure offenders' overall motivation for treatment. Scores ranged from 19 to 95, with higher scores indicating greater motivation for treatment. Data from a multisite clinical sample and a test–retest study provided support for the reliability of SOCRATES scales.[34]

County of residence was recorded at treatment assessment. In order to maintain the confidentiality and anonymity of participating counties, each was arbitrarily assigned a letter from A to E. Detailed information on county characteristics is provided elsewhere.[26]

During treatment

Treatment retention was defined by the number of days from admission to the last day of treatment. Statewide administrative data indicate that a majority of Prop 36 offenders receive more than 90 days of treatment.[22] Thus, a median split was conducted on all calendar days of treatment received to distinguish *longer treatment retention* (≥ 113 days) from shorter treatment retention (<113 days).

The number of treatment services received was calculated from data collected by the Treatment Services Review (TSR). Administered at the 3-month follow-up interview, the TSR captured services received in the previous 3 months (either during or after treatment) in each of the seven domains of the ASI (e.g., alcohol and drug use, employment, family, etc.), including the number of professional services and discussion sessions received. The number of times an individual self-reported receipt of services in any domain (either in the program or through other sources) was summed (range = 0–1,407 services) and the mean number of treatment services received during the 3 months following assessment for treatment were calculated. Test–retest studies on the TSR indicated satisfactory reliability, and tests of concurrent validity showed the ability to discriminate different levels of treatment services and good correspondence with independent measures of treatment provided.[35]

Administrative records contained in the California Alcohol and Drug Data System (CADDS) were analyzed to determine *modality of care* (outpatient, residential, methadone maintenance) at treatment entry and *completion status* at treatment discharge.

Before and after treatment assessment

Mental health services utilization was calculated using administrative records acquired on all individuals from the California DMH Client and Service Information system. This database tracks services and psychiatric diagnoses for clients treated in community-based mental health facilities that receive DMH funds. Services received prior to the baseline assessment for Prop 36 treatment were analyzed.

Recidivism was calculated using DOJ administrative records on arrests. The recidivism rate and the number of re-arrests included all arrests that occurred in the 12 months and in the 30 months following the date each individual was assessed for treatment. The 12-month time period was chosen to examine patterns for an outcome time period that is typically used in related research, while the 30-month time period was utilized to replicate prior research on high-risk Prop 36 offenders.[2]

Statistical Analyses

Statistical analyses were conducted to examine differences in characteristics between high-risk and low-risk Prop 36 offenders and to identify factors associated with the number of re-arrests (as recorded in DOJ records) 12 and 30 months after intake assessment.

To test differences among the high-risk and low-risk offenders, ANOVA on continuous measures and chi-square tests on categorical measures were conducted. Controlling for county variation (as a set of dummy variables) and adjusting for several demographic covariates (age, gender, race/ethnicity), multiple regression analyses were conducted to examine predictors of more re-arrests as recorded in DOJ records in the 12 and 30 months following the baseline interview date. Four separate models were run to examine predictors of re-arrest during the two time periods of interest and before and after inclusion of an interaction term indicating high/low-risk level × longer/shorter treatment retention (described below).

Selection of variables for inclusion in the multiple regression models was informed by the relevant literature as well as by the descriptive analysis of characteristics. When indicators of similar behaviors were correlated, only one indicator was chosen for inclusion. To check that no potential multicollinearity biases existed among the selected predictors, diagnostic analysis with variance inflation factor (VIF) was also conducted. The VIF values of the selected predictors were below 5, indicating no multicollinearity biases among the predictors. Predictors examined in the model included age, gender, race/ethnicity, county of residence, employment status at intake, primary drug type, motivation for treatment, treatment modality, urine testing, services received during treatment, and mental health services utilization prior to Prop 36 entry. In addition, high-/low-risk level and longer/shorter treatment retention as well as their interaction [i.e., four strata were created ("high risk with longer treatment retention," "high risk with shorter treatment retention," "low risk with longer treatment retention," "low risk with shorter treatment retention") and included as an interaction term using "low risk with shorter treatment retention" as the reference group] were included as primary predictors in the multiple regression models. Unless otherwise stated, the significance level for all statistical tests was set at $p < 0.05$.

Results
Characteristics of High-risk Offenders

At assessment for treatment, high-risk offenders were distinguishable from low-risk offenders on several characteristics. As shown in Table 1, compared to low-risk offenders, high-risk offenders were younger (33.4 vs. 37.3 years old), fewer were female (14.1% vs. 28.9%), more were taking psychiatric medication (17.8% vs. 10.2%), more had been incarcerated in the prior 30 days (65.3% vs. 49.7%), first arrest occurred at a younger age (18.5 vs. 20.9 years old), the number of arrests (13.0 vs. 8.9 arrests) and convictions (8.4 vs. 4.7 convictions) accumulated over the lifetime was greater, and more had received mental health services (47.4% vs. 26.2%) according to services utilization data from the Department of Mental Health. There were no significant differences at intake between high-risk and low-risk offenders on the other variables that were examined, including race/ethnicity, education, marital status, employment status, homelessness, parole status, motivation level, severity of problems in all of the domains measured by the ASI composite scores, primary drug type, recent drug use and arrests and psychiatric problems, age at first primary drug use, years of primary drug use, receipt of prior treatment, number of prior treatments, and months incarcerated in lifetime. Of note is that about half of offenders in both groups reported no use of any drugs (excluding alcohol) in the 30 days prior to treatment assessment.

Treatment Received and Recidivism

As shown in Table 2, several measures of treatment received were examined, but only one measure indicated differences between high-risk and low-risk offenders. Fewer high-risk offenders were urine tested during treatment than low-risk offenders (70.1 percent vs. 82.6 percent). Except for this difference, the treatment experiences of offenders were similar regardless of risk classification. For both groups, most offenders were treated in an outpatient setting, average time

Table 1 Offender Characteristics at Assessment for Treatment

Variables	High-risk ($\geq$5 prior convictions, $n = 78$)	Low-risk (<5 prior convictions, $n = 1,009$)	Test statistic, p value
Age, mean (SD)	33.4 (8.9)	37.3 (9.7)	$F(1,1085) = 11.43, p < 0.01$
Female (percent)	14.1	28.9	$\chi_1^2 = 0.88, p < 0.01$
Ethnicity (percent)			$\chi_3^2 = 0.49, p = 0.92$
White	53.9	50.9	
African American	18.0	19.1	
Hispanic	23.0	23.1	
Other	5.1	6.8	
Education, mean (SD)	11.8 (2.0)	11.8 (1.9)	$F(1,1055) = 0.01, p = 0.92$
Married (percent)	12.2	16.3	$\chi_1^2 = 0.88, p = 0.35$
Employed (full- or part-time, percent)	36.5	39.0	$\chi_1^2 = 0.18, p = 0.67$
Homeless (percent)	12.3	7.7	$\chi_1^2 = 1.70, p = 0.19$
Taking psychiatric medication	17.8	10.2	$\chi_1^2 = 4.10, p = 0.04$
On parole (percent)	15.6	11.0	$\chi_1^2 = 0.14, p = 0.70$
Motivation level, mean (SD)	77.5 (11.2)	77.3 (12.5)	$F(1,1071) = 0.03, p = 0.86$
ASI Composite Scores, mean (SD)			
Alcohol	0.09 (0.16)	0.10 (0.18)	$F(1,1040) = 0.02, p = 0.88$
Drug	0.14 (0.11)	0.13 (0.11)	$F(1,1017) = 0.40, p = 0.53$
Employment	0.77 (0.26)	0.71 (0.29)	$F(1,1059) = 2.94, p = 0.09$
Family	0.16 (0.22)	0.16 (0.20)	$F(1,1033) = 0.00, p = 0.98$
Legal	0.28 (0.22)	0.26 (0.18)	$F(1,1058) = 1.17, p = 0.28$
Medical	0.20 (0.29)	0.26 (0.34)	$F(1,1062) = 1.79, p = 0.18$
Psychiatric	0.19 (0.22)	0.18 (0.22)	$F(1,1040) = 0.20, p = 0.65$
Primary drug (percent)			$\chi_4^2 = 7.60, p < 0.11$
Methamphetamine	43.2	50.6	
Cocaine	17.6	12.5	
Marijuana	10.8	13.4	
Heroin	10.8	8.5	
Alcohol	14.9	7.2	
Past 30 days (percent)			
Used any drug (excludes alcohol)	54.1	48.5	$\chi_1^2 = 0.84, p = 0.36$
Arrested	50.7	43.7	$\chi_1^2 = 1.31, p = 0.25$
Incarcerated	65.3	49.7	$\chi_1^2 = 6.82, p < 0.01$
Had psychiatric problems	41.0	39.4	$\chi_1^2 = 0.07, p = 0.78$
Lifetime			
Age at first primary drug use, mean (SD)	18.9 (7.5)	20.5 (8.0)	$F(1,1057) = 2.86, p = 0.09$
Years of primary drug use, mean (SD)	17.4 (25.5)	22.2 (33.5)	$F(1,1036) = 1.42, p = 0.23$
Received prior drug treatment, percent	73.0	65.0	$\chi_1^2 = 1.95, p = 0.16$
No. of prior drug treatments, mean (SD)	0.40 (1.1)	0.50 (1.5)	$F(1,1060) = 1.40, p = 0.24$
Age at first arrest, mean (SD)	18.5 (5.3)	20.9 (7.9)	$F(1,1074) = 6.80, p < 0.01$
No. of arrests, mean (SD) (data source: DOJ)	13.0 (11.3)	8.9 (12.0)	$F(1,1060) = 7.81, p < 0.01$
No. of convictions, mean (SD) (data source: DOJ)	8.4 (3.7)	4.7 (3.7)	$F(1,1085) = 72.44, p < 0.01$
Months incarcerated, mean (SD)	29.9 (30.4)	26.4 (34.4)	$F(1,1057) = 0.76, p = 0.38$
Received mental health services (percent) (data source: DMH)	47.4	26.2	$\chi_1^2 = 16.36, p < 0.01$

Data source: All variables were extracted from the baseline assessment interview unless stated otherwise

High-Risk Offenders Participating in Court-Supervised Substance Abuse Treatment by Elizabeth Evans, David Huang, and Yih-Ing Hser

195

Table 2 Treatment Received and Recidivism

Variables	High-risk (≥5 prior convictions, $n = 78$)	Low-risk (<5 prior convictions, $n = 1,009$)	F test or chi-square
Treatment received			
Modality (percent) (data source: CADDS)			$\chi^2_2 = 2.75, p = 0.25$
Outpatient	73.1	78.8	
Residential	24.4	17.2	
Methadone maintenance	2.6	4.0	
Longer treatment retention (≥113 days, percent) (data source: CADDS and follow-up interview)	46.2	42.4	$\chi^2_1 = 0.41, p = 0.52$
No. of services received, mean (SD) (data source: follow-up interview)	129.2 (169.1)	137.9 (138.7)	$F(1,1079) = 0.28, p = 0.60$
Urine tested during treatment (percent) (data source: follow-up interview)	70.1	82.6	$\chi^2_1 = 7.40, p < 0.01$
No. of urine tests, mean (SD) (data source: follow-up interview)	5.8 (7.7)	7.0 (7.1)	$F(1,1079) = 1.77, p = 0.18$
Completed treatment (percent) (data source: CADDS)	31.3	39.3	$\chi^2_1 = 1.59, p = 0.21$
Recidivism over 12 months after assessment for treatment (data source: DOJ) Re-arrested (percent)	64.1	53.8	$\chi^2_1 = 3.08, p = 0.07$
No. of re-arrests, mean (SD)	1.6 (1.8)	1.1 (1.6)	$F(1,1085) = 7.14, p < 0.01$
Recidivism over 30 months after assessment for treatment (data source: DOJ) Re-arrested (percent)	78.2	69.6	$\chi^2_1 = 2.58, p = 0.11$
No. of re-arrests, mean (SD)	3.4 (3.6)	2.3 (2.6)	$F(1,1085) = 12.45, p < 0.01$

in treatment was approximately 4.5 months—during this time between 129.2 and 137.9 services were received on average—less than half of offenders received a longer period of treatment, about one third completed treatment, and slightly more than half stayed in treatment for 90 or more days or completed treatment. To better understand the type of treatment received by offenders in the sample, services and retention data were analyzed by modality (data not shown). This analysis revealed that compared to offenders in outpatient treatment settings, offenders in residential treatment settings received almost twice as many services over a fewer number of days (an average of 212 services over 86 days for residential vs. an average of 121 services over 148 days for outpatient), and this was the case for both high-risk and low-risk offenders.

Also shown in Table 2, a similar proportion of high-risk and low-risk offenders were re-arrested in the 12 months (64.1% and 53.8%) and in the 30 months (78.2% and 69.6%) following intake assessment; however, the mean number of re-arrests that occurred was greater among high-risk offenders compared to low-risk offenders for both time periods (1.6 vs. 1.1 re-arrests over 12 months and 3.4 vs. 2.3 arrests over 30 months). Very few (<1%) re-arrests over 12 and 30 months were due to a probation or parole violation, but instead mostly reflected a new offense (drug-related offenses were most common, data not shown).

Offender and Program Factors Associated with Number of Re-arrests

Shown in Table 3 are four models which were run to examine factors associated with the number of re-arrests over 12 months (models 1 and 2) and over 30 months (models 3 and 4) before (models 1 and 3) and after (models 2 and 4) inclusion of an interaction term indicating high-/low-risk level × longer/shorter treatment retention as a predictor.

As shown in model 3, high-risk offender classification was associated with more re-arrests over the 30 months following intake assessment (0.061). A similar association was evident over the 12-month time period (model 1), but this result was not statistically significant. White race/ethnicity (−0.069) and employment at intake (−0.072) were associated with a fewer number of re-arrests over the 12-month time period. These associations were evident for the 30-month time period, but were not statistically significant. Report of methamphetamine as the primary drug problem (vs. other drug types such as heroin and cocaine) was associated with a fewer number of arrests over 30 months, as was also evident (but did not reach statistical significance) over the 12-month time frame.

Table 3 Multiple Regression Models Predicting Number of Re-arrests Over 12 and 30 Months after Assessment for Treatment

Variables	Over 12 months		Over 30 months	
	Estimates			
	Model 1	Model 2	Model 3	Model 4
Age at intake	−0.126**	−0.130**	−0.163**	−0.168**
Female (vs. male)	−0.076*	−0.076*	−0.092**	−0.092**
White (vs. non-White)	−0.069*	−0.066*	−0.038	−0.035
Employed (vs. not employed) at intake	−0.072*	−0.069*	−0.061	−0.058
County B (vs. County A)	−0.005	−0.001	0.013	0.018
County C (vs. County A)	−0.016	−0.021	0.001	−0.004
County D (vs. County A)	−0.109**	−0.108**	−0.092**	−0.090*
County E (vs. County A)	0.136**	0.139**	0.174**	0.177**
Primary drug is methamphetamine (vs. all other drug types)	−0.019	−0.021	−0.068*	−0.070*
Motivation level	0.004	0.004	0.014	0.013
Treatment setting is residential (vs. methadone maintenance)	0.004	0.002	0.053	0.050
Treatment setting is outpatient (vs. methadone maintenance)	0.038	0.033	0.033	0.027
Received mental health services prior to intake	0.017	0.014	0.036	0.033
No. of urine tests received during treatment	−0.001	Less than −0.001	−0.018	−0.016
No. of services received during treatment	−0.102**	−0.105**	−0.063*	−0.066*
High-risk offender (vs. low-risk offender)	0.029	–	0.061*	–
Longer treatment retention [≥113 days vs. shorter treatment retention (<113 days)]	−0.248**	–	−0.179**	–
High-risk offender and longer treatment retention (vs. low-risk offender and shorter treatment retention)	–	−0.109**	–	−0.074*
Low-risk offender and longer treatment retention (vs. low-risk offender and shorter treatment retention)	–	−0.223**	–	−0.158**
High-risk offender and shorter treatment retention (vs. low-risk offender and shorter treatment retention)	–	0.067*	–	0.099**

Standardized betas are shown. R^2 was 0.16 for models 1, 3, and 4 and 0.17 for model 2
*$p < 0.05$;
**$p < 0.01$

For both the 12- and 30-month time periods, the number of re-arrests was increased by residing in County E (vs. County A, 0.136 and 0.174) and decreased by older age (−0.126 and −0.163), being female (−0.076 and −0.092), residing in County D (vs. County A, −0.109 and −0.092), receipt of more services during treatment (−0.102 and −0.063), and longer treatment retention (−0.248 and −0.179).

A significant interaction effect between risk classification and treatment retention on the mean number of re-arrests was found for both the 12- and 30-month time periods (Figs. 1 and 2). When this interaction effect was included in multiple regression analyses (Table 3, models 2 and 4), additional significant predictors emerged. For both time periods, a shorter treatment length for high-risk offenders increased the number of re-arrests (0.067 and 0.099), whereas a longer treatment length decreased the number of re-arrests for both high-risk offenders (−0.109 and −0.074) and low-risk offenders (−0.223 and −0.158).

Discussion
Summary of Findings
In summary, high-risk offenders were distinguishable from low-risk offenders (defined as having five or more and less than five convictions in the 5 years prior to the current offense, respectively) on several characteristics at assessment for treatment including younger age, male gender, prior contact with the mental health services system, and more frequent contact with the criminal justice system. Treatment received and the proportion of offenders who recidivated were mostly similar across groups, but fewer high-risk offenders were urine tested during treatment and high-risk offenders had more re-arrests over 12 and 30 months following intake assessment. Consistent with prior research, multiple regression analysis showed that high-risk classification was a significant predictor of more re-arrests over 30 months after intake (results for the association between

high-risk classification and re-arrests over 12 months pointed in the same direction, but did not reach statistical significance). Significant predictors associated with fewer re-arrests over 12 months after intake included White race/ethnicity and employment at intake. Regardless of the length of the outcome observation time period, the number of re-arrests was smaller with older age, being female, residing in a particular county, receipt of more services during treatment, and receipt of a longer length of treatment. Moreover, congruent with expectations, the interaction between risk classification and treatment length had a significant effect on the mean number of re-arrests. The number of re-arrests was greater with shorter treatment retention lengths for high-risk offenders and was smaller with longer treatment retention lengths for both low-risk and high-risk offenders.

Limitations

The present study has several limitations. Offender risk classification relied on a single indicator (number of prior convictions)—and it is not intended to serve as definitive criteria for classifying offenders in the future—but use of this indicator permitted constructive comparisons with existing Prop 36 evaluation reports. The treatment received measure primarily relied on one indicator (treatment retention), and potential effects associated with the quantity and quality of treatment services were omitted; however, other indicators of treatment received (treatment modality, urine testing, number of services received) were also examined and described. Also, for ethical and feasibility reasons, offenders were not randomly assigned to receive different lengths of treatment, as would have been the case with an experimental study design, and thus self-selection biases may have contributed to group differences that emerged; however, key factors that have been associated with outcomes were examined and included in the analyses. Another limitation is that group comparisons

yielded a medium effect size, suggesting that some differences may not have reached statistical significance because of low power. Findings were congruent with general trends, but replication of analyses with larger sample sizes is warranted. Also, information on periods of incarceration was not available, and thus, re-arrest data were not adjusted to account for possible group differences in time-at-risk periods. Similarly, re-arrest may be influenced by contextual differences in criminal justice policing, supervision practices, or other environmental factors. Except for inclusion of "county" in the models, data were not adjusted to account for potential contextual biases. Also, this study captured a relatively small proportion of the larger statewide population of Prop 36 offenders and focused on only one outcome measure (re-arrest). Findings may vary with analysis of a larger sample and inclusion of additional outcome indicators. The study utilized administrative data, a data source vulnerable to over- or underreporting of behaviors.[36,37] For example, measures of arrest and drug treatment/mental health services utilization that relied on administrative data did not capture events that may have occurred outside of California. Also omitted from the analysis were any events that may have occurred but did not come to the attention of the institution from which the data were acquired (e.g., utilization of health services in non-publicly funded settings; crimes for which there was no arrest). Finally, future research that aims to isolate causal factors related to outcomes would likely be strengthened by the application of propensity scoring or other approaches to adjust for differences in offender characteristics. Despite these and other limitations of administrative data, it is generally believed to be a valuable resource for the evaluation of substance abuse treatment outcomes.[27,36–38] The findings support and extend existing knowledge on drug treatment for offenders and new aspects of a unique and costly offender subgroup were documented.

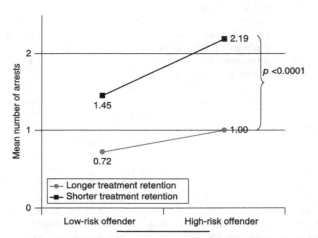

Figure 1 Interaction effect between risk level and treatment retention on re-arrests over 12 months after assessment for treatment

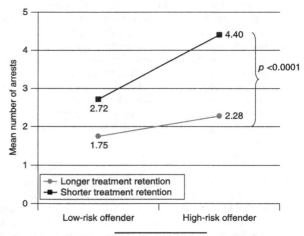

Figure 2 Interaction effect between risk level and treatment retention on re-arrests over 30 months after assessment for treatment

Implications for Behavioral Health

The study findings pose several important implications for future program planning and research on court-supervised drug treatment for offenders. Examining conviction history to assign offenders to a risk level is a clear-cut and pragmatic tool, yet the classification of offenders based on the number of convictions alone is problematic. The results showed that recidivism was associated with risk classification at intake, but it was also associated with individual demographic variables (i.e., age, sex, race/ethnicity, employment status), history of interactions with the mental health services system and criminal justice system, and county of residence. Using the number of convictions as the sole criteria for program exclusion/inclusion would not only overlook the range of personal characteristics, system interactions, and environmental factors that influence behavior but would also represent a significant change in current eligibility criteria which looks beyond conviction frequency to consider offense type and the timing of conviction occurrence in the life course.

Another study implication is that using recidivism as the only measure of program outcomes is problematic. Variation in Prop 36 program operations has been documented,[39] and community-level differences in program practices and approach likely impact criminal justice outcomes differentially. Also, differences between groups may appear in one behavioral domain but not in another. For example, for this study, separate analysis of self-reported use of any drug (excluding alcohol) in the 30 days prior to the 12-month follow-up interview indicated no significant differences in the proportion of high- and low-risk offenders who had used (about one quarter of both groups had used drugs). As has been done in other similar work,[40] future treatment outcomes research would be strengthened by the examination of a range of behaviors impacted by drug use, including not only recidivism but also employment, family and social relationships, and general health and well-being.

The intent to spend Prop 36 public resources efficiently is a valid reason for omitting high-risk offenders from the program, but it is also the case that by excluding those with more prior convictions, there is the risk of omitting individuals who are most in need of treatment. Prior research indicates that few offenders in prisons and jails have access to substance abuse services,[41] drug treatment programs have been shown to reduce criminal behavior,[42] and judicial mandates can provide an opportunity for substance-using offenders to access and benefit from needed treatment.[43] A significant added economic benefit is the cost savings that are consistently associated with substance use treatment.[44]

Risk classification based on conviction history might be best suited for use as a clinical tool for identifying offenders who are most in need of longer lengths of drug treatment. The findings indicated that the number of re-arrests was decreased by receipt of more services and longer lengths of treatment, and most notably, the results showed that the number of re-arrests was less when high-risk offenders received longer lengths of treatment. Also, although not a significant predictor of re-arrest, fewer high-risk offenders were urine tested during

treatment. Undoubtedly, the provision of more treatment, especially high-intensity treatment, is expensive[14] and offenders may drop out of treatment prematurely, effectively choosing to receive less treatment. Yet it is also evident that a standardized risk assessment is not used by the Prop 36 program, as is the case in many community-based substance abuse treatment programs that treat drug-involved offenders,[45] and about one-third of counties report that special strategies to manage Prop 36 high-risk offenders are not used.[2] So it may not be surprising to find that in the sample that was studied, Prop 36 treatment retention lengths were not significantly different by risk level and that similar proportions of high-risk and low-risk offenders received longer treatment stays. The provision of longer treatment to low-risk offenders was not shown to harm outcomes. But the overtreatment of some low-risk offenders, when there is an undertreatment of others who are in greater need, is wasteful of scarce resources and is an indication that there is room to improve efforts to retain high-risk offenders in treatment. Tools to engage and retain offenders in court-supervised community-based treatment have been identified and include a range of strategies such as the use of incentives and sanctions, adequate monitoring, participation in mutual self-help groups, and development of relapse prevention skills.[46]

In recent years, fiscal constraints have obliged many counties to shorten the expected length of treatment stay for Prop 36 offenders and, in some areas, to eliminate certain costlier modalities, such as residential treatment, from Prop 36 programming altogether. The data indicated that residential treatment often appears to be a setting where Prop 36 offenders receive more services in a shorter amount of time, a practice that can "intensify" the treatment experience but may not be as important for enhancing outcomes as the provision of a sufficient length of time in treatment. Some research indicates that a highly controlled environment may precipitate treatment dropout for some high-risk offenders.[47] Also, for many drug offenders, recovery from drug dependence is a lengthy process and the effects of treatment require adequate time to develop and sustain in order to have long-term impacts on overall health, quality of life, and social functioning.[48–50] In the absence of adequate residential treatment (for example due to limited residential treatment capacity or offender ineligibility), lengthened engagement with the type of treatment that is available (e.g., outpatient, self-help groups) may be warranted. More research is needed to understand how risk level may interact with treatment setting, as well as services received and level of supervision, to impact outcomes. Criminal justice mandated treatment clients face numerous obstacles to treatment compliance[51] and barriers to implementing client treatment matching exist,[52] but taken together, the information presented here indicates that more can be done to evaluate the risk level of Prop 36 offenders at program entry and that this information could be used to ensure that treatment, especially length of treatment, is better matched to need.

Finally, receipt of mental health services was one of the few client characteristics that differentiated high-risk offenders from low-risk offenders at assessment for treatment. Offenders diagnosed with both mental illness and drug dependence are particularly challenging to treat, and Prop 36 stakeholders have expressed concerns regarding their ability to effectively address the needs of these offenders.[53] Evidence-based treatment practices for individuals with co-occurring disorders can be difficult to implement within criminal justice settings.[54] Yet finding ways to integrate treatments for drug and mental health disorders (e.g., assessment of mental health needs, co-location of services, on-site service delivery, adequately trained mental health professionals) will likely improve outcomes. Also, no studies have been published on offenders with mental illness who participate in drug treatment through Prop 36. More research is needed to identify special needs and strategies for improving outcomes among this population.

In conclusion, alternative sentencing policies that focus on the rehabilitation of drug offenders in lieu of imprisonment appear to be gaining in popularity among the general public. In the past decade, more than 20 states have considered legislation that is similar to Prop 36.[55] In California, voters were recently given the opportunity to consider a new drug diversion option, the Nonviolent Offender Rehabilitation Act,[56] and the debate continues over whether to solve the state's overcrowded prison problem through early prisoner release programs that would presumably route significant numbers of drug offenders to community-based treatment programs. Stakeholders desire sentencing options that save taxpayer money and also perform better than incarceration in reducing recidivism and improving longer term outcomes. However, the effectiveness and financial benefits of such programs are in jeopardy when treatment lengths are inadequate. To improve outcomes among high-risk offenders who receive court-supervised treatment, efforts are needed to address psychiatric problems and criminal history and to ensure receipt of appropriate lengths of treatment. The findings may be useful for optimizing the effectiveness of criminal justice diversion programs for treating drug-addicted offenders.

References

1. California Department of Alcohol and Drug Programs. *Substance Abuse and Crime Prevention Act of 2000 (Prop. 36)*. 2008. Available at: www.adp.ca.gov/sacpa/prop36.shtml. Accessed October 8, 2009.

2. Hawken A. *High-risk and high-cost offenders in Proposition 36*. 2008. Available at: www.uclaisap.org/Prop36/html/reports .html. Accessed October 9, 2009.

3. California Department of Finance. *Governor's Budget 2008–2009*. 2008. Available at: www.ebudget.ca.gov/Enacted/ BudgetSummary/BSS/BSS.html. Accessed October 8, 2009.

4. Little Hoover Commission. *Addressing addiction: Improving and integrating California's substance abuse treatment system. A report to the California Legislature*. 2008. Available at: www .lhc.ca.gov/lhcdir/report190.html. Accessed October 8, 2009.

5. Evans E, Li L, Hser YI. Client and program factors associated with dropout from court mandated drug treatment. *Evaluation and Program Planning*, 2009; 32: 204–212.

6. Hser YI, Evans E, Teruya C, et al. Predictors of short-term treatment outcomes among California's Proposition 36 participants. *Evaluation and Program Planning*, 2007; 30: 187–196.

7. Taxman FS, Thanner M, Weisburd D. Risk, need, and responsivity (RNR): It all depends. *Crime & Delinquency*, 2006; 52: 28–51.

8. Thanner MH, Taxman FS. Responsivity: The value of providing intensive services to high-risk offenders. *Journal of Substance Abuse Treatment*, 2003; 24: 137–147.

9. Taxman FS, Bouffard J. Treatment inside the drug treatment court: The who, what, where, and how of treatment services. *Substance Use & Misuse*, 2002; 37: 1665–1688.

10. Marlowe DB. Integrating substance abuse treatment and criminal justice supervision. *Science and Practice Perspectives*, 2003; 2: 4–14.

11. Marlowe DB. Judicial supervision of drug-abusing offenders. *American Journal of Drug and Alcohol Abuse*, 2006; 29: 337–357.

12. Marlowe DB, Festinger DS, Dugosh KL, et al. Adapting judicial supervision to the risk level of drug offenders: Discharge and 6-month outcomes from a prospective matching study. *Drug and Alcohol Dependence*, 2007; 88: 4–13.

13. Marlowe DB, Festinger DS, Lee PA, et al. Matching judicial supervision to clients' risk status in drug court. *Crime & Delinquency*, 2006; 52: 52–76.

14. Chen S, Barnett PG, Sempel JM, et al. Outcomes and costs of matching the intensity of dual-diagnosis treatment to patients' symptom severity. Journal of Substance Abuse Treatment. 2006; 31: 95–105.

15. Thornton CC, Gottheil E, Weinstein SP, et al. Patient-treatment matching in substance abuse drug addiction severity. *Journal of Substance Abuse Treatment*, 1998; 15: 505–511.

16. Tiet QQ, Ilgen MA, Byrnes HF, et al. Treatment setting and baseline substance use severity interact to predict patients' outcomes. *Addiction*, 2007; 102: 432–440.

17. Timko C, Sempel JM. Short-term outcomes of matching dual diagnosis patients' symptom severity to treatment intensity. *Journal of Substance Abuse Treatment*, 2004; 26: 209–218.

18. Babor TF. Treatment for persons with substance use disorders: Mediators, moderators, and the need for a new research approach. International Journal of Methods in Psychiatric Research, 2008; 17: 45–49.

19. Karno MP, Longabaugh R. Does matching matter? Examining matches and mismatches between patient attributes and therapy techniques in alcoholism treatment. *Addiction*, 2007; 102: 587–596.

20. Lowenkamp CT, Latessa EJ. Increasing the effectiveness of correctional programming through the risk principle: Identifying offenders for residential placement. *Criminology & Public Policy*, 2005; 4: 263–290.

21. Farabee D, Hser Y, Anglin D, et al. Recidivism among an early cohort of California's Proposition 36 offenders. *Criminology & Public Policy*, 2004; 3: 563–584.

22. Urada D, Evans E, Yang J, et al. *Evaluation of the Substance Abuse and Crime Prevention Act 2009 Report*. 2009. Submitted to the California Department of Alcohol and Drug Programs. Los Angeles, CA: UCLA Integrated Substance Abuse Programs.

23. Hser YI, Teruya C, Brown AH, et al. Impact of California's Proposition 36 on the drug treatment system: Treatment capacity and displacement. *American Journal of Public Health*, 2007; 97: 104–109.

24. Urada D, Hawken A, Conner B, et al. (2008). *Evaluation of the Substance Abuse and Crime Prevention Act 2008 Report. 2008*. Available at: www.uclaisap.org/Prop36/html/reports.html. Accessed October 8, 2009.

25. Grella CE, Greenwell L, Prendergast M, et al. Organizational characteristics of drug abuse treatment programs for offenders. *Journal of Substance Abuse Treatment*, 2007; 32: 291–300.

26. Hser YI, Teruya C, Evans E, et al. Treating drug-abusing offenders: Initial findings from a five-county study on the impact of California's Proposition 36 on the treatment system and patient outcomes. *Evaluation Review*, 2003; 27: 479–505.

27. Hser YI, Evans E. Cross-system data linkage for treatment outcome evaluation: Lessons learned from the California Treatment Outcome Project. *Evaluation and Program Planning,* 2008; 31: 125–135.

28. Longshore D, Urada D, Evans E et al. *Evaluation of the Substance Abuse and Crime Prevention Act: 2004 report.* 2005 Available at: www.uclaisap.org/Prop36/html/reports.html. Accessed October 9, 2009.

29. McLellan AT, Luborsky L, Woody GE, et al. An improved diagnostic evaluation instrument for substance abuse patients: The Addiction Severity Index. *Journal of Nervous and Mental Disease,* 1980; 168: 26–33.

30. McLellan AT, Kushner H, Metzger D, et al. The fifth edition of the Addiction Severity Index. *Journal of Substance Abuse Treatment,* 1992; 9: 199–213.

31. Bovasso GB, Alterman AI, Cacciola JS, et al. Predictive validity of the Addiction Severity Index's composite scores in the assessment of 2-year outcomes in a methadone maintenance population. *Psychology of Addictive Behaviors,* 2001; 15: 171–176.

32. Kosten TR, Rounsaville BJ, Kleber HD. Concurrent validity of the Addiction Severity Index. *Journal of Nervous and Mental Disease,* 1983; 171: 606–610.

33. McLellan AT, Cacciola JC, Alterman AI, Rikoon SH, Carise D. The Addiction Severity Index at 25: Origins, contributions and transitions. *American Journal of Addictions,* 2006; 15: 113–24.

34. Miller WR, Tonigan JS. Assessing drinkers' motivation for change: The Stages of Change Readiness and Treatment Eagerness Scale (SOCRATES). *Psychology of Addictive Behaviors,* 1996; 10: 81–89.

35. McLellan AT, Alterman AI, Cacciola J, et al. A new measure of substance abuse treatment: Initial studies of the treatment services review. *Journal of Nervous and Mental Disease,* 1992; 180: 101–110.

36. McCarty D, McGuire TG, Harwood HJ, Field T. Using state information systems for drug abuse services research. *American Behavioral Scientist,* 1998; 41: 1090–106.

37. Saunders RC, Heflinger CA. Integrating data from multiple public sources: Opportunities and challenges for evaluators. *Evaluation: International Journal of Theory, Research, and Practice,* 2004; 10: 349–65.

38. Evans E, Grella C, Murphy D, Hser YI. Using administrative data for longitudinal substance abuse research. *Journal of Behavioral Health Services & Research,* 2010; 37: 252–271.

39. Evans E, Anglin MD, Urada D, Yang J. Promising practices for delivery of court-supervised substance abuse treatment: Perspectives from six high-performing California counties operating Proposition 36. *Evaluation and Program Planning,* 2011; 34: 124–134.

40. Evans E, Li L, Urada D, Anglin M.D. Comparative effectiveness of California's Proposition 36 and drug court programs before and after propensity score matching. *Crime & Delinquency,* 2011 (in press).

41. Taxman FS, Perdoni ML, Harrison LD. Drug treatment services for adult offenders: The state of the state. *Journal of Substance Abuse Treatment,* 2007; 32: 239–254.

42. Holloway KR, Bennett TH, Farrington DP. The effectiveness of drug treatment programs in reducing criminal behavior: A meta-analysis. *Psicothema,* 2006; 18: 620–629.

43. Kelly JF, Finney JW, Moos R. Substance use disorder patients who are mandated to treatment: Characteristics, treatment process, and 1- and 5-year outcomes. *Journal of Substance Abuse Treatment,* 2005; 28: 213–223.

44. Ettner SL, Huang D, Evans E, Ash DR, Hardy M, Jourabchi M, Hser YI. Benefit-cost in the California Treatment Outcome Project: Does substance abuse treatment "pay for itself?" *Health Services Research,* 2006; 41: 192–213.

45. Friedmann PD, Taxman FS, Henderson CE. Evidence-based treatment practices for drug-involved adults in the criminal justice system. *Journal of Substance Abuse Treatment,* 2007; 32: 267–277.

46. Center for Substance Abuse Treatment. Substance Abuse Treatment for Adults in the Criminal Justice System. Improvement Protocol (TIP) Series 44. DHHS Publication No. (SMA) 05–4056. Rockville, MD: Substance Abuse and Mental Health Services Administration, 2005.

47. McKellar J, Kelly J, Harris A, et al. Pretreatment and during treatment risk factors for dropout among patients with substance use disorders. *Addictive Behaviors,* 2006; 31: 450–460.

48. Laudet AB. The road to recovery: Where are we going and how do we get there? Empirically driven conclusions and future directions for service development and research. *Substance Use & Misuse,* 2008; 43: 2001–2020.

49. Laudet AB, White W. What are your priorities right now? Identifying service needs across recovery stages to inform service development. *Journal of Substance Abuse Treatment,* 2010; 38: 51–59.

50. McLellan AT. Have we evaluated addiction treatment correctly? Implications from a chronic care perspective. *Addiction,* 2002; 97: 249–252.

51. Sung HE, Belenko S, Feng L, et al. Predicting treatment noncompliance among criminal justice-mandated clients: A theoretical and empirical exploration. *Journal of Substance Abuse Treatment,* 2004; 26: 315–328.

52. Merkx MJ, Schippers GM, Koeter MJ, et al. Allocation of substance use disorder patients to appropriate levels of care: Feasibility of matching guidelines in routine practice in Dutch treatment centres. *Addiction,* 2007; 102: 466–474.

53. Hardy M, Teruya C, Longshore D, et al. Initial implementation of California's Substance Abuse and Crime Prevention Act: Findings from focus groups in ten counties. *Evaluation and Program Planning,* 2005; 28: 221–232.

54. Chandler RK, Peters RH, Field G, et al. Challenges in implementing evidence-based treatment practices for co-occurring disorders in the criminal justice system. *Behavioral Sciences & the Law,* 2004; 22: 431–448.

55. The Avisa Group. *Comparing California's Proposition 36 (SACPA) with similar legislation in other states and jurisdictions.* 2005 Available at: www.prop36.org/pdf/ ComparisonProp36OtherStates.pdf. Accessed October 8, 2009.

56. California Secretary of State. *Voter information guide.* 2008. Available at: www.voterguide.sos.ca.gov/title-sum/prop5-title -sum.htm. Accessed October 8, 2009.

Critical Thinking

1. Discuss key differences between high and low risk drug offenders.

2. Discuss important treatment program factors for drug users at high risk for relapsing.

3. Discuss this study's implications for future court mandated treatment programs.

Create Central

www.mhhe.com/createcentral

High-Risk Offenders Participating in Court-Supervised Substance Abuse Treatment by Elizabeth Evans, David Huang, and Yih-Ing Hser

201

Internet References

The Drug Reform Coordination Network (DRC)
www.drcnet.org

National Institute on Drug Abuse
www.nida.nih.gov

Acknowledgments—The study was supported in part by the National Institute on Drug Abuse (NIDA; grant no. R01DA15431 & P30DA016383). Also, Dr. Hser is supported by a Senior Scientist Award (K05DA017648) and Dr. Huang is supported by the National Institute of Mental Health (NIMH, grant no. R03MH084434-01A1 & R03MH084434-02). The content of this publication does not necessarily reflect the views or policies of NIDA or NIMH.

Address correspondence to ELIZABETH EVANS, MA, UCLA Integrated Substance Abuse Programs, Semel Institute for Neuroscience and Human Behavior, Department of Psychiatry and Biobehavioral Sciences, David Geffen School of Medicine, 1640 S. Sepulveda Blvd., 200, Los Angeles, CA 90025, USA. Phone: +1-310-267-5315; Email: laevans@ucla.edu.

DAVID HUANG, DrPh, UCLA Integrated Substance Abuse Programs, Semel Institute for Neuroscience and Human Behavior, Department of Psychiatry and Biobehavioral Sciences, David Geffen School of Medicine, Los Angeles, CA, USA. Phone: +1-310-267-5288; Email: yhuang@ucla.edu.

YIH-ING HSER, PhD, UCLA Integrated Substance Abuse Programs, Semel Institute for Neuroscience and Human Behavior, Department of Psychiatry and Biobehavioral Sciences, David Geffen School of Medicine, Los Angeles, CA, USA. Phone: +1-310-267-5388; Email: yhser@ucla.edu.

Journal of Behavioral Health Services & Research, 2011. © 2011 National Council for Community Behavioral Healthcare.

Article

Prepared by: Mary Maguire, *California State University—Sacramento*
Clifford Garoupa, *Fresno City College*

The Needle and the Damage Done

The Case for the Self-Destructing Syringe

The WHO says 1.3 million people a year die because of the re-use of syringes. A British designer aims to change that.

SARAH BOSELEY

Learning Outcomes

After reading this article, you will be able to:

- Explain how many people die each year from using contaminated syringes.
- Discuss how many people in Africa each year contract HIV/AIDS from using contaminated syringes.
- Understand what the cost is to provide clean syringes.

Tanzania is to become the first country in the world to move exclusively to using syringes that self-destruct after a British entrepreneur played the health minister undercover footage of children being injected with used needles.

Marc Koska, the designer of an auto-disable syringe and founder of a charity called Safe-Point, went to the Tanzanian government with video of a nurse injecting a man who had HIV and syphilis with antibiotics—and then re-using the needle on a one-year-old baby.

"I went to see the minister of health in Tanzania and showed her the film. She was so distraught and said: What are we talking about here? She said, What's the solution? Let's get on with it. A meeting scheduled for 10 minutes went on for two hours," Koska told *The Guardian*.

Koska is a man on a mission. He hopes to persuade four other countries in east Africa to follow suit—Kenya, Uganda, Burundi and Rwanda—before he takes on the rest of the world.

The stakes are higher than most people imagine. Some 1.3 million people die every year because of the re-use of syringes, according to the World Health Organisation. That's more than malaria kills, Koska points out. "This is not mosquito-borne disease. This is man-made," he said. There are 23m transmissions of hepatitis, which cost $119bn (£74bn) every year in medical and lost production costs. In Africa,

around 20m injections contaminated with HIV are given every year. In the developing world, every syringe is used on average four times. That's Russian roulette, he says.

Koska goes to health ministries armed with figures. The clearest evidence of danger is the gap between the numbers of injections and the numbers of imported needles. "Tanzania has 45 million people and they are importing 40m syringes. With an average of five injections each a year, they need 220m," he said.

This is not about routine childhood immunisation, for which safe syringes such as Koska's are provided along with the vaccines, usually by Unicef, the biggest procurer.

But "they forgot the other 90%", he said. Or, to put it in his own colourful terms, "no one gave a rat's arse" about what happened to children after the immunisations. In developing countries, treatment is often by injection rather than pills.

"The village quack has one syringe for 200 people," he said. "I've seen him take it out of his hair, use it and then stick it back in the roof of the hut where the insects are." The healthy start to life that children are given is so easily undermined.

There is a commercial conundrum at the heart of the problem. At 3p each, syringes are very cheap to make. They are manufactured by a small number of big companies which use them as a loss leader—they package the syringe together with blood bags or catheters and charge more. Although auto-disable syringes are now as cheap to make, it involves changing over the production process, which is expensive. Companies also sell fewer syringes in the long run—because people get well.

Koska has his own company, but his charity supports the use of any quality-assured brand of auto-disable syringe. Koska hopes to persuade families to demand safe injections from needles carrying a LifeSaver kitemark. In Tanzania, health workers will ask people given such injections to send a free text to the health ministry. Health workers who get 500 text "votes" receive congratulations and a status-conveying badge. Koska tells of seeing parents asked to choose the needle to be used on their child from a tray of re-used ones. If families understood the danger, they would insist on a new one, Koska believes.

Twenty-seven years ago, he was kicking his heels in the Caribbean after a privileged upbringing, looking for something interesting to do with his life. "I had first-class honours in beach bumming," he said. "Then in May 1984, I read an article—in *The Guardian* as it happened—predicting in the future, syringes would be a major transmission route for HIV. Immediately I knew that was my calling."

It took years of studying the problem and learning about plastics, before he hit on his design, in which the plunger breaks as soon as it is pulled back for re-use. He has now sold 3bn of them and last month, he finally signed a contract with the world's biggest syringe-maker to produce his auto-disable design.

Next in his sights are the UN and aid agencies that provide medicines to the developing world, such as the Global Fund for AIDS, TB and Malaria and Pepfar, the US president's emergency plan for AIDS relief. They do not specify to the countries they help that the drugs must be safely injected, he says. But no doubt they soon will.

Critical Thinking

1. Why are so many people in Africa becoming ill from contaminated syringes?

2. What is a "self-destructing syringe"?

3. Why is it so important that a syringe only be used once?

Create Central

www.mhhe.com/createcentral

Internet References

Safe Point
  safepointtrust.org
Harm Reduction Works
  www.harmreductionworks.org.wk